Muslims and Political Participation in Britain

Muslims play a prominent role in British political life and yet little is known about this participation beyond the existence of a handful of Muslim MPs. What is unique about political participation in Muslim communities? How do they contribute to electoral politics and civil society initiatives? All the major parties actively seek to court a 'Muslim electorate' but does such a phenomenon exist? Despite the impact that Muslims have had on election campaigns and their roles in various political institutions, research on this topic remains scant. The chapters in this volume address this lacuna by highlighting different aspects of Muslim participation in British politics. They investigate voting patterns and election campaigns, civil society and grassroots political movements, the engagement of young people and the participation of Muslims in formal political institutions. Written in an accessible style, this book will be of interest to students and scholars of political participation and religious studies.

Timothy Peace is Lecturer in Comparative European Politics at the University of Stirling.

Routledge Studies in Religion and Politics

Edited by Jeffrey Haynes, London Metropolitan University, UK

This series aims to publish high quality works on the topic of the resurgence of political forms of religion in both national and international contexts. This trend has been especially noticeable in the post-cold war era (that is, since the late 1980s). It has affected all the 'world religions' (including, Buddhism, Christianity, Hinduism, Islam, and Judaism) in various parts of the world (such as, the Americas, Europe, the Middle East and North Africa, South and Southeast Asia, and sub-Saharan Africa).

The series welcomes books that use a variety of approaches to the subject, drawing on scholarship from political science, international relations, security studies, and contemporary history.

Books in the series explore these religions, regions and topics both within and beyond the conventional domain of 'church-state' relations to include the impact of religion on politics, conflict and development, including the late Samuel Huntington's controversial – yet influential – thesis about 'clashing civilisations'.

In sum, the overall purpose of the book series is to provide a comprehensive survey of what is currently happening in relation to the interaction of religion and politics, both domestically and internationally, in relation to a variety of issues.

Politics and the Religious Imagination
Edited by John Dyck, Paul Rowe and Jens Zimmermann

Christianity and Party Politics
Keeping the faith
Martin H. M. Steven

Religion, Politics and International Relations
Selected essays
Jeffrey Haynes

Religion and Democracy
A worldwide comparison
Carsten Anckar

Religious Actors in the Public Sphere
Means, objects and effects
Edited by Jeffrey Haynes and Anja Hennig

Politics and Religion in the United Kingdom
Steve Bruce

Politics, Religion and Gender
Framing and regulating the veil
Edited by Sigelinde Rosenberger and Birgit Sauer

Representing Religion in the European Union
Does God matter?
Edited by Lucian N. Leustean

An Introduction to Religion and Politics
Theory and practice
Jonathan Fox

Religion in International Relations Theory
Concepts, tools, debates
Johnathan Fox and Nukhet Sandal

Religion in the Context of Globalization
Essays on concept, form, and political implication
Peter Beyer

Muslims and Political Participation in Britain
Edited by Timothy Peace

Religion and the Realist Tradition
From political theology to International Relations theory and back
Jodok Troy

Cosmopolitanism, Religion and the Public Sphere
Maria Rovisco and Sebastian Kim

Religion, Identity and Human Security
Giorgio Shani

Christians and the Middle East Conflict
Edited by John Rowe, John Dyck and Jens Zimmerman

Conservative Religious Politics in Russia and the United States
Dreaming of a Christian nation
John Anderson

Muslims and Political Participation in Britain

Edited by
Timothy Peace

Routledge
Taylor & Francis Group
LONDON AND NEW YORK

First published 2015
by Routledge
2 Park Square, Milton Park, Abingdon, Oxon OX14 4RN

and by Routledge
711 Third Avenue, New York, NY 10017

Routledge is an imprint of the Taylor & Francis Group, an informa business

© 2015 Timothy Peace for selection and editorial matter; individual contributors for their contributions

The right of Timothy Peace to be identified as the author of the editorial material, and of the authors for their individual chapters, has been asserted in accordance with sections 77 and 78 of the Copyright, Designs and Patents Act 1988.

All rights reserved. No part of this book may be reprinted or reproduced or utilised in any form or by any electronic, mechanical, or other means, now known or hereafter invented, including photocopying and recording, or in any information storage or retrieval system, without permission in writing from the publishers.

Trademark notice: Product or corporate names may be trademarks or registered trademarks, and are used only for identification and explanation without intent to infringe.

British Library Cataloguing in Publication Data
A catalogue record for this book is available from the British Library

Library of Congress Cataloging in Publication Data
Muslims and political participation in Britain / edited by Timothy Peace.
  pages cm. -- (Routledge studies in religion and politics)
Includes bibliographical references and index.
  1. Muslims--Great Britain--Politics and government. 2. Political participation--Great Britain. I. Peace, Timothy, editor of compilation, author.
  DA125.M87M875 2015
  323'.0420882970941--dc23
             2014033898

ISBN: 978-0-415-72531-6 (hbk)
ISBN: 978-1-315-85685-8 (ebk)

Typeset in Times New Roman
by Taylor & Francis Books

Contents

List of illustrations ix
List of contributors xi
Foreword xiii

Introduction 1
TIMOTHY PEACE

PART I
Voting and elections 13

1 The paradox of patronage politics: Biraderi, representation and political participation amongst British Pakistanis 15
PARVEEN AKHTAR

2 Muslim electoral participation in British general elections: an historical perspective and case study 32
JAMIL SHERIF, ANAS ALTIKRITI AND ISMAIL PATEL

3 Mosques and political engagement in Britain: participation or segregation? 53
SIOBHAN MCANDREW AND MARIA SOBOLEWSKA

PART II
Social Movements 83

4 Women from Muslim communities in Britain: political and civic activism in the 9/11 era 85
KHURSHEED WADIA

5 'Islamic' environmentalism in Great Britain 103
ROSEMARY HANCOCK

6 British Muslims and the anti-war movement 124
TIMOTHY PEACE

PART III
Exploring the political amongst young people — 139

7 Diversity in political perspectives and engagement among young British Muslims — 141
ASMA MUSTAFA

8 Facebook groups as potential political publics? Exploring ideas of the political amongst young British Muslim Facebook users — 156
BROOKE STORER-CHURCH

9 From crisis to opportunity – 9/11 and the progress of British Muslim political engagement — 174
KHADIJAH ELSHAYYAL

PART IV
Representation — 193

10 The Muslim Council of Britain and its engagement with the British political establishment — 195
EKATERINA BRAGINSKAIA

11 Muslims in Parliament: a myth of futility — 215
EKATERINA KOLPINSKAYA

12 The political behaviour of minority councillors across London boroughs: comparing Tower Hamlets, Newham, and Hackney — 237
EREN TATARI AND AHMET YUKLEYEN

Index — 257

List of illustrations

Figures

3.1	Frequency of attendance by affiliation (British ethnic minority and Muslim, or British ethnic minority and non-Muslim religious adherent)	59
3.2	Frequency of British ethnic minority Muslims' mosque attendance by sex	60
3.3	Frequency of British ethnic minority Muslims' mosque attendance by ethnic origin	60
3.4	Diversity of British ethnic minority Muslims' and non-Muslims' places of worship	61
3.5	Differences between regular mosque attenders and less frequent attenders on three social distance measures (Muslim respondents only)	63
11.1	Legislative roles of Muslim MPs by session	219

Tables

3.1	Summary of variables of interest for Muslims in the EMBES sample	69
3.2	Drivers of mosque attendance	74
3.3	Political engagement, religious involvement, basic values and perceived prejudice: bivariate associations	75
3.4	Drivers of political engagement and political effect: multivariate analysis	76
3.5	Tests for mediating effect of religious attendance and confounding effect of co-ethnic density	78
11.1	MPs from under-represented groups in the 2010 Parliament by role type	221
11.2	Members of Parliament with Muslim background on leadership roles, 1997–2012	222
11.3	Members of Government from Muslim backgrounds, 1997–2012	224
11.4	Membership in Select and Public Bills Committees	226

11.5	Private Members' Bills, number per session	230
11.6	Private Members' Bills introduced by Muslim MPs	231
12.1	Percentage of Muslims in parliamentary constituencies in England and Wales	241
12.2	Comparison of Tower Hamlets, Newham, and Hackney	244
12.3	Ethnic breakdown of Tower Hamlets, Newham, and Hackney, mid-2005	244
12.4	Hackney data	247

List of contributors

Parveen Akhtar is Lecturer in Sociology in the School of Social and International Studies at the University of Bradford.

Anas Altikriti is the Founder and CEO of The Cordoba Foundation. He holds a doctorate in Political Studies from Westminster University in London.

Muhammad Anwar OBE is Emeritus Professor in the Department of Sociology at the University of Warwick.

Ekaterina Braginskaia has a PhD in Politics from the University of Edinburgh. She has previously worked as a Research Fellow on the ESRC-funded project "Radicalisation and Islam: the Russian dimension."

Khadijah Elshayyal is a Postdoctoral Fellow (Muslims in Britain) at the Alwaleed Centre, University of Edinburgh.

Rosemary Hancock is a PhD candidate at the University of Sydney. She holds a teaching fellowship at The Women's College (University of Sydney) and is an Associate Lecturer in Philosophy at the University of Notre Dame, Sydney.

Ekaterina Kolpinskaya is an Associate Lecturer (E&S) in Quantitative Methods at the Q-Step Centre, University of Exeter.

Siobhan McAndrew is Lecturer in Sociology with Quantitative Research Methods within the School of Sociology, Politics and International Studies at the University of Bristol.

Asma Mustafa is Research Fellow on Muslims in Britain at the Oxford Centre for Islamic Studies and Senior Tutor and Senior Research Fellow at Linacre College, University of Oxford.

Ismail Patel is the Chairman of Friends of Al-Aqsa (UK) and Director of YouElect.

Timothy Peace is Lecturer in Comparative European Politics at the University of Stirling.

Jamil Sherif is a data analyst and was founding chair of the Muslim Council of Britain's Research & Documentation Committee.

Maria Sobolewska is Lecturer in Politics (Quantitative Methods) at the University of Manchester and a member of the Centre on Dynamics of Ethnicity (CoDE).

Brooke Storer-Church is Higher Education Policy Advisor (Postgraduate Policy) and the project manager of the Postgraduate Support Scheme for the Higher Education Funding Council for England (HEFCE).

Eren Tatari is Assistant Professor of Political Science at Rollins College in Florida.

Khursheed Wadia is Principal Research Fellow in the Centre for the Study of Safety and Well-Being at the University of Warwick.

Ahmet Yukleyen is Associate Professor of International Relations at Istanbul Commerce University.

Foreword

Muhammad Anwar

Britain is now a well established multi-ethnic and multi-faith society. This is a result of a long tradition of migration and integration. There have been migrants in Britain for two thousand years. However, except in the last 67 years, most of those who migrated to this country were white people. It is only since 1948 that Britain has received large numbers of people from the former colonies; workers and their dependents whose colour differs from the native population. They are largely from the 'New Commonwealth' countries which include several Muslim majority countries. Commonwealth citizens had free entry into Britain before the Commonwealth Immigrants Act 1962. After the Second World War many workers from the New Commonwealth countries came to work in expanding British industries. The start of the mass migration from these countries was the arrival of the ship *Empire Windrush* in June 1948 at Tilbury docks with 492 immigrants from Jamaica. After this, migration from the West Indies progressed slowly by air and sea. It is worth mentioning that, in addition to the voluntary movement of people, some institutional arrangements also helped the process of migration. These included the recruitment of workers for London Transport and for the National Health Service from the West Indies. Migration from India and Pakistan started later. Two developments in the region contributed to this process of migration to Britain: the partition of India in 1947, when Pakistan was created, and the construction of the Mangla Dam. In both cases large numbers of people were displaced and some looked for work opportunities in Britain (Anwar 1979).

The mass migration of Muslims to Britain started mainly from Pakistan in the 1960s followed by Muslims from other Commonwealth and, later on, from non Commonwealth countries as well. In 1951 the estimated number of Muslims in Britain was only 10,000, which increased to 50,000 in 1961. However, with the increased migration from some Muslim countries in the 1960s and 1970s the number of Muslims grew significantly and by 1981 it was estimated to be one million. Mosques were built and organisations were formed at local, regional and national levels. Some of them encouraged and helped their members to participate in politics. Another development which helped this participation was the diminishing myth of return to their countries of origin. This myth was quite common among some larger Muslim communities such as Pakistanis in the 1970s (Anwar 1979). In this context the right of dual nationality has also helped Pakistanis and Bangladeshis because they feel that their property rights in their countries of origin are secure, as they can keep the citizenship of those countries. This has helped them to feel more settled in Britain and participate in British life including civic activities.

Based on the 2011 Census, which for the second time included a voluntary question on religion, I estimate that in 2015 the number of British Muslims is over 3 million. Most of them have a right to vote as Commonwealth or British citizens. British Muslims are not a homogenous group. They come from different countries, belong to different ethnic groups, speak different languages and have different migration experiences. The largest number of British Muslims, over one million, originate from Pakistan followed by Bangladeshis (402,428). Other Muslims come from India, Cyprus, Africa and Arab countries. However, it is worth mentioning that almost 8 per cent of British Muslims are White. Muslims have the youngest age profile compared with other religious groups in Britain. For example, 36.4 per cent of the Muslim population is under 18 years of age compared with 21.3 per cent of the general population. At the other end only 4 per cent of British Muslims are over 65, compared with 16.4 per cent of this age group in the general population. It is also relevant to mention here that almost half of British Muslims are now British born (Office for National Statistics 2013).

Muslims are highly concentrated in certain areas and regions. In 2011, for example, over one million Muslims lived in London, over half a million lived in the Midlands and about 700,000 Muslims were living in the North West and Yorkshire and Humber regions. Moreover, they are highly concentrated within these regions. There are several local authority areas in England where Muslims make up over 20 per cent of the total population. Therefore, there are several local wards and Parliamentary constituencies in Britain with a significant number of Muslims (Office for National Statistics 2013). For example, there are 50 Parliamentary constituencies where the Muslim population is more than 14 per cent (two with more than 50 per cent). These numbers and their concentrations have increased the statistical significance of Muslims in the political process. I believe that, with the generational change amongst British Muslims, their attitudes are also changing. Young Muslims are becoming more assertive and active in the civic life of the country and British Muslims see themselves as British and as an integral part of Britain.

Some national and global events involving Muslims have made British Muslims more visible and politically more active, in particular the Rushdie affair in 1989 and the tragic events of 11 September 2001 in New York and 7 July 2005 in London. In addition, the Gulf wars of 1991 and 2003, the genocide of Muslims in Bosnia in the early 1990s, the urban unrest in Oldham, Burnley and Bradford, all with large Muslim populations, in 2001, the war in Afghanistan since 2001 and more recent developments in Syria, Iraq and Gaza have kept British Muslims politicised and in the news. This means that

British Muslims need to be seen in a global context. In fact, since the Rushdie affair, I have not known a period in which British Muslims have not been in the news. In this the role of the media in terms of projecting and presenting Muslims is important. Unfortunately the media's tone has generally been negative and this has resulted in an increase in Islamophobia and created a sense of insecurity amongst British Muslims (Anwar 2008). This situation has no doubt encouraged Muslims to participate in politics to counter anti-Muslim propaganda.

I strongly believe that the participation of British Muslims and other ethnic minorities in Britain in the electoral system gives them the opportunity to express their views. Their representation in politics is crucial to achieve equality of opportunity in the political system, as well as in other fields. It was with this belief that I started research on the political participation of ethnic minorities in the early 1970s (Anwar 1973, 1974; Anwar and Kohler 1975), which I have continued to this day. In fact, since the early 1970s, I have monitored all the general elections and some local elections to find out the progress being made in terms of the participation and representation of ethnic minorities and, more recently, of British Muslims. In addition to their progress in educational, economic and other fields, British Muslims' integration into the political process is of fundamental importance. I also believe that the integration of British Muslims into the political process requires their effective, not token, representation and involvement at all levels. They need to feel part of and participate fully in the decision making process in order to feel that they are accepted as full citizens of this country. Slow progress has been made to provide British Muslims representation at local, national and European levels. Currently nearly 300 out of almost 21,000 councillors, nine out of 650 MPs (the first MP of Muslim origin was elected in 1997), four MEPs and 14 out of 774 members of the House of Lords are of Muslim origin. However, to reflect the number of Muslims in the population, there should be at least 30 MPs and another 20 members of the House of Lords of Muslim origin.

In terms of participation of British Muslims in the electoral process, four trends are worth noting. First, that British Muslim turn outs at elections are generally higher than non-Muslims in the areas where they are concentrated. Second, while at the local level the majority of Muslim origin councillors belong to the first generation, at national and European levels the Muslim origin MPs and MEPs tend to belong to the second generation. Third, in the 1970s and 1980s if a British Muslim became a Mayor or Lord Mayor it was seen as big news but now it is quite a common occurrence, and currently there are several towns and cities which have Mayors and Lord Mayors of Muslim origin. Fourth, unlike the 1970s, 1980s or even 1990s, when most British Muslims supported and represented the Labour Party, now they are supporting and representing all the main political parties. A British Muslim (Amjad Bashir) has even represented the United Kingdom Independence Party (UKIP) in the European Parliament. However, while there is slow progress in terms of representation of Muslims at all levels, overall it still does not reflect the number of Muslims in the population. Therefore, I feel that the main political parties need to do more to correct this deficit, as I believe that they cannot afford to ignore the statistical significance of British Muslims in the inner city areas of British cities where elections are often decided. So what is the way forward? I suggest that Muslims need to join the political parties in greater numbers and seek office. The political parties must make sure that they are treated as party candidates and not as token Muslim candidates. British Muslims, including Muslim women, need to be selected for both 'safe' and 'winnable' seats. Muslim candidates should not be seen as representing only their own communities, but all communities where they contest and win. Once elected, Muslim origin representatives should represent the interests of all their electorate, not just the interests of British Muslims. *Muslims and Political Participation in Britain* is a welcome, timely and important contribution to our understanding of the participation of British Muslims in politics in a wider context. The book is a crucial resource for academics, students, political parties, equality workers, and the general public, including British Muslims, who are interested in ethnicity and politics. It will also enable readers in other countries to understand the specificities of the British case as well as provide a useful comparison to what is happening in other European states with similar multi-ethnic and multi-faith situations.

Bibliography

Anwar, M. (1973) 'Pakistani Participation in the 1972 Rochdale By-Election', *New Community*, 2: 4.
Anwar, M. (1974) 'Pakistani Participation in the 1973 Rochdale Local Elections', *New Community*, 3: 1–2.
Anwar, M. (1979) *The Myth of Return: Pakistanis in Britain*. London: Heinemann.
Anwar, M. (2008) 'Muslims in Western States: The British Experience and the Way Forward', *Journal of Muslim Minority Affairs*, 28(1).
Anwar, M. and Kohler, D. (1975) *Participation of Ethnic Minorities in the General Election, October 1974*. London: Community Relations Commission.
Office for National Statistics (2013) *2011 Census*. London: ONS.

Introduction

Timothy Peace

There is increasing interest in the political participation and representation of religious and ethnic minorities in Europe (Bird, Saalfeld and Wüst 2010; Benbassa 2011; Givens and Maxwell 2012; Nielsen 2013). While in many countries this is quite a new topic, such research in Britain actually dates back to the early 1970s. This can firstly be explained by the settlement of large numbers of migrants from its former colonies in the immediate post-war period which meant that issues of immigration, race and ethnicity became prominent relatively early. Also, unlike other European countries which denied voting rights to migrants, many of those arriving in Britain had full political rights as either citizens of the UK or Commonwealth citizens. It was in this context that Muhammad Anwar started his research on political participation amongst minorities in Britain by firstly monitoring the participation of Asians in Rochdale in the parliamentary by-election of 1972 and then participation by all ethnic minorities during the 1974 general election (Anwar and Kohler 1975). His work has been crucial in our understanding of this phenomenon and it is fitting that his foreword begins this current volume. Other important landmarks in this field include works by Anthony Messina (1989), Shamit Saggar (1991) and Andrew Geddes (1995).

These authors were concerned with issues of race in British politics at a time when 'race relations' was still the dominant narrative in terms of the position of minorities in society. Philip Lewis' (1994) account of local politics in Bradford showed that religion could be an equally, if not more, important factor. Campaigns for halal meat in schools and the protests against the head teacher Ray Honeyford in the early 1980s can be seen as the early signs of a developing Muslim identity. The true watershed moment, though, was the Rushdie affair which certainly led to the creation of a distinct 'Muslim consciousness' (Meer 2010). Lewis' observations of developments in Bradford 'post-Rushdie' would apply to other urban conurbations with a significant Muslim population, in particular how many were now entering local government:

> Residential clustering has also provided a constituency which ensures the appointment of Muslim councillors. The 1980s saw a dramatic increase in their numbers, ensuring that local services began to respond to their

> special needs ... in 1981 only three of Bradford's 90 councillors were Muslim. By 1992 it had 11, all Labour, including the deputy leader of the ruling group. These included both a Gujarati woman and a Bangladeshi. This already indicates co-operation across national and regional groupings.
>
> (Lewis 1994: 21, 24)

The emergence of Muslim councillors was studied in detail by Kingsley Purdam who carried out his PhD research between 1994 and 1998. He was the first scholar to look specifically at Muslim identities in British politics and electoral participation as 'Muslims' rather than ethnic minorities. By 1996 he had estimated that there were 160 Muslim councillors in Britain, the majority of whom had been elected in wards with large Muslim populations. The success of Muslim councillors was therefore a result of Muslim demographic concentration and the first past the post electoral system which meant that Muslim political participation was of direct electoral significance (Purdam 1996). He also noted the prominence of being Muslim as a primary identity for these councillors (Purdam 2000) and how they attempted to invoke loyalties of kinship and caste in their appeals to voters (Purdam 2001).

Muslims have been participating in British politics for many years but it is only relatively recently that they have come to be defined as such. The semantic shift from an ethnic to a religious identity has the potential to clarify and also confuse. Part of the problem with past political research on 'immigrants' and then later 'ethnic' or 'visible' minorities is that it tended to treat all non-white voters/candidates/citizens as a reified category when they may have had very little in common. Using such categories obscures the inherent diversity within a given population and ignores the subtleties of how different groups actually interact with the political process and why we may observe significant differences between them. This is illustrated by research on the political participation of ethnic minorities in the UK which shows that there are major differences between various ethnic groups (Heath *et al.* 2013). On the other hand, by referring to 'Muslims' rather than say 'South Asians' or 'Pakistanis' we are making assumptions about the importance of religion when other factors such as kinship networks could have a much stronger influence on political behaviour. Indeed, the use of a religious marker is inherently problematic. When we talk about a 'Muslim MP' does this imply that the person in question represents Muslims or that his/her own religious beliefs or cultural background is more important than party affiliation? Indeed, it is rare to see references to 'Jewish MPs' or a 'Christian Vote'.

This discussion of identities and labels is not new however. Scholars have been grappling with this issue in relation to Muslims and political participation for a long time. In his research in the 1990s, Kingsley Purdam noted that:

> Muslims invoke various interpretations and rhetorics of Islam to justify and inspire particular political strategies. They operate both inside and

beyond the *liberal democratic* system. It is evident that in Britain a majority of Muslim voters vote Labour but within this general alignment there are various political and cultural positionings. Muslims are not an undifferentiated group, they are not, in the language of political science a single-issue pressure group. Identities are more complex than this: they are negotiated, contested, unstable historical positionings. Muslims themselves are debating and contesting exactly what it means to be a Muslim, what Islam means and how it should be constructed and reproduced both in the *West* and in the rest of the world.

(Purdam 1996: 130)

Later, even after 9/11, Stefano Allievi pointed to the dangers of seeing voters in purely religious terms:

If we refer to the electorate of these communities as Muslims, the religious variable must prevail: but the success of specific lists characterised in this way has been inconsistent to date and the degree of identification poor. The basic illusion of these parties is that of the very existence of homogeneous religious communities: it does not take into account the fact that many presumed Muslims are often not Muslims and if they are, they are Muslims in a highly diversified way. In addition, there is often only an instrumental use of the Muslim reasoning by leaders, with the aim of achieving some visibility, thus producing Islamisation of a debate which, up to now, has only tenuous religious characteristics and which is often short lived.

(Allievi 2003: 187)

While both statements are still valid, the intervening years have seen the development of a distinct Muslim identity in Britain which has been used in the political arena, as evidenced from the chapters in this volume which point to the need for looking at Muslims as a separate political category despite its inherent problems and contradictions. Social science must take account of such developments as there is now an undeniable salience of religion in British political life, particularly amongst voters who identify as Muslim. The existence of civil society groups which mobilise Muslims to vote is just one example of this phenomenon.[1]

Scholarly interest in Britain's Muslim communities has proliferated since the events of 11th September 2001 but there has been a surprising lack of work on Muslims and political participation since the work of Purdam. This volume seeks to fill that gap in the literature by looking specifically at how Muslims have participated in British politics in an attempt to go beyond the over-studied issues of identity, terrorism, headscarves and other items that often make the headlines. Muslims have, in fact, been quietly participating in local politics since the 1970s. Free from the barriers to participation found in other countries, they availed themselves of the ability to vote and subsequently stand for election. The pioneers in this respect were Bashir Maan, elected to represent Glasgow's Kingston ward for Labour in 1970, and Karamat Hussain, elected to Brent Council in London in 1972 (Anwar 1996: 126). Bashir Maan was also put forward by Labour for the East Fife parliamentary constituency in 1974, and in 1979 the Conservative candidate for Glasgow Central was Farooq Saleem. Unsurprisingly both lost but during the 1980s Muslim candidates made significant inroads in local politics with election to posts as councillors. Some went on to become mayors, including the aforementioned Karamat Hussain who became mayor of Brent in 1981, and Councillor Muhammad Ajeeb, first elected to Bradford Council in 1979, who became Lord Mayor of Bradford in 1985. However, it wasn't until 1997 that Britain got its first Muslim MP when Mohammad Sarwar was elected to the seat of Glasgow Govan for Labour. This was followed one year later by the first Muslim life peers in the House of Lords (Baroness Uddin, Lord Alli and Baron Ahmed) who also represented the Labour Party.

It is this party that has continuously attracted the support of Muslim (and indeed all non-white) voters in the UK and the majority of elected Muslim politicians have represented the Labour Party. In the early years of Muslim political participation it was natural for them to support Labour because of the stance it took on immigration and that the fact that many first generation Muslims were factory workers who would have had strong links with the unions (Hussain 2004). The Labour Party built on its early success of attracting a minority vote by developing a distinct ethnic electorate which included promoting ethnic minority elites (Garbaye 2005). For example, in the case of Pakistani communities, the consequence was a system of patronage whereby local Labour politicians built links with community leaders who were expected to deliver bloc votes. These local leaders were often given minor positions of power and mentored in the ways of the political system. Later they could stand for council seats or at least hold influential roles as subaltern aides. Some community leaders negotiated for community provisions such as neighbourhood centres, whilst others were content with the status conferred on them in the eyes of their compatriots (Akhtar 2013). They also put pressure on their parliamentary representatives to raise issues in parliament relating to international issues such as the Kashmir dispute. In 1990 a Kashmir Human Rights Committee was formed in the House of Commons and subsequently an All Party Kashmir Group was set up, most members being Labour MPs who represented large Pakistani/Kashmiri communities (Ellis and Khan 1998). In Birmingham a political party was subsequently set up in 1998 that grew out of the Justice for Kashmir campaign group. The People's Justice Party (PJP) went on to elect a handful of local councillors before disbanding in 2006. This demonstrated that loyalty to the Labour Party could not be taken for granted amongst Muslim voters, as was proved by the success of the Respect Party.

The development of Respect represented a new era in the participation of Muslims in British politics. Appeals were now being made to a specific religiously defined electorate rather than an ethnic community.[2] Respect was branded as the 'party for Muslims' and candidates claimed they were backed by 'Muslim scholars' (Peace 2013). In the 2005 election campaign, George Galloway constantly referred to the invasion of Iraq as a 'war against Muslims' and forced his Labour rival Oona King to also appeal to voters through their Muslim identity (Glynn 2008). This has now become the norm and political parties have set their sights on capturing a 'Muslim vote' as if Muslims formed some kind of unified constituency. For example, the Conservative Muslim Forum was 'founded by Lord Sheikh in 2005 when the Conservative Party recognised that it needed to do more to appeal to Muslim voters'.[3] Since then a number of landmarks have been passed including the first Muslim minister in 2007 (Shahid Malik as Parliamentary Under-Secretary of State for International Development), the first Muslim to attend a meeting of the Cabinet in 2009 (Sadiq Khan upon his appointment as Minister of State for Transport) and the first Muslim woman to serve in the Cabinet in 2010 (Baroness Warsi as Minister without portfolio). The general election of 2010 also saw the arrival in parliament of the first female Muslim MPs and Conservative Muslim MPs. So Muslims are playing a prominent role even at the highest levels of British political life. Yet Muslim political participation is about much more than national and local party politics and the chapters in this volume showcase current research into Muslim political participation both in terms of electoral politics and civil society initiatives.[4]

The chapters

In Chapter 1, Parveen Akhtar tackles the importance of biraderi networks which are key to understanding political activity amongst Pakistani communities in Britain. She discusses the concept of political representation and the idea of minorities within minorities in relation to Muslim politicians. She argues that the demographic make-up of Muslim political representatives largely mirrors that of the wider British political spectrum, usually middle class and middle aged men, but that things are beginning to change including the election of more women. She describes how biraderi (or kinship) networks function in the diasporic context and their importance in the migration and settlement process. Local politicians became aware of the electoral potential of such close-knit communities in the 1970s and patronage relationships were subsequently formed. Akhtar makes an important distinction between the use of biraderi networks in everyday life and the use of biraderi-politicking whereby kinship networks are used as a mechanism for political control. Although this practice did limit the political role marginalised sections of the community could play in the political process, there is some recognition that it allowed Muslims to gain representation for their community and its specific concerns. Nevertheless, there is now a perception, particularly among the younger generation, that Muslim representatives may have held the community back because the focus was on narrow community specific issues and not wider social problems which could unite people across different communities.

Chapter 2 continues the theme of electoral participation with a historical look at how Muslim organisations in Britain have made interventions in the political sphere in relation to general elections. Jamil Sherif, Ismail Patel and Anas Altikriti trace the history of these organisations including the Union of Muslim Organisations (UMO) founded back in 1970. Its interventions in the political sphere may have gone largely unnoticed at the time but this reminds us that even if other ethnic or racial labels were more common in that period, some Muslims were still mobilising on a religious basis. The authors demonstrate that there has been a 'Muslim lobby' since at least 1979 when the UMO general secretary wrote a letter to the leaders of the main political parties prior to that year's general election. The list of concerns presented in this letter and the one sent in 1983 was a taste of things to come regarding Muslim political mobilisation at the end of the 1980s, particularly regarding the provision of halal food and a proposed change to blasphemy laws in the wake of the Rushdie affair. As Sherif, Patel and Altikriti explain, the aftermath of this mobilisation of the Muslim community was disappointing for its representative organisations as the political establishment was unwilling to take any action to have the book banned. They show however that from 1997 onwards there has been a concerted effort by the Muslim Council of Britain (MCB), and its predecessor the UKACIA, to state what British Muslims expect from their parliamentary representatives by producing a series of policy documents or manifestos. The MCB has been a key player in driving Muslim voter registration and participation in elections through its website and affiliate network. Over the years these attempts to get Muslims involved in elections have become more sophisticated and the second half of the chapter details the work of the YouElect project run by a network of Muslim civil society activists prior to the 2010 general election. Such attempts to shape Muslim voting intentions are likely to continue during 2015 and beyond.

The third chapter in the volume by Siobhan McAndrew and Maria Sobolewska looks at the importance of mosques and their role in the political integration of Muslims into British society. They do so by comparing Muslims who do not regularly attend mosques with those who do to see how this affects political participation. Research from the US in fact demonstrates a positive link between attendance at religious services and civic and political activity. To test their hypotheses with the British Muslim case, the authors draw on the Ethnic Minority British Election Study (EMBES) of 2010. They discovered that mosque attendance is associated with self-reports of having voted and is not a cause of political alienation as often described in the tabloid press. Indeed, more accurate predictors of political disengagement include a feeling of prejudice and being socially distant from the majority white group. However, on other matters, such as the duty to vote, religious attendance was not significant and mosque attendance does not predict many other indicators of political engagement. It is therefore important not to try to read too much into religiosity and political participation where British Muslims are concerned.

The second section of the volume is concerned with social movements and in Chapter 4 Khursheed Wadia looks at the role of Muslim women as political actors in the UK since 9/11. She points out that the state encouraged Muslim women to get active in community organisations as a means to prevent radicalisation and state-funding provided the opportunity to create new groups and projects. Wadia identifies three main types of participants among Muslim women: 'stay-home political activists', 'civic activists' and 'intense political activists'. The first category concerns those women who made a contribution through actions such as donating money to campaigns or signing petitions, some of whom were also drawn to action outside of the home. The second category includes women who wanted to use their position within the community to counter negative stereotypes. They were often involved in various community organisations and took part in marches, rallies and political demonstrations. The third category refers to those who gained public visibility because of their political activism and often had a history of involvement in social movements.

In Chapter 5 Rosemary Hancock explores the involvement of British Muslims in the environmental movement and the emergence of green Muslim organisations such as the Islamic Foundation for Ecology and Environmental Sciences (IFEES) and Wisdom in Nature (WiN). She firstly explores how Social Movement Theory has dealt with the issue of religion and notes how religious movements tended to be left out of social movement studies until quite recently. This was especially true with Islamic activism although that situation has now been redressed with the wave of studies that have surfaced in the wake of 9/11. Hancock looks at some of the central concepts in Islamic environmental discourse and then turns to her case studies of Islamic Environmental Organisations in Britain by outlining their goals and means for achieving them. She then elaborates on the ideology and framing of both IFEES and WiN showing that the former is more formally grounded in Islamic beliefs while the latter is more influenced by left-wing political activism associated with more mainstream environmental groups. Where IFEES is more international and seeks to work with governments and institutions, WiN prefers a bottom-up approach that remains committed to local grassroots action. The two groups demonstrate the diversity of options available to those Muslims interested in saving the planet where they can meet like-minded individuals who share their faith. However, Hancock also points out the similarity of these groups to the larger secular environmental organisations such as Greenpeace and Friends of the Earth which Muslims are now increasingly likely to join.

Timothy Peace's chapter concludes the section on social movements with an overview of the participation of British Muslims in the anti-war movement. He traces the history of this participation with a focus on some of the key figures and activists that were involved. He argues that the involvement of Muslims in the anti-war movement acted as a springboard to the development of what is now referred to as 'Muslim civil society' and created opportunities for a new generation of Muslim leaders to emerge from the shadows of the first generation. He contrasts the mobilisation against the 'war on terror' with protests during the Rushdie affair, the success of the former being based on successful partnerships being built with organisations that formed the Stop the War Coalition. The formation of Just Peace, a small London-based group, started the ball rolling for Muslim participation in the anti-war movement. Its role is often forgotten due to the later exposure given to groups such as the Muslim Association of Britain (MAB). Peace also demonstrates that Muslim participation in the movement was not as straightforward as many leaders have publically claimed. Nevertheless the anti-war movement, and in particular the massive demonstration of 15th February 2003, is a key moment in the history of British Muslim political participation and directly led to the formation of the Respect Party.

Part 3 of the volume looks at the political involvement of young people, an important topic given the demographics of the British Muslim population. Asma Mustafa's contribution analyses the perception of young second generation British Muslims regarding political violence, foreign policy, citizenship and political engagement. She shows how many young Muslims use religious teachings, morals and values to inform their political perspectives and activities. Some respondents directly referred to the Qur'an but Mustafa highlights the diversity of religious interpretation and subsequent broad range of views espoused by those she interviewed. She notes that despite their loyalty being called into question, many young Muslims feel a shared sense of Britishness and engage in moments of national pride. Others may perceive their citizenship in purely instrumental terms and feel that their only allegiance is to the 'ummah' or global Muslim community. Irrespective of their emotional attachment to the country, most respondents did feel passionate about politics and in particular elections and the right to vote. Boycotting was also a method that many used to signal their discontent on certain political issues.

Chapter 8 looks at how young Muslims use Facebook to explore ideas of the political. Brooke Storer-Church used Facebook Groups to recruit participants for her study and observed the discussions that they engaged in on this social media platform as well as conducting online and offline interviews. Facebook afforded her participants the opportunity for education and engaging in conversation with people who hold a wide range of political views. This even includes engaging with political groups that are hostile to Muslims such as the English Defence League (EDL) Facebook Group. Other groups more focused on British Muslims provided a point around which respondents could gather, debate and discuss the terms of their identity and representation. They also were used as tools for participation in collective action through particular political campaigns. Facebook therefore provides a space for the articulation of reflexive politics and an arena for democratic debate as well as a springboard for offline political action such as street protests.

Political engagement is explored further by Khadijah Elshayyal and in particular the development of British Muslim identity politics. Her focus is on the reactions to 9/11 both among Muslim advocacy groups and the British government. Prior to this, she recounts how the 1990s were a period of religious discovery and self-assertion of young Muslims. The formation of the MCB meant that for the very first time the British government had a privileged Muslim interlocutor, however the period of 2001–2005 saw a host of new initiatives that were designed to represent British Muslims. Elshayyal also discusses how Muslims have reacted to the emergence of the far-right which traded particularly heavily on stoking fears of Muslims. The means for dealing with this problem became the source of tension between those who believed people of faith need protection against incitement to hatred and those who sought to protect freedom of expression, even of those they might disagree with.

Chapter 10 takes an even deeper look at the Muslim Council of Britain as part of the final section on participation in institutions. Ekaterina Braginskaia examines the MCB's relationship with successive British governments in the period from 1997–2013. She analyses the changing nature of its engagement with the political establishment in light of the opportunities and constraints offered by a rapidly changing political climate. She notes that the initial years of the MCB could be considered as a honeymoon period as there was successful cooperation between senior politicians and the Council. This coincided with an effort by the government to demonstrate a greater receptivity to faith and faith-based identities. The MCB became the unquestioned representative organisation for Muslim interests and successfully lobbied for a religious question to be included in the 2001 census. As Braginskaia points out, this was a notable achievement on behalf of the MCB as it paved the way for the recognition of a Muslim identity in the public sphere with statistics to back it up. The events of September 2001 would merely confirm the salience of this identity and this event also provided the MCB with its biggest challenge. Braginskaia documents how the relationship between the Council and the government gradually broke down. She also details how the change from a Labour to Coalition government led to a pluralising of state-Muslim relations.

In her chapter (Chapter 11), Ekaterina Kolpinskaya analyses the role of Muslim MPs in the Westminster parliament. She challenges the assumption that Muslim politicians may lack opportunities to contribute to legislative decision making. She also shows that belonging to a religious minority does not determine how they engage with the legislative process. The chapter adopts an institution-centred approach and demonstrates that Muslim MPs are more than able contributors to the legislative process including the introduction and scrutiny of legislative proposals and policies. They are thus involved in decision-making at the heart of British parliamentary democracy. Indeed, it is noted that by 2012 four of the six Labour and one of the three Conservative Muslim MPs had held either ministerial or Parliamentary Private Secretary (PPS) positions. Although Muslim MPs have not been particularly successful at introducing Private Members' Bills, this again is not due to their background but rather their disengagement with this type of parliamentary activity. This is more than balanced out by preparing and passing government legislative proposals as either ministers or PPS, and conversely scrutinising such proposals as members of the opposition. In fact, this chapter reminds us that Muslims are actually over-represented on the frontbench when compared to other MPs with a minority background. This is a measure of the progress that has been made since the very first Muslim MP was elected in 1997.

Finally, Chapter 12 deals with Muslim representatives in local government with a case study of the London boroughs of Hackney, Newham and Tower Hamlets which are all home to large Muslim populations. Eren Tatari and Ahmet Yukleyen examine the extent to which ethnic minorities engage in community politics and represent the interests of their own communities rather than the entire constituency. They argue that while substantive representation is necessary, it is not sufficient for Muslim political representation. Their research draws on original data from in-depth interviews with a range of Muslim leaders, political activists and city councillors as well as a quantitative analysis of all Muslim councillors across the three boroughs. The data show that Tower Hamlets Council has the highest local government responsiveness to specific Muslim demands. The authors also demonstrate that party fragmentation among Muslim councillors can impact their cohesion and effectiveness in terms of their responsiveness to Muslim demands. The research does however show that Muslim councillors do not focus exclusively on Muslim interests. So while they might articulate and pursue the concerns of the Muslim community, they also devote time to working on issues that have no religious, ethnic or racial content. Tatari and Yukleyen also remind us that these Muslim elected officials encourage civic involvement among Muslim youth and are alternative role models to the extremists who shun democratic institutions.

Notes

1 A good example is the YouElect campaign run by a network of Muslim civil society activists in the lead up to the UK general election to promote Muslim voter registration and political engagement (see Chapter 2). The Muslim lobbying group MEND (formerly iENGAGE) has an initiative called Get Out & Vote! www.getoutandvote.info while the Muslim Council of Britain runs www.mcb.org.uk/muslimvote.
2 It could be argued that the first party to do this was the Islamic Party of Britain, established in 1989 by convert David Musa Pidcock. It stood candidates in Bradford at the 1992 general election and received just over 1,000 votes.
3 www.conservativemuslimforum.com/about-us/overview/.
4 Many of the chapters in this volume were first presented in April 2012 at a conference in Edinburgh organised by the Alwaleed Centre at the University of Edinburgh in partnership with the Muslims in Britain Research Network (MBRN). As part of the conference, the Centre also organized a public debate called 'Muslims and the political process in Scotland' held at the Scottish Parliament; the speakers included Hamira Khan, Hanzala Malik MSP, Shabnum Mustapha and Humza Yousaf MSP and was chaired by Professor Mona Siddiqui, OBE. www.ed.ac.uk/schools-departments/literatures-languages-cultures/alwaleed/muslims-in-britain/conference/.

Bibliography

Akhtar, P. (2013) *British Muslim Politics: Examining Pakistani Biraderi Networks*. Basingstoke: Palgrave Macmillan.
Allievi, S. (2003) 'Muslims and Politics', in B. Maréchal *et al.* (eds) *Muslims in the Enlarged Europe: Religion and Society*. Leiden: Brill.
Anwar, M. (1986) *Race and Politics: Ethnic Minorities and the British Political System*. London: Routledge.
Anwar, M. (1996) *British Pakistanis: Demographic, Social and Economic Position*. Warwick: CRER.
Anwar, M. and Kohler, D. (1975) *Participation of Ethnic Minorities in the General Election, October 1974*. London: Community Relations Council.
Benbassa, E. (2011) *Minorités Visibles en Politique*. Paris: CNRS Editions.
Bird, K., Saalfeld, T. and Wüst, A.M. (2010) *The Political Representation of Immigrants and Minorities: Voters, Parties and Parliaments in Liberal Democracies*. London: Routledge.
Ellis, P. and Khan, Z. (1998) 'Diasporic Mobilisation and the Kashmir Issue in British Politics', *Journal of Ethnic and Migration Studies*, 24(3): 471–488.
Garbaye, R. (2005) *Getting Into Local Power: The Politics of Ethnic Minorities in British and French Cities*. Oxford: Blackwell.
Givens, T. and Maxwell, R. (2012) *Immigrant Politics: Race and Representation in Western Europe*. Boulder, CO: Lynne Rienner Publishers.
Geddes, A. (1995) *The Politics of Immigration and Race*. Manchester: Baseline Books.
Glynn, S. (2008) 'East End Bengalis and the Labour party – the End of a Long Relationship?', in C. Dwyer, and C. Bressey (eds) *New Geographies of Race and Racism*. Aldershot: Ashgate.
Heath, A. *et al.* (2013) *The Political Integration of Ethnic Minorities in Britain*. Oxford: Oxford University Press.
Hussain, D. (2004) 'Muslim Political Participation in Britain and the 'Europeanisation' of Fiqh', *Die Welt des Islams*, 44(3): 376–401.
Lewis, P. (1994) *Islamic Britain: Religion, Politics, and Identity Among British Muslims*. London: I.B. Tauris.
Meer, N. (2010) *Citizenship, Identity and the Politics of Multiculturalism: The Rise of Muslim Consciousness*. Basingstoke: Palgrave.
Messina, A. (1989) *Race and Party Competition in Britain*. Oxford: Clarendon Press.
Nielsen, J. (ed.) (2013) *Muslims and Political Participation in Europe*. Edinburgh: Edinburgh University Press.
Peace, T. (2013) 'Muslims and Electoral Politics in Britain: The Case of Respect', in Nielsen, J. (ed.) *Muslims and Political Participation in Europe*. Edinburgh: Edinburgh University Press, pp. 426–454.
Purdam, K. (1996) 'Settler Political Participation: Muslim Local Councillors', in W.A.R. Shadid, and P.S. Van Koningsveld (eds) *Political Participation and Identities of Muslims in Non-Muslim States*. Kampen: Kok Pharos.
Purdam, K. (2000) 'The Political Identities of Muslim Local Councillors in Britain', *Local Government Studies*, 26(1): 47–64.
Purdam, K. (2001) 'Democracy in Practice: Muslims and the Labour Party at the Local Level', *Politics*, 21(3): 147–157.
Saggar, S. (1991) *Race and Public Policy: A Study of Local Politics and Government*. Aldershot: Avebury.

Part I
Voting and elections

1 The paradox of patronage politics
Biraderi, representation and political participation amongst British Pakistanis

Parveen Akhtar

Introduction

This chapter examines a paradox at the heart of British Pakistani politics. On the one hand, the use of biraderi (kinship networks) within the political process has excluded specific subsections of British Pakistanis, namely, women and young people, whilst benefitting others, particularly older males. On the other hand, a consequence of biraderi electoral mobilisations, has been the relative success of British Pakistani politicians in attaining local and national level positions in office. This, in turn, has been symbolically significant for many young British Pakistanis, including women, raising aspirations and inspiring a belief amongst a new generation of British Pakistanis, that they too, can 'make it' in politics. In this way, biraderi practices have, indirectly, contributed to the political aspirations and successes of the very sub-sections of individuals they had traditionally excluded. The descriptive representation of British Pakistanis in the political institutions, has then, been significant for a generation of potential political candidates.

The chapter starts by examining the debates around minority political representation as a normative ideal and in practice. This is followed by a section detailing the concept of biraderi (broadly defined as kinship networks) and biraderi-politicking (a patronage style relationship between politicians and some parts of the British Pakistani community). It is argued that in the period after large scale Pakistani migration to the UK in the 1960s, a corporatist relationship of mutual benefit developed between some Pakistani community leaders and local politicians, so that bloc community votes were exchanged for political patronage. Biraderi networks were used as a mechanism through which Pakistani electoral support could be mobilised. The use of biraderi networks in this way, in effect, disenfranchised Pakistani women and young people from the electoral politics. Biraderi leaders are invariably male elders and it is they, who, as intermediaries between the state and the community had visibility amongst, and access to, local politicians and policy makers (Akhtar 2013). The mobilisation of the biraderi vote, nevertheless, was the means through which many British Pakistani politicians gained a foothold into the political system – access that many British Pakistanis themselves (including politicians) believe they could not have achieved without the support of the Pakistani community and the mobilisation of electoral support through kinship networks. Whilst biraderi politicking is an exclusive process of attaining and maintaining power, often only benefiting specific subgroup interests, it did however, provide an avenue of representation for the British Pakistani community in mainstream politics. An unintended consequence of biraderi-politicking, insofar as it enabled British Pakistani politicians to gain office and therefore Pakistani representation in politics, was that it generated a self-belief amongst younger Pakistanis that they too could achieve political success. The symbolic value of descriptive representation provides community role models and contributes to the burgeoning of political aspirations amongst some young British Pakistanis, including women. Indeed, many young British-Pakistani politicians in the British political system today believe that the first generation of Pakistani politicians in the UK influenced their journey into politics, if not their political beliefs.

The chapter draws on original ethnographic research with British Pakistanis in Birmingham over a seven year period (2005–2012). The author worked with community organisations in the city, specifically, a Muslim radio station, 'Unityfm', and, 'Saheli', a women's empowerment group. This involved discussing ongoing research on a special program on Unityfm where listeners phoned the station with comments on the topic of Muslims and civic and political engagement. Links made through the organisations facilitated contact with British Pakistani community activists, aspiring politicians and parliamentarians in Birmingham. Data was collected through semi-structured interviews and participant observation research conducted at a variety of events in a number of different contexts; including, election campaigns, local street canvassing and at community initiatives. This longitudinal research material helped to contextualise the one-off research collected at a public event on 'Muslims and the political process' which took place in Edinburgh in 2012. Organised by the University of Edinburgh, the occasion formed part of a public discussion on Muslims in the Scottish politics in particular, but also Muslims in British politics more widely.

The research brings attention to the complex and multi-faceted nature of community representation. It is clear that a demographically representative democratic chamber does not necessarily correspond to the substantive representation of minorities. Indeed, the research shows that when British Pakistanis are in representative positions they are heavily criticised from within their community (Akhtar 2013). They are accused of selling out and of being in office for reasons of personal power and prestige, rather than for the good of the community. In this sense, there is a deep mistrust of community representation (Werbner 1991). Minorities may often expect that once a member of their community has made it into the system they will be able to put forward the interests of the group without constraint. This is especially the case since biraderi allegiances are evoked for political mobilisation by aspiring British Pakistani politicians which means that once in power; they are expected to reciprocate biraderi loyalty.

Political representation: the concept

For Hilary Pitkin, whose work on the concept of political representation is an insightful and important contribution to the debate, the concept of representation implies a paradox: 'being present yet not present' (Pitkin 2004: 335). It is often equated with democracy and Pitkin is critical of what she sees as a 'thoughtless equation' of democracy and participation, arguing that the two ideas have in fact conflicting origins. Democracy, coming from Ancient Greece has its roots in struggles 'from below'. Representation, on the other hand, is a more recent concept, dating from the late medieval period and was a duty imposed by the monarch. Pitkin contends that the two concepts became linked only relatively recently, during the English civil war and the democratic revolutions of the eighteenth century. Whilst in contemporary politics, representation and democracy are harmoniously paired together; this then belies a more contentious history. The UK is a model of representative democracy which has emerged over time. For many normative theorists, democratic institutions that are representative of the population they serve, are an ideal type. Jane Mansbridge, for example, in an article entitled, 'Should blacks represent blacks and women represent women? A contingent "yes"', argues that the demographic make-up of parliament could significantly impact upon group interests within representative systems.

Scholars in the field of philosophy and politics have constructed a number of typologies of representation. In another article, 'Rethinking Representation', Jane Mansbridge (2003) identifies four main forms of representation arguing that all four are legitimate ways to represent citizens. Alongside the traditional model of representation which she calls 'promissory' representation (the electoral promises made by representatives before elections), she identifies 'anticipatory' representation (where representatives focus on what they anticipate their constituents will want in the next election), 'gyroscopic' representation (where representatives looks to their own life histories for values and principles), and, finally, 'surrogate' representation (where representatives represent individuals outside of their own constituencies, so individuals with whom they do not have a direct electoral relationship). Others too have devised typologies of representation. In scholarship focusing on women and political representation, the work of Anne Phillips (1994) provides a useful distinction between a 'politics of presence' (denoting descriptive representation of the citizenry) and a 'politics of ideas' (denoting individuals' views and beliefs). That across the world, women make up such small proportions of the legislature, Phillips argues, suggests that we need both types of representation. Taking a critical realist standpoint she argues that unobservable structures, namely, patriarchy, constrain the ability of women to take part in this level of politics. Consequently, this de-legitimises the validity of the decisions taken by these legislatures: there is a limit to their representativeness since the balance of representation suggests differing interests, leading to the assumption that the interests of some are not adequately addressed (Phillips

1994). Research by Joni Lovenduski and Pippa Norris has examined the differences between male and female politicians in terms of their attitudes and values. This study was made possible after 1997 because of the number of female Labour MPs who entered the British Parliament. It offered a test case of whether and how female politicians had the ability to 'make a substantive difference'. Lovenduski and Norris (2003) argued that whilst there were no major differences between the sexes on issues such as the economy, Europe and moral traditionalism, on issues traditionally sees as 'women's issues', such as affirmative action and gender equality scales, male and female politicians differ significantly within each party.

With regards to ethnic minorities in the UK political process, Anwar, writing in the 1990s, argued that their successful integration into the political mainstream: 'requires their 'effective' representation and involvement and not 'tokenism' (Anwar 1990: 46). Indeed, it is only when they feel themselves to be an equal part of the decision-making process that they will feel that: 'they are accepted as full citizens of this country, rather than a 'problem' and one which is 'deplored'. In discussing how this integration can be achieved, Anwar suggested that the: 'political parties need to open their door to ethnic minorities and welcome them as members by removing all the obstacles', and that, at the same time, minorities need to 'feel free to join the political parties and take initiatives without any fear of rejection or prejudice' (Anwar 1990: 46). In the aftermath of the 2001 General Election when turnout amongst ethnic minorities stood at 47 per cent (Richards and Marshall 2003), there was concern over the trend of low participation amongst some minority communities. The report *Voter Engagement among Black and Minority Ethnic Communities* (Purdam *et al.* 2002) recommended various policy responses and possible initiatives for increasing engagement among Black and Minority Ethnic (BME) communities. Amongst these were measures to: make registration and voting easier; encourage political parties and others to review BME representation within UK politics; and ensure that public-awareness campaigns reflected the diversity of BME communities and their consumption of culture and media. Longer running initiatives to involve more ethnic minorities in politics include, for example; Operation Black Vote (OBV), which began in July 1996 as a collaboration between two organisations: Charter 88, which campaigns for democratic reform; and the 1990 Trust, the only national-level and generic Black policy research and networking organisation. Operation Black Vote is a non-party political campaign and, in March 2006, Operation Black Vote and the Electoral Commission launched an MP-shadowing scheme which allowed 21 people from BME communities to shadow high-profile MPs. The aim was to 'demystify' the role of politicians, to encourage those from BME groups to vote and potentially stand for public office and ultimately to: 'promote participation ... and make clear that politics is accessible to all' (Electoral Commission 2006). A study by the Electoral Commission in 2002 suggested that one explanation for political abstinence amongst minority communities was representation: lack of Black and minority ethnic (BME) representation within the political elite was a barrier to participation. Nearly half of those questioned said that better representation of Black people within politics would be the most important factor in encouraging them to vote (Electoral Commission 2002). Similarly, two-thirds of Muslim respondents in Anwar's research felt that Muslims lacked a sufficient voice in the political process (Anwar 2005: 38). Some have argued that minority communities are politically disengaged because the: 'equitable, representative decision-making institutions' are not multicultural (Viswanathan 2002 cited in Electoral Commission 2005: 16). This is a view shared by Marsh *et al.* who argue:

> Racialised political discourses, mono-ethnic political and public institutions and ethnic segregation shaped young people's perceptions of political and public institutions.
>
> (2007: 208)

Even when utilising a limited conception of representative democracy, engagement is a minimum pre-requisite. Moreover, it has been argued that political disengagement can itself be a form of social exclusion (Electoral Commission 2005). Yet, a more ethnically diverse House of Commons would not necessarily reflect greater political representation for ethnic minority interests, or substantive representation. As Crewe noted long ago:

> Whether coloured councillors or MPs could act – or would wish to act – as ethnic spokesmen is far from certain ... no doubt the first Black MPs would be treated willy-nilly as minority spokesmen.
>
> (Crewe 1983: 276)

This raises the question of the ambiguous concept of representation, sometimes taken to mean that ethnic minority councillors are there to represent their own ethnic community. The notion of 'under-representation' of ethnic minorities draws on this assumption (Garbaye 2005: 40). This is deeply problematic not least because it implies that minority politicians can not represent the majority opinion and its logical conclusion appears to be that majority politicians cannot represent minority communities.

Research by Heath *et al.* (2013) indicates that ethnic minorities in the UK are as electorally active as wider British society. In the most recent General Election (2010) Britain's elected chamber saw in 27 ethnic minority MPs out of 649, nearly doubling the figures from the 2005 General Election which stood at 15 (Fieldhouse and Sobolewska 2013: 236). Research comparing the content of all parliamentary questions asked by ethnic minority MPs between 2005 and 2011 and a matching sample of non-minority MPs by Saalfeld and Bischof (2013) found that minority MPs do ask more questions relating to the right of ethnic minorities and issues of immigration, suggesting that descriptive representation could lead to more substantive representation in Parliament.

Importantly, however, their research also showed that all British MPs were responsive to minority interests in constituencies with a high proportion of ethnic minorities, demonstrating that majority politicians were capable and willing to represent minority interests.

Minorities within minorities: which identity is most important?

An important factor in the debate on who legitimately represents ethnic-minority communities is that of multiple subjectivities: the idea that there are minorities within minorities. Thrasher *et al.* note that whilst local level politics in the UK can be characterised as 'male, pale and stale' (2013: 286) reflecting the under-representation of women, minorities and young people, it is the case that minority political candidates are more likely to be younger and better educated. This supports claims made by Durose *et al.* that where under-representative candidates have been successful securing party candidature, it is because they are 'acceptably different', defined as having characteristics 'which are seen to mitigate the electoral disadvantages of being from a minority group' such as a university education (2013: 258). British Pakistani politicians, like British politicians more widely, are not representative of the community from which they are drawn, being largely middle class (in terms of education) and in this respect they have more in common with the elite within the wider British society (Werbner 1990: 321). Furthermore, Purdam (2000) argues that for Muslim councillors: 'the civic tradition of middle-aged male control is not only maintained but increased in their case'. He suggests that this may be a result of 'the limited direct public role of women in certain Islamic traditions, and, more generally, a consequence of the male-led process of settlement and community establishment' (ibid.: p. 48). The 2010 cohort of MPs did however, include three new female Muslim MPS: Rushanara Ali, Shabana Mahmood and Yasmin Qureshi (Operation Black Vote 2010) all have a university education. The demographic make-up of political representatives of the Muslim community largely mirrors that of the wider British political spectrum: dominated by economically well-off, middle-class and middle-aged men, but is beginning to include more women.

Group or interest specific political representation has become an important feature of contemporary UK politics. In the 1980s multiculturalism emerged to protect the interests of minority groups. Within the British context, multiculturalism developed within the arena of education and it's (policy) focus was on schools: so for example, initiatives which addressed the cultural heritage of the ethnic minorities included the inclusion of black history, mother-tongue teaching and parity rights such as holidays for non-Christian religions (Modood and Ahmad 2007: 188). As a normative theory of social justice, multiculturalism espoused equality between groups by recognising differences. A prominent theorist in this area, Charles Taylor argued that our identities as individuals are located in our specific cultures and moral codes and these should be recognised because not doing so was discriminatory (Taylor 1994).

The aim of cultural rights was to prevent the dominant majority from forcing its norms and practices on the minority.

This posed problems for some feminists who argued that in giving legitimacy to religious and cultural groups, there was a danger that multiculturalism promoted the power of men over women (since ethnic minority leadership is often male dominated). A key concern is whether ethnic minority women are excluded from politics, and the relationship between their political exclusion and a state-sponsored framework of cultural relativism. Some academics have questioned the claims to representation made by the first-generation leaders of minority communities and rejected the idea that such leaders represented the interests of all (Macey 2009).

The issue is particularly pertinent in a political context where relationships of patronage developed between largely male Pakistani community leaders and local politicians and it is to the issues of biraderi (kinship) in the political sphere of diaspora Pakistani communities to which we now turn.

Biraderi in the political system

> My biraderi is my wider family – they are closer than friends but not close as family.
>
> (Interviewee, Ali)

A system of kinship networks found in Pakistan and the Indian subcontinent more broadly, biraderi has two constituent parts. On the one hand, biraderi has an element of patrilineage, of descent through a single blood line: 'all men who can trace their relationships to a common ancestor' (Raza 1993: 2). On the other, biraderi can include non-blood relatives 'ties between contemporaries' (Shaw 1988). Amongst the diaspora, ties between contemporaries can often be inclusive of 'our Pakistani community' where the boundary of 'our community' is not fixed or defined. Sometimes 'our community' is Mirpuri, sometimes Kashmiri, and at other times linked to specific villages in Pakistan, highlighting the malleable nature of community boundaries and the context-bound nature of inclusion and exclusion. Biraderi does not have a religious element, it is not a feature of Islam (Raza 1993). It is a cultural system popular in Pakistan and the Indian subcontinent more widely, in which context it functions (in the absence of any meaningful contract between the state and civil society) as a welfare system. Biraderi members turn to each other in times of economic need and for social support, and, as Alison Shaw has pointed out in her research in Pakistan, the biraderi network is trusted more than the justice system and the police (1988: 136, 2000).

Biraderi relations were pivotal in the migration trajectories of Pakistanis who moved to the UK (Werbner 1990; Ballard 1994; Akhtar 2013). Biraderi was the mechanism through which rural Pakistanis became 'migrant entrepreneurs' (Ballard 2003). Pioneer migrants sponsored biraderi members in Pakistan to share in the opportunities of Britain's postwar boom. Settled biraderi members found work for the new arrivals, helped with accommodation and in dealing with the state. Migrants relied on biradari connections in times of need. In the aftermath of family reunification in the 1970s and the arrival of wives and children, welfare and voluntary organisations were set up to help migrants deal with life in the UK. The leaders of these organisations were often those who had been in the country the longest and had the language skills required to deal with state bureaucracy (Rex *et al.* 1987). Such individuals acted as intermediaries between new migrants and officials, often emerging as community leaders through positions in voluntary and community organisations. In the sphere of politics, such community leaders were often seen by local politicians as the link to, what were sometimes regarded, as impenetrable communities (Ellis 1991), and eventually, to provide potential gateways into increasing minority votes.

Whilst Commonwealth migrants were allowed to vote, many, nevertheless, did not participate in electoral politics for a number of reasons. Akhtar (2013) identifies four broad reasons for this: the myth of return – the belief that as temporary economic migrants, they would eventually return to their country of origin; unfamiliarity with the political process; lack of time through long working hours; and finally, preference for the politics of the home country. If the Pakistani migrants were not interested in the British political process, it is also the case that the British political elite were not interested in the new migrants. Indeed, the attitude of the main political parties towards migrants in the immediate post-war years has been described as 'benign neglect' (Garbaye 2005: 16). Like the migrants themselves, the political elite thought that they were sojourners. History proved otherwise. That migrants did not return to their homelands but remained (and increased in number) in specific constituencies had implications for local politics. Their political rights and, more specifically, voting rights meant that migrant minorities constituted a potential interest group for British politicians. From the vantage point of the migrants, such inalienable rights hugely facilitated the genesis of their political claims. This helped the formation and advent of ethnic minority elites on the political scene and the automatic right to vote provided a strong resource for participation.

The first concerted effort to court minority voters occurred after 1974 when it appeared that some marginal seats in inner-city areas were won by Labour with support from minorities (Saggar 2003: 234–5; Garbaye 2005: 42). A report by written by Anwar and Kohler (1975) for the *Community Relations Commission* concluded that ethnic minorities played a significant part in determining the outcome of the election; the swing to Labour amongst minorities was more than the electorate as a whole, and this was at least partly in response to Labour's actions to benefit minorities. The report suggested that although most voters from minority communities conformed to their socio-economic group in voting Labour, other parties were able to attract support among minorities when they made the effort to do so. It also argued that the anti-immigration candidates made little or no progress at the election. The report was a success in bringing minorities to the attention of the main parties, and in particular, the Conservatives by highlighting: 'the fact that many Black voters resided in marginal constituencies and that they were a fast expanding part of the electorate and should not be ignored' (Layton-Henry 1992: 50).[1]

In a context in which politicians believed that the ethnic bloc vote could swing elections in particular urban constituencies, a patron-client relationship between Pakistani community leaders and politicians developed. In exchange for promising community votes en mass, biraderi leaders gained the prestige of being endorsed by politicians (Akhtar 2012).

Biraderi and biraderi politicking

It is important to make a distinction between biradari, biraderism and biradari politicking. Elsewhere, I elaborate on this distinction (Akhtar 2013). Biraderi and biraderism are 'indigenous' words, used by Pakistanis themselves. Often, though not exclusively, biraderism is used as a derogatory term, encapsulating the idea that biraderi as a community regulatory structure is outmoded and not relevant in the UK context. 'Biraderi-politicking' is the term used specifically with reference to the mobilisation of biraderi networks as a system of patronage and mechanism for political control within the Pakistani diasporic public sphere. Whilst it is the case that biraderi and biraderi-politicking are connected – biraderi-politicking cannot take place without biraderi networks – nevertheless, there is no causal link. Indeed, biraderi networks do not necessarily lead to biraderi-politicking. They are analytically distinct.

The paper does not address the multifaceted roles that networks of kinship reciprocity and patronage play at the level of the everyday in the lives of British Pakistanis; in the sphere of economics, or family relationships (Shaw 2000). The focus is on biraderi in the political arena, and specifically biraderi-politicking. The use of kinship networks for political gain flourished in the UK. Many Pakistanis believed that their local leaders were acting on their behalf in a political system that they did not understand. On occasions, biraderi politicians helped local residents to obtain grants for double glazing or heating (benefits they were entitled to through national level schemes) but many Pakistanis believed their biradari leaders had gone out of their way and felt obligated towards them. Interviews with first generation Pakistanis reveal that they had a naïve trust in leaders and believed that intermediaries were necessary to help them navigate the political landscape of the UK (Akhtar 2013).

The use of biraderi networks in the political sphere has been described as an impurity within the electoral system (Wilks-Heeg 2008) a form of clientelism that can lead to the political disenfranchisement of specific groups (Akhtar 2013). Since it is often a male elder within the community, someone of prestige or influence, who fills the role of the biraderi elder, it is extremely difficult for those outside the biraderi system to break into mainstream local politics where biraderi politicking is in existence.

Biraderi-politics: excluding or inspiring?

Whilst patronage politics was beneficial for the two groups which propagated biradari-politicking (local politicians and biradari leaders), the patriarchal and hierarchical nature of the system meant then that it alienated many young people and women. One young British Pakistani interview suggested that biradari elders had 'sold out' to patronage politics (Interviewee, Azik). Yet the biradari system can also be viewed as an effective mechanism to pool together limited resources. Indeed, such a practice is not unique to Pakistani communities and has been used by other migrant communities for effective political representation (McDonald 1994). By mobilising the biraderi vote, Pakistanis have achieved positions of power in local politics. Biraderi politicking has increased descriptive representation especially at the local level.

It is often assumed that greater descriptive representation within the political structures would be beneficial for minority communities. One reason, which Crewe highlighted over thirty years ago, was that: 'their election would probably raise the status of the minorities in the eyes of the country – and themselves' (1983: 276). The underlying assumption here is that a representative political elite is good because it raises the community profile and helps minority individuals feel a part of the political process. This symbolic importance of political representation was picked up by one of my interview respondents who worked in local politics:

> The key thing is how many Asians or how many Muslims do we have in cabinet or in government …you know if we have more it's always a good thing – you know a cabinet which will reflect the population that's always a good thing.
>
> (Interviewee, Asif)

An event in April 2012 at the Scottish Parliament entitled 'Muslims and the political process in Scotland' brought together four guest speakers, all British Pakistani Muslims, to talk about their routes into politics: Humza, Yousaf, MSP for the Scottish National Party; Hamira Khan, former candidate for the Scottish Conservative Party; Shabnum Mustapha, a former Scottish Liberal Democrat candidate and now special advisor to the Deputy Prime Minister and, Hanzala Malik, MSP for the Scottish Labour Party. Each of the four speakers spoke about their particular pathways into politics and experiences of the political system. For Humza Yousaf, Muhammad Sarwar, the first Muslim MP, was his inspiration for getting into politics. Yousaf stated that whilst he did not agree with Sarwar's opinions and views, the fact that 'he was there' and was 'somebody from our culture' made him believe that such a position was attainable. It helped to raise aspirations and the belief that 'if they can do it so can I'.[2]

Hamira Khan pointed to Sayeeda Warsi (former chairman of the Conservative Party) as a role model: 'when I saw her in her shalwar kameez outside number 10, I was a very proud Muslim that day'. The positives of having Muslim representatives in politics and parliament pointed out by both Yousaf and Khan link into the point about the symbolic value of representation. However, on the question of whether a more demographically representative political elite translates into a greater diversity of political interests, or, substantive representation, views from my wider research appeared to be mixed. So, for example, as one interviewee put it, community representatives risk becoming Uncle Toms:

> Malcolm X – you've got to hear his speeches about house slaves and field slaves – he put it far better than I could ever put it, he said whenever the slave master was ill the house slaves would always say 'our master's ill' or 'our fields' – you know, the crops aren't growing, but the field slave would always say 'the master' or 'the fields'…you know and it is their government, you know, it is Khalid Mahmood's government – he's gonna turn around and say our government is in trouble, whereas most people, most working class Muslims say 'the government'.
>
> (Interviewee, Salman)

Here, the local Muslim MP is equated with 'the system', he is seen as serving the state, not the Muslim people, the assumption being that there are clear Muslim interests. Salman forcefully argues that politicians and wider community representatives have their own interests at heart:

> Khalid Mahmood, Trevor Philips have got a vested interest, they're professional anti-racists or whatever, these people they benefit from this system, yeah, and therefore they've go no interest to challenge it, yeah, you know they've taken their 30 pieces of silver or whatever analogy you want to use, yeah, and that's what they do.
>
> (Interviewee, Salman)

They may be important symbolically, but the Muslim politicians already in positions of power were not seen by many Muslims to substantively represent their concerns. Being seen as part of the system can sometimes de-legitimise community representatives' claims of being 'one of the people'. Second, it was pointed out by some during the course of the research that having Muslim representatives actually held the community back because the focus was on narrow community specific issues and not wider social issues which could unite people across different communities. Here, Muslim politicians did focus on the issues which concerned Muslims, but these were the 'wrong issues' (Interviewee, Shoaib) such as visas and immigration. One young Pakistani Muslim male involved in local politics commented that: 'People do go to the (MPs) surgeries, but they ask for visas: please help with visas, visas, visas' (Interviewee, Shoaib). This was an issue that some younger Muslims found frustrating, in their opinion the 'right issues' were education, health and crime. As my interviewee Shoaib described: 'There are piles of rubbish this high on street corners and rats as big as cats running around the streets at night…'. These were the 'bread and butter issues' which affected the lives of Muslims, the focus on visas, immigration and politics in Pakistani was symptomatic of a 'limboland' mentality (interviewee, Yasser). In other words, Pakistanis were hovering on the outskirts of the society in which they had chosen to live, all the while looking backwards, often nostalgically – and usually through rose-tinted spectacles – at a land which they had left behind. Shoaib, provided a diagnosis for the problem of Muslim politics as well as a prognosis: 'The priorities of the Muslim community are wrong. They have not grasped the important issues. They are just concerned with getting as many relatives into the country as possible.' A way to overcome this, he suggested, was to educate people about what the problems are:

> There are two kinds of MPs, the ones who go to the community and ask 'what is it that you want?' … and those who tell the community what they need … what we need is the latter, because people need to be told what the problems are.

Yet, in spite of this, another interviewee, a journalist involved in political activism suggested that there were: 'a lot more young people at [council] meetings: they air their views that way, and not through voting' (Interviewee, Mufti). Clearly, young British Pakistani Muslims are finding their own alternative routes around the traditional system, routes that allow them to express themselves politically.

Made to work harder

Speaking to local British Pakistani politicians, it became clear that they felt under particular scrutiny from within their own communities, a belief that they were judged by a different standard. One British Pakistani councillor in Birmingham told me: 'You go to a white area and they don't know who their local councillor is; here, everybody knows, same in all these Asian areas' (Interviewee, Kamal). Kinship politics may well be utilised to mobilise electoral support, but this does mean that support is given on the assumption that the 'favour' will be returned. British Pakistanis have been effective in gaining local positions of political office, there are a large number of local councillors for example. Many have achieved their positions through biraderi-politicking. Some of them work tirelessly for their constituencies whilst others are happy just to attain office. The idea that 'he's one of our own' means that sometimes expectations from within the British Pakistani community of British Pakistani MPs is that: 'they are already familiar with the issues so should get on and represent Muslim interests' (Interviewee, Hanif). In putting forward their opinions about the performance of Muslim MPs representing Muslim interests, many individuals speak as though the interests of all Muslims in the UK were the same, which given the heterogeneity within Muslim communities, is of course unlikely.

Research by Purdam (2000) and Klausen (2005) on Muslim politicians in the UK and in Europe respectively, has shown that many of the South Asian Muslims who become involved in local politics are, in fact, secular Muslims although they may use religion as a mobilising force. In my research, a number of local British Pakistani councillors stated that whilst they were not practising Muslims themselves, they did canvass in mosques during election time.

Having British Pakistani politicians in parliament through the use of biraderi-politicking was seen by some British Pakistanis as better than not having them there at all. Some of my interviewees believed that although things were much better for them than their parents' generation, racism and discrimination were factors which were important in keeping Muslims out of politics. Furthermore, political parties, in viewing minorities as potential vote losers are less willing to select them at the local level (Sobolewska 2013) thereby compounding (the impression of) discrimination. Many British Pakistani politicians argued that if it was a level playing field, then biraderi-politicking would not be acceptable. But since the playing field was not level, birderi-politicking is an effective strategy for pooling community resources.

Many British Pakistanis also believe that it is only through the mobilisation of kinship networks that a significant number of aspiring Pakistani politicians have been successful, especially at the local level. This success has been important in contributing to the aspirations of a new generation of British Pakistanis. Whilst some British Pakistanis believe that this unintended consequence of biraderi-politicking has been important for the symbolic representation of British Pakistanis in the arena of politics, many believe that there is now a need to turn away from such practices. Indeed, some have argued that the change has already started to take place. Shabnum Mustapha, speaking at the Scottish Parliament noted that:

> Whereas in the past ... many of our politicians of our past generation used to bring in that system of politics ... traditional ways of doing politics which were largely brought over from the subcontinent ... it was often in the media called biraderi politics ... it was that idea that there was one gatekeeper there and you had to be part of that person's camp ... and I think that has changed.
>
> (Shabnum Mustapha)

Now, there have been British Pakistani right at the top of politics, the strategic use of biraderi politicking is less relevant. What this points to is the perception amongst some that the British Pakistani vote has matured away from religious identity politics, Mustapha explains:

> I remember growing up in Glasgow, many Muslims blindly voted Labour because family members voted Labour or someone rang them up the night before the election to say vote Labour and they did it. It shows a level of maturity within the Muslim community that they're actually

gonna think about who they're gonna vote for...moving away from that old adage that there is this bloc Muslim vote for the Labour Party, in the same way that people used to say that the Catholic vote was a vote for the Labour Party.

(Shabnum Mustapha)

Conclusion

In a majoritarian 2-party political system, such as in the UK, ethnic minorities aspiring for political office have the odds stacked against them. Yet, whilst British political institutions are far from reflective of the population at large, ethnic minorities, have, in recent years, been successful in securing office at both the local and national level (Heath et al. 2013). This has been particularly true for British Pakistanis. In the 2010 General Election, minority candidates attained seats in constituencies without significant ethnic minority populations. Yet, for most minority candidates their success is still often in constituencies with large minority concentrations, suggesting that Saggar and Geddes's (2000) finding at the start of the century that: race matters, but only for minorities, still holds true.

Amongst the British Pakistani population, aspiring parliamentarians and local politicians have mobilised support within their own communities through kinship networks. The patriarchal and hierarchical nature of biraderi functions within the political sphere as an exclusionary mechanism for specific sub-sections within the British Pakistani community, most notably women and young people. Nevertheless, many British Pakistani politicians believe that as a result of discrimination in the political system, drawing on kinship ties is the only way to secure a career in mainstream British politics. Indeed, the use of kinship networks has been a highly successful strategy in securing the political representation of British Pakistanis, particularly at local council level. The mobilisation of biraderi in the political sphere has contributed to the descriptive representation of Pakistanis in the UK's political institutions, and seemingly paradoxically, inspired the very subsections which biraderi-politicking excludes. Seeing individuals from within their communities holding positions of local and national level power has been symbolically significant in demonstrating to British Pakistani women and young people that they too can 'make it'.

Notes

1 It should be noted that in this era the term 'Black' encompassed all non-white minorities and was not restricted to those of Afro-Caribbean heritage.
2 Muslims and Political Participation in Britain: Conference 2012, John McIntyre Conference Centre, Edinburgh, 20th and 21st April 2012. The event website can be accessed: www.ed.ac.uk/schools-departments/literatures-languages-cultures/alwaleed/muslims-in-britain/conference/.

Bibliography

Akhtar, P. (2012) 'British Muslim Politics: After Bradford', *Political Quarterly*, 83(4): 762–766.
Akhtar, P. (2013) *British Muslim Politics*. Basingstoke: Palgrave Macmillan.
Anwar, M. and Kohler, D. (1975) *Participation of Ethnic Minorities in the General Election, October 1974*. London: Community Relations Commission.
Anwar, M. (1990) 'Ethnic Minorities and the Electoral Process: Some Recent Developments', in H. Goulbourne (ed.) *Black Politics in Britain*. Aldershot, Gower Publishing Company.
Anwar, M. (2005) 'Muslims in Britain: Issues, Policies and Practice', in T. Abbas (ed.) *Muslim Britain: Communities Under Pressure*. London: Zed Books.
Ballard, R. (1994) 'Introduction', in R. Ballard (ed.) *Desh Pardesh: The South Asian Presence in Britain*. London: Hurst.
Ballard, R. (2003) 'A Case of Capital-rich Under-development: The Paradoxical Consequences of Successful Transnational Entrepreneurship From Mirpur', *Contributions to Indian sociology*, 37(1–2): 25–57.
Baston, L. (2013) *The Bradford Earthquake: The Lessons From Bradford West for Election Campaigning and Political Engagement in Britain*. Liverpool: Democratic Audit.
Crewe, I. (1983) 'Representations and Ethnic Minorities in Britain', in N. Glazer, K. Young and C. Schelling (eds) *Ethnic Pluralism and Public Policy: Achieving Equality in the United States and Britain*. Lexington, KY: Lexington Books.
Durose, C. *et al.* (2013) '"Acceptable Difference": Diversity, Representation and Pathways to UK Politics', *Parliamentary Affairs*, 66(2): 246–267.
Electoral Commission (2002) 'Campaign to Increase Electoral Registration Amongst Black and Minority Ethnic Communities', available at: www.electoralcommission.org.uk/media-centre/newsreleasecampaigns.cfm/news/63 (accessed 15 January 2007).
Electoral Commission (2005) 'Social Exclusion and Political Engagement', available at: www.electoralcommission.org.uk/files/dms/Socexclfinalrept_19491-14052__E__N__S__W__.pdf (accessed 15 January 2007).
Electoral Commission (2006) 'Operation Black Vote and Electoral Commission Launch MP Shadowing Scheme', *Electoral Commission*, 21 February, available at: www.electoralcommission.org.uk/media-centre/newsreleasecampaigns.cfm/news/527 (accessed 20 January 2007).
Ellis, J. (1991) *Meeting Community Needs: a Study of Muslim Communities in Coventry*. Coventry: Centre for Research in Ethnic Relations.
Fieldhouse, E. and Sobolewska, M. (2013) 'Introduction: Are British Ethnic Minorities Politically Under-represented?', *Parliamentary Affairs*, 66(2): 235–245.
Garbaye, R. (2005) *Getting Into Local Power: The Politics of Ethnic Minorities in British and French Cities*. Oxford: Blackwell.
Heath, A. *et al.* (2011) 'Ethnic Heterogeneity in the Social Bases of Voting at the 2010 British General Election', *Journal of Elections, Public Opinion and Parties*, 21(2): 255–277.
Heath, A. *et al.* (2013) *The Political Integration of Ethnic Minorities in Britain*. Oxford: Oxford University Press.
Klausen, J. (2005) *Islamic Challenge: Politics and Religion in Western Europe*. Oxford: Oxford University Press.
Layton-Henry, Z. (1992) *Politics of Immigration: Race and Race Relations in Postwar Britain*. Oxford: Blackwell.

Lovenduski, J. and Norris, P. (2003) 'Westminster Women: The Politics of Presence', *Political Studies*, 51(1): 84–102.

Macey, M. (2009) *Multiculturalism, Religion and Women: Doing Harm by Doing Good?* Basingstoke: Palgrave Macmillan.

Marsh, D., O'Toole, T. and Jones, S. (2007) *Young People and Politics in the UK: Apathy or Alienation?* Basingstoke: Palgrave Macmillan.

McDonald, T. (1994) 'Introduction: How George Washington Plunkitt Became Plunkitt of Tammany Hall', in W. Riordon (ed.) *Plunkitt of Tammany Hall*. Boston, MA: Bedford Books.

Mansbridge, J. (1999) 'Should Blacks Represent Blacks and Women Represent Women?', *The Journal of Politics*, 61: 628–657.

Mansbridge, J. (2003) 'Rethinking Representation', *American Political Science Review*, 97: 515–528.

Modood, T. and Fauzia, A. (2007) 'British Muslim Perspectives on Multiculturalism', *Theory, Culture & Society*, 24(2): 187–213.

Operation Black Vote (2010) 'An Historic Political Night for Black Britain', *Press release*, available at: www.obv.org.uk/index.php?option=com_content&task=view&id=1560&Itemid=5 (accessed 1 February 2014).

Phillips, A. (1994) 'Dealing With Difference: A Politics of Ideas Or A Politics of Presence?', *Constellations*, 1(1): 88–91.

Pitkin, H. (2004) 'Representation and Democracy: Uneasy Alliance', *Scandinavian Political Studies*, 27(3).

Purdam, K. (2000) 'The Political Identities of Muslim Councillors in Britain', *Local Government Studies*, 26(1): 47–64.

Purdam, K., Fieldhouse, E., Kalra, V. and Russell, A. (2002) *Voter Engagement Amongst Ethnic Minority Communities in the UK*. London: UK Electoral Commission.

Raza, M. (1993) *Islam in Britain: Past, Present and the Future*. Leicester: Volcano.

Rex, J., Joly, D. and Wilpert, C. (1987) *Immigrant Associations in Europe*. Aldershot: Gower.

Richards, L. and Marshall, B. (2003) 'Political Engagement Among Black and Minority Ethnic Communities: What We Know and What We Need To Know', available at: www.electoralcommission.gov.uk/files/dms/BMEresearchseminarpaper_11354-8831__E__N__S__W__.pdf (accessed 2 November 2006).

Saggar, S. (2000) *Race and Representation: Electoral Politics and Ethnic Pluralism in Britain*. Manchester: Manchester University Press.

Saggar, S. (2003) 'Race Relations', in J. Hollowell (ed.) *Britain Since 1945*. Malden, MA: Blackwell.

Saggar, S. and Geddes, A. (2000) 'Negative and Positive Racialisation: Re-examining Ethnic Minority Political Representation in the UK', *Journal of Ethnic and Migration Studies*, 26: 25–44.

Saalfeld, T. and Bischof, D. (2013) 'Minority-Ethnic MPs and the Substantive Representation of Minority Interests in the House of Commons, 2005–2011', *Parliamentary Affairs*, 66(2): 305–328.

Shaw, A. (1988) *Pakistani Community in Britain*. Oxford: Basil Blackwell.

Shaw, A. (2000) *Kinship and Continuity: Pakistani Families in Britain*. Amsterdam: Harwood.

Sobolewska, M. (2013) 'Party Strategies, Political Opportunity Structure and the Descriptive Representation of Ethnic Minorities in Britain', *West European Politics*, 36(2).

Taylor, C. (1994) *Multiculturalism: Examining the Politics of Recognition*. Princeton, NJ: Princeton University Press.
Thrasher, M. *et al.* (2013) 'BAME Candidates in Local Elections in Britain', *Parliamentary Affairs*, 66(2): 286–304.
Werbner, P. (1990) *The Migration Process: Capital, Gifts and Offerings Among British Pakistanis*. Oxford: Berg.
Werbner, P. (1991) 'Black and Ethnic Leadership in Britain: A Theoretical Overview', in P. Werbner and M. Anwar (eds) *Black and Ethnic Leadership: The Cultural Dimensions of Political Action*. London: Routledge.
White, I. (2012) *Postal Voting and Electoral Fraud 2001–09*. Standard Note: SN/PC/3667. London: House of Commons Library.
Wilks-Heeg, S. (2008) *Purity of Elections in the UK: Causes for Concern*. Joseph Rowntree Reform Trust, available at: www.jrrt.org.uk/publications/purity-elections-uk-causes-concern.

2 Muslim electoral participation in British general elections

An historical perspective and case study

Jamil Sherif, Anas Altikriti and Ismail Patel

Introduction

The record of Muslim individuals and community organisations participating in British political life and elections begins with the earliest days of settlement at the turn of the nineteenth century. Deeper engagement began in the post-World War II period when there was an increase in the population of Britain's ethnic minorities. The Union of Muslim Organisations (UMO) presented the Muslim communities' concerns at the time of the 1979 general election, a role taken up in a more extensive manner by successor bodies such as the UK Action Committee for Islamic Affairs (UKACIA) and the Muslim Council of Britain (MCB) in general elections held in the late 1990s and subsequent decade. In addition to national-level activity, the number of Muslims participating in local government politics as elected councillors has steadily increased since the 1970s. The first part of this chapter traces the progress of Muslim participation in mainstream politics, focussing on the activities of UMO, UKACIA and MCB in the run-up to general elections. Drawing on archival sources, the chapter seeks to convey the changes of style and substance in the way representative bodies have prepared for general elections and the responses, from within the community and the political establishment. The second part of this chapter describes the YouElect project, established by a network of community organisers to mobilise Muslim voters for the 2010 general election. While building on past experiences of Muslim representative bodies and advocacy groups, it also broke new ground in providing campaigning know how and electoral information to local activists. It made use of 2001 Census data, promoted hustings and conducted polls on voting intentions. The chapter concludes with some of the lessons from the YouElect project pertinent to the 2015 General Election.

A historical perspective

The first Muslim to put himself forward as a parliamentary candidate was perhaps Maulvi Rafiuddin Ahmed, who stood as a Conservative in the 1895 general election. A London journal of the day published his picture, with the note, 'he is a celebrated Moslem jurist and founded the *Anjuman-i-Islam* (Islamic Association) in London'.[1]

The Central Islamic Society, a successor body to the *Anjuman*, organising meetings in 1917 to voice criticisms of the Balfour Declaration is an example of an early pressure group on matters of foreign policy (Sherif 2011a). The issue of Palestine remained at the forefront in the interwar years and Lord Lamington, a trustee of the London Mosque Fund, chaired a meeting in July 1931 at which speakers hoped for a change at the Colonial Office, 'should Conservatives regain power', in the forthcoming general election.[2] The *Jamiat-ul-Muslimin* (Association of Muslims), a community association in the East End, displayed 'street power' in August 1938 by organising a march to protest about sacrilegious statements in *A Short History of the World* by H. G. Wells (Ahmed and Stadtler 2012). The Muslim community pre-World War II comprised mainly of settled seamen (lascars) and their families. Workers' organisers like Surat Alley and Aftab Ali rose from these lascar ranks and made their name pressing ship owners and government for fair labour rights and concessions. In July 1939, 'Alley planned an Indian Workers' Conference at the United Ladies Tailors' Union Hall in Whitechapel, to be addressed by ... Aftab Ali, president of the All-India Seamen's Federation' (Visram 2002). The seamen from British India settled in London, including many Sylheti Muslims, formed a backbone of the India League, making it a 'serious political force in Britain ... their tactics included lobbying MPs and key figures in the Labour movement such as Harold Laski, Bertrand Russell and Fenner Brockway, and raising political consciousness with information campaigns and public meetings' (Lahiri 2007).

Britain's need for manpower after World War II led to an inflow of labour from the Commonwealth. The estimated population of Pakistanis (including East Pakistan, which in 1971 became the independent nation Bangladesh) in 1951 was 5,000, rising to 24,900 in 1961 and 119,700 in 1966 (Anwar 1996: 14). Race and immigration were to become potent factors in British politics. The Conservative Party, in power since the 1951 general election, changed its policy of free entry for all Commonwealth citizens to a policy of controls implemented by the 1962 Commonwealth Immigration Act. A Conservative Party candidate in the 1964 general election gained notoriety through use of slogans like 'If you want a nigger neighbour, vote Labour'.[3] Muslims within the ethnic minorities felt beleaguered by racist 'skinhead' attacks on Pakistanis, Enoch Powell's 'rivers of blood speech' calling for repatriation of immigrants[4] and articles mocking Islam and Muslims, such as Auberon Waugh's reference to 'Allah-catchers' in *The Times* in March 1970.[5] In April 1974, Roy Jenkins, the newly elected Labour government's Home Secretary, introduced an amnesty for illegal immigrants who were Commonwealth citizens and new rules to relax the conditions for the admission of husbands and fiancés of women settled in Britain. The measures were welcomed by the ethnic minorities and the Community Relation Commission (CRC) reported that their 'overwhelming majority' voted for the Labour Party in the October 1974 general election (Anwar 1986: 88). The 1976 Race Relations Act that strengthened provisions against racial discrimination and the creation of the Commission for Racial Equality (CRE) further enhanced support for Labour within ethnic minorities.

Many Muslim civil society groups at the time were named 'welfare association' or 'overseas workers league', with a national or ethnic identity. A broader-based platform emerged in July 1970 when 38 regional and local Muslim associations formed the Union of Muslim Organisations (UMO), 'to unite and represent the Muslim community living in the United Kingdom and Ireland' (UMO 1995: 7). UMO gave Muslims a voice in politics at the national level and began lobbying Government departments and agencies, ministers and parliamentarians. For example in 1975 it made representations to the National Health Service on provisions for male circumcision (UMO 2001). UMO also put forward a memorandum to parliamentarians in January 1976, making a case for recognition of Muslim family law. The new Home Secretary, Merlyn Rees, who took over from Roy Jenkins, was invited to address its annual conference in 1977. Civil servants however, advised against taking this up:

> Since, if he attended the conference, the Home Secretary will be expected to give some indication of the Government's reaction to the Union's overtures, our view is that it would be more preferable if neither the Home Secretary nor (junior minister) Mr John were able to find room in their timetables to be present.
>
> (National Archives 1977)

UMO also started building links with the Anglo-Asian Conservative Society, an association established by the Conservative Central Office 'to assure its members and other Asians about the good intentions of the Conservative Party ... to recruit Asians directly into the Party' (Anwar 1986: 85–86). In January 1977, UMO jointly sponsored a meeting with the Society at the House of Commons, with support from Conservative MPs Bernard Weatherill and Ian Percival (National Archives 1977). The Society's efforts to build bridges with the ethnic minorities were to some extent undone by Margaret Thatcher – Conservative Party leader and also honorary president of the Anglo-Asian Conservative Society – who referred to fears 'that this country might be swamped by people with a different culture' in a TV interview in January 1978 (Anwar 1986: 87).

In April 1979 UMO's general secretary, Dr Syed Aziz Pasha, wrote an unprecedented one-page letter to the leaders of the three main parties a month prior to the general election. This document serves as the first formal record of a Muslim lobby in a British general election:

> Right Honourable Mr. James Callaghan, Prime Minister and Leader of the Labour Party.
> Right Honourable Mrs. Margaret Thatcher, Leader of the Conservative Party.

Right Honourable Mr. David Steel, Leader of the Liberal Party.

As the General Election is drawing closer, we, the citizens of the United Kingdom, are naturally anxious to see that the next Government will give adequate consideration to the rights of the minorities, particularly the religious minorities.

Being the representative body of British Muslims, it has been the endeavour of our Union to bring to the attention of the Authorities concerned the problems facing the Muslim community in this country and seeking their solution. As our Union is a religious organisation with no political affiliations, we have been seeking the support of all political parties for obtaining our religious rights in this land of democracy and religious freedom to which we are happy to belong and for whose prosperity we are making our humble contribution. We are anxious to know the position of your Party with regard to the following important issues affecting the Muslim community here:

1. Application of Muslim Family Law to the Muslim community through parliamentary legislation.
2. Declaring the two Muslim religious Festivals, namely, *Eid-ul-Fitr* (Ramadan festival) and *Eid-ul-Adha* (Festival of Sacrifice) as official holidays to Muslim workers and employees in Government and non-Government establishments.
3. Extending the Law on Blasphemy to protect non-Christian religions as well.
4. Provision of single-sex schools at secondary school level, particularly for girls.
5. Provision of *halal* food to Muslim children during lunch at schools.
6. Imparting of lessons on Islamic education to be taught by Muslim teachers to Muslim children in State schools.
7. Giving a slightly-extended lunch break to Muslim employees on Fridays enabling them to perform congregational prayers in Mosques.
8. Allowing circumcision of male Muslim children under the National Health Act.

We would be grateful to receive an early reply to this letter.

(UMO 1995: 36)

In its response, the office of the Labour Party leader indicated that in order to provide 'the most comprehensive reply possible' it would need to consult Ministers, but this would not be possible before polling day; the Liberal Party responded by providing a copy of its manifesto, 'the Rights of Minorities'; Richard Ryder from Mrs. Thatcher's office replied on 2 May 1979:

May I take your points in order.

1. As for applying Muslim Family Law to the Muslim Community in this country through Parliamentary legislation is concerned, we have no proposals to do so at present.
2. We certainly believe that religious feelings of employees should be registered by employers but is something that would have to be worked out between the employer and employee concerned.
3. If the Law on Blasphemy were to be amended, we would certainly take into consideration extending it to include non-Christian religions as well.
4. We believe in the maximum choice in education as a Party but unfortunately there has been a trend towards new systems of education by this Government. We would certainly allow independent schools of the single sex type to continue to exist.
5. This is something that children of other religious communities have had to cope with and it seems unlikely that any other system can be arranged in individual schools.
6. It would obviously be difficult to arrange for Muslim teachers to teach Islamic education in every state school.
7. Extended lunch break – again this is something to be worked out between individual employer and employee.
8. This question should be addressed to the incoming Secretary of State.

I hope this helps answer your questions.

(UMO 1995: 36)

By end of the 1970s and early 1980s there was a sea change in the nature of Muslim settlement in Britain. In their early years in Britain, 'most Pakistanis felt they were here to save enough to return to Pakistan after a few years. Therefore, they did not get involved in the British political system in any significant way. However, because of the future of their children as well as for economic reasons the "myth of return" diminished, and their participation in British political life (has) gradually increased' (Anwar 1996: 119). The end of the 'myth of return' was accompanied by a growing network of mosques, *madrasas* and *halal* meat shops as well as the movement for Muslim faith schools.[6] The ethnic minority population in 1981 was estimated to be 2.1 million, with about 400,000 of Pakistani and Bangladeshi origin and hence predominantly Muslim heritage (Owen 1996). The Muslim presence became marked in local politics, with rapid increase in the number of councillors in the 1980s and early 1990s.

Prior to the June 1983 general election, UMO submitted a one-page letter to the leaders of the four main political parties (now including Roy Jenkins MP, leader of the Social Democratic Party) with a list of eight concerns. It was similar to its submission in 1979, though with two differences: the request for consideration of Muslim Family Law previously at the top of the list was now at the bottom, and the reference to NHS services for male circumcision removed and replaced with a new concern of more general import – the need for 'extending the scope of the Race Relations Act to cover discrimination on grounds of religion as well' (UMO 1995: 33). The latter was a reference to legislation introduced in 1976 which outlawed discrimination at the workplace and in the provision of goods and services, in both the public and private sectors, on racial but not religious grounds. It was a measure of UMO's success in cultivating links with the political establishment that this time Prime Minister Thatcher's reply began with the hand-written salutation in her own hand, 'Dear Dr Syed Aziz Pasha', continuing:

> I well recall meeting with you when we were discussing these questions with Sir Ian Percival and Bernard Weatherill, and I know that they and many of my parliamentary colleagues have worked closely with you, and have a deep interest and affection for the Muslim community.
> (UMO 1995: 32)

Notwithstanding these friendly sentiments, Mrs. Thatcher did not concede to UMO's requests, and referring to the issues of blasphemy and religious discrimination observed, 'the Government would be reluctant to alter the existing legislation until a precise case has demonstrated the inadequacy of the law as it stands'. At the end of her response, the Prime Minister noted, 'I hope your members will take advantage of the Election campaign to ask all the candidates their views on these matters. My very best wishes to you and to UMO in the future'. The UMO continued these high-level political contacts in Margaret Thatcher's second term and followed precedent in writing to the party leaders again prior to the May 1987 general election. The Prime Minister's reply to UMO now extended to two pages and included a reference to shared values and multiculturalism:

> There is, I believe, an increasing awareness on the part of both the Conservative Party and the Moslem community in Britain about the extent to which our values and priorities coincide. We share a firm belief in the importance of a strong family unit as the foundation of a stable and responsible society. ... I would like to underline too the importance the Conservative Party attaches to recognising and respecting the cultural diversity and traditions of each of the main communities in our countries. Conservatives well understand the importance of tradition and of enabling each religious grouping to practice its faith where this is consistent with the law of this country. ... I am grateful to you for providing me with an opportunity to stress the concern of my party for the interests of the Moslem community and our determination to build a united and peaceful Britain for all our citizens.
> (UMO 1995: 39)

The Prime Minister's reference to practices being acceptable 'where this is consistent with the law of this country' put an end to Dr Pasha's oft-repeated goal of carving out a jurisdiction for Muslim Family Law within

English law, as was the case in the days of the Raj in British India with 'Anglo-Mohammedan Law'.

During the Rushdie Affair (*Satanic Verses* was first available for sale in the UK in September 1988) the mantle of political activism within Muslim communities passed on from UMO to the newly-founded UK Action Committee on Islamic Affairs (UKACIA). This was a network bringing together many of UMO's members as well as mosques and Islamic centres that had remained unaffiliated. In November 1989 UKACIA initiated a new form of political engagement by launching a 'National petition to Parliament', collecting signatures from the public, because

> Up to now, the many attempts to obtain legal sanctions against the book have not been successful. The Home Office has spoken of 'difficulties' in extending any existing law to deal with this offensive publication and continue to emphasise the principle of the freedom of expression under the law. The Government at the moment does not seem to have the inclination or the will to take any action to redress the situation ... we hope to fix, in cooperation with concerned and sympathetic MPs, a specific date on which the National Petition will be presented to Parliament.
> (UKACIA 1989)

The early 1990s were a despondent period for Muslims because of several factors. In the aftermath of the 1992 general election there was a feeling that the Labour Party was reluctant to select Pakistanis for safe and winnable parliamentary seats, and 'this applies to the other two parties as well ... this is seen as deliberate by some, and anti-Pakistani and anti-Muslims policy, by others' (Anwar 1996: 129). The feeling of disempowerment was exacerbated by the inability to build a base of political support for a ban on *Satanic Verses,* and later for the lifting of the arms embargo placed on Bosnian forces during the war in the Balkans. The first Gulf War in 1991 also brought Hizb-ut-Tahrir into prominence in Britain (Genovese 2012), a group that turned its back on electoral politics, and believed voting to be *haram* (forbidden). The main community voices urging participation in the democratic processes of the land were UMO and UKACIA, though neither launched any significant initiatives in the run up to the 1992 general election. The latter published an 11-page 'Muslim manifesto', *For a Fair and Caring Society*, in time for the May 1997 general election. It referred to the findings of the survey to provide 'an overall picture of community needs':

> The forthcoming General Elections will see a significant number of Muslims eligible to vote, including, for various demographic reasons, a greater than average proportion of young Muslim voters. The UK Action Committee on Islamic Affairs (UKACIA), representing Muslim organisations and mosques throughout Britain, strongly supports the full participation of British Muslims in the electoral process. The UKACIA will be

urging Muslims to exercise their right to vote. There are few constituencies today without a Muslim presence, and in some wards they are a majority. We hope that parliamentary candidates of the respective parties will be able to explain their stand on the matters raised in this statement, so that the Muslim voter can make an informed decision on polling day.
(UKACIA 1997: 3)

UKACIA was able to draw on the findings of the 1991 Census, which included a question on ethnicity for the first time. Using ethnicity as a proxy, the size of the Muslim population was estimated to be 1.5 million (Ansari 2004). Age-sex demographics and socio-economic profiles of Pakistani and Bangladeshi-origin respondents also provided information on the characteristics of Muslim communities, raising issues of academic attainment and unemployment. Twelve 'needs' or calls for action were presented in *For a Fair and Caring Society*: Political Representation, Education, Protection against religious discrimination, Vilification and Incitement to Religious Hatred, Socio-economic Deprivation and its Impact on the Young, The National Lottery, Muslim stereotyping and 'Islamophobia', Family & Morality, International and Humanitarian Concerns. This was a quantitative and qualitative change from the one-page letters submitted by UMO to party leaders. Unlike previous communications at general election time, UKACIA's eleven-page statement was robust and challenged the politicians seeking the Muslim vote:

> There is no law in Great Britain that makes discrimination on grounds of religion unlawful. In Northern Ireland there is such a law. Why not introduce a similar law in Great Britain? ... In the autumn of 1993, the UKACIA for example, submitted a detailed memorandum, *The Need for Reform*, calling for such legal measures. However, in a speech in July 1994 the Home Secretary said that he would only consider making discrimination on religious grounds unlawful if he was shown evidence that such discrimination was indeed occurring. This insistence on the production of numbers is a demonstration of the government's unprincipled position. Moreover, even one case of unjustified discrimination is one too many.
> (UKACIA 1997: 6)

The document was sent to each Member of Parliament. Under 'Political Representation', it noted:

> Muslims are the second largest religious community in the UK but have no representation in either the Lower or Upper House. Many believe that this marginalisation of Muslims is by design, on the part of all the major political parties. There is no dearth of Muslims who have a record of public service and who are capable to contribute in the highest political and democratic institutions of this country. So far the response from the

political parties has been disappointing to say the least. Some positive steps to redress this situation need to be taken.

(UKACIA 1997: 4)

In addressing issues such as the National Lottery, *For a Fair and Caring Society* showed that Muslims had a point of view on issues to do with the common good: 'We strongly deplore the introduction of the National Lottery and the further aggressive extension of gambling to mid-week draws and other "games". The lottery is having a massively detrimental impact on the lives and health of millions of people, encouraging false expectations and attitudes to individual worth, effort and achievement' (UKACIA 1997: 8). Meetings were also organised with prominent PCs (Parliamentary Candidates), including the Home Secretary Michael Howard MP and the Shadow Home Secretary Jack Straw MP. UKACIA's specific aim was to obtain a number of commitments from the next government, particularly to expedite voluntary-aided status for Muslim faith schools, place discrimination on grounds of being Muslim on par with the protection afforded to Jews and Sikhs and inclusion of a religion question in the 2001 Census.

The general election was a landslide victory for the Labour Party under Tony Blair. The Muslim Council of Britain, inaugurated in November 1997 as an umbrella body within Muslim civil society, soon organised a meeting with the Home Secretary, Jack Straw MP, (MCB 1998) and a large-scale community reception for the Prime Minister the following year (MCB 1999). On both occasions, Iqbal Sacranie (later Sir), MCB's first secretary general and a joint-convenor of UKACIA, reminded the guests of their various pre-election commitments. The outcomes were positive: 'perhaps as a testimony to its institutional status, the MCB was largely successful in achieving these highly strategic and symbolically important goals' (O'Toole *et al.* 2013). The 1997 general election also resulted in Mohammad Sarwar winning the Glasgow Govan seat for Labour; a year later the Labour government also conferred peerages on two party activists, Nazir Ahmed and Manzila Pola Uddin. The MCB published a policy document prior to the June 2001 general election, entitled *Electing to Listen: promoting policies for British Muslims*, similar in scope and format to UKACIA's 'manifesto' of 1997. Its foreword noted:

> *Electing to Listen* is designed as a positive contribution to our representative democracy. In this document the Muslim Council of Britain highlights issues and principles to help shape debate and policy agendas in the run up to the next general election. Based on consultations with Muslim community representatives, it seeks to initiate dialogue articulate the ideas and needs of Britain's one and a half million Muslims in the context of a multi-faith, multi-cultural Britain.
>
> (MCB 2000)

Maintaining the non-partisan stand of earlier representative bodies, the MCB also met the Rt Hon William Hague MP, presenting the Conservative leader with a copy of *Electing to Listen* in November 2000 (MCB 2001). The MCB promoted voter registration through its website and affiliate network and prepared a 'voter card' for distribution outside mosques listing questions to raise with prospective party candidates. Labour was returned to power; Mohammad Sarwar held his seat, and a new Muslim-heritage MP, Khalid Mahmood, was elected for the Perry Barr constituency in Birmingham.

By the time of the May 2005 General Election, there was much resentment and disaffection within Muslim communities with the Labour government to do with the 'War on Terror', anti-terrorism laws and the use of stop-and-search powers by the police. Its pre-2005 general election 'manifesto', *Electing to Deliver – working for a representative Britain* was a 21-page policy paper urging Muslims, as in the 2001 general election, 'to take an active part in all the issues of the election campaign…active engagement in civil society is basic duty in Islam' (MCB 2005a: 3–4). It took note of the increased politicisation within the community:

> This election takes place in the wake of the Iraq war and the deep divisions it has created. It is the single issue that galvanised British Muslims. Those who participated in or watched the huge demonstration of 15 February 2003 found they stood side-by-side with Britons of all ages, backgrounds and persuasions. This mobilisation has been carried through to increased involvement in subsequent by-elections across the country. This presents a challenge and an opportunity to all political parties.
> (MCB 2005a: 6)

The MCB's positive approach to participation in the nation's political processes was opposed by sections of young Muslims – an event to launch the document at the Baker Street mosque in London was disrupted by those opposed to such electoral participation.[7] The MCB responded by publishing a statement on its website:

> Just forty eight hours before the nation goes to the polls, leading Islamic scholars and prominent community leaders will be urging the British Muslim community to do their citizens duty and to take the fullest part in the General Election on the 5 May 2005. There has arguably never been a more important time for British Muslims to engage in the mainstream political process. We know there is a lot of disaffection in the community particularly with the way the anti-terror laws have been applied and with respect to the war against Iraq as well as concerns on inclusion and equality. We believe that by not participating in the political process we will only be further marginalised.
> (MCB 2005b)

The 2005 general election also heralded a new force in British politics, the Respect Coalition, that had captured the imagination of many Muslims (Peace 2013). A post-election survey conducted by Mori for the Electoral Commission reported that Muslims 'are the group most likely to have voted against a party that did not like (14 per cent), and are also the group most likely to want to send a message to the government with their vote (17 per cent)' (Electoral Commission 2005: 11). In the MCB's view, a noteworthy development in the 2005 general election was a more participative and informed citizenship:

> The issues raised by British Muslims were mainstream concerns and not peripheral as the results around the country show clearly. We are encouraged that despite this negative background the British Muslim community have reaffirmed their commitment to a fuller participation in the civic and political life of the country to work for the common good. The election results show that no single party can any longer take the Muslim community's votes for granted. The Muslim electorate has become more discerning and that is good news for the health of our democracy.
>
> (MCB 2005c)

The number of Muslim candidates standing in the 2005 general election was 48, more than double compared to 2001, 'but despite the rise, Muslims remain under-represented, particularly in being selected for safe or winnable seats' (*The Muslim News* 2005). An outcome of the election was an increase in the number of Muslim-heritage MPs from two to four. Apart from the re-election of Sarwar and Mahmood the newly elected Labour MPs were Shahid Malik and Sadiq Khan. The Respect Coalition candidate, the anti-war, hijab-wearing Salma Yaqoob, came second to the Labour PC in the Birmingham Sparkbrook and Small Heath constituency, but causing a swing of 11 per cent away from Labour to Respect

The YouElect project

The YouElect project was initiated in July 2009 by a network of Muslim civil society activists in anticipation of the 2010 general election. Its distinct features were the pooling of resources and expertise of a number of community bodies and the forging of stronger links between a central coordinating team and local grassroots activists. It was a modestly resourced, volunteer-driven venture that came into being at a unique moment in British political history. First, the 2005 General Election had resulted in a large number of marginal constituencies that offered local Muslim community organisations an opportunity to make a difference if they were to mobilise. Second, larger than normal number of incumbent MPs had announced their intention to retire from politics, some because they were tainted by the 'Expenses Scandal' that broke in 2009 relating to excessive monetary claims for maintaining a second residence. Third, the 2010 General Election offered a further opportunity for the Respect Party, fielding 11 candidates, including Salma Yaqoob standing in Birmingham Hall Green. In the field of parliamentary hopefuls were 89 Muslims standing in 61 constituencies (*The Muslim News* 2010). The 2001 Census (of England and Wales), which included a religion question for the first time in modern British history, indicated that there were 10 constituencies where the Muslim population formed 20 per cent or more of the total population: Birmingham Sparkbrook and Small Heath (49 per cent), Bethnal Green and Bow (39 per cent), Bradford West (38 per cent), East Ham (30 per cent), Birmingham Ladywood (30 per cent), Blackburn (26 per cent), Poplar and Canning Town (25 per cent), West Ham (24 per cent), Bradford North (21 per cent), Ilford South (20 per cent).[8]

The 2010 General Election also provided a strategic opportunity: political commentators were discussing the possibility of a hung parliament and while at the time it was uncertain whether this would lead to minority government or a coalition of either Labour or Conservatives with the Liberal Democrats, the general feeling within the Muslim community towards the end of 2009 was that such an outcome was one worth striving for. This was because a minority or coalition government would be obliged to listen to voices from all sections of society, including Muslim concerns with domestic and foreign policy. YouElect was both an outcome of the unique circumstances of 2010 and also an extension of the community initiatives during previous general elections described above. It was non-partisan but having obtained information on PCs by various means (questionnaires, hustings, local feedback) it aimed to inform voters to assess who was committed to shared values such as social justice, the rule of law and solidarity with the disadvantaged. The work of Operation Black Vote[9] and London Citizens[10] provided role models and care was taken not to duplicate electoral initiatives of other community bodies. The first phase involved data collection and the specification and commissioning of a website with an underlying constituency and parliamentary candidates database. The starting point for data collection was the 2001 Census and statistics available from the Electoral Commission website.[11] The results of the 2005 General Election were analysed to obtain an estimate of Muslim voting strength, for example in the case of Birmingham Sparkbrook:

(a) 2005 turnout – 51.8%
(b) 2005 Eligible electorate – 73,721
(c) 2005 Total Population – 117,507
Therefore Total votes cast – (d) 38,161 [(a) x (b)]
Votes cast as % of Population (e) 32.48 – (d) as % of (c)
Therefore if Total Muslim Population is 57,354 (from 2001 Census), Muslim voter estimate is 32.38% of 57,354 i.e. 18,629.

It was assumed that the increase in population between 2001–2010 would be offset by the acknowledged lower turnout of 'Black and Minority Ethnic' populations (BME) at elections – the BME turnout rate in the 2005 general election was around 47 per cent compared to 61 per cent for the national turnout (Electoral Commission 2005: 8). The YouElect analysis was restricted to about 100 constituencies, including those with sizeable Muslim populations and also those that were marginal after the 2005 General Election. Of particular interest were constituencies where the Muslim voter estimate exceeded the margin of victory of the elected MP. Further data was collected on the select constituencies' PCs in 2005 and their electoral performances. The YouElect database was supplemented with data on each confirmed candidate standing in 2010 obtained through questionnaires, web searches and other sources such as Hansard, Early Day Motion records and the 'They Work For You' site.[12] The websites and blogs maintained by many candidates also provided data on their affiliations, causes supported and priorities. This data collection exercise proceeded in tandem with the specification and commissioning of a website. For accounting transparency and legal requirements, YouElect was registered as a limited company in February 2010 and a 07578 telephone number was also obtained (to enable transfer across networks if necessary). A design company was also commissioned for a YouElect logo to appear on all print and Internet publications.[13] The project was formally launched in East London at a meeting of community organisers and media representatives on 9 March 2010. A veteran community activist, Ismail Patel, was called on to coordinate activities, and two workgroups emerged under his direction: one for website content management and the other assigned community-facing tasks such as organising flyer distribution, providing local groups with hustings support and conducting polls. In many cases the political parties were still finalising their PC details throughout the month of March. In order to update entries on the website, a second questionnaire was sent to candidates via email – supplemented with some telephone interviews – to solicit 'Strongly Agree/Agree/No View/Disagree/Strongly Disagree' responses to 10 short statements:

- An All-Party Parliamentary Group to counter Islamophobia is needed.
- Anti-Terrorism Laws have affected civil liberties and should be revised.
- Frontline social services (e.g. Health, Social Care) should be protected.
- Faith schools contribute positively and should be supported by Government.
- The 'Prevent' agenda has stereotyped Muslims and should be scrapped.
- Everyone, including faith groups, have a right to dress as they choose.
- Britain needs to have tougher regulations for the Banking industry.
- There should be an immediate end to the siege of Gaza.
- British foreign policy in Afghanistan and Iraq has been counterproductive.
- The Climate crisis requires more national coordination.

A back office team managed content, including PC updates, campaign news at the national and constituency levels, a moderated discussion forum and a central diary of all known hustings in mosques and community centres and meeting reports. The site also included original commissioned features, for example an analysis of the manifestos provided by the three main parties (Conservative, Labour and Liberal Democrats). The themes considered were: Health Services; Education; Immigration; Anti-Terrorism Legislation, Defence and Security; Foreign Policy; Families; Jobs; the Economy and the Deficit; The Constitution (e.g. relating to an elected House of Lords); Social Policy and Crime.[14]

Communication channels

YouElect's first press release was issued on 18 March 2010:

> National Muslim Voter Registration Drive Launched
> YouElect, a national grassroots initiative to encourage, inform and empower the Muslim community at the forthcoming General Elections has been launched. Ismail Patel, Project Co-ordinator, explained that YouElect aims to 'help make the election process easier by providing individuals with tools to make an informed decision when voting'.
> YouElect has also launched a dedicated website, www.youelect.org.uk, which provides profiles of nearly three hundred candidates spread across approximately a hundred constituencies nationally. The website will also feature a blog, to encourage debate and discussion closer to the election.
> YouElect hopes to offer advice on all aspects of the upcoming elections, 'getting people to register to vote remains a priority at this stage. We also hope to assist individuals and local organisations with their queries and facilitate local hustings' concluded Patel.

Subsequently YouElect adopted a mix of traditional and new media channels to fulfil the aims set out in this first press release. YouElect was timely and tapped into a reservoir of creative energy within the community. Apart from institutional responses there were many creative ideas from individuals that warranted promotion, such as the witty film directed by Tre Azam, 'I am a Muslim and the BNP got my vote'.[15] YouElect became known within the community through Muslim media coverage[16] as well as beyond through an item in Al-Jazeera (Wander 2010) However it remained off the radar of the mainstream media with the exception of the *The Guardian* (Altikriti 2010) and some coverage in the Irish Times.[17] Collaborative links were set up with other like minded Muslim and BME civil society projects. For example, constituency data was shared with the MCB's www.muslimvote.org.uk website, the community portal www.salaam.co.uk, and the British Muslim Initiative (BMI). These various community initiatives built on their strengths and interests: the MCB for example collaborating with the Electoral Commission to promote voter registration; the Salaam website leveraging on its site traffic and BMI on its political campaigning role and suggestions for tactical voting.

Flyers and posters were produced for mass distribution, through the mosques across the UK: in late February to promote voter registration[18] and in late March to promote engagement with PCs and turn-out on Polling Day. The website was updated several times a day and included a variety of text and video content. The home page included images and quotes from civil society personalities, for example:

> As Muslim citizens it is not only an option but an *amanah* (obligation) to be engaged in the political process to make an effort in bringing about positive socio-economic and political change.
> (Shaikh Ibrahim Mogra, Imam)

> Politics is the best non-violent way of creating change. War, violence or apathy occur when politics fail. Voting is the method used for the governed to give consent to the government.
> (Neil Jameson, London Citizens)

> The future belongs to those who prepare for it today – it is time to engage.
> (Mahdi Adib, Youth Club leader)

The YouElect message was broadcast on community radio stations in three cities, Birmingham (on Unity FM, a not-for-profit service), Bradford and Leicester. A 30-second advert was also prepared for ethnic and faith media channels and social media.[19]

YouElect subscribed to an email management service, and having obtained access to a large Muslim individuals' address list, sent general election news including reminders for voter registration prior to the deadline. The e-mail communications starting off weekly, becoming twice-weekly as Polling Day approached. The contents included details of hustings, links to items on the YouElect website and any key political developments. Access to a database of mobile phone numbers enabled SMS broadcasts. Various texting suggestions emerged from a brainstorming session, of which one was selected: 'Salaams. The Muslim vote can make a difference if you put X in the right place on 6 May – check www.youelect.org.uk to decide who deserves your vote. Please forward this on. JZK' (JZK being an abbreviation of an Arabic phrase of appreciation). YouElect established a Facebook and Twitter presence though the outcomes were modest because of a lack of resources.

Grassroots interaction

YouElect produced toolkits for local community groups comprising Ulema statements endorsing participation in electoral politics, a practical guide for planning and running a hustings, flyers downloadable from the YouElect website and a summary of Party manifestos.

YouElect volunteers co-hosted around 20 hustings, taking a leading role in some sensitive constituencies such as Bethnal Green and Bow that had swung to Respect in 2005 but whose future direction was uncertain and seen as winnable for several parties. The YouElect website also carried reports of hustings, thus providing role models for organisers. A notable husting for the Harrow East and Harrow West constituencies was organised at the Mahfil Ali Islamic community centre in North Harrow by the Middlesex Forum of Mosques that had had 300 participants.[20] A feature of the 2010 General Election were the passionate and informed debates at hustings, a reflection of a more politicised and informed Muslim voter.

YouElect conducted an on-line and telephone poll of Muslim households in London, Leicester, Bradford and Birmingham following the three TV debates between Gordon Brown, David Cameron and Nick Clegg that were held between 15–29 April 2010. This was the first time such a survey was undertaken by a Muslim group within the community. A YouElect press release (30 April 2010) noted:

> In the biggest Poll of its kind, 940 Muslims from across Britain took part in an Opinion Poll revealing that 70% of respondents believe the Lib Dems have the fairest policies on domestic issues which concern them the most. There was also overwhelming support for the Lib Dems on foreign policy, with 74% stating that they believed the Lib Dems would address the issues of foreign policy most fairly. 19% were in favour of Labour on this point, and a mere 5% in favour of the Conservatives. Despite this support on Lib Dem policies, faith in the leadership of the parties was less pronounced with 43% stating they were not sure which leader would make the most effective Prime Minister. 32% were in favour of Nick Clegg, with 17% and 6% supporting Gordon Brown and David Cameron respectively.
>
> Domestic policies would 'very strongly' influence 37% and 'strongly' influence 48% in their voting choice, while foreign policy would 'very strongly' influence 53% and 'strongly' influence 32%. On the domestic front, a majority of 38% were most concerned about policies for tackling Islamophobia, with 70% having most faith in the Lib Dems to tackle it most fairly. On foreign policy, Palestine was of the greatest concern to pollsters, with an overwhelming 72% stating it concerned them more than all other foreign issues including Afghanistan, Iraq, Iran and Kashmir....Other findings included 80% saying they would be voting in the election, a figure much higher than previously thought. Only 7% stated they would not vote.

Reflections

The YouElect venture in the 2010 General Election extended British Muslim civil society's record of engagement and participation in the democratic processes of the land. Each successive General Election has seen increasing campaigning know-how and mobilisation. While the first efforts were modest one-page letters to party leaders, these were soon superseded by manifestos offering a Muslim policy perspective on a wide range of issues, from Foreign Policy to the Environment and Health. Efforts were also needed to counter a small but vocal minority that rejected mainstream political participation on the grounds that it was somehow contrary to Islam or the interests of Muslims. The religion question, first introduced in the 2001 Census has made its impact felt, not just in matters of public policy making and advocacy work but in YouElect's case in alerting the community to its potential political strength and the power of the ballot box (Sherif 2011b). It has enabled constituencies with high Muslim populations to be more precisely identified, as well as marginal constituencies where the Muslim population could be sufficiently large to make a difference to the end result.

Political analysts have noted that voter turnout in 2010 was slightly higher than 2005 (65 per cent compared to 61 per cent), while within the 18–24 year group, the greatest swing was for the Liberal Democrats (Kavanagh and Cowley 2010). The outcome of a hung Parliament was also achieved. In broad-brush terms, the YouElect team would not complain about the outcomes. The doubling of the number of Muslim-heritage MPs, as well as the re-election of MPs outspoken in their pursuit of social justice and ethical foreign policy was also welcomed by those involved in the initiative. The struggle to ensure Muslims in Britain acquire political muscle commensurate with their population and demographics remains a challenging one, which needs to take into account some political realities. For example the national swing of 5 per cent from Labour to Conservative in 2010 overwhelmed the potential king-making role of Labour supporting Muslim voters in Conservative marginals. Even in Battersea, the incumbent Labour MP Martin Linton lost to Jane Ellison of the Tories, in spite of his strong stand for an ethical foreign policy and in support of faith schools: the Labour to Conservative swing in this constituency was 7.5 per cent, wiping out Linton's margin of 163 whatever the voting decisions of the estimated 1,618 Muslim voters. In Rochdale, a Liberal Democrat incumbent MP with many shared values with his Muslim constituents lost to Labour – in spite of the Gillian Duffy 'bigot' episode.[21] The 2010 General Election indicates the continued loyalty for Labour amongst Muslim communities. The Bagehot columnist in *The Economist* noted, 'Labour enjoyed a crushing dominance among ethnic-minority voters – even among British blacks and Asians whose affluence, or robust views on crime and public spending, might make them natural Conservative voters' (Bagehot 2012). Similar research by Runnymede (2011) has concluded that 'only 16 per cent of ethnic minorities voted for the Conservative party at the last election, compared to 37 per cent of white British people; 14 per cent of ethnic minorities voted for Liberal Democrats in comparison to 22 per cent of white British people; In contrast, 68 per cent of ethnic minorities voted Labour, compared to 31 per cent of white British people'.

The YouElect team was disappointed that Salma Yaqoob could not win Birmingham Hall Green, though the number of votes she obtained indicated support from both Muslims and non-Muslims. The outcome was possibly affected by the new boundaries that split the Small Heath ward with a 35 per cent Muslim population with the Ladywood constituency, which was won by female Muslim candidate Shabana Mahmood. Other Respect candidates were similarly unsuccessful: George Galloway in Poplar and Limehouse and Abjol Miah in Bethnal Green and Bow. The results of May 2010 were 'disastrous' for the Respect Party (Peace 2013). The roller coaster world of politics however saw Galloway succeed spectacularly in the Bradford West by-election held in March 2012.

The results from the latest decennial census highlight the challenges and opportunities ahead: after the 2001 Census, there were 10 constituencies with a Muslim population of 20per cent or more of the total population; the 2011 Census has increased this to 26.[22] Of the 10 in 2001, seven remain on the updated list, while three having been abolished due to boundary changes – Sparkbrook and Small Heath, Poplar and Canning Town and Bradford North.[23] The 19 additions (with percentage of the Muslim population) are: Birmingham Hodge Hill (52 per cent), Birmingham Hall Green (47 per cent), Bradford East (37 per cent), Poplar and Limehouse (34 per cent) Manchester Gorton (29 per cent), Leicester South (28 per cent), Edmonton (25 per cent), Luton South (25 per cent), Oldham West and Royton (25 per cent), Walthamstow (25 per cent), Rochdale (24 per cent), Slough (24 per cent), Birmingham Perry Barr (23 per cent), Leyton and Wanstead (23 per cent), Westminster North (23 per cent), Luton North (22 per cent), Brent Central (21 per cent), Birmingham Yardley (21 per cent) and Leicester East (20 per cent). YouElect analysts need to avoid naive arithmetic and recognise the other factors at play in marginal constituencies where the estimated number of Muslim voters is larger than the majority to be overturned.

British Muslims find themselves at the intersection of several overlapping circles – living in impoverished areas (ODPM 2006), part of BME (almost one in three BMEs are Muslim), with a sizeable proportion of the nation's young population in an ageing society (*The Muslim News* 2013). No doubt many of the concerns to be raised with PCs and in hustings will be ones shared with other Britons, such as jobs and the economy, but what unites minorities 'against the white British status quo' is their priority on equal opportunities and redress for racial discrimination (Heath *et al.* 2013). Racism persists, but now with the added dimension of 'the attribution to all Muslims of pejorative group characteristics', or Islamophobia (Meer and Modood 2010). An effective coalition is taking shape to ensure these matters are on the political agenda of the main parties, prompted by the analysis undertaken by Operation Black Vote, identifying 168 marginal seats in the 2015 general election where the BME electorate is larger than the majority in which the seat was won in 2010 (OBV 2013). With experiences such as those gained in the YouElect venture, Muslim activists can approach the 2015 General Election with greater realism, ready to form alliances based on shared values, and better informed of the multi-faceted nature of political campaigning and the level of resources needed to be effective.

Notes

1. *The Graphic*, London. Issue 1313, 26 January 1895. Archive at the British Library, London.
2. *The Islamic Review*, Woking. Issue XIX, September 1931, pp. 336–337. www.wokingmuslim.org/work/islamic-review/1931/sep31.pdf/.
3. *The Times*, March 9 1964. The Conservative Party candidate making the statement was Peter Griffiths, contesting the Smethwick constituency.
4. Enoch Powell delivered this speech on April 20 1968. www.telegraph.co.uk/comment/3643823/Enoch-Powells-Rivers-of-Blood-speech.html/.
5. *The Times*, March 14 1970. Auberon Waugh's article was entitled 'A leaf from the Koran'.
6. For an account of the campaign for the Islamia Primary School in the early 1980s, see www.salaam.co.uk/blogs-new/?p=1093.
7. For an account of the disruption see http://news.bbc.co.uk/1/hi/4460565.stm.
8. Nomis website – Parliamentary constituency data based on the 1995 boundaries and 2001 Census findings. www.nomisweb.co.uk.
9. Operation Black Vote (www.obv.org.uk), established in 1996 promotes voter registration within ethnic minorities and also commissions research studies e.g. Ethnic Minorities and the British Electoral System, 1998.
10. London Citizens is a network of the Citizen Organising Foundation (www.citizensuk.org) that has organised candidates' hustings at times of mayoral and parliamentary elections. It has been effective in obtaining political commitment for social justice, such as an equitable minimum wage.
11. www.electoralcommission.org.uk/find-information-by-subject/elections-and-referendums/past-elections-and-referendums/uk-general-elections/2005-uk-general-election-results.
12. They Work for You website – see www.theyworkforyou.com.
13. The London-based communications strategy and design company *MDUKmedia* provided branding and e-mail marketing services.
14. http://youelect2010.org.uk/akfiles/YouElect_Manifesto_Analysis.pdf.
15. http://www.youtube.com/watch?v=wYDuQLm-9IA.
16. http://muslimmatters.org/2010/04/19/uk-general-election-2010-the-muslim-vote/.
17. *The Irish Times*, May 1 2010, 'On the Hustings'.
18. http://youelect2010.org.uk/akfiles/You_Elect_A3_Poster.pdf.
19. Viewable on YouTube. www.youtube.com/watch?v=ieEdS9qUQ-A.
20. For a report see http://youelect2010.org.uk/constituency/harrow-west/news/9th-april-harrow-muslims-grill-their-parliamentary-hopefuls.
21. Not realising his lapel microphone was switched on while campaigning in Rochdale, Gordon Brown referred to pensioner Gillian Duffy as a 'bigot' after she had questioned him over the financial crisis.
22. Nomis website – Table KS209EW.
23. The updated list includes three new parliamentary constituencies in 2010: Hall Green, Poplar and Limehouse and Bradford East.

Bibliography

Ahmed, R. and Stadtler, F. (2012) 'Muslims Protest Against H.G. Wells Book in the 1930s', *Huffpost Culture*, September 19, available at: www.huffingtonpost.co.uk/rehana-ahmed/muslims-protest-against-h_b_1895942.html (accessed 30 May 2014).

Altikriti, A. (2010) 'Muslim Voters Come of Age', *The Guardian*, April 27, available at: www.theguardian.com/commentisfree/belief/2010/apr/27/general-election-muslim-vote.

Ansari, H. (2004) *The Infidel Within*. London: Hurst, p. 171.

Anwar, M. (1986) *Race and Politics*. London: Tavistock.

Anwar, M. (1996) *British Pakistanis, Demographic, Social and Economic Position*. Coventry: University of Warwick.

Bagehot (2012) 'David Cameron's Race Problem', *The Economist*, March 3, available at: www.economist.com/node/21548940.

Electoral Commission (2005) *Black and Minority Ethnic Survey*, May–July, p. 11, available at: www.electoralcommission.org.uk/__data/assets/pdf_file/0019/47260/ECBMEReport FINAL2_18810-13883__E__N__S__W__.pdf.

Genovese, D. (2012) 'Representation and self-Representation of radical Islamism in the UK', in C. Flood, S. Hutchings, G. Miazhevich and H. Nickels (eds) *Political and Cultural Representations of Muslims*. Leiden: Brill.

Heath, A. Fisher, S.D. Rosemblatt, G. (2013) *The Political Integration of Ethnic Minorities in Britain*. Oxford: Oxford University Press.

Kavanagh, D. and Cowley, P. (2010) *The British General Election of 2010*. Basingstoke: Palgrave Macmillan, Table 16.3.

Lahiri, S. (2007) 'From Empire to Decolonisation, 1901–1947', in M.H. Fisher, S. Lahiri and S.S. Thani (eds) *A South-Asian History of Britain*. Oxford: Greenwood World Publishing, pp. 136–137.

Meer, N. and Tariq Modood, T. (2010) 'The Racialisation of Muslims', in S. Sayyid and A. Karim Vakil (eds) *Thinking through Islamophobia: Global Perspectives*. London: Hurst, p. 82.

Muslim Council of Britain (1998) 'MCB Delegation Meets Home Secretary', *MCB Press Release*, June 17, available at: www.webarchive.org.uk/wayback/archive/20050715120000/http://www.mcb.org.uk/index.html (accessed 30 May 2014) (follow link to Media, Press Releases).

Muslim Council of Britain (1999) 'Secretary General's Address at Reception for Prime Minister', *MCB Press Release*, May 5, available at: www.webarchive.org.uk/wayback/archive/20050715120000/http://www.mcb.org.uk/index.html (accessed 30 May 2014) (follow link to Media, Press Releases).

Muslim Council of Britain (2000) *Electing to Listen: Promoting Policies for British Muslims*, p. 1.

Muslim Council of Britain (2001) *MCB Newsletter*, 1(3), March, p. 8.

Muslim Council of Britain (2005a) *Electing to Deliver – Working for a Representative Britain*, p. 3–4, available at: www.webarchive.org.uk/wayback/archive/20050715120000/http://www.mcb.org.uk/index.html (accessed 30 May 2014) (follow link to Committees, Public Affairs).

Muslim Council of Britain (2005b) 'Islamic Scholars Urge British Muslims to Vote', *MCB Press Release*, May 3, available at: www.webarchive.org.uk/wayback/archive/20050715120000/http://www.mcb.org.uk/index.html (accessed 30 May 2014) (follow link to Media, Press Releases).

Muslim Council of Britain (2005c) 'Muslims Congratulated Over Robust Participation', *MCB Press Release*, May 6, available at: www.webarchive.org.uk/wayback/archive/20050715120000/http://www.mcb.org.uk/index.html (accessed 30 May 2014) (follow link to Media, Press Releases).

National Archives (1977) *PRO, File HO 342/259. Letter from J.M. Gose to Miss Crabb*, 14 July. Introductory Paper presented by Dr Syed Aziz Pasha, General Secretary of UMO at a meeting held at the House of Commons, 20 January.

OBV (Operation Black Vote) (2013) *Power of the Black Vote in 2015 – the Changing Face of England and Wales*. Available at: www.obv.org.uk/sites/default/files/images/downloads/Powerofthe%20BlackVotev3.pdf (accessed 30 May 2014).

ODPM (Office of the Deputy Prime Minister) (2006) *Review of the Evidence Base on Faith Communities*. Research by the Mercia Group: Professor James A. Beckford, University of Warwick.

O'Toole, T., Modood, T., DeHanas, D. (2013) *Taking Part, Muslim Participation in Contemporary Governance*. Centre for the Study of Ethnicity and Citizenship: University of Bristol. Available at: www.bristol.ac.uk/ethnicity/projects/muslimparticipation/documents/mpcgreport.pdf.

Owen, D. (1996) 'Size, Structure and Growth of Ethnic Minority Populations', in D. Coleman and J. Salt (eds) *Ethnicity in the 1991 Census*. London: HMSO, p. 85.

Peace, T. (2013) 'All I'm Asking, is for a Little Respect', *Parliamentary Affairs*, 66(2): 405–424.

Runnymede (2011) *Runneymede Trust and Embes Press Release*, 26 October, available at: www.runnymedetrust.org/uploads/EMBESpressreleasefinal.pdf (accessed 30 May 2014).

Sherif, M.A. (2011a) *Brave Hearts, Pickthall and Philby: Two English Muslims in a Changing World*. Kuala Lumpur: Islamic Book Trust, pp. 19–20.

Sherif, J. (2011b) 'A Census Chronicle', *Journal of Belief & Values*, 32(1): 1–18.

The Muslim News (2005) '2005 Elections a Milestone in British Muslim Calendar', Issue 192, April 29, available at: http://archive.muslimnews.co.uk/archives/paper.php?issue=192&article=1925.

The Muslim News (2010) 'Election 2010 Statistics', Issue 263, May 28, available at: http://archive.muslimnews.co.uk/archives/paper.php?issue=253&article=4645.

The Muslim News (2013) 'Census Finding: Muslim Population – Young and Diverse', Issue 293, September 27, available at: www.muslimnews.co.uk/newspaper/home-news/census-finding-muslim-population-young-and-diverse/.

UK Action Committee on Islamic Affairs (UKACIA) (1989) *Bulletin*, October.

UK Action Committee on Islamic Affairs (UKACIA) (1997) *Elections 1997 and British Muslims – For a Fair and Caring Society*.

Union of Muslim Organisations (UMO) (1995) *A record of achievement 1970–1995, 25 Years Silver Jubilee Magazine*.

Union of Muslim Organisations (UMO) (2001) *Muslims in Britain, General Election 2001*. Pamphlet, p. 12.

Visram, R. (2002) *Asians in Britain, 400 Years of History*. London: Pluto, p. 219.

Wander, A. (2010) 'UK Muslims 'Backing Lib Dems'', *AlJazeera*, 4 May, available at: www.aljazeera.com/focus/britishelection/2010/05/20105312436485579.html (accessed 30 May 2014).

3 Mosques and political engagement in Britain
Participation or segregation?

Siobhan McAndrew and Maria Sobolewska

Introduction

Are mosques insular? Do they encourage living 'parallel lives' and breed disaffection with Britain and the mainstream political process? Media portrayals have depicted some mosques as fostering traditionalism, radicalisation, and cultural divides between British Muslims and others. But is this picture of mosques in Britain representative? When discussing radical Islam, integration and the role of mosques, politicians are often careful to emphasise that most Muslims in Britain are peace-loving and loyal Britons. Evidence regarding public distrust of Muslims (Field 2007) by non-Muslims, however, suggests that these caveats are empty in effect. With the belief that Islam constitutes a threat to British values so widespread, the possibility that mosques may play an important role in the integration of Muslims into British society and politics may appear counterintuitive.

At the same time, research shows that religious participation produces better citizens. People who participate in group religious events – such as attending a place of worship – tend to be more active in civic and political associations, have more social capital, and more political resources. This has been shown for native, immigrant and ethnic minority origin populations alike in the US and elsewhere. It therefore seems plausible that mosques in Britain perform the same positive role. In this chapter, we will compare Muslims who do not regularly attend mosques with those who do, to see whether the latter are more insular and suspicious of white Britain, with fewer friends outside their ethnic group, or whether contrarily they have more social capital, more contact with people outside their ethnic group, and participate more in civic and political associations and activities.

Negative stereotypes surrounding mosques in Britain

Islam is perceived widely as a source of cultural threat (Phillips 2006; Bawer 2006; Caldwell 2009), and mosques in particular are perceived as sites where difference is fostered. Examples in the mainstream media include a pair of documentaries broadcast for the Channel 4 series *Dispatches* (*Undercover*

Mosque in January 2007; *Undercover Mosque: The Return* in January 2008). These featured material filmed at the Green Lane Mosque in Birmingham and the London Central Mosque in Regent's Park, and suggested that radical ideologies propagated in Britain had been diffused by clerics, speakers and writers with links to Saudi Arabia.[1]

The think tank Policy Exchange also wrote a report based on visits to almost one hundred mosques suggesting that 'radical' literature had been found at about a quarter, although some of the evidence was disputed subsequently in a *Newsnight* broadcast for BBC2. Both the authors of the preface and the report itself suggested that radical material tended to hail from Saudi Arabia; the report also suggested that direct funding of British mosques from Saudi Arabia should be monitored (MacEoin 2007: 16, 5, 170). A report by the counter-extremism think tank Quilliam Foundation, based on a survey of over 500 mosques, found that the overwhelming majority of imams came from outside Britain and were trained abroad.[2] The author suggested that they were likely to be ill-equipped 'to help young British Muslims integrate into a democratic, multi-faith society, of which [the imams] have a limited understanding, and leaves them powerless to challenge Islamist extremist rhetoric propagated by young, English-speaking, and articulate Muslims' (Hart Dyke 2009: 8).

This link between mosques and the threat of Islamist extremism is apparently ever-present. At the time of writing, the threat from terrorism to the UK is graded as 'substantial' from international terrorism, and radical Islamist organisation Al Qa'ida is considered the most serious threat (May 2011: 13).[3] A small number of mosques have been associated with radical Islamism, most notably the former Finsbury Park mosque with Abu Qatada and Abu Hamza in the 1990s and early 2000s, and which a number of terrorists attended, including 'shoebomber' Richard Reid and Zacarias Moussaoui, the 'twentieth hijacker' from the 9/11 attacks (Dean and Allen 2006). The police, Home Office and Charity Commission monitor mosques' links and political ideologies closely (Bradley 2012). The 2011 version of the *Prevent* Strategy also suggested that 'radicalising locations' include mosques as well as university campuses, homes, cafes, and bookstores (May 2011: 108). At the same time, a good deal of academic research shows that religious participation is generally pro-social: people who participate in communal religious events tend to be more active in civic and political associations, and have more social and political capital.

Theories of religious and civic engagement

Most of the existing research into the role of religion for civic and political participation is based in the US, which is natural given its religious exceptionalism. However, as we will argue later, because of the high level of religiosity of British Muslims, we believe theories developed in the US may be applicable here too.

Most importantly for our argument regarding mosques as the social context for worship, it appears that embeddedness in the moral communities provided by religious groups, rather than personal religiosity *per se*, is the crucial variable. Putnam and Campbell have found that more religious Americans are more civically-active, with religious social networks serving as 'echo chambers' (Putnam and Campbell 2010: 456–469). Moreover, research has also suggested that places of worship can integrate minority groups into civic and social life. The history of black churches in the United States is suggestive of how minority religiosity translates into progressive political action (Calhoun-Brown 1996). Harris has analysed how religion provides both organisational and psychological resources for individual and collective political action among Black Americans, largely through churches providing the 'leadership base, social interaction, and communication networks required for collective action' (Harris 1994: 45).

For a variety of reasons it might be thought that mosques foster the political involvement of British Muslims. Some US-based work on Muslims also found positive effects of attending a mosque similar to those shown by the broader literature (Jamal 2005; Ayers and Hofstetter 2008). This relationship has been underexplored in Britain, and particularly for British Muslims. Some recent British research suggested that for all ethnic minorities religion may have a moderately positive impact on political engagement, but Muslims were not separately looked at systematically (Sobolewska *et al.* 2011; Heath *et al.* 2013).

Besides Putnam and Campbell's work analysing the 'Faith Matters' surveys, much American research has established that those more active in church decision-making are more interested in politics and more politically active. The effects are similar across the sexes, races and denominations, and relate primarily to political spill-over from church-level engagement rather than doctrinal differences (Peterson 1992: 137–138). Examining the National Election Surveys of 1994, 1996 and 1998, Wilcox and Sigelman found that one in 10 members of each of the four major US Christian traditions reported that a moral or religious group had tried to influence their vote; in 1996 the figure was one in seven (Wilcox and Sigelman 2001: 529). While religious contacts did not always increase turnout among all denominations in all elections, it often did (Wilcox and Sigelman 2001: 533). Examining a sample of congregations, Beyerlein and Chaves found that political activism at the congregation level took place in over 40 per cent of congregations (a substantially higher figure than that for non-religious organisations); and that furthermore there are differences in modes of political participation across religious traditions. Evangelical congregations tend to distribute Christian Right voter guides; Black Protestant congregations register voters, welcome candidates, and distribute alternative voter guides; Catholic congregations organise demonstrations and marches, and lobby elected officials; while mainline Protestant congregations organize discussion groups around political issues and host political candidates (Beyerlein and Chaves 2003: 229, 242).

Church congregations also supply personal friendship networks which affect social incentives to be active, and additionally enhance civic skills so that effort is more effectively translated into political impact (Verba, Schlozman and Brady 1995). Beyerlein and Hipp suggest that the main pathways may be via sermons on civic engagement and systematic listing of opportunities for civic engagement in religious service programmes by congregations (Beyerlein and Hipp 2006: 115). They also examined the extent to which religious involvement is associated with bridging as opposed to bonding social capital.[4] They found that participation in Black Protestant, Mainline Protestant and Catholic congregations facilitates involvement in organisations serving the larger community and establishing broader bridging ties, while greater participation in evangelical Protestant congregations does not appear to do so, suggesting that the wider community will not benefit from the growth in evangelical Protestantism in the US.

Unlike Jones-Correa and Leal, Calhoun-Brown found in her analysis of the 1984 National Black Election Study that attendance itself was not a strong predictor of political involvement; however, attendance at a political church was, suggesting that context is integral. Regular attendance in the more politicised black churches provided worshippers with psychological resources as well as organisational resources: political trust, a sense of political efficacy, and a group racial consciousness (Calhoun-Brown 1996). Djupe and Gilbert also make the point that the relationship between church attendance and political involvement is under-theorised. They suggest that the mechanisms may be as follows: clergy seek to address perceived under-representation of their congregants directly; social networks fostered among congregants are infused with political information and these encourage political involvement; and finally, they reaffirm the spill-over effect, considering that it works in a manner similar to involvement in secular organisations so that 'a turn inward to the church does not mean a turn away from civic and political life' (Djupe and Gilbert 2006: 118). Involvement in small groups within the congregation was a key driver of civic skills development, and further, social homogeneity within these small groups supported skills acquisition. Finally, feeling religiously different from one's neighbourhood, and perceiving one's congregation's beliefs not to be represented there, both increase the acquisition and use of civic skills in church: local minorities find a social outlet through church which often translates into political knowhow (Djupe and Gilbert 2006: 126).

It has also been suggested that the direction of causality may run from politics to religion rather than the converse; where governments seek dialogue with Muslim organisations, religion can become a tool for political activists just as it was for Black American civil rights leaders, in turn encouraging religious participation (Voas and Fleischmann 2012: 530). Another complicating issue highlighted by Van der Meer and Van Ingen (2009) is that people who participate in politics and religious worship are mobilised to do both by their general tendency to engage in social activity of all sorts. There is also a strong possibility that attendance in a place of worship affects engagement not through the sheer fact of religious participation, but by other, confounding factors, such as contact with co-ethnics in that place of worship. Data from the Netherlands collected for the Integration of the Second Generation (TIES) project suggest that the presence of co-ethnics in a given neighbourhood is directly related to the presence of a mosque and its effectiveness at fostering religiosity. To put it another way, the social networks fostered by mosques reinforce behavioural norms differing between the co-ethnic minority and the secularised majority, and this in turn depends on ethnic concentration and bonding social capital (Maliepaard and Phalet 2012; Fleischmann 2012: 531). Since Cutts *et al.* (2007) have also found that a higher residential concentration of co-ethnic members promotes electoral turnout in the UK, we might expect mosque attendance to be confounded by ethnic density in Britain as in the Netherlands.

By comparison with the US, there is relatively little similar work conducted for Britain, or Western Europe more broadly. More specifically, despite the great interest in European Muslims and their political and civic attitudes as well as the risk of extremism, apart from specific case studies of certain radicalising mosques, little has been done to investigate systematically whether mosque attendance has a negative or a positive effect on democratic involvement. On the one hand, although they did not look at non-Christian religions, Jones-Correa and Leal (2001) found that in the US the simple act of attending a place of worship has a bigger impact on political participation than belonging to a particular denomination. Therefore, we may expect that British Muslims will develop a greater political involvement as a result of their religious attendance. On the other, Beyerlain and Hipp (2006) show that some evangelical Protestant communities in the US do not develop an overall civic and pro-democratic orientation; we may conversely question whether mosques similarly encourage self-segregation from other – non-religious – forms of engagement.

Some recent research into how these theories might apply to British ethnic minorities may cast some light into which of these contradictory expectations seems more likely. Heath *et al.* have recently found that attendance at a place of worship significantly predicts responses that 'it is every citizen's duty to vote in an election' among British visible ethnic minority members (Heath *et al.* 2013: 49). McAndrew and Voas have suggested that immigrant religiosity promotes civic integration among visible ethnic minorities in Britain, with civic engagement measured by self-reports of generalised social trust, political volunteering, and volunteering for non-political groups (McAndrew and Voas 2014). Caveats include the fact that the analysis pooled different ethnic and religious groups, and did not distinguish whether this effect worked similarly for Pakistanis and Bangladeshis (overwhelmingly Muslim) as for Black Caribbeans (largely Christian), Black Africans (Christian and Muslim) and Indians (largely Hindu, with sizeable Sikh and Muslim subpopulations). Sobolewska *et al.* (2011) found that these effects are present for all ethnicities and religions for non-electoral political participation, with effects for Sikhs and Muslims significantly stronger. Storm (2013) found that communal religious practice, along with private prayer and affiliation, was positively associated with volunteering in general, but that this was only the case for 'bonding', i.e. co-ethnic, organisations. Religious affiliation and weekly attendance were negatively associated with 'bridging' participation, although private prayer remained positive and significant. She suggested that involvement in ethnic and religious minority organisations and places of worship might be unlikely to promote 'civic spillover'. This leaves us with a conflicting picture of the role that mosque attendance may have on British Muslims' political engagement.

Data and analytical strategy

To test these hypotheses, we draw upon the Ethnic Minority British Election Study 2010 (EMBES), to examine the relationship between religious participation and political engagement for the largest British Muslim communities – those of South Asian and Black African origin.[5] EMBES is the largest and most comprehensive survey of visible ethnic minorities in Britain, heavily focused on their socio-political attitudes, behaviour and integration. It drew a stratified probability sample, including areas of relatively low ethnic diversity, although for cost and feasibility reasons excluding all areas where the ethnic minority population is less than 2 per cent of the total (Heath *et al.* 2012). A summary of the key variables of interest for our analysis in this chapter is given in Table 3.1 in the Data Appendix.

Before we proceed with our analysis of any political and civic effects of mosque attendance, we examine who attends and why. The measure in the EMBES survey specifically asks:

> In the past 12 months, how often did you participate in religious activities or attend religious services or meetings with other people, other than for events such as weddings and funerals?

This does not specify whether the place of communal worship is one that others would recognise as a mosque open to the faithful; respondents might reasonably interpret this to include prayer rooms in private houses and institutions. Gilliat-Ray clarifies that 'mosque' is 'a universal term referring to any place or building used for prayer' which requires ritual cleanliness but no other specific ritual. Mosques are also commonly-understood to have a wider function than hosting prayers, for example as spaces for discussion and debate, education, and provision of social welfare (Gilliat-Ray 2010: 182–183). Nevertheless, we use the measure of 'participation with other people' as a proxy for mosque attendance on the assumption that respondents understand the question to mean participation at a public place of worship.

British Muslims exhibit a high rate of attendance, both compared with the white community in Britain, and non-Muslims represented in the EMBES. Of white respondents reporting a (non-Muslim) religious affiliation in the 2006–2010 British Social Attitudes surveys, 10.4 per cent reported that they attended church at least weekly. By comparison, 39.3 per cent of Muslims over the same period reported that they attended a mosque at least weekly.[6] Among EMBES respondents, 45.0 per cent of non-Muslim adherents reported that they attended at least weekly and 6.8 per cent that they attended at least daily. By comparison, 32.6 per cent of Muslims reported at least weekly attendance, and 24.4 per cent at least daily attendance, as Figure 3.1 illustrates.

The apparently high rate of attendance for Muslims overall may mask some gender and ethnic heterogeneity. Figure 3.2 illustrates the difference in rates between male and female Muslims, and Figure 3.3 differences by ethnic group. Males largely report that they attend at least weekly; for females, the distribution is more equally distributed across categories ranging from never to daily, which is to be expected as some mosques exempt women from attendance requirements in favour of private prayer. Larger mosques often make some provision for women, although Hart Dyke suggested that only 54 per cent of British mosques were accessible to women (Hart Dyke 2009: 20).

By contrast, expected differences in attendance across ethnic groups is not strongly apparent in the sample, even though mosques are anecdotally considered to being largely ethnically segregated, and more recent immigrants from Africa might have been thought to find it harder to access mosques than those from longer-established communities. Figure 3.3 suggests that Black African and Bangladeshi Muslims are slightly less likely to attend regularly, although this difference was not statistically significant.[7] We provide results of a full multivariate model of frequency of attendance by British ethnic minority Muslims in the Appendix to this chapter (see Table 3.2); the results confirm that females attend less frequently than males, and Bangladeshis slightly less frequently than Pakistanis. Married people attend more frequently. Age,

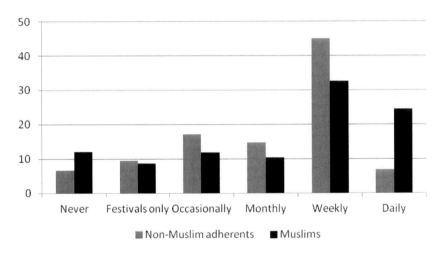

Figure 3.1 Frequency of attendance by affiliation (British ethnic minority and Muslim, or British ethnic minority and non-Muslim religious adherent)
Source: Ethnic Minority British Election Study and authors' analysis.

60 *Siobhan McAndrew and Maria Sobolewska*

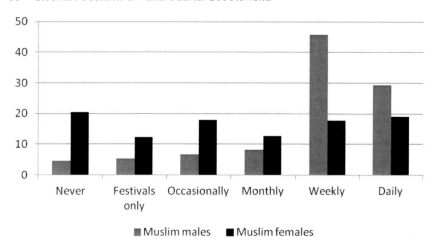

Figure 3.2 Frequency of British ethnic minority Muslims' mosque attendance by sex
Source: Ethnic Minority British Election Study and authors' analysis.

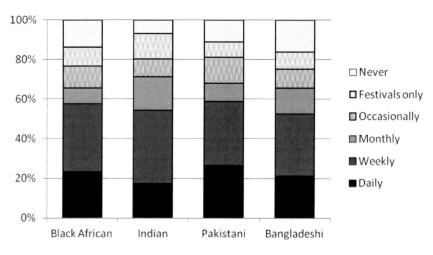

Figure 3.3 Frequency of British ethnic minority Muslims' mosque attendance by ethnic origin
Source: Ethnic Minority British Election Study and authors' analysis.

generational status, employment status and educational achievement are not significant predictors of attendance.

Of those respondents both reporting an affiliation and at least some attendance at a place of worship, Figure 3.4 does illustrate that British Muslims are slightly more likely to attend with others of a similar ethnic background than non-Muslims. This however masks great variation between Christians attending more diverse churches, and Sikhs or Hindus, where places of worship are overwhelmingly South Asian and even more co-ethnic than mosques.[8] Apart from 'ethnic preference', residential concentration may be the main driver of homogeneity in a place of worship. Analysis by the University of Manchester's Centre on Dynamics of Ethnicity has found that the geographical 'Index of Dissimilarity' for Pakistanis and Bangladeshis at local authority level was a little higher than those for Indians, Caribbeans and Africans in the 1991–2011 Censuses. In other words, on this indicator, Pakistanis and Bangladeshis appear to be slightly more residentially-concentrated than the other three groups. Nevertheless, the Index of Dissimilarity has declined for all ethnic groups over the three Censuses (except for the very small Chinese population in Britain; see Simpson 2012: 1–4).

Are British Muslims socially segregated in their mosques?

We now know that British Muslims are more likely than other religious groups to attend their place of worship regularly, and that they are a little more likely to do so predominantly with other co-ethnics. But does this attendance serve to separate them from a wider community and create a sense of separation from other Britons? Or does it increase their bridging social capital and participatory orientation towards British democracy?

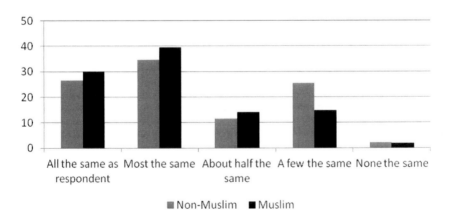

Figure 3.4 Diversity of British ethnic minority Muslims' and non-Muslims' places of worship
Source: Ethnic Minority British Election Study and authors' analysis.

We can measure whether British Muslims are more likely than other ethnic minority members to feel socially distant to British Whites and other ethnic groups more broadly. The EMBES survey includes measures of the ethnic diversity of organisations to which respondents belong, as gauged and reported by the respondents themselves. It also includes measures of their attitudes towards out-groups as well as to cultural diversity in the abstract; and measures of the ethnic diversity of their residential areas using data from the 2001 Census. First, we examine how the extent of 'ethnic bridging' varies between Muslims who attend a mosque regularly and those who do so only occasionally.

We used an attitudinal measure of social distance, namely whether the respondent would mind if a relative married a white person; a behavioural measure of social capital, namely the proportion of friends with a different ethnicity; and an attitudinal measure of belonging – whether the respondent felt that they have anything in common with other British people. While we see that regularly attending Muslims say that they would mind more if their relative married a white person that those who do not go to mosque regularly, they do not have statistically different levels of belonging and they are in fact less likely to say that they have no friends of other ethnicities. As we can see in Figure 3.5, regular attendance either makes very little difference or significantly decreases the social isolation of British Muslims. Taking the three items together, the proposition that mosque attendance encourages an insular mindset and 'separate' lives, in which no contact takes place between Muslim and non-Muslim Britons, does not find unambiguous support.

Are British Muslims politically mobilised by mosque attendance?

Having shown that mosque attendance does not correlate with tendencies to self-segregate, we now turn to testing theories on the role of places of worship in political and civic mobilisation. Our outcome measures include self-reported voting and four non-electoral political acts: signing a petition, taking part in a boycott, in a protest and donating money to a political cause; and three attitudinal measures: the level of satisfaction with democracy, belief that voting is a duty and support for violent political protest.

In addition to mosque attendance, our other explanatory variables relate to the many theories discussed above on the mechanisms and potential confounders of the influence of attendance on political engagement. These variables includes cross-ethnic bridging and perceived social distance between groups, generalised social trust, the perception that non-whites or Muslims in particular are victims of prejudice, and radical religious ideology measured by respondents' support for the introduction of sharia law in the UK. Since the issue of sharia law is rather controversial this last measure is designed to test the furthest extent to which religiosity may influence political attitudes of British Muslims.

As a first step, we conduct bivariate correlations between our explanatory variables and outcomes of interest. Because our variables are almost all binary (with respondents offered only 'yes' or 'no' responses), we dichotomise the

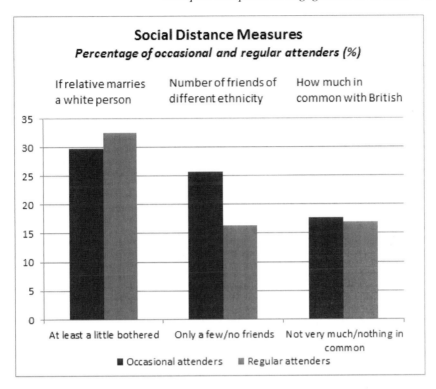

Figure 3.5 Differences between regular mosque attenders and less frequent attenders on three social distance measures (Muslim respondents only): whether the respondent is bothered by a relative marrying a white person; the proportion of friends of a different ethnicity; and how much the respondent feels they have in common with British people[9]

Source: EMBES and authors' analysis.

remaining non-dichotomous items and use tetrachoric correlation. Table 3.3 presents the results. The outcome variables are given in columns and explanatory variables in rows; by reading across the rows, we can see whether the proposed explanatory variables frequently predict our outcomes of interest.

At the bivariate level, attending the mosque at least weekly only correlates significantly with two outcomes: having protested within the last twelve months (at the 1 per cent level of significance), and having made a political donation within the last twelve months (at the 10 per cent level of significance). Weekly attendance does not significantly predict reporting having voted, attitudes to democracy and voting, or support for violent protest. Neither does generalised social trust predict significantly many of the outcomes of interest beyond satisfaction with democracy and agreement with the duty to vote. By comparison, the measures of perceived prejudice and political Islam possess stronger predictive power. Reporting that non-whites are 'held back' by ethnic prejudice, that Muslims in particular are victims of racial prejudice, and that sharia should be implemented in all cases in Britain is associated with being more likely to report dissatisfaction with democracy and disagree that citizens have a duty to vote; more likely to report having protested and signed a petition in the last twelve months; and more likely to report support for political violence. It appears that conventional Islamic religiosity, as measured by mosque attendance, is not the root cause of political alienation. By contrast, adherence to a radical religious ideology does appear to be associated with political oppositionalism.

Mosque attendance, social distance and political engagement: multivariate analysis

We now turn to a multivariate analysis of a set of political engagement measures (see Table 3.4 in appendix). In this set of models, we combine the following: first, the reports of having protested, supported a boycott, signed a petition, or donated money to a political cause, into a measure of 'any other political involvement'. The variables for support for violent protest are also combined into one measure of 'any support for violent protest' – namely whether the respondent supports violent protest in any of the three cases suggested (a controversial war, an unpopular tax, or job cuts). Accordingly, we have five dependent variables: having voted, satisfaction with democracy, agreeing that citizens have a duty to vote, any other political involvement, and any support for violent protest.

We then seek to test the effect of attendance at a place of worship on engagement for Muslims, once controlling for 'religious salience', or how important the respondent reports religion is in their daily life. Second, we include controls for ethnic bridging and social distance. Third, we include a control for a sense that Muslims are the recipients of prejudice. Fourth, in addition to the controls described above, we also control for two aspects of Verba *et al.*'s (1995) civic voluntarism model: whether the respondent has experience of non-political civic engagement (capturing the possibly confounding tendency to participate in general); and whether somebody they know has tried to persuade them how to vote, capturing a mobilisation effect. Finally, we include a control for support for the full implementation of sharia in Britain, to take account of the influence of holding a radical religious ideology.

We found the following. In the model predicting whether the respondent voted in 2010, sex, age, marital status, employment status and second-generational status were significantly and positively associated with having voted, as was religious attendance, albeit at the ten per cent level of significance. The ethnic bridging, social distance and civic voluntarism predictors were not significant; neither was perception of Islamophobia, or support for the full implementation of sharia. The results suggest that, unlike in the US, socio-structural factors are more important for turnout in Britain while the expected effects of psychological resources, social distance and spill-over from religious to civic engagement are not found.

In the model predicting satisfaction with democracy, the terms for religious attendance and religious salience were not significant. Being of second-generation status was associated with significantly lower satisfaction; earlier work by Heath *et al.* (2013: 195) confirms, however, that this generational effect works to converge ethnic minority attitudes to the White British level, rather than indicating divergence. Those with fewer friends of a different ethnicity reported lower satisfaction with democracy, as did those who had not volunteered in the past few years for a non-political cause. Perception of prejudice against Muslims and support for sharia were both associated with dissatisfaction. Psychological and civic resources appear most significant for this outcome, although it is conceivable that personality differences drive the tendency to join in, make diverse friendships and feel happy with the state of democracy alike.

In the model predicting agreement that citizens have a duty to vote, effects were somewhat similar: again, religious salience and religious attendance were not significantly associated with agreeing that citizens have a duty to vote. Being of second-generation status, being more bothered by the notion of a close relative marrying a white person, perceiving that Muslims were recipients of racial prejudice and support for the full implementation of sharia all predicted a lower sense of duty to vote. These findings are relatively reassuring: while greater social distance, perception of poor treatment and holding a more radical religious ideology are associated with a lower sense of electoral engagement, higher religiosity and more frequent mosque attendance are not. This suggests that to the extent that political disengagement is a problem, it is largely affective and identity-based, rather than arising through mosque attendance.

We now turn to the models predicting non-electoral political involvement, and support for violent protest. In the model predicting non-electoral political involvement, being older, employed and of second-generation immigrant status were associated with having protested, signed a petition, engaged in a boycott or donated money to a political cause in the previous twelve months. Greater ethnic bridging via an organisational membership was associated with greater involvement. Attempted mobilisation, measured by the respondent reporting that somebody outside a place of worship had attempted to persuade them how to vote, was also associated with such involvement, as was civic engagement via non-political volunteering. Concern at a close relative marrying a white person, and a perception that Muslims were the recipients of prejudice, were also associated with non-electoral forms of political involvement. Support for the full implementation of sharia, and higher religious salience were also associated with this form of political engagement; notably, however, higher mosque attendance was not. These effects are all intuitively plausible and accord with the theories presented in the literature; non-electoral political engagement requires political know-how, acquired through contact with others and associational involvement. Having a 'cause', greater group consciousness and religious ideology are also motivators of non-electoral political involvement. However, contrasting with the US findings for Black Protestants, these effects appear separable from frequency of attendance.

Support for violent protest is perhaps the strongest indicator of disengagement with democratic processes available in the dataset; 18.8 per cent of Muslim respondents supported violent protest in at least one of the three cases offered. The predominant finding in our model is that few drivers were significant. While support for sharia does predict support for violent protest at the ten per cent level of significance, religious salience and greater mosque attendance did not. Younger respondents were more likely to be supportive (likely to be an attitude they will outgrow), as were the employed, and those who had not reached tertiary education either within Britain or abroad. Notably, having more ethnic bridging links via civic involvement predicted greater support for violent protest, suggesting that contact with people outside the respondent's ethnic group does not necessarily foster harmony: instead, it may be a by-product of involvement in more radical campaigning groups with cross-ethnic appeal, such as anti-war groups. The terms for social distance and perception of prejudice were not significant, suggesting that the associations found here differ somewhat from those for satisfaction with democracy and holding a voting norm. Neither were the terms for having volunteered, or attempted mobilisation, found to be significant. Again, our conclusion is that having a particular worldview appears to matter more than religious behaviour, and the case for mosques in general fostering such worldviews appears weak to non-existent.

There is a remaining issue – namely, that mosque attendance may not be the 'true' driver of turnout, but rather act as a proxy for an underlying factor. The natural candidate is residential concentration of ethnic groups: mosques are more likely to be located where South Asians are clustered. Ethnic concentration can occur for a number of reasons and is not necessarily a by-product of 'white flight' or segregation; people often choose to live with or close to relatives, or within close distance of particular employers, schools or community centres. It is also known that residential concentration is associated with higher turnout, lower experienced racism and better health, suggesting that living in areas of higher co-ethnic concentration has some benefits for minorities (Cutts *et al.* 2007; Bécares *et al.* 2009). If mosques then proliferate in areas with higher ethnic concentration of South Asians or Black Africans, our model would capture this effect as one relating to religious behaviour rather than residential choice. It is also conceivable, although less plausible, that mosque attendance might act to suppress the effects of residential concentration, and so it is important to check how these factors relate to each other.

As an additional check, we therefore tested whether mosque attendance merely serves to mediate the effect of co-ethnic concentration, as measured by the percentage of people with the same ethnicity as the respondent living within their Lower Super Output Area (LSOA) in the 2001 Census (geographical areas which in 2001 hosted an average of 1,500 people). By doing this, we were testing whether the effect of attendance acts predominantly as a proxy for concentration, or instead may be the means whereby the effect of residential concentration has impact. It is plausible that respondents' residential choices were not driven primarily by the availability of a local mosque; controlling for co-ethnic concentration therefore helps us better identify the causal relationship between mosque attendance and political engagement more clearly. As a first step, we included in our multivariate analysis a term for co-ethnic concentration (Table 3.5 in the appendix presents full results). To keep the model tractable, we measured this via a binary measure of whether the LSOA was relatively 'co-ethnically dense', which we defined as 15 per cent or more of the LSOA being of the same ethnicity as the respondent. While we cannot strictly compare effects between probit models having added additional terms, we did find that no terms lost significance once the residential concentration measure had been included. We do also find that residential concentration is associated with significantly higher reported turnout, and a higher perception that there is a duty to vote.

We then conducted our formal test in two ways: first, by examining how the effect of mosque attendance is affected when adding a control for residential concentration to the model; and second, by examining how the effect of residential concentration is affected when adding a term for mosque attendance. Because our outcome variables are dichotomous, we used the Karlson-Holm-Breen (KHB) decomposition method, which splits the effect of co-ethnic density between a direct part and an indirect part via religious attendance.[10] Second, we examined whether including co-ethnic density as an additional control variable appeared to be the cause of religious attendance as a key variable – namely calculating the 'spurious effect' of religious attendance, again using the KHB method. The results for both tests are displayed in Table 3.5: they affirm that co-ethnic density and mosque attendance as reported in Table 3.4 indeed have separate effects. Moreover, they are overwhelmingly direct rather than indirect: the confounding percentage is low in all cases, while the difference between terms in the reduced and full models are not significant in any case. Accordingly, we can conclude that the beneficial effect of residential concentration on turnout and the voting norm does not work via mosque attendance; and neither is it the case that the effect of more frequent mosque attendance on voting is spurious, due to mosque attenders more often living among more people of a similar ethno-religious background. We can therefore be more confident that our findings regarding mosque attendance are causal in the case of electoral turnout, and furthermore that mosque attendance is neither the agent nor suppressor of the effects of residential concentration on political engagement.

Conclusion

Taken together, what do our results tell us? We find that more frequent mosque attendance is associated with self-reported turnout, but does not predict our other indicators of political engagement. Our overall impression is that second-generation status, perceived prejudice and radical religious ideology (as measured by support for sharia) are most consistently associated, whether positively or negatively, with political activity or a sense that democratic engagement is worthwhile. Ethnic bridging and civic voluntarism are predictive in some of the models, but not others. There is little clear evidence for a 'young Muslim male' problem, apart from the model explaining support for violent protest, where being younger is significant, but as Heath *et al.* (2013) show this is the case for all minorities and not just for Muslims. We might in any case expect to see a similar age effect for the White British; and furthermore do not find a gender effect. Having received higher education is significantly associated with lower support for political violence, reaffirming the civic value of education.

Most interestingly, it is the non-religious predictors, such as the perception of prejudice and the feeling of social distance from whites, that are a more solid predictor of political disengagement and oppositional engagement than religious involvement. This is an important finding that deserves further examination. The perception that racial discrimination holds minorities back was shown to predict lower political integration for minorities in general (Sanders *et al.* 2013), and we confirm this effect for Muslims, as it encourages less democratic and more oppositional engagement: engagement in protest and support for violent protest. This then, not the role of the mosques, should perhaps be the focus of any future policy on improving Muslims' integration.

Our findings are in the spirit of Wright and Bloemraad (2012) and Heath and Demireva (2014), who found no evidence for multiculturalist policy weakening integration and who emphasised the social and political importance of such 'null' findings. Here, we find no evidence that more frequent mosque attendance hinders the political integration of British Muslims, and some that it promotes it. To the extent that mosque attendance encourages or at least does not prevent social contact with other ethnic groups and a sense belonging, lower attendance correlates with a sense of disengagement, perceived Islamophobia, and a sense of social distance. Since young Muslims seem to attend mosques much less than their parents this relationship might be of interest, as we also found some worrying evidence that young Muslims have lower levels of engagement. However, we want to underline that the finding that British Muslims who were born and raised in Britain have a lower satisfaction with democracy, sense of duty to vote, and greater non-electoral political involvement, is suggestive of possible convergence to a White British norm. This convergence has been shown in many Western European countries (Maxwell 2013) and is thought to be caused by a sense of optimism of immigrants who are often favourably comparing their experiences with European democracies with their non-democratic countries of origin, but which is not shared by their European-born offspring, rather than a particular scepticism on the part of the second and third generation.

When presenting our previous work on the relationship between religion and political participation we often encountered a question: are mosques that encourage voting and strong Muslim political participation a good thing for Muslim integration, or do they perhaps encourage a separate political agenda and a sense of separate political community among Muslims? We hope that in this chapter we answered this question by showing that those Muslims who attend mosques do not live separate lives away from mainstream society. The set of findings presented here are extensive and the picture is not unambiguous. However, they crucially show that frequent attenders are as likely as those who do not attend to feel that they have something in common with other British people; more likely to have friends outside their ethnic or religious group; and overall more likely to engage in mainstream British politics given rates of engagement among British Muslims which are already high. In sum, our results support an optimistic interpretation of Muslim civic and political integration in Britain, and the pro-social benefits of religious involvement.

Data Appendix: summary of the data

Here we provide the detailed tables summarising the EMBES variables of interest to our analysis reported above, and the multivariate analyses of political behaviour and attitudes. We also provide a table of the results of the Karlson-Holm-Breen tests for mediation and confounding.

Table 3.1 Summary of variables of interest for Muslims in the EMBES sample[1]

Variable	Question wording	Mean or %	Unweighted N
Whether R is Muslim	Do you regard yourself as belonging to any particular religion? If yes, which one?	39.2%	1,140 of 2,787
Male	Interviewer observes and records	50.6%	584 of 1,140
Age	What was your age last birthday?	36.2	1,140
Black Caribbean	... which of these best describes your ethnic group? ... Black British – Caribbean	0.2%	5 of 1,140
Black African	Black British – African	14.3%	153 of 1,140
Indian	Asian British – Indian	11.6%	77 of 1,140
Pakistani	Asian British – Pakistani	52.6%	640 of 1,140
Bangladeshi	Asian British – Bangladeshi	21.3%	265 of 1,140
Married or partnered	... which of these applies to you at present? Married; living with a partner; separated after being married; divorced; widowed; single (never married)	65.5%	1,140

Table 3.1 (continued)

Variable	Question wording	Mean or %	Unweighted N
Employed	Which of the descriptions on this card best applies to you? ... In paid work	43.7%	475 of 1,088
Full-time education	In full-time education	13.7%	122 of 1,088
At least some tertiary education, in Britain or abroad	Taking your answers from this card, which is the highest British qualification you have? [Any of] postgraduate degree; first degree; university/ polytechnic diploma; teaching qualification; nursing qualification; HNC/HND, City & Guilds level 4, NVQ/SVQ 4/5. Do you have any qualifications you have not yet told me about that you gained overseas? [Either of] first degree; higher degree.	23.0%	259
First generation status	In which country were you born? In which year did you first move to Britain?	44.6%	510 of 1,094
1.5 generation status	Respondent defined as 1.5 generation if arrived in Britain before aged 16	21.4%	228 of 1,094
Second generation status	Using country of birth question	34.0%	356 of 1,094
Attends mosque at least weekly	In the past 12 months, how often did you participate in religious activities or attend religious services or meetings with other people, other than for events such as weddings and funerals? ... at least once a day; at least once a week	55.6%	640 of 1,129
Never attends mosque	... not at all	13.4%	150 of 1,129
Reports religion is extremely important	How important is your religion to you? ... extremely important	51.1%	566 of 1,136
Reports religion is not at all important	... not important at all	1.0%	14 of 1,136
Reports that they voted in 2010 General Election	... did you manage to vote in the General Election?	71.1%	801 of 1,140

Variable	Question wording	Mean or %	Unweighted N
Reports satisfaction with democracy	On the whole, are you satisfied or dissatisfied with the way that democracy works in this country?... (replies very satisfied; fairly satisfied)	78.9%	835 of 1,084
Reports citizens have duty to vote	It is every citizen's duty to vote in an election (replies strongly agree; agree)	87.7%	982 of 1,123
Protested in last twelve months	In the last 12 months, have you participated in a protest, like a rally or a demonstration, to show your concern about a public issue or problem?	8.6%	87 of 1,140
Signed petition in last twelve months	In the last 12 months, have you signed a petition?	19.6%	204 of 1,140
Supported boycott in last twelve months	In the last 12 months, have you participated in a boycott of a particular product or service?	9.6%	102 of 1,140
Donated money to political cause in last twelve months	In the last 12 months, have you given money to a political cause or advocacy organisation (other than a political party)?	6.2%	66 of 1,140
Any non-electoral political involvement on four measures above	Responding 'yes' to at least one of the four preceding items	27.4%	291 of 1,140
Supports violent protest in case of war	Would you ever support violent demonstrations or protests... ... if the British government was about to start a war that you didn't agree with?	9.8%	105 of 1,140
Supports violent protest in case of unpopular tax	... if the British government passed a tax increase which you thought was unfair?	8.4%	97 of 1,140
Supports violent protest in case of job cuts	... to protest against job cuts?	8.1%	91 of 1,140
Reports that other people can be trusted	Generally speaking, would you say that most people can be trusted or that you can't be too careful in dealing with people?	22.8%	252 of 1,102

Table 3.1 (continued)

Variable	Question wording	Mean or %	Unweighted N
Reports that non-Whites are 'held back' in Britain	Non-White people don't have the same opportunities and chances in life as White people, as they are held back by prejudice and discrimination (agrees or strongly agrees)	39.9%	466 of 1,140
Reports that Muslims are recipients of racial prejudice	Which groups, if any, do you think there is prejudice against? (respondent replies 'Muslims' unprompted)	34.8%	409 of 1,140
Supports full implementation of Sharia in Britain	Looking at these statements about Sharia courts being introduced in Britain, which of these come closest to your view? … Introduce Sharia law, that is traditional Islamic law, in all cases	17.4%	202 of 1,140
Ethnic bridging link via civic involvement	How many members of the [non-religious organisation(s) of which R is a member] are from the same ethnic or religious group as you? (reports membership where co-ethnics constitute about half, a few, or none of the members)	20.8%	220 of 1,140
Ethnic bridging link via friends	How many of your friends are from the same ethnic or religious group as you? (reports co-ethnics constitute about half, a few or none of their friends)	40.9%	453 of 1,140
Bothered by close relative marrying White person	How much would it bother you if one of your close relatives were to marry a White person? (reports 'not very much' or 'not at all')	67.3%	673 of 1,140
Contact (other than at place of worship) attempted to persuade them how to vote	Did anyone, for example, a friend, a member of your family, or someone at work, try to persuade you to vote for a particular party in the recent general election?	20.5%	226 of 1,140

Variable	Question wording	Mean or %	Unweighted N
Volunteered in the past few years for a non-political organisation	Over the past few years, have you volunteered to get involved in politics or community affairs?	38.8%	417 of 1,140
Lower Super Output Area (LSOA), percentage African, 2001	Percentage of LSOA recorded as of Black African ethnicity in 2001 Census	3.11%	1,140
LA percentage Indian, 2001	Percentage of LSOA recorded as of Indian ethnicity in 2001 Census	9.36%	1,140
LA percentage Pakistani, 2001	Percentage of LSOA recorded as of Pakistani ethnicity in 2001 Census	16.80%	1,140
LA percentage Bangladeshi, 2001	Percentage of LSOA recorded as of Bangladeshi ethnicity in 2001 Census	5.19%	1,140
% African if R is African	Percentage of LSOA recorded as of African ethnicity if R is African in 2001 Census	7.26%	153 of 1,140
% Indian if R is Indian	Percentage of LSOA recorded as of Indian ethnicity if R is Indian in 2001 Census	26.36%	77 of 1,140
% Pakistani if R is Pakistani	Percentage of LSOA recorded as of Pakistani ethnicity if R is Pakistani in 2001 Census	23.99%	640 of 1,140
% Bangladeshi if R is Bangladeshi	Percentage of LSOA recorded as of Bangladeshi ethnicity if R is Bangladeshi in 2001 Census	14.26%	265 of 1,140

Source: EMBES and authors' analysis.

Note: [1] Data weighted to correct for unequal probability of selection and for non-response using weight designed for analysis of all ethnic groups as one population.

Table 3.2 Drivers of mosque attendance[1]

Variable	Frequency of mosque attendance
Female	-0.814***
	(0.000)
Age	-0.005
	(0.180)
Black African	-0.124
	(0.356)
Indian	-0.134
	(0.253)
Bangladeshi	-0.308**
	(0.002)
Married or partnered	0.409***
	(0.000)
Employed or in full-time education	-0.097
	(0.296)
At least some tertiary education	-0.097
	(0.283)
1.5 generation	0.044
	(0.668)
Second generation	0.066
	(0.520)
Cut 1	-1.683***
	(0.000)
Cut 2	-1.318***
	(0.000)
Cut 3	-0.929***
	(0.000)
Cut 4	-0.598**
	(0.003)
Cut 5	0.309**
	(0.131)
N	1043
Log likelihood	-1613.9
Pseudo R^2	0.047

Source: EMBES and authors' analysis.

Notes: [1] Ordinal probit model predicting frequency of mosque attendance. The five 'cut' terms reflect the predicted cumulative probabilities at covariate values of zero; there are five because the outcome variable has six categories (from never attends to daily attendance). The base category is male, Pakistani, not currently married, not in employment or education, with secondary education or less, and a first-generation immigrant. Design weight applied as above. P-values in parentheses. * $p<0.10$, ** $p<0.05$, *** $p<0.001$.

Table 3.3 Political engagement, religious involvement, basic values and perceived prejudice: bivariate associations[1]

	Whether R voted in 2010 (self-report)	Satisfaction with democracy	Duty to vote	Protested in last 12 months	Petition in last 12 months	Boycott in last 12 months	Donated to political cause in last 12 months	Supports violent protest in case of war	Supports violent protest in case of unfair tax	Supports violent protest in case of job cuts
At least weekly attendance	0.015 (0.794)	0.025 (0.662)	0.013 (0.856)	0.262*** (0.000)	0.073 (0.213)	0.038 (0.602)	0.157* (0.055)	0.055 (0.412)	0.080 (0.242)	-0.031 (0.661)
Social trust	0.008 (0.937)	0.197*** (0.001)	0.183** (0.012)	-0.052 (0.592)	0.051 (0.406)	-0.020 (0.901)	-0.135 (0.170)	-0.062 (0.459)	0.020 (0.800)	-0.053 (0.600)
Perceives prejudice vs. non-Whites	-0.081 (0.114)	-0.172*** (0.001)	-0.156** (0.010)	0.069 (0.364)	0.065 (0.239)	0.004* (0.066)	-0.079 (0.367)	0.162** (0.016)	0.020 (0.829)	0.175** (0.010)
Perceives prejudice vs. Muslims	-0.070 (0.177)	-0.255*** (0.000)	-0.193*** (0.001)	0.275*** (0.000)	0.240*** (0.000)	0.306*** (0.000)	0.086 (0.290)	0.129* (0.054)	-0.012 (0.912)	0.098 (0.171)
Support for Sharia	-0.048 (0.398)	-0.157** (0.010)	-0.139** (0.044)	0.142* (0.058)	0.109* (0.085)	0.116 (0.134)	0.090 (0.317)	0.157** (0.031)	0.154** (0.037)	0.181** (0.015)

Source: EMBES and authors' analysis.

Notes: [1] Tetrachoric correlations of indicators of political engagement, political attitudes, religious involvement, basic values and perceived prejudice. P-values in parentheses, number of cases in italics. * $p<0.10$, ** $p<0.05$, *** $p<0.001$.

Table 3.4 Drivers of political engagement and political effect: multivariate analysis[1]

Variable	Voted in 2010	Satisfaction with democracy	Sense of duty to vote	Other political involvement	Support for violent protest
Constant	-0.689 (0.169)	2.126*** (0.000)	1.726** (0.003)	-3.520*** (0.000)	-0.563 (0.312)
Female	0.372** (0.004)	-0.080 (0.553)	0.232 (0.101)	0.141 (0.296)	0.066 (0.626)
Age	0.016** (0.003)	0.003 (0.588)	-0.001 (0.842)	0.010** (0.062)	-0.024*** (0.000)
Married or partnered	0.212** (0.064)	-0.156 (0.214)	0.056 (0.668)	0.063 (0.614)	-0.101 (0.438)
Employed or in full-time education	0.239* (0.069)	0.019 (0.896)	0.187 (0.217)	0.244* (0.071)	0.398** (0.008)
At least some tertiary education	-0.060 (0.610)	-0.084 (0.534)	-0.050 (0.721)	0.133 (0.296)	-0.334** (0.015)
Second-generation immigrant status	0.181 (0.135)	-0.578*** (0.000)	-0.628*** (0.000)	0.421*** (0.001)	0.022 (0.867)
Ethnic bridging link via civic involvement	0.003 (0.981)	-0.147 (0.286)	0.207 (0.181)	0.405** (0.004)	0.343** (0.026)
Ethnic bridging link via friends	-0.025 (0.679)	-0.146** (0.013)	-0.067 (0.328)	-0.056 (0.424)	-0.015 (0.823)
Attempted vote suasion other than via place of worship	0.049 (0.709)	-0.062 (0.666)	-0.196 (0.180)	0.284** (0.035)	0.146 (0.271)
Whether volunteered for non-political organisation	0.143 (0.275)	-0.251* (0.036)	0.058 (0.663)	0.886*** (0.000)	0.185 (0.151)
Bothered by close relative marrying White person	0.005 (0.907)	0.022 (0.604)	-0.064* (0.133)	0.115** (0.011)	-0.010 (0.797)

Table 3.4 (continued)

Variable	Voted in 2010	Satisfaction with democracy	Sense of duty to vote	Other political involvement	Support for violent protest
Perceives that Muslims are recipients of racial prejudice	-0.149 (0.177)	-0.352** (0.003)	-0.359** (0.006)	0.353** (0.003)	-0.104 (0.408)
Support for full implementation of sharia	-0.121 (0.402)	-0.385** (0.006)	-0.262* (0.073)	0.196 (0.162)	0.269* (0.053)
Religious attendance	0.061* (0.080)	-0.032 (0.382)	-0.033 (0.415)	0.052 (0.169)	0.065 (0.106)
Religious salience	-0.016 (0.845)	-0.056 (0.517)	0.027 (0.774)	0.178** (0.052)	-0.004 (0.962)
Whether R lives in Local Super Output Area where at least 15 % are of the same ethnicity as R	0.302** (0.005)	0.064 (0.600)	0.306** (0.027)	0.174 (0.144)	0.043 (0.721)
N	972	931	972	972	972
Log likelihood	-523.4	-414.5	-314.5	-452.0	-413.8
Pseudo R-squared	0.053	0.109	0.101	0.200	0.124

Source: EMBES and authors' analysis.

Notes: [1] Probit regression analysis of political behaviour and attitudes. P-values in parentheses. * $p<0.10$, ** $p<0.05$, *** $p<0.001$. The base category is male, not currently married, not in employment or education, with a secondary education or less, first or 1.5 generation immigrant, does not possess a bridging link via civic membership, has not experienced a contact attempting to persuade them how to vote, has not volunteered in the past few years for a non-political organisation, does not perceive that Muslims are at the receiving end of racial prejudice; either does not support the implementation of sharia or only does so where not in conflict with British law; and lives in a neighbourhood where fewer than 15 per cent of the residents are of the same ethnicity. Design weight applied as above.

Table 3.5 Tests for mediating effect of religious attendance and confounding effect of co-ethnic density[1]

Testing whether effects of co-ethnic density work via religious attendance	Effect of co-ethnic density in reduced model (excludes mosque attendance)	Effect of co-ethnic density in full model (includes mosque attendance)	Difference	Confounding percentage (%)
Whether R voted in 2010 general election	0.310** (0.004)	0.302** (0.005)	0.008 (0.338)	2.71
Whether R is satisfied with democracy	0.060 (0.625)	0.064 (0.600)	-0.004 (0.489)	-7.38
Whether R perceives there to be a duty to vote	0.301** (0.029)	0.306** (0.027)	-0.005 (0.507)	-1.53
Whether R has engaged in non-electoral politics	0.182 (0.129)	0.174 (0.144)	0.007 (0.379)	4.00
Whether R supports violent protest	0.052 (0.665)	0.043 (0.721)	0.009 (0.350)	17.29
Testing whether effects of religious attendance are spurious, caused by co-ethnic density	Effect of mosque attendance in reduced model (excludes density)	Effect of mosque attendance in full model (includes density)	Difference	Confounding percentage (%)
Whether R voted in 2010 general election	0.065* (0.062)	0.061* (0.080)	0.004 (0.290)	6.01
Whether R is satisfied with democracy	-0.031 (0.394)	-0.032 (0.382)	0.001 (0.634)	-2.76
Whether R perceives there to be a duty to vote	-0.029 (0.472)	-0.033 (0.415)	0.004 (0.310)	-13.37
Whether R has engaged in non-electoral politics	0.055 (0.152)	0.052 (0.169)	0.002 (0.368)	4.11
Whether R supports violent protest	0.066 (0.102)	0.065 (0.106)	0.001 (0.733)	0.85

Source: EMBES and authors' analysis.

Notes: [1] All other variables held constant as concomitant variables. Design weight applied as above. P-values in parentheses. * p<0.10, ** p<0.05, *** p<0.001.

Notes

1 Following investigations by the West Midlands police and Crown Prosecution Service (CPS) into both the clerics featured in the first documentary, and subsequently into the documentary-makers for inciting religious hatred, the broadcast was referred to OFCOM which judged that the documentary had been made responsibly.
2 Note that without an official directory of mosques we cannot be sure how representative this sample was; it is likely to be biased towards larger mosques because these are more easily identifiable and more likely to have the personnel to respond.
3 As of 17 August 2013, www.gov.uk/terrorism-national-emergency/terrorism-threat-levels.
4 Bridging capital refers to ties formed within heterogeneous groups and bonding capital are the links within homogenous groups (Putnam 2000).
5 The sample excludes those of mixed heritage where one ethnic identity is white. Accordingly, it does not sample the 8 per cent of British Muslims who are ethnically white. A further 14.5 per cent identified as mixed or 'other' than Black, White or Asian (ONS 2013).
6 Authors' analysis. Data were pooled for the most recently-available five years of the BSA to ensure an adequate sample of Muslims (Muslim n = 438; White non-Muslims n = 15,283).
7 A chi-squared test found no relationship between ethnicity and frequency of attendance: χ^2 (15, 1124) = 16.673, p = 0.309.
8 A chi-squared test corroborated a relationship between religious adherence (Muslim vs non-Muslim) and ethnic homogeneity of co-worshippers: χ^2(4, 1140) = 80.069, p < 0.001.
9 Whether feeling positive about a relative marrying a white person varies with frequency of attendance for British Muslim attenders: χ^2(16, 885) = 32.964, p = 0.007. Whether diversity of friends varies with frequency of attendance: χ^2(16, 952) = 27.779, p = 0.034. Whether feeling more in common with British people varies with frequency of attendance: χ^2(12, 969) = 41.630, p < 0.001.
10 If the outcome variables were continuous we could simply compare how coefficients change once the additional control is added to the model. However, where outcome variables are binary, the estimated coefficients of the models, and their significance, are not strictly comparable between different models. Hence we use the KHB method with results presented in Table 3.5.

Bibliography

Allum, N., Read, S. and P. Sturgis (2011) 'Evaluating Change in Social and Political Trust in Europe', in E. Davidov, P. Schmidt and J. Billiet (eds) *Cross-Cultural Analysis: Methods and Applications*. Hove: Routledge, 35–54.

Ayers, J.W. and Hofstetter, C.R. (2008) 'American Muslim Political Participation Following 9/11: Religious Belief, Political Resources, Social Structures, and Political Awareness', *Politics and Religion*, 1: 3–26.

Bawer, B. (2006) *While Europe Slept: How Radical Islam is Destroying the West from Within*, New York: Random House.

Bécares, L. Nazroo, J. and Stafford, M. (2009) 'The Buffering Effects of Ethnic Density on Experienced Racism and Health', *Health and Place*, 15: 670–678.

Beyerlein, K. and Chaves, M. (2003) 'The Political Activities of Religious Congregations in the United States', *Journal for the Scientific Study of Religion*, 42(2): 229–246.

Beyerlein, K. and Hipp, J.R. (2006) 'From Pews to Participation: The Effect of Congregation Activity and Context on Bridging Civic Engagement', *Social Problems*, 53: 97–117.

Bradley, J. (2012) "Mosque's terror links' investigated by Charity Commission', *BBC News London*, 7 June, available at: www.bbc.co.uk/news/uk-england-london-18355721 (accessed 17 August 2013).

Calhoun-Brown, A. (1996) 'African-American Churches and Political Mobilization: The Psychological Impact of Organizational Resources', *Journal of Politics*, 4: 935–953.

Caldwell, C. (2009) *Reflections on the Revolution in Europe: Immigration, Islam and the West*. London: Allen Lane.

Cutts, D., Fieldhouse E., Purdam, K., Steel, D. and Tranmer, M. (2007) 'Voter Turnout in British South Asian Communities at the 2001 General Election', *British Journal of Politics and International Relations*, 9(3): 396–412.

Dean, N. and Allen, N. (2006) 'Finsbury Park Mosque's Terrorist Roll Call', *The Independent*, 7 February, available at: www.independent.co.uk/incoming/finsbury-park-mosques-terrorist-roll-call-465867.html (accessed 18 August 2013).

Djupe, P.A. and Gilbert, C.P. (2006) 'The Resourceful Believer: Generating Civic Skills in Church', *Journal of Politics*, 68(1): 116–127.

Field, C. (2007) 'Islamophobia in Contemporary Britain: The Evidence of the Opinion Polls, 1998–2006', *Islam and Christian-Muslim Relations*, 18: 447–477.

Fieldhouse, E. and Cutts, D. (2008) 'Diversity, Density and Turnout: The Effect of Neighbourhood Ethno-Religious Composition on Voter Turnout in Britain', *Political Geography*, 27(5): 530–548.

Gilliat-Ray, S. (2010) *Muslims in Britain: An Introduction*. Cambridge: Cambridge University Press.

Harris, F.C. (1994) 'Something Within: Religion as a Mobilizer of African-American Political Activism', *The Journal of Politics*, 56(1): 42–68.

Hart Dyke, A. (2009) *Mosques Made in Britain*. London: Quilliam Foundation.

Heath, A.F. and Demireva, N. (2014, forthcoming) 'Has Multiculturalism Failed in Britain?', *Ethnic and Racial Studies*, DOI:10.1080/01419870.2013.808754.

Heath, A.F., Fisher, S.D., Rosenblatt, G., Sanders, D. and Sobolewska, M. (2010) *British Election Study Ethnic Minority Survey*, UK Data Service, SN 6970, 10.5255/UKDA-SN-6970–6971 (first release, April 2012).

Heath, A.F., Fisher, S.D., Rosenblatt, G., Sanders, D. and Sobolewska, M. (2013) *The Political Integration of Ethnic Minorities in Britain*. Oxford: Oxford University Press.

Jamal, A. (2005) 'The Political Participation and Engagement of Muslim Americans: Mosque Involvement and Group Consciousness', *American Politics Research*, 33: 521–544.

Jones-Correa, M. and Leal, D. (2001) 'Political Participation: Does Religion Matter?', *Political Research Quarterly*, 4: 751–770.

MacEoin, D. (2007) *The Hijacking of British Islam: How Extremist Literature is Subverting Mosques in the UK*. London: Policy Exchange.

Maliepaard, M. and Phalet, K. (2012) 'Religious Identity Expression Among Dutch Muslims: The Role of Minority and Majority Group Contact', *Social Psychology Quarterly*, 75/2: 131–148.

Maxwell, R. (2013) 'The Integration Trade-offs of Political Representation', *European Political Science*, 12(3): 467–478.

May, T. (2011) *Prevent Strategy*, Presented to Parliament by the Secretary of State for the Home Department by Command of Her Majesty, Cmnd 8092 (June), available at: www.gov.uk/government/uploads/system/uploads/attachment_data/file/97976/p Revent-strategy-review.pdf (accessed 17 August 2013).

McAndrew, S. and Voas, D. (2014) 'Immigrant Generation, Religiosity, and Civic Engagement in Britain', *Ethnic and Racial Studies*, 37(1).

Office for National Statistics (2013) 'Full Story: What Does the Census Tell Us About Religion in 2011?', *Briefing Notes* (May).

Peterson, S.A. (1992) 'Church Participation and Political Participation: The Spillover Effect', *American Politics Quarterly*, 20: 123–139.

Phillips, M. (2006) *Londonistan: How Britain is Creating a Terror State Within*. New York: Encounter Books.

Putnam, R.D. (2000) *Bowling Alone: The Collapse and Revival of American Community*. New York: Simon and Schuster.

Putnam, R.D. and Campbell, D.E. (2010) *American Grace: How Religion Divides and Unites Us*. New York: Simon and Schuster.

Sanders, D., Heath, A.F., Fisher, S. and Sobolewska, M. (2013) 'The Democratic Engagement of Britain's Ethnic Minorities', *Ethnic and Racial Studies* (early view publication online 19 September).

Simpson, L. (2012) 'More Segregation or More Mixing?', Briefing Note, *Dynamics of Diversity: Evidence from the 2011 Census*, ESRC Centre on Dynamics of Ethnicity (December).

Sobolewska, M., Heath, A.F., Sanders, D. and Fisher, S. (2011) 'Religion and Minority Political Participation: Evidence from Great Britain', Paper presented to 6th European Consortium of Political Research General Conference, University of Iceland, Reykjavik, 24–27.

Storm, I. (2013) 'Civic Engagement in Britain: The Role of Religion and Inclusive Values', Mimeo, University of Manchester.

Van Der Meer, T. and Van Ingen, E. (2009) 'Schools of Democracy? Disentangling the Relationship Between Civic Participation and Political Action in 17 European Countries', *European Journal of Political Research*, 48: 281–308.

Verba, S., Schlozman, K.L., and Brady, H.E. (1995) *Voice and Equality: Civic Voluntarism in American Politics*. Cambridge, MA: Harvard University Press.

Voas, D. and Fleischmann, F. (2012) 'Islam Moves West: Religious Change in the First and Second Generations', *Annual Review of Sociology*, 38: 525–545.

Wilcox, C. and Sigelman, L. (2001) 'Political Mobilization in the Pews: Religious Contacting and Electoral Turnout', *Social Science Quarterly*, 82: 524–535.

Wright, M. and Bloemraad, I. (2012) 'Is There a Trade-Off Between Multiculturalism and Socio-Political Integration? Policy Regimes and Immigrant Incorporation in Comparative Perspective', *Perspectives on Politics*, 10: 77–95.

Part II
Social Movements

4 Women from Muslim communities in Britain

Political and civic activism in the 9/11 era[1]

Khursheed Wadia

Introduction

The events of 9/11 cast a spotlight on Muslims as never before. In Britain, it influenced the way in which individuals, families and entire communities lived day-to-day and how they saw themselves and others. Most importantly, 9/11 and the 'war on terror' determined how Muslims came to be seen by majority British society; that is, as bearers of a menacing, destabilising religion whose principles and practice clashed with western liberal democratic values and systems. Over the last 13 years, the war on terror has generated various measures aimed at combating terrorism and violence, including the introduction of harsh immigration legislation, rules and an array of control orders dubbed 'prisons without bars'. This has had a particularly negative impact on those arriving at British border ports from Muslim-majority countries in the Middle East and North Africa. It has also meant that long-established black and minority ethnic (BME) communities have become the target of increased policing while an all-out attack has been launched on their 'failure' to integrate into British society. The principles and practices of liberal multiculturalism introduced since the late 1960s and which created the framework in which ethnic and cultural diversity was managed in Britain, came under an unprecedented attack.[2]

Where Muslim women are concerned, their lives were transformed by the events of 9/11 (and 7/7) and by the cumulative effects of racism, Islamophobia and an anti-terror legal system targeted at their communities. Two things happened and arguably these are among the unintended consequences of the war on terror. On one hand, large numbers of Muslim women who had led an 'ordinary life', having little or no direct involvement with political institutions and processes beyond voting, were suddenly and brutally exposed to the public gaze. Struggling to cope with this unwanted exposure, they developed various strategies, including those of resistance. There is little doubt for example (although there are no statistics to hand) that after 9/11, increasing numbers of women from Muslim communities in Britain took up wearing Islamic dress (mainly the headscarf/*hijab* and to a lesser extent the full face veil/*niqab*) as an assertion and banner of their religion in the face of rising hostility although many also wore it as it lent a sense of anonymity and safety.[3] The assertion of an Islamic identity, whether through changed dressed codes or other means, more often than not, went hand-in-hand with increased political awareness and activism on the part of Muslim women in both grassroots organisations, social movements and campaigns and institutional politics. Our study revealed that a significant number of women who wore *hijab* did so because it allowed them to assert their Muslim identity and the politics which flowed from it. According to one respondent, 'Back in those days [before 9/11] when people saw a girl wearing the hijab, everybody used to think "poor her, her parents must be very strict" ... now it's almost a political statement for these girls to wear the hijab' (Indameera).

The second effect is that Muslim women were called on by the British state to help counter the growth of terrorism in their communities and thereby reinforce social cohesion processes. The thinking behind this was that young Muslim men, considered susceptible to fundamentalist Islamic logic and attracted by extremist networks, were the product of failed integration and that mothers, wives, sisters could stop sons, husbands, brothers from subscribing to extremist thought and action; that the women would constitute a bridge between alienated Muslim communities and potential 'home-grown terrorists' and majority British society. The British state's call to Muslim women was framed within the Prevention of Violent Extremism (PVE) or Prevent programme, established in 2007.[4] This programme incorporated state funding for the empowerment and advancement of Muslim women in public life as a means of de-radicalising Muslim communities. The state's call to Muslim women to be active in their communities and become 'empowered' produced varying responses from Muslim women's groups and community organisations. Some argued women were being bought off to spy on families and communities (Woolf 2008). Others voiced doubts about pairing up community engagement with counter-terrorism measures while, at the same time, feeling that the lack of funds for women's organisations meant that there was an obligation to use this opportunity; as one women's Midlands-based project manager stated, 'All the doors to obtaining funding for work with Muslim women were shutting and all the signposts were pointing to Prevent' (Demos 2010). Yet others took a more pragmatic approach towards Prevent (at least initially): 'If the process of empowering Muslim women also helps tackle extremism, then surely this is a positive outcome that we should all welcome – so it is difficult to understand why some are opposing this idea' (Gohir 2008). Whatever the response, the Prevent programme brought a significant number of Muslim women into civic and political life through the creation of new women's organisations and projects at local level or the reinforcement of existing ones,[5] although those benefitting from PVE funding were constrained vis-à-vis the issues over which they were consulted by government. In addition to the state courting Muslim women through the Prevent programme, Muslim women who had experience of civic and political activism began to be considered by political parties as community interlocutors and even election candidates in constituencies with large Muslim populations.

The effects of the 9/11 events, 7/7 London bombings and the war on terror coupled with the state's call to Muslim women to play a part in the de-radicalisation of their communities meant that more women from Muslim communities than at any time previously became engaged in the polity and civil society. This chapter aims to understand Muslim women's activism in the 9/11 era. It explores this activism by using a broad definition of political participation which includes the involvement of citizens in civic arenas and by locating Muslim women in three distinct but intersecting contexts (that of post-war family migration from South Asia; that of new migrations in the 1990s and 2000s; that of second and subsequent generation BME populations in Britain) which bear different influences on their participation. It focuses on the types of political and civic activism in which British Muslim women are involved through an examination of specific cases and, in doing so, constructs a three-way typology of activists.

About the research

The findings presented here are based on an empirical study of women from Muslim communities and politics in Britain and France funded by the Economic and Social Research Council.[6] The study compares the political participation and civic engagement of Muslim women in two major European countries although the focus in this chapter is on Britain alone.[7]

The fieldwork in Britain involved gathering data from: 40 semi-structured interviews with women from Muslim communities of whom half had attained a level of public visibility at local or national level through their political and civic activism, and half of whom were (for want of a better term) 'ordinary women'; a programme of focus group meetings[8]; and direct observation of public meetings and events organised by community organisations and political campaigns in which Muslim women were involved.

Interviewees and focus group participants were initially recruited through purposive sampling though the target sample size was eventually reached through convenience sampling. Consequently, the total sample of respondents (interviewees and focus group participants) reflected an age range between 18 and 55.[9] They were all educated up to the age of 16 at least, in the UK or elsewhere and all but two possessed a high if not native level of English.[10] Our total sample of respondents was composed of married and single women mainly; of students, those who cared for home and family, women in or in search of employment. It included women from Bangladesh, Pakistan (Punjab and *Azad Kashmir*), India, East Africa, Bosnia, Turkey and Iraqi Kurdistan. Women from both Sunni and Shi'a communities were represented as were *hijabis* and non-*hijabis* (the majority). Three women did not practise Islam and of these one declared herself atheist although she was happy to be interviewed as a woman from an Islamic republic and culture.[11] The fieldwork took place in Birmingham, Bradford, Coventry, London, Manchester, Glasgow and Cardiff. All bar four of our respondents were born in the UK or had acquired UK citizenship through marriage or patriality or had the right to reside indefinitely in the UK and were therefore entitled to vote or stand for election.

Women from Muslim communities/Muslim women

The term 'women from Muslim communities' was the preferred terminology within the study because it permits the inclusion of women who are religious and those who are not; practising and non-practising Muslims. Despite the intensification of Islamic belief in the UK, there are women from Muslim communities who do not describe themselves as Muslim first and foremost but for whom the celebration of Islamic culture and history remains important – it was important to represent those women also. However, the phrase 'women from Muslim communities' can be cumbersome and is therefore used interchangeably with 'Muslim women' throughout this chapter.

Political participation and civic engagement

While there now exists a vast body of literature on women, political participation and civic engagement in Britain, that on women from black and minority ethnic/faith communities and politics is small; and while public and academic interest in Muslim women in Britain has increased over the past decade for the reasons explained above, so far it has translated into a rather slim body of work. For the most part, this body of work covers Muslim women's participation in areas of public life other than the polity; for instance, education, employment, organised religion and culture (Ahmad 2001; Bhimji 2012; Brah 2001; Cheruvalli-Contractor 2012; Dyke and James 2009; Haw 1998; Jawad and Benn 2003; Peach 2006; Tyrer and Ahmad 2006). Some work focuses on particular issues, for example, Muslim women and feminism (Afshar *et al.* 2005; Cheruvalli-Contractor 2012, Chapter 6); Islamic dress code and identity (Cheruvalli-Contractor 2012, Chapter 5; Dwyer 1999; Hopkins and Greenwood 2013) or dress code and the law (Malik 2008; Ward 2006); marriage/family legal codes and practices (Bano 2012); Muslim women, Islamophobia and racism (Allen *et al.* 2013; Williamson and Khiabany 2010; Ryan 2011); and Muslim women, counter-terrorism and social cohesion policies (Rashid 2014; Jones *et al.* 2014). Of course, the areas of public life and issues mentioned above can be politicised and involve 'doing politics'. There is also a small number of works which deals more explicitly with the question of Muslim women and politics (e.g. Allen and Guru 2012; Belli 2013; Takhar 2013; Werbner 1996) but none take a political participation-civic engagement approach in examining and accounting for Muslim women's participation in political and civic life.

Political participation and civic engagement

The involvement of citizens in public life has been approached and categorised in a number of ways. Traditional political science has focused on the polity and conventional political activity aimed at influencing government thinking, policy and action either directly or indirectly (Verba, Schlozman and Brady 1995: 38). Hence activity aimed at directly influencing government would include lobbying MPs or demonstrating against specific government policies, while indirect influence, through selecting people who make policy decisions, would include voting. However, women's movements of the 1970s challenged traditional, narrow definitions of what 'doing politics' involved. Their claim that 'the personal is political' brought new issues onto the political agenda and also expanded the definition of the political to include activities in which women were involved.

In the 1980s, feminist scholars, explaining the absence of women in politics through reasons other than 'political apathy' and/or a 'lack of political knowledge' as defined by traditional political science (Goot and Reid 1984) or arguing that women were differently active from men (Hernes 1984: 21–31; Lovenduski 1986: 126–7), de-emphasised methods of study of mass and elite political behaviour and instead placed value on the combined searches of historical archives and primary materials, interviews with activists and studies of the law and policy-making processes in order to reveal a rich history of women's political participation. An important finding of early feminist studies was that a gender gap (in men's favour) did exist concerning participation in political institutions and elections (Randall 1987: 57) but that this gap was explicable by examining the structural barriers women faced in entering the political arena. Such studies also found that women participated at grassroots level in social movements and protest politics, unstructured community organisations, voluntary organisations, etc. and that they often addressed issues of social and political importance through the legal system and by targeting specific policies.

Thus feminist scholars expanded the definition of the political to include not only electoral and institutional (elite) politics but also so-called unconventional political activity such as direct action and protest at grassroots level, in favour of social and political transformation.

In this chapter, Muslim women's activism will be examined and understood through this expanded definition of politics. However, within this broader conceptualisation of 'doing politics', we use the term and concept 'civic engagement' to refer to involvement which takes place in civic arenas as opposed to within explicitly political structures and processes. While civic engagement has been variously defined (Adler and Goggin 2005), we use the definition provided by Zukin *et al.* (2005: 7) where it is seen as organised voluntary activity, undertaken by citizens, individually or collectively, which is aimed at helping others within a community in order to find solutions to social and other problems and eventually bring about societal change.

Whether or not civic engagement can be considered political has been the subject of lengthy academic discussion. For instance, while scholars such as Burns, Schlozman and Verba concede that 'voluntary activity in both the religious and secular domains outside of politics intersects with politics in many ways' (2001: 58), they ultimately conclude that political activity is that which 'seek[s] to influence either directly or indirectly what the government does' (Ibid.). Hence, they argue that serving in a community soup kitchen may be a precursor to political activity through the development of transferable skills but that it is not a political activity in itself. However, it can also be argued that the context in which serving in a soup kitchen occurs must be considered; that the act of volunteering in a soup kitchen is not necessarily apolitical but may express disapproval of a government's economic and welfare policies and also constitute an attempt to shame politicians and influence public policy. Supporting an expanded definition of politics to include activities undertaken in the civic sphere, by voluntary organisations and unstructured community groups, Pippa Norris argues:

> While these groups are not conventionally seen as political, their status should be redefined since as part of their work they can engage in activity which is designed to influence public policy, understood in broad terms.
>
> In response, traditionalists might argue that these activities ... should not all be considered instances of political participation ... Participants in these activities may not necessarily see themselves as engaging in 'politics' since their actions are not directed, in the first instance, towards influencing the state. Nor are they using the conventional political mechanisms of parties and elections. The level of involvement may be relatively trivial and undemanding. Nor may they necessarily see themselves as formal members of an organized group or voluntary association ...
>
> Nevertheless in a broader conception participation in these groups can be seen as political since, as part of their functions, they address policy issues of public concern. These organizations can have a significant indirect impact on conventional politics.
>
> (Norris 1991: 60)

We have introduced the term and concept civic engagement within a broad conceptualisation of 'doing politics' for a number of reasons. First, because both explicitly political and civic activity/activism are equally important forms of public involvement and, on their own, neither can tackle the innumerable problems and issues arising in advanced industrial societies nor produce the solutions and decisions which must be formulated in response to them; second, it provides a detailed picture of changing citizen involvement in public life over time as groups or individuals stick to one form, move from one to another or are both politically and civically involved. Such an understanding may be useful in assessing the legitimacy accorded to democratic systems by citizens and also the impact of different forms of public involvement on policy; most importantly, in terms of the population under study here, it allows the inclusion, within the ambit of citizen participation, populations which historically have been excluded from the polity (women, BME populations, young people) and because often those very social actors may see themselves as non-political or even anti-politics. However, the fact that their involvement occurs in the public arena and that they engage with community organisations and indirectly with political institutions and thereby influence public policy means that they are acting politically and thus the intentionality of individual actors is not a crucial element in the definition of 'doing politics'.

Women from Muslim communities: contexts of political participation and civic engagement in Britain

Muslim women's political participation and civic engagement will be influenced by the varying contexts in which they operate: their family and local community; the historical and prevailing socio-cultural and political conditions in Britain and to some extent by what is going on in Muslim-majority countries where they have connections through family or their ethnic group. Thus three distinct but intersecting contexts shape their political attitudes and activist behaviour.

In the first context, one may identify women who are active in political and civic life, long-settled in Britain (of first generation labour and family migration in the 1960s and 1970s), who originated from the New Commonwealth countries of Pakistan, Bangladesh, India, East and South Africa and who have drawn political inspiration, know-how and resources from national independence struggles in which they or their families were involved. Women's participation in post-war independence movements (in South Asia as elsewhere) was deeply gendered and unequal but promises of equality in a post-independence world reinforced their commitment. This generation of women worked alongside men during independence struggles and after decolonisation, although almost always in positions of little or no power. After immigrating to Britain, they often became active in UK branches of South Asian political parties (Awami League, National Socialist Party of Bangladesh) and organisations (e.g. All Pakistan Women's Association UK, Mohila Samity Women); but over time they also became active around issues related to their presence in Britain; for example, immigration (right of entry, family reunifications, etc.), deportation, race discrimination and equality in the political, social and economic spheres.

The second context is that of new migrations and involves populations of women who have arrived in the UK over the past 20 years, from Muslim-majority countries as asylum seekers and refugees or dependants of primary migrants, bringing vastly different experiences from those of first generation women marriage/family migrants of the New Commonwealth. For these women, experience of direct or indirect political, ethno-cultural or religious persecution may generate political views and behaviour that are uncommon among marriage/family migrant women who came to Britain in the 1960s and 1970s. For example, asylum seeking women (who do not have the same political, economic and social rights as British-born women or as those who have acquired British citizenship) find themselves excluded from mainstream political and civic structures and processes and are therefore unable to participate fully. Therefore, these women will be active in unstructured community organisations and campaigns, often organised around country of origin politics or in migrant support organisations and campaigns on specific issues in which they have a stake (Allwood and Wadia 2010).

The experience of Muslim women within the two contexts described above involves a history and tradition of political struggle alongside men, in male dominated organisations and movements and the continuation of such organisations and politics in Britain. However, increased political activity and activism, independent from that of men, is becoming more visible among Muslim women from newer migrant communities and recent years have seen the emergence (and disappearance due to lack of funding) of Somali, Sudanese, Eritrean, Kurdish and Iranian women's organisations in London, Birmingham and other large UK cities.

The third context, intersecting with those described above, is characterised by women born and/or raised in Britain's long-established Muslim communities whose families have a migrant background. These women have had to tread an uneasy path between western ideals of modernity and Islamic values and traditions – something that not only women from Muslim-majority countries and non-Muslim women in the West find difficult to grasp but which is also not always understood by their own mothers/grand-mothers who are the product of South Asian migration, who did not feel caught between cultures, who were certain of their Pakistani, Bangladeshi or Indian identity and who had settled in Britain for better or worse. Deniz Kandiyoti (1991) argues that these Muslim women have come to represent a kind of 'inner sanctum' of Islamic identity and a visible cultural marker against the West's values and ambitions and particularly so in the urban heartlands of western societies.

These Muslim women have searched for facilitators within Islam and resisted obstacles in their ethnic culture in order to negotiate a means of living in the private sphere of family and close community and the public spaces of western society where they grew up but which have become increasingly inhospitable to Muslims after 9/11. The fact that some Muslim women wear *hijab* or *niqab*, perceived by many as a symbolic affront to the liberal democratic state and its values, has made all Muslim women the target of not just outright racists but also of many secularists and liberals fearing that personal freedom, secularity and women's rights are being undermined by them.

Moreover, as Muslim communities in Britain came under heavy surveillance and control in the 9/11 era, the wives, mothers, sisters of men suspected of and/or imprisoned for terrorist activity have had to take on traditional male roles in their family. They have also established or supported campaigns for the fair treatment and release of male relatives and friends and increasingly, women have been the object of direct surveillance, questioning and arrest by the state (Brittain 2013).

In this context, Muslim women have become rapidly politicised and this has been evidenced by their increased visibility in political and civic arenas. While our respondents are related to all three contexts described above, it is Muslim women in the third context, 'British Muslim' women, on whom we will focus below to ascertain to what extent 9/11 marked a turning point in their political participation and civic engagement and to determine what kind of activists they are and the forms of activism in which they engage.

Muslim women and politics post 9/11

For the majority of our respondents, the events of 9/11 marked an important moment in their life and in the development of their political awareness and action. Most had voted at a general and/or local election while some also had experience of political and civic activism before 9/11. Below, we consider what kind of participants/activists Muslim women are and the activities they undertake through a selection of cases.[12]

In a context of voter apathy and decline in conventional political activity (particularly among young people) scholars who examine types of participants and what they do have tended to paint a dismal picture; on the one hand focusing on those who do not participate at all or, alternatively, on citizens who participate intensively in such politics. More recently, some important work has been undertaken to move beyond this non-participant/intense participant binary in order to identify other types of participants whose aim may not be to influence state authorities but who operate in civic arenas and in those of contentious politics and who may target political influencers and decision makers in the public, voluntary and private sectors (Bang 2005; Li and Marsh 2008; Pattie, Seyd and Whiteley 2004; Norris 2002, 2005). Acknowledging the contribution of the work cited here on participants/activists in non-explicitly mainstream politics and adhering to the expanded definition of politics (including civic engagement) set out above, we identify three main types of participants among the Muslim women in our study: 'stay-home political activists'; 'civic activists' and 'intense political activists'.

Stay-home political activists

Located in this category are women who told us that prior to September 2001, they had taken little if any interest in politics apart from voting occasionally when persuaded by extended family or friends. For them politics was a man's world in which only a few exceptional women succeeded. The majority of the 'ordinary' respondents (whether in employment, at college/university, at home with children) fell into this category. For them, politics was about mainstream political institutions (parties, elected politicians and government were most frequently mentioned) and about what was referred to as 'high up issues' (Tabasam) such as the economy and foreign affairs. After 9/11, for the first time, these women experienced a real and deep uneasiness about their presence in British society.

The events of 9/11 and London 7/7 made them visible outside their home and family in a way that they had not experienced before. For women who wore non-western clothes the feeling of exposure was more acute and those who wore *hijab* feared for their safety. Whether out shopping or at the school gates with their children they felt scrutinised, on trial by people. They found themselves having to explain to people they had known over years that they did not support Al-Qaeda or the London 7/7 bombers. They were having to coach their children about what to say at school when friends asked what they thought about the terrorists. For those living in the areas where the 7/7 bombers or terrorist suspects came from it was even more difficult. One respondent spoke of the difficulty in going about one's daily business in the Leeds area of Beeston, home to three of the 7/7 bombers. She said, 'the whole world's media was in Leeds to film where the bombers came from' (Rabiya). Others living in the Alum Rock and Sparkhill areas of Birmingham told similar stories of repeated police raids. Almost all the respondents knew someone with a male relative who had been stopped and searched or knew of families who had experienced a police raid.

Also, for the first time, many women directly experienced hate speech in public areas. While always aware of the racism that existed in British society, they had felt protected from its worst effects in their close-knit families and communities. For many, racism and hate crime happened to others but now they were the direct target on an almost daily basis.

It was therefore impossible for women who claimed to know and do nothing about politics and current affairs, to remain so. Many felt they had to learn about British politics and the world beyond in order to make sense of events and counter the hostility they encountered; so they started to follow radio-TV and print news closely and gained sufficient confidence to discuss current affairs with family and friends. In the 9/11 era, among the women in the category of 'stay-home political activists, involvement in politics increased from the more passive end of the scale – wearing political badges, donating money to political campaigns, signing and sharing (e-)petitions – to the more active end of the scale – contacting politicians, boycotting/'buycotting' products for political or ethical reasons, etc.

While stay-home political activists with internet access found it easier to 'do politics' at home, over time some were drawn to action outside the home as internet activism became limiting and the desire to become part of an activist community increased. Hence, it appeared that some women were outgrowing this category and found themselves wanting to do more outside the home. This suggests that this is not an impervious category and that outward movement can take place over time.

Civic activists

A number of respondents fell into the category 'civic activists'. These women had been involved in voluntary activity outside the home before 9/11 – e.g. in ethnic or migrant community organisations or their mosque. The issues which drew them into these local structures commonly included children's education, domestic violence, poverty and aid to developing countries especially where they had family connections. This category included women in public sector employment, in particular health and social welfare, and also women who did not work. Despite their civic activism these women saw themselves as non-political.

A common sentiment among this group of women, after 9/11, was that they should use their position within their community and public sector to counter negative stereotypes of Muslim communities, to act as positive role models and involve more Muslim women in civic life. For example, Reema, a social worker, persuaded many of her Muslim women friends and relatives to take part in an annual 'sleep-out' organised by homelessness charities aimed at raising awareness about people who slept rough in Birmingham. She explained that not only did this action lead to more Muslim women engaging with homelessness issues but also that it showed white British people that Muslims were a part of British society and not all bent on its destruction through terrorism.

The headteacher of a girls' school in London explained that after 9/11 she made a conscious effort to act to as a positive role model for Muslim girls and women. She contributed to public debates and events in order to 'publicise what is being done by Muslim pupils, to be able to say "Look what Muslim pupils are able to do"' (Bilkis).

Sultana who worked in the health service and helped at a local homework club said that after 9/11 she did what she had wanted to do for a long time but about which she had lacked confidence; that is, to be a governor at her son's school in order to position a female Muslim voice among a majority white/male governing body.

For the women in this category, the events of 9/11 and 7/7 led to an intensification of civic engagement but also to involvement in political activity they would not have contemplated otherwise: marches, demonstrations, political rallies against the wars in Afghanistan (October-November 2001), Iraq (February 2003) and Gaza (January 2009). For many this was facilitated by mosques and Muslim community organisations which organised coaches to national anti-war demonstrations in London.

As with the first category, one must be cautious in viewing the category 'civic activists' as entirely discrete as many of the women within it engaged in wider political action at times. Also, they were regular voters and by virtue of their civic activism over issues like poverty, homelessness etc. came into contact with political institutions.

Intense political activists

Included in the category, 'intense political activists', are women who have gained high public visibility at local or national level since the events of 9/11. Almost all the respondents in this category had been politically active before 9/11 in student, local party or social movement politics. Their activism had developed because of a family history of political and/or civic activism, going to university and getting into student politics or because of particular personal experiences such as being racially attacked. However, none had attained a high public profile before 2001. The trajectory of these women from unknown political activists (and in one case of not politically active beyond voting) to publicly recognised activists is remarkable.

Two different examples illustrate this below; one woman had been highly active before 9/11 while the other had had little political interest beyond keeping informed about current affairs and little experience outside of voting.

The first example is of a young woman, Rabiya, who at the time of our interview helped run the constituency office of a Respect Party MP. Rabiya came from a highly religious, non-political family but started taking an interest in current affairs when she was at school through the influence of 'the incredibly good teachers' she had – 'old white men' as she described them. It was due to her teachers that she took politics at A-Level and became involved in the UK Youth Parliament. When she was doing her A-Levels, the events of 9/11 took place and she explains '9/11 and the 7/7 bombings were defining moments in my political career'. She took part in anti-war demonstrations, met lots of interesting people and made the 'political decision', to study journalism at a northern English University where she became heavily involved in student politics and anti-racism campaigns.

After graduating, just before the London 7/7 bombings, she became her university's National Union of Students Education Officer and consequently a point of call not only for Muslim students caught up in the tensions of the 7/7 events but also for the University authorities who were responding indecisively to Muslim students and the hostility against them. She believes she helped prevent a backlash against Muslim students in the city. After her stint as education officer Rabiya moved to London and became a Respect Party activist. For Rabiya, the events of 9/11 and 7/7 intensified both her political activism and faith because she felt that people would judge her religion by who she was and what she did. To break their false perceptions, she had to prove she was 'normal' and be a better human being than most. But she also felt that she had to make her life as beneficial as possible to others, non-Muslims and Muslims, in order 'to be up to the Islamic ideal'. Thus, Islam became the driving force behind her activism: 'It affects my politics as such, everything I have done: anti-war, [anti]racism, getting people involved, I don't feel there is any contradiction in that' (Rabiya).

The second example is of Sabreena who at the time of interview was leader of a national anti-war organisation and local councillor. Sabreena revealed, 'I only became politically active after September the 11th. After the terrorist attacks, everything changed. Suddenly, all the things about Muslim terrorism, Islamic terrorism were just everywhere. ... We just shifted into a different area after that. It was the first time I actually experienced it personally'.

Sabreena, a practising psychotherapist and part-time PhD student, was spat at in the street just days after 9/11, her friend was deliberately was pushed roughly at a cinema entrance by a group of white men while another friend had a beer can opened in her face. It was after a series of such incidents that Sabreena decided to attend a local meeting against the invasion of Afghanistan. From there on her activism snow-balled and because she was a confident speaker she began to be invited to community meetings, on stage at rallies and eventually to comment on radio and TV. Sabreena's move from someone who kept abreast of current affairs and who voted Labour to the leadership of an anti-war campaign group, of a minor political party and to a councillorship in a large English city was unprecedented and she strongly doubts this would have happened had the events of 9/11 and 7/7 not taken place. Like Rabiya, Sabreena made strong connections between her faith and politics and how the articulation of both became crystallised after 9/11. She stated, 'I think as Muslims, it is our duty to act in a humanitarian capacity' and that after 9/11 she connected humanitarian action with issues of democracy and social justice. She explained:

> So all these questions started coming up you know, I didn't normally think of myself as the kind of person that would talk about this; privatisation [of the NHS and other services] was a long boring word to me, you know before all of this [9/11] but it started to make sense, that the links are there with foreign policies and domestic policies, there are choices about that we make as a nation, or that politicians make on our behalf as to where our money goes and who benefits and who doesn't. It becomes very clear that a few people are benefiting from a system which really exploits the majority of people.
>
> (Sabreena)

The majority of the women in this category tended to be more involved in explicitly political institutions and processes (whether conventional or unconventional) and identified themselves as 'political'. They also felt that they would always remain politically active unless particular circumstances prevented their activism. The possession of a clear political identity and intention to remain active suggests that this is the most stable of the three categories presented and explains the progression of many of the women from unknown activists to high-profile political actors.

Conclusion

The events of 9/11 and their repercussions constituted a catalyst for Muslim women's increased political and civic participation. They disrupted relations between Muslims and majority British society. The intensive surveillance and control of Muslim men and rise in Islamophobia led Muslim women to resist, to help families cope with hostility and repressive counter-terror measures, to oppose negative stereotypes of their communities and call for just treatment. The events also disturbed gender relations within Muslim communities so that women began organising separately and challenging the political strictures imposed by male 'community leaders'. Thus many took up the state's offer to be 'empowered' through the Prevent programme. Muslim women 'do politics' in different ways, in different arenas and this chapter provides an understanding of their activism through an expanded definition of political participation, by exploring the social and political contexts shaping their politics and presenting a framework of the type of activists they are.

Notes

1 The '9/11 era', starting with the Al-Qaeda attacks in New York and Washington, DC on 9th September 2001, includes the short to medium term consequences following world reaction to them. Hence, the 9/11 era includes the 'war on terror' and the wars in Afghanistan (declared in October 2001) and Iraq (declared in 2003), the terrorist attacks in London (7th July 2005) and the fall-out from them.
2 The attack on liberal multiculturalism had started after the 'northern riots' of May and July 2001 involving disaffected young men from disadvantaged Muslim communities. The government-commissioned Cantle report among others had laid blame for the social conflict at the door of BME communities reportedly living 'parallel lives' to those in majority society (Cantle 2001: 9). See Kundnani (2002); Wadia and Allwood (2012).
3 No research exists on why Muslim women in Britain wear the *hijab* or *niqab* but studies undertaken in France and the USA (Bouteldja 2011; Read and Bartowski 2000) suggest that an important reason for adopting Islamic dress is that women feel protected from sexual objectification.
4 Prevent formed one strand of the counter-terrorism strategy CONTEST aimed at preventing terrorism against the public and British interests within and outside the UK. The other strands included: Pursue (identifying and isolating those involved in extremist activity); Protect (building measures to protect the public from terrorist attacks); and Prepare (developing public resilience to the negative impact of terrorism) (DCLG 2007; HM Government 2006). Prevent underwent review in 2010 following the Coalition government's accession to power so that its focus on women's empowerment and other 'soft' de-radicalisation activities has shifted to a narrower range of actions targeting men.
5 Between 2007 and 2011, an estimated £80 million was allocated by government to PVE whereby almost 80% of funds passed through local authorities to grassroots organisations and projects (Kundnani 2009: 11). The Tax Payers Alliance (a Conservative Party affiliated critic of Prevent) listed organisations/projects receiving PVE funding in 2007/8 and 2008/9. Their list includes over 90 groups and projects specifically involving Muslim women (TPA 2009).
6 'Women from Muslim Communities and Politics in Britain and France' (RES062–23–0380), June 2007 to May 2011.
7 Both countries are covered, in comparative perspective, in *Muslim Women and Power: Political and Civic Engagement in West European Societies* (co-authored with Danièle Joly), to be published by Palgrave Macmillan in Autumn 2015.
8 Two focus groups (of 8 and 13 women plus invited interlocutors) met regularly over a period of two months and four months respectively. The focus group programme was based on Touraine's sociological intervention methodology where the researched (social and political) action is meaningfully and subjectively driven by the responses to a situation and the commitment of social/political actors to certain values, principles and rules. It is constructed through the unity of three principles: 'identity' (how the actors define themselves); 'opposition' (how the actors define their opponents and allies); and 'totality' (the main issues, debates, interests

impacting on the relationship(s) between the social actors and their opponents and/or allies within particular spheres of action) (Dubet and Wieviorka 1996).
9 We were unable to recruit older respondents even through convenience sampling.
10 It was not possible to include women who spoke little or no English as there was no funding to support interpreters.
11 The respondent belongs to a workers' communist party banned in her country of origin.
12 Pseudonyms are used when referring to particular cases.

Bibliography

Adler, R.P. and Goggin, J. (2005) 'What Do We Mean By 'Civic Engagement'?', *Journal of Transformative Education*, 3(3): 236–253.

Afshar, H., Aitken, R. and Franks, M. (2005) "Feminisms', Islamophobia and Identities', *Political Studies*, 53(2): 262–283.

Ahmad, F. (2001) 'Modern Traditions? British Muslim Women and Academic Achievement', *Gender and Education*, 13(2): 137–152.

Allen, C. and Guru, S. (2012) 'Between Political Fad and Political Empowerment: A Critical Evaluation of the National Muslim Women's Advisory Group (MWMAG) and Governmental Processes of Engaging Women', *Sociological Research Online*, 17(3). Available at: www.socresonline.org.uk/17/3/17.html (accessed 10 May 2014).

Allen, C., Isakjee, A. and Ogtem, O. (2013) *Maybe We Are Hated. The Experience and Impact of Anti-Muslim Hate on British Muslim Women*. Report. Birmingham: University of Birmingham, Institute of Applied Social Studies.

Allwood, G. and Wadia, K. (2010) *Refugee Women in Britain and France*. Manchester: Manchester University Press.

Bang, H. (2005) 'Among Everyday Makers and Expert Citizens', in Newman, J. (ed.) *Remaking Governance: Peoples, Politics and the Public Sphere*. Bristol: The Policy Press, 159–179.

Bano, S. (2012) *Muslim Women in Shari'ah Councils: Transcending the Boundaries of Community and Law*. Basingstoke: Palgrave Macmillan.

Belli, A. (2013) 'Limits and Potentialities of the Italian and British Political Systems Through the Lens of Muslim Women in Politics', in J. Nielsen (ed.) *Muslim Political Participation in Europe*. Edinburgh: Edinburgh University Press.

Bhimji, F. (2012) *British Asian Muslim Women, Multiple Spatialities and Cosmopolitanism*. Basingstoke: Palgrave Macmillan.

Bouteldja, N. (2011) *Unveiling the Truth: Why 32 Muslim Women Wear the Full-face Veil in France*. New York, Budapest and London: Open Society Foundations.

Brah, A. (2001) 'Race', and 'Culture' in the Gendering of Labour Markets: Young South Asian Women and the British Labour Market, WLUML Dossier 23–34. Available at: www.wluml.org/sites/wluml.org/files/import/english/pubs/pdf/dossier23-24/D23-24.pdf (accessed 10 May 2014).

Brittain, V. (2013) *Shadow Lives: the Forgotten Women of the War on Terror*. London: Pluto Press.

Burns, N., Schlozman, K. and Verba, S. (2001) *The Private Roots of Public Action: Gender, Equality and Political Participation*. Cambridge, MA: Harvard University Press.

Cantle, T. (2001) 'Community Cohesion: A Report of the Independent Review Team', chaired by Ted Cantle. London: Home Office. Available at: www.tedcantle.co.uk/publications/001%20Cantle%20Report%20CCRT%202001.pdf (accessed 10 May 2014).

Cheruvalli-Contractor, S. (2012) *Muslim Women in Britain: De-mystifying the Muslimah.* London: Routledge.
DCLG (Department of Communities and Local Government) (2007) *Preventing Violent Extremism – Winning Hearts and Minds.* London: DCLG. Available at: www.tedcantle.co.uk/publications/021%20Preventing%20violent%20extremism%20%20winning%20hearts%20and%20minds,%20.pdf (accessed 10 May 2014).
Demos (2010) 'Abolishing Prevent will Make UK Safer', Press Release. Available at: http://webcache.googleusercontent.com/search?q=cache:http://www.demos.co.uk/press_releases/abolishingpreventwillmakeuksafer (accessed 10 May 2014).
Dubet, F. and Wieviorka, M. (1996) 'Touraine and the Method of Sociological Intervention', in J. Clark, and M. Diani (eds) *Alain Touraine.* London: Falmer Press: 55–76.
Dwyer, C. (1999) 'Veiled Meanings: Young British Muslim Women and the Negotiation of Differences [1]', *Gender, Place and Culture: A Journal of Feminist Geography,* 6(1): 5–26.
Dyke, A.H. and James, L. (2009) *Immigrant, Muslim, Female: Triple Paralysis?* Report. London: Quilliam Foundation. Available at: www.quilliamfoundation.org/wp/wp-content/uploads/publications/free/immigrant-muslim-female-triple-paralysis.pdf (accessed 10 May 2014).
Gohir, S. (2008) 'Can Muslim Women Tackle Extremism?', *Muslim Women's Network,* February, available at: www.mwnuk.co.uk/resourcesDetail.php?id=8 (accessed 10 May 2014).
Goot, M. and Reid, E. (1984) 'Women: If Not Apolitical Then Conservative', in Siltanen, J. and Stanworth, M. (eds) *Women and the Public Sphere.* London: Hutchinson.
Haw, K. (1998) *Educating Muslim Girls: Shifting Discourses.* Buckingham: Open University Press.
Hernes, H.M. (1984) 'The Role of Women in Voluntary Associations and Organisations', in *The Situation of Women in the Political Process in Europe Part 3.* Strasbourg: Council of Europe.
HM Government (2006) *Countering International Terrorism: the United Kingdom's Strategy.* London: TSO. Available at: www.gov.uk/government/uploads/system/uploads/attachment_data/file/272320/6888.pdf (accessed 10 May 2014).
Hopkins, N. and Greenwood, R.M. (2013) 'Hijab, Visibility and the Performance of Identity', *European Journal of Social Psychology,* 43: 438–447.
Jawad, H. and Benn, T. (2003) *Muslim Women in the United Kingdom and Beyond: Experiences and Images.* Leiden: Brill.
Jones, S.H., O'Toole, T., DeHanas, D.N., Modood, T. and Meer, N. (2014) 'Muslim Women's Experiences of Involvement in UK Governance' (Public Spirit Project: 'Has UK Policy Succeeded in "Empowering" Muslim Women?'). Available at: www.publicspirit.org.uk/muslim-womens-experiences-of-involvement-in-uk-governance (accessed 10 May 2014).
Kandiyoti, D. (ed.) (1991) *Women, Islam and the State.* Philadelphia, PA: Temple University Press.
Kundnani, A. (2002) 'The Death of Multiculturalism', *Race & Class,* 43(4): 67–72.
Kundnani, A. (2009) *Spooked: How Not to Prevent Violent Extremism.* London: Institute of Race Relations. Available at: www.irr.org.uk/pdf2/spooked.pdf (accessed 10 May 2014).
Li, Y. and Marsh, D. (2008) 'New Forms of Political Participation: Searching for Expert Citizens and Everyday Makers', *British Journal of Political Science,* 37: 247–272.
Lovenduski, J. (1986) *Women and European Politics.* Brighton: Wheatsheaf.

Malik, M. (2008) 'Complex Equality: Muslim Women and the "Headscarf"', *Droit et Société*, 1(68): 127–152.

MWNUK (Muslim Women's Network UK) (2010) 'Memorandum: Written Evidence Submitted to the House of Commons, Select Committee Report 2010 on Preventing Violent Extremism PVE20'. Available at: www.publications.parliament.uk/pa/cm 200910/cmselect/cmcomloc/65/65we17.htm (accessed 10 May 2014).

Norris, P. (1991) 'Gender Differences in Political Participation in Britain: Traditional, Radical and Revisionist Models', *Government and Opposition*, 26(1): 56–74.

Norris, P. (2002) *The Demographic Phoenix*. Cambridge: Cambridge University Press.

Pattie, C., Seyd, P. and Whiteley, P. (2004) *Citizenship in Britain: Values, Participation and Democracy*. Cambridge: Cambridge University Press.

Peach, C. (2006) 'Muslims in the 2001 Census of England and Wales: Gender and Economic Disadvantage', *Ethnic and Racial Studies*, 29(4): 629–655.

Randall, V. (1987) *Women and Politics: An International Perspective*, 2nd edn. Chicago, IL: University of Chicago Press.

Rashid, N. (2014) 'Initiatives to Empower Muslim Women as Part of the UK's 'War on Terror'' (Public Spirit Project: 'Has UK Policy Succeeded in "Empowering" Muslim Women?'). Available at: www.publicspirit.org.uk/initiatives-to-empower-muslim-women-as-part-of-the-uks-war-on-terror-2/ (accessed 10 May 2014).

Read, J.G. and Bartowski, J.P. (2000) 'To Veil or Not to Veil? A Case Study of Identity Negotiation Among Muslim Women in Austin, Texas', *Gender and Society*, 14(3): 395–417.

Ryan, L. (2011) 'Muslim Women Negotiating Collective Stigmatization: 'We're Just Normal People'', *Sociology*, 45(6): 1045–1060.

Salway, S.M. (2007) 'Economic Activity Among UK Bangladeshi and Pakistani Women in the 1990s: Evidence for Continuity or Change in the Family Resources Strategy', *Journal of Ethnic and Migration Studies*, 33(5): 825–847.

Takhar, S. (2013) 'Conceptualising the Uneasy Relationship of Religion to Political Agency', in S. Takhar (ed.) *Gender, Ethnicity and Political Agency: South Asian Women Organising*. London: Routledge, 158–196.

TaxPayers' Alliance (2009) 'Council Spending Uncovered II: No 5 the Prevent Strategy'. Available at: www.taxpayersalliance.com/waste/2009/09/council-spending-uncovered-ii-no-5-preventing-violent-extremism-grants.html (accessed 11 May 2014).

Tyrer, D. and Ahmad, F. (2006) *Muslim Women and Higher Education: Identities, Experiences and Prospects* (Liverpool John Moores University and European Social Fund Report). Available at: www.educacionenvalores.org/IMG/pdf/muslimwomen.pdf (accessed 10 May 2014).

Verba, S., Schlozman, K.L. and Brady, H. (1995) *Voice and Equality: Civic Voluntarism in American Politics*. Cambridge, MA: Harvard University Press.

Wadia, K. and Allwood, G. (2012) 'The Crisis of Multiculturalism in the UK', in M. Labelle, J. Couture, and F. Remiggi (eds) *La Communauté Politique en Question. Regards Croisés sur l'Immigration, la Citoyenneté, la Diversité et le Pouvoir*. Montréal: Presses de l'Université du Québec, 97–119.

Ward, I. (2006) 'Shabina Begum and the Headscarf Girls', *Journal of Gender Studies*, 15(2): 119–131.

Werbner, P. (1996) 'Public Spaces, Political Voices: Gender, Feminism and Aspects of British Muslim Participation in the Public Sphere', in W.A.R. Shadid and P.S. Van Koningsveld (eds) *Political Participation and Identities of Muslims in Non-Muslim States*. Leiden: Kok Pharos.

Williamson, M. and Khiabany, G. (2010) 'UK: The Veil and the Politics of Race', *Race & Class*, 52(2): 85–96.

Woolf, M. (2008) 'Muslim Women to Curb Terror', *The Times*, 6 January, available at: www.timesonline.co.uk/tol/comment/faith/article3137633.ece (accessed 11 May 2014).

Zukin, C., Keeter, S., Andolina, M., Jenkins, K. and Delli Carpini, M.X. (2006) *A New Engagement? Political Participation, Civic Life and the Changing American Citizen*. Oxford and New York: Oxford University Press.

5 'Islamic' environmentalism in Great Britain

Rosemary Hancock

Introduction

The environmental movement arose as a social movement engaged in resisting hegemonic ways of life and societal structures, including post-industrial capitalism, which caused multiple environmental crises and issues of social justice globally. Environmental organisations in Great Britain have historically been politically active, operating as organisers of collective action and as lobbyists for environmental policy change. The emergence of specifically Islamic environmental organisations has provided a platform from which Muslims resist and struggle to transform British society into a society reflective of their Islamic, and environmental, values. It is noteworthy to see that many of the critiques, in particular those against the capitalist economic system, made by environmental organisations and activists are remarkably similar to those made by Muslims in Great Britain concerned with aligning a compassionate, religio-ethical worldview with the reality of life in a Western post-industrial nation.

This chapter utilises Social Movement Theory (SMT) as an overarching framework. SM theorists have studied the environmental movement extensively and attention to Islamic movements has increased in last 10 years. Here I focus upon a movement that is both Islamic and environmental simultaneously. Islamic Environmental Organisations (IEOs) and activists share in the language and codes of both Islamic religious movements and the broader environmental movement, and they express the desire for varying degrees of social-political change. The theoretical tools of SMT are a new avenue of analysis for these organisations, offering the opportunity to find commonality between Islamic movements and secular movements.

Firstly, this chapter explicates how SMT is a useful theoretical framework for understanding Muslim involvement in the environmental movement and contentious politics. Following this, I make a brief explanatory note on contemporary understandings of religion and civil society; and discuss the Islamic discourse on environmentalism which informs Muslim responses to environmental crises. Finally, two case studies of British Islamic environmental organisations illuminate the participation of British Muslims in environmentalism and contentious politics. The Islamic Foundation for Ecology and Environmental Sciences (IFEES) is an internationally recognised environmental organisation; and Wisdom in Nature (WiN, formerly the London Islamic Network for the Environment) is a successful local organisation. The organisational structure, participants, action forms, ideology and framing, and goal orientations of both organisations are compared with each other, and also with Greenpeace and Friends of the Earth, the two most significant secular environmental organisations in Great Britain.

Theoretical framework: Social Movement Theory

Social Movement Theory emerged in the late twentieth century as an analytic tool in sociology in response to the significant social uprising in Europe and the United States of America during the 1960s and 1970s. In Europe sociologists developed a theory of New Social Movements (NSMs), whilst American theorists worked on Resource Mobilisation (RM) theories.[1] NSM theorists viewed the environmental movement as the 'new' social movement *par excellence* (Alain Touraine 1984 in Eggert and Giugni 2012: 337). The environmental movement has a progressive political orientation, large-scale membership from across a range of social classes, a sophisticated administrative apparatus, and environmental organisations actively promote membership and support for their causes (Yearly 2005: 11–12). Furthermore, environmental movements are often 'value-oriented' and require participants to embrace a lifestyle in keeping with these values. For NSM theorists, the environmental movement proved to be 'a useful starting point for the discussion of the relationship between changes in the social structure and collective action' (Della Porta and Diani 1999: 24).

Social movement theorists offer competing explanations for the motivations behind the emergence of the environmental movement. Some argue that the environmental movement reflects the values of post-industrial society.[2] In their view, issues of distribution or the provision of social welfare are no longer politically contentious in the more affluent post-industrial societies. Rather, an emphasis on 'lifestyle values' predominates, of which environmental protection is one of the most prominent (Inglehart 1977). This view, however, can only explain social movements in the very limited context of a truly 'post-industrial society', and ignores the great social and economic discrepancies that exist within these countries. A second explanation contends that the environmental movement, like older social movements, is still fundamentally about distributive justice. However rather than being concerned with the distribution of public 'goods', it is concerned with the distribution of 'bads' – namely environmental degradation and associated public costs (Johnson and Frickel 2011: 318; Beck 1995).

Early SMT scholars largely subscribed to Karl Marx's (1967: 71–72) maxim that religion is 'the opium of the people'.[3] Religion, in the eyes of these social movement theorists, was 'seen as the pillar of the status quo, and religious movements are treated as withdrawals from, rather than encounters with, social change' (Hannigan 1991: 317). However, the last twenty years has seen an increase of attention on religiously-grounded movements in SMT, and indeed recent studies have shown that religious movements *can* be politically revolutionary, 'transforming the basic institutions of society in line with their own ideological vision'(Hannigan 1991: 318).

The 'central and overpowering' role of the black church during the American Civil Rights movement (Morris 1984: xii) proves the effectiveness of religiously grounded movements in political action. The black church provided the institutional base from which the Civil Rights movement could operate: clergy were leaders both within their communities and in major Civil Rights movement organisations; the pulpit was an efficient and reliable way to transmit information and gave the movement legitimacy amongst the black community; the church raised money to financially support the movement; church property was used for mass meetings; and, finally, the church was seen as an autonomous institution, being owned and controlled by blacks (Morris 1984: 4, 12, 86).

Islamic movements have, of course, engaged in political action throughout much of the twentieth and twenty-first centuries. Indeed Islamic activism may be 'one of the most common examples of activism in the world', referring to the plethora of collective actors operating under the banner 'Islam' such as 'prayer groups, propagation movements, study circles, political parties, non-governmental organizations, cultural societies etc.' (Wiktorowicz 2004b: 4–5). Such events as the 1979 Iranian revolution – perhaps the most studied phenomenon of Islamic revolutionary activism – along with the popularity of Islamist movements and religiously grounded political parties such as Hamas and Hezbollah are evidence of Islam's engagement in politics. In fact, like the black church during the Civil Rights movement, the social institutions that structure Islamic practice aid in the organisation of collective action. Thus the widespread protests around the Muslim world following the invasion of Afghanistan in October 2001 were organised through the communal Friday prayer in Mosques (Wiktorowicz 2004b: 4–5) and the Friday prayer was similarly utilised in Egypt during the uprisings of 2011 (Aouragh and Alexander 2011: 1354).

In the study of Islamic environmental activism, SMT provides the ability to compare Islamic and secular environmental movements. In particular, commonality can be found in the process of mobilisation: the organisation of contention, the framing of ideas, ideological propagation, and organisational structures (Singerman 2004: 143; Wiktorowicz 2004a: 34). Islamic movements will always differ in terms of their ideology from non-Islamic movements, yet it is important to recognise that this alone does not make Islamic social movements *sui generis* (Wiktorowicz 2004b: 3; Wiktorowicz 2002: 189).

There is a valid concern that, in applying a theory constructed upon the study of social movements occurring in politically and culturally different environments to the majority of Islamic social movements, one may be in danger of theoretical 'colonisation' by importing a hegemonic social science framework in a new territory with little sensitivity for the importance of the empirical difference of the new territory (Wiktorowicz 2002: 207). As

Singerman (2004: 149) has convincingly argued, 'the universality that implicitly underpins many strands of social movement theory has obscured some of the more distinctive elements of Islamist movements.' The organisations in this chapter operate within Great Britain, and to a degree within the broad environmental movement upon which so much SMT has been developed, providing a test for SMT – occurring in a location eminently suitable for its application, yet grounded in Islamic ideology.

Many 'outside' analyses of Islamic movements have succumbed to generalisations about both Islam and Islamism, which are regarded as static and unique (Bayat 2005: 899). It is common knowledge that there is not one Islam but rather many Islams, and from this one can deduce that Islamic movements will be heterogeneous, depending on which Islam is utilised to build ideology. Further, even *within* movements and organisations, there will be difference. Asef Bayat (2005: 901) writes that Islamic movements are 'internally fluid, fragmented and differentiated.' He argues that consensus in Islamic movements comes, not from homogeneity of ideology and interests, but rather from imagined solidarities and the convergence of partial interests (Bayat 2005: 902, 903).

Civil society and religion

James (2007: 3) defines civil society as 'the level of governance between the state and the governed', a definition that has room for religion. Certainly the last 40 years has seen religion become deinstitutionalised, with the expansion of religious plurality and religion becoming a voluntary association. James' definition is, however, vague, and has been expanded upon by Mark Juergensmayer to more accurately reflect how the term 'civil society' is really understood today.[4] Juergensmayer (2005: 12) has a two-part definition including a structural aspect and a cultural aspect. Structurally, civil society refers to 'the ensemble of institutions' that stand *in between* the private sphere (which notably includes the family), on the one hand, and the macro-institutions of the state and the economy, on the other hand. Culturally, civil society refers to those 'in between' institutions that are indeed *civil* – that is, institutions that mitigate conflict and foster social peace' (Juergensmeyer 2005: 12). This definition is in keeping with the many contemporary commentators on civil society who implicitly assume that civil society's characteristics are derived from its associated teleological functions (Hudson 2007: 149). Civil society is thus equated with 'the good society' and with 'social vitality, pluralism, and democracy' (Juergensmeyer 2005: 12), in other words, all concepts which have themselves been deemed 'good'.

Islamic discourse on environmentalism

The contemporary environmental movement emerged during the 1960s following a significant shift in publicly available information about environmental degradation and crises, and an accompanying shift in public values relating to the environment. We find Muslim engagement with the environmental crisis from the outset. Influential Islamic philosopher Seyyed Hossein Nasr (1976) argues that contemporary environmental crises are a reflection of humankind's spiritual crisis (see also Nasr 1996). He believes that the instrumentalisation of the environment by modern industry is 'the usurpation, from the religious point of view, of man's role as the custodian and guardian of nature' (Nasr 1976: 19). In his many writings on religion and the environment, Nasr emphasises in particular the Islamic concepts of *tawḥīd*, *khilāfa*, and *mizān*. These concepts have formed the core of Islamic responses to environmental crises, and are consistently referenced by IEOs in their construction of ideology.

Nasr (1976: 94) calls *tawḥīd* 'the principle of unity' that binds all modes of being and knowing together. Man and nature are inseparably linked, as are the two types of revelation: the 'cosmic revelation' which is the recorded *Qur'ān*, and the '*Qur'ān* of nature' (Nasr 1976: 94). Ibrahim Abdul-Matin (2010: 20) phrases this in more accessible terms, 'We come from Allah, and so does the universe and everything in it. Everything emanates from the same source ... the Oneness of Allah and His creation.'

Where the Hebrew Bible gives to humankind 'dominion' over nature (Genesis 1:26, 1:28), the *Qur'ān* emphasises humankind's role as *khālifa*, a representative of God on earth. Muslim writers on the environment frequently quote Verse 2:30 (Abu-Hola 2009; Abu-Sway 1998; Setia 2007). It reads, 'when your Lord told the angels: "I am putting a successor on earth," they said "How can You put someone there who will cause damage and bloodshed, when we celebrate Your praise and proclaim Your holiness?"'[5] Most writers on the Islamic worldview and the environment discuss the concept of stewardship and the responsibilities this role entails. Indeed, some acknowledge that the role of *khālifa* entails accountability to God, and some even believe it to be a 'test' from God (Abu-Sway 1998: 3; Khalid 2002: 4). For Nasr, *khilāfa* signifies an intimate link between humankind and nature:

> Man is the channel of grace for nature; through his participation in the spiritual world he casts light into the world of nature ... Because of the intimate connection between man and nature, the inner state of man is reflected in the external order.
>
> (Nasr 1976: 96)

The final central concept in Islamic environmental discourse is *mizān*, balance. A verse commonly used by Muslim writers discussing *mizān* is 15:19: 'As for the earth, We have spread it out, set firm mountains on it, and made everything grow there in due balance'. *Mizān* is used by Islamic environmentalists to explain the complex eco-systems and physical laws of the universe much discussed in secular environmental literature. Fazlun Khalid (2005: 103–4), the founder of IFEES, talks about the 'dynamic balance' of the natural world, which he states is 'Muslim in the original, primordial sense' because it is in submission to God.

Invariably, Islamic literature on the environment, including that produced by IEOs, refers back to the scriptural sources of the *Qur'ān* and collections of *Hadith* (traditions of the Prophet Muhammad). Nasr's argument that the environmental crisis is a reflection of a spiritual crisis in modern humanity is largely echoed in subsequent Islamic environmental literature. Certainly, the *Qur'ān* clearly discusses the changing states of nature as signs of divine reward or punishment for human behaviour. The words of biblical scholar Jeanne Kay are as applicable to the *Qur'ān* as they are to the Hebrew bible. She writes that nature is a 'tool of divine justice: beneficent nature is a reward for religious observance, and a deteriorating environment is God's punishment for idolatry or immorality' (Kay 1989: 215). This 'injustice' framing, commonly used in other NSMs, allows IEOs, and indeed other religious groups, to explain the environmental crisis in religious terms and in some cases use environmentalism to achieve religious aims.

Methodology and case studies

The following section presents two case studies of IEOs in Great Britain, the Islamic Foundation for Ecology and Environmental Sciences (IFEES), and Wisdom in Nature (WiN). Case studies, being 'constituted in part by empirical and analytical focus on an instance or variant of some more generic phenomena' (Snow and Trom 2002: 151–152) require the use of mixed methods and triangulation, aiming to 'generate richly detailed, thick, and holistic elaborations and understandings of instances or variants of bounded social phenomena' (Snow and Trom 2002: 151–152). The collected data upon which this analysis is based takes the form of indigenously produced textual material – including their websites, newsletters, blogs, and educational resources developed by the organisations – and semi-structured interviews conducted with the founders of both organisations.

There exist a small number of studies discussing environmentalism amongst Muslims in Great Britain, notably DeHanas' (2010) article on environmental broadcasting by a Muslim women's radio program during Ramadan 2007, and Gilliat-Ray and Bryant's (2011) overview of Islamic environmentalism in Great Britain which focuses on the development of Islamic gardens. Both studies note that environmental activism amongst Muslim in Great Britain is small in scale, although experienced growth in the late 2000s. Where IFEES is the only international Islamic environmental organisation in Great Britain, a number of small local organisations were founded during late 2000s (Gilliat-Ray and Bryant 2011: 291). In addition to organisations that are exclusively environmental, there have been some environmental projects run by non-environmental Islamic organisations or mosques – notably the establishment of 'Green' or 'Eco' Mosques (iEngage 2013).[6] Where Gilliat-Ray and Bryant (2011: 291) emphasise the difficulty Muslim environmentalists face promoting and encouraging environmentalism in a largely environmentally apathetic community, DeHanas (2010: 141) focuses upon the way in which the radio presenters 'sacralised' the environment for their viewers, 'imbuing environmental ethics with religious meaning.'

This chapter is informed by critical discourse analysis, in particular the pragmatic use of discourse analysis which goes beyond the literal meaning of words themselves and attempts to understand what people mean by their choice of words (Paltridge 2006: 179). The context in which the discourse occurs is thus significant in the analysis. Discourse is not only an act of communication, but is a 'social construction of reality' (Paltridge 2006: 9). What we write and speak is shaped by the world we inhabit, but, importantly, discourse also shapes the world we inhabit (Paltridge 2006: 9). Muslim environmentalists attempt not only to appeal to people with existing environmental beliefs, but also try to 'convert' non-environmentalist Muslims to an environmental viewpoint through their literature.

An important factor in my analysis is identifying the framing of the texts: that is, 'how the context of the text is presented and the sort of angle or perspective the writer ... is taking' (Paltridge 2006: 45) In the context of a social movement such as environmentalism, framing is used by movement organisations to ensure they communicate their grievances, goals, and actions in a way that will resonate with potential and actual participants. It is vital to remember, however, that although activists consciously use frames to appeal to their peers or the broader community, frames are also 'constitutive aspects of the subjectivity of social agents which those agents cannot get behind or detach themselves from' (Crossley 2002: 140). In other words, activists *genuinely believe* in the reality they present through their frames.

The two environmental organisations are compared using the descriptive categories for NSMs proposed by John Hannigan. These categories are: goal orientations or aspirations; action forms; participants or support base; and values and ideology (Hannigan 1993: 2). These categories are also useful in comparing the two IEOs to secular environmental organisations.

IFEES was founded by prominent Muslim environmentalist Fazlun Khalid and the organisation operates from a small office in Burton-upon-Trent. It has an annual operating budget of approximately 15,000 GBP excluding in-kind contributions (such as the time given by trustees and long-term volunteers, which Khalid estimates at over 150,000 GBP in value each year) (Khalid and Price 2012). IFEES has spawned numerous local 'chapters' in the UK since 2005. These operate from Edinburgh, South Wales, Leicester, Manchester, London, and Birmingham. Internationally, IFEES had direct involvement with the establishment of Islamic environmental groups in Washington and Toronto. IFEES has no formal links to any of these organisations or groups; however they provide regular support in the form of education materials and advice. Wisdom in Nature (WiN) began life as the London Islamic Network for the Environment in 2003, changing its name to Wisdom in Nature some years later. The founder, Muzammal Hussain, was active in the anti-GM movement and radical left activism, and was involved with IFEES prior to founding WiN. It has a small operating budget of no more than 500 GBP (Hussain 2013a) and is run entirely by volunteers.

Goal orientations or aspirations

The goals of IFEES are split into changes made by the individual, and changes at the social and political level. Firstly, IFEES emphasises the revival of traditional Islamic or indigenous lifestyles and practices. These lifestyles are, they argue, more connected to nature and living sustainably. In the IFEES newsletter *EcoIslam*, an article on *sharī'ah* conservation models states: 'preserving the environment is a priority that requires creative solutions, including the revival of traditional ways of conserving our natural surroundings' (Mangunjaya 2009: 4). In another issue of *EcoIslam*, the Muslim figure SM Mohamed Idris says, 'we need to rediscover our lost heritage and critically examine the knowledge systems and the institutions we have inherited from our colonial past. We need to be creative and develop institutions based on our religious values and traditions' (Lubis 2007: 7). These institutions include establishing *ḥimā* and *al-ḥarīm* land designations and the revival of the *mustaḥib* in Muslim communities.[7] In an article on water management from an issue of *EcoIslam*, IFEES argues that 'an integrated approach to water, using *sharī'ah* guidelines, would help in water management and allocation in areas which might be more resistant to "foreign" conservation models' (Khan 2011: 4). In a similar vein, they promote a return to sustainable farming practices – growing food locally and gaining independence from agri-business. IFEES also calls upon Muslim majority nations to support international climate change agreements such as the Kyoto Protocol and the Bali agreement. Further, they argue that oil-producing nations in the Middle East should ration oil to make it last longer, and invest oil wealth into alternative energy industries.

At the individual level, IFEES calls for Muslims to live a life guided by moderation, not consumerist impulses. Muslims are seen as much a part of the environmental crisis as other peoples:

> Mainly concerned with the routine and drudgery of life if not with survival they [Muslims] play their part in frittering away finite natural resources ... it is interesting to note that the two Eids in the Islamic calendar are rapidly becoming consumer fests not far removed from what Christmas is to the West.
>
> (Khalid 2009a: 3)

The *EcoIslam* newsletter calls in many articles for Muslims to disengage from consumerism, arguing that 'Islam encourages moderation and forbids excess' (Khalid 2008: 4).

WiN consciously seeks to dismantle the current political, economic, and social system to be replaced with new inclusive systems informed by Islamic principles. Politically, they aim for an inclusive democratic society where power is shared equally, and argue that the current political system does not work in favour of its constituents: 'we as a diverse society must come together to challenge the political system and claim our collective, rightful ownership of it, as after all it is there to serve us' (Hussain *et al.* 2010: 10). This includes a focus on the power of corporations in contemporary society, and the consumerism that WiN identifies as marking our time:

> At WiN we would like a power shift – *away* from large power-hungry corporations; and *towards* community; *away* from consumerism *towards* sharing and simplicity; *away* from corporate power and privilege, *towards* corporate constraints, accountability and grassroots cooperative-type movements.
>
> (Wisdom in Nature 2013a)

Like many Islamic groups (both environmental and non-environmental), both WiN and IFEES advocate reform of the economy focusing in particular upon the use of 'usury' in modern banking. WiN argue that an Islamic system of finance would be both more sustainable and more equitable:

> In an Islamic economics, the unit of transaction that takes the form of money would have real value ... any medium could be used ... the power would thus shift away from banks, and back to the people ... money would remain connected to the real wealth of the finite physical world.
>
> (Wisdom in Nature 2013a)

As expected from an organisation that began with an environmental focus, WiN promotes the use of renewable energy: 'the *Climate Justice* strand comprises an intention to move: a*way from* dependence on fossil fuels; *towards* non-polluting energy, needs above profit, and low impact living' (Wisdom in Nature 2013a). Yet interestingly, WiN argues that addressing environmental crises such as climate change requires changes at multiple levels of society: 'the problem of climate change [needs] to be tackled from a number of different levels. It would require a personal response that integrates the spiritual and the rational, a response at the community level, and at the economic one' (Hussain 2007: 31).

Finally, the formation of WiN was initially intended by Muzammal Hussain to bring together environmentally minded Muslims to grow environmental consciousness and action in the Muslim community. Writing about the decision to form WiN (then known as LINE) Hussain says:

> The path seemed obvious: people had to meet up regularly, get to know one another, and thus be empowered to build their own networks within which they could work together and thus engage more creatively and effectively in their local communities.
>
> (Hussain 2013a)

Action forms

IFEES works primarily on education initiatives, running workshops internationally on Islam and the environment. These workshops are tailored to the needs of the country – for example they have presented workshops in Nigeria on desert reclamation; on water conservation in Yemen and Indonesia; habitat reclamation in Pakistan; sustainable fishing in Zanzibar; and run Islamic environmental training days in Indonesia. Fazlun Khalid and some IFEES participants also speak to media about Islam and the environment, for example on Radio Ramadan, Sky TV, and Channel 4's Shariah TV. They are also called upon to speak to university Islamic Societies in Great Britain, community organisations, public bodies, and interfaith groups. Finally, IFEES volunteers have participated in a number of collective protests against climate change: the Climate Chaos March in December 2005, where Fazlun Khalid was an official speaker; and a climate change demonstration in London coinciding with the Copenhagen summit in December 2009.

When WiN began, regular monthly forums were the focus of their activities. These involved a speaker or panel, *Qur'ān* readings or readings from environmental literature, and facilitated group discussion. These forums have not continued in recent years, however, WiN Representatives still participate in workshops with outside organisations (for example at the Climate Camp in London) and speak on various environmental and activist panels. Members of WiN have participated in protest marches and actions, including a publicity stunt on Brick Lane where members dressed up in snorkels to draw attention to the consequences of climate change. WiN also participates in collaborative projects with other grassroots organisations (not necessarily environmentally focused) such as the Spitalfields City Farm, Seeds for Change, and Fast for the Planet. WiN now focuses upon training for other grassroots community activists and organisations, offering training and workshops in Permaculture, Islam and Ecology, and Facilitation. They do, however, remain committed to grassroots action (Hussain 2013a).

Organisation and participants

IFEES has two formal positions – Fazlun Khalid, who as the founder is the leader of the organisation working full time (unpaid), and a part-time administrative employee (paid). There is a volunteer board of trustees, and between 15–25 long-term volunteers. Depending on their local activities there can be up to 50 short term volunteers working with IFEES at any time. IFEES has no formal membership structure, and participants do not pay membership dues. Most volunteers are aged between 18–35 years old, are scattered across the United Kingdom, and all are Muslim (Khalid and Price 2012). The main driver of IFEES activities is Fazlun Khalid, to the extent that the organisation revolves around his prominent presence in the Islamic environmental movement. IFEES is currently facing the challenge of deciding how the organisation will operate when Khalid, now a pensioner, is no longer able to play an active role (Khalid and Price 2013).

IFEES and WiN both share a concern to ensure their financial independence from political groups or organisations that may have a different worldview to their own. NSM Theory has highlighted the problem of autonomy, and the desire of movement organisations to be free from 'manipulation, control, dependence, bureaucratization, regulation, etc.' (Offe 1985: 829). These IEOs are both highly cognisant of the potential for their financial backers to attempt to influence and control the actions of their organisations. IFEES receives its funding from various grants for community organisations, and they express concern about taking money from wealthy Gulf Arab nations – although they have sought funding from these sources in the past (Khalid and Price 2012). WiN on the other hand operates without any significant funding source, receiving small monthly donations from a few members, and occasionally receiving payment for workshops they run to cover the costs of that workshop.

WiN has undergone a number of structural changes since its foundation in 2003 as LINE. The organisation was initially non-hierarchical with no leadership positions. This changed early in the organisation's history:

> Due to considerably varying levels of commitment and attendance – especially in the early stages of the group forming – and with a quite limited degree of face to face contact amongst members, we found that an entirely horizontal structure was not working for us ... We thus decided to open up two roles: a 'Chair' role, and a 'Support to Chair' role.
> (Wisdom in Nature 2012)

However the core members remained committed to the ideal of a flat organisational structure and in 2012, when Muzammal Hussain expressed a desire to step down from holding the position of Chair, the core members decided through consensus to revert to the original, non-hierarchical structure.

There are currently 3 WiN 'Representatives', who form the core membership of the organisation. During the monthly forums attendance came from regular participants (estimated at 7–15) and varying numbers of irregular participants with an age range similar to IFEES (Hussain 2013b). There is no formal membership structure and participants do not pay membership dues. In the early days of LINE, membership involved simply showing up to meetings regularly, 'essentially anyone who regularly attends WiN forums and who believes and works within its ethos, Muslim or of another belief, can consider themselves to be an informal member of the group' (Wisdom in Nature 2013b). However Hussain states that the group has become more selective about those involved, expecting a greater degree of commitment and experience in grassroots activism (Hussain 2013b).

Interestingly, WiN is not and never has been exclusively Muslim, 'being an Islamic group does not negate the probability of working with others that are not labeled Islamic'(Wisdom in Nature 2013b). The group is decidedly ecumenical, with Christian, Buddhist, Jewish, and non-religious participants as regular attendees of WiN events. However, the WiN representatives have always been Muslim. A blog post discussing the name change from LINE to WiN, removing the word 'Islamic' from the name of the organisation states, 'we were also aware that we were sometimes wrongly considered a "Muslim-only group" by those somewhat over-enthusiastic to compartmentalize, yet we enjoy and are grateful to have the presence of participants that do not call themselves Muslim' (Wisdom in Nature 2011).

Framing and ideology

IFEES clearly identifies the cause of environmental crises as the global capitalist system and the nation state model. In the April 2010 issue of *EcoIslam* Khalid writes: 'our problem is systemic. At the root of this debacle [referring here to climate change and the poor outcome from the Copenhagen Climate Summit] is a competing nation state model locked into a capitalist economic paradigm which encourages a consumer culture which in turn sets no limits on growth' (Khalid 2010: 3). This quotation also demonstrates the negative stance of IFEES towards consumerist culture, which they argue is an unsustainable habit that divorces humanity from both the environment and from God.

IFEES grounds its ideology in Islamic belief, and they believe Islam to be a self-contained religion – the solutions to environmental crises can be found *within* the Islamic tradition, whether this is in scripture, law, or even traditional lifestyles: 'there is much in the Islamic system that can show the way to a more considered approach to our relations with the natural world' (Khalid 2009a: 3). They make reference to institutions such as *ḥimā* and *mustaḥib,* as discussed previously, and also write extensively on the concepts on applying the concepts of *tawḥīd* and *khilāfa* to the environmental debate. Further, IFEES argues that a 'true' Muslim will be connected to nature – moderate, humble, respectful of creation, and not prone to excess. Were Muslims to practice an 'authentic' Islam, as per their understanding of Islam, environmental crises would be ameliorated.

The ideology and framing of WiN has been heavily influenced by radical left-wing political activism and grassroots organising through its founder Muzammal Hussain. This includes their operating principles – flat, non-hierarchical structure, consensus decision making, and process orientated – and their framing of the environmental crisis. WiN takes an integrated approach, framing environmental crises as intertwined with and inseparable from social, political, and economic structures. They believe the entire framework of contemporary society needs changing and environmental justice and action cannot be isolated from other issues. In the booklet *Islam and Climate Change,* they state, 'we … recognise that individual and societal transformation is an essential basis for meaningful ecological work' (Hussain *et al.* 2010: 11). They list four 'strands' of focus: earth and community; deep democracy;

whole economics; and climate justice. The descriptors for all four strands use transformative language – a 'moving away from' and opposition to excessive consumption and waste, the use of usury and 'big-banking' style economics, social inequality and the concentration of power in the hands of a few, and dependence on fossil fuels (Wisdom in Nature 2013a).

These four strands of focus are underpinned by 'engaged surrender' which they define as 'non-violent, process-oriented activism, expressed through a contemplative dimension within the framework of Islam (surrender to the divine)' (Wisdom in Nature 2013a). It is this strand that encompasses the 'religious' ideology of WiN. WiN also finds in the Islamic traditions approaches to overcome the ills of contemporary society:

> The thread of materialism and individualism that ran through the society into which Islam initially spread ... seems to exist to an appreciable extent within many societies today ... the practical implementation of this message [in the *Qur'ān*], through experiencing and reflecting on the natural world, therefore offers a vehicle that Islamically can be viewed as culturing a reverence towards nature and strengthening one's connection to the Creator, whilst simultaneously providing an antidote to the effects of living in a culture fixated on production, profit and the growth of the economy.
>
> (Hussain 2007: 11)

Further, WiN finds deep similarities between Islamic teachings and that of ecology:

> Islamic teachings are ... clear in presenting human beings as a part of creation, and place importance on the value that each aspect of creation has in contributing to the overall whole. It can thus be concluded that Islam does not view human beings as central to creation, and the world is not solely for humankind and it seems safe to say that the non-human world does have intrinsic value.
>
> (Hussain 2004: 3)

Hussain goes on to write about Islam on the one hand, and ecology on the other: 'fundamental similarities between the two ideologies are apparent and the reader may conclude that there might be plenty of room for people in both camps to not just learn from each other but also to work more closely together' (Hussain 2004: 7).

Analysis

By comparing the above four characteristics, it is clear the IFEES and WiN approach environmental activism in different ways. IFEES has an international, outward focus driven in large part by the prominence of Fazlun

Khalid, and works *with* governments and institutions in advisory and advocacy roles to achieve their objectives. In contrast, WiN is process-oriented and inward facing, more collaboratively driven, and does not engage with institutional politics. This is also reflected in their organisational structures: where IFEES conforms to a more traditional centralised structure revolving around Fazlun Khalid as the primary figure and driver of IFEES' work, WiN is non-centralised and non-institutional, and, although the role of Muzammal Hussain as founder and active member is undoubtedly significant, he actively works to ensure a non-hierarchical structure that does not revolve around himself.

Ideologically both IFEES and WiN believe that the contemporary political and economic systems are the cause of environmental destruction and are flawed on moral and theoretical levels. They are both vocal in their critique of the hegemony of consumerism in British (if not global) society. In this area both organisations clearly align with Habermas' (1981: 36) definition of the 'alternative praxis' of New Social Movements, as they are opposed to 'the consumerist redefinition of private life spheres and personal lifestyles.' However, only WiN actively promotes withdrawal from these systems.

Further, IFEES is far more religiously oriented than WiN. Not only are their participants exclusively Muslim, and their actions targeted towards the Muslim community, IFEES members have expressed that environmentalism may be a useful way to bring people to Islam (Khalid and Price 2012). Their discourse is all, therefore, framed through an Islamic lens and Islamic teachings and theology are the key touchstone of their literature to appeal to Muslims as current and potential participants. WiN, however, is not only more diverse in terms of the religious background of participants, it also engages in mostly secular actions with a focus on environmental and social justice as opposed to religiously grounded education. This is particularly evident in the way WiN frames its beliefs in language influenced by grass-roots social justice organisations, language that will be familiar to their current participants and appeal to potential participants who have experience in grassroots activism.

Because of their greater focus upon religion, IFEES utilises Islamic institutions in their actions more than WiN. Where IFEES works with Imams and religious leaders internationally to teach environmentalism and Islamic ecology, WiN draws more heavily upon their connections with secular grassroots groups to recruit participants. Although WiN has engaged with local mosques and Muslim community groups, they do not rely upon Islam to legitimate their cause. IFEES in this sense more clearly represents a 'religious' social movement, conforming to the expectation to utilise pre-existing religious networks and institutions to mobilise and legitimate their actions.

It is important to note that, because both organisations are grounded in at least some Islamic teachings, and patronised by Muslims, both organisations are 'hubs' where like-minded Muslims debate and discuss Islam in the context of British society. Negotiating their commitment to the practice of Islam, along with the practicalities of life in an industrialised nation – whose value system and organisation does not align well with their religious beliefs and environmental concerns – is a complex process. 'Islamic' organisations like IFEES and WiN play a valuable role in promoting active engagement in British society by Muslims without downplaying the importance of finding ways to live in harmony with Islamic beliefs.

The work of WiN, in particular, is evidence of a religiously grounded organisation embracing both Islamic teachings and a commitment to environmental and social justice. WiN's collaboration with numerous secular grassroots political and social justice organisations shows an engagement in civil society that overcomes religious exclusivity and promotes pluralism. Further, their intense focus on justice: environmental, economic, political, and social, lends credence to the SM theorists who contend that the causes of the environmental movement are still inherently about distributive justice.

A comparison of IFEES and WiN to two popular secular environmental organisations in Great Britain – Greenpeace and Friends of the Earth – shows many similarities. Both Greenpeace and Friends of the Earth frame the capitalist economic system as being a root cause of environmental crisis:

> Our whole economic system is built on the belief that a thing is only of value if it creates money. By these standards a forest is worthless unless it is cut down and sold. When economists balance the books, they don't take into account the value of the work that forests do to provide rainfall, regulate the climate and provide habitat for most of the world's plants and animals, not to mention food and shelter for millions of local people.
> (Greenpeace UK 2013)

Like the IEOs, the ideology of both secular organisations places a high priority on independence (in particular financial independence from government or corporate-sponsored grants). On their website Greenpeace writes, 'We are independent. That means we can tackle power, not problems' (Greenpeace UK 2013). Friends of the Earth states, 'Over 90% of our income comes from individuals – people like you' (Friends of the Earth UK 2013).

The four organisations all participate in similar forms of action: direct actions for publicity; collective action in the form of protest marches; educational workshops and trainings; and public meetings and seminars. Similarly, all four organisations make use of multiple channels for communication with existing and potential participants – be it the publication of newsletters, maintaining an organisational website, writing blogs, and the use of social media.

Of course, both Greenpeace and Friends of the Earth have a dramatically greater numbers of participants, and – by necessity – more rigorous, institutionalised organisational structures than either IEO. The greatest difference lies in the use (or not) of religious concepts in ideological underpinnings and framing. The main focus of the secular EMOs is upon the health of people and planet and does not refer back to any religious or spiritual foundation. Greenpeace writes, 'The underlying goal of all our work is a green and peaceful world – an earth that is ecologically healthy and able to nurture life in all its diversity' (Greenpeace UK 2013). The value of the earth is not grounded in sacredness or a created nature, or in that it is a sign from God – the starting point for much Islamic environmentalism.

A few activists involved in WiN and IFEES have participated in Greenpeace or Friends of the Earth. In fact, Elizabeth, one of the WiN representatives, first heard about WiN through her involvement with Greenpeace and was taken to one of their forums by a Greenpeace member. Her involvement with Greenpeace waned after she began participating in WiN, and she spoke of Greenpeace as 'really a way in for people to get more active in things that are a bit deeper' (Lymer 2013). WiN has also collaborated with Friends of the Earth, hosting speakers at their monthly forums and sending speakers to their public meetings, and collaborating in Friends of the Earth's Big Ask campaign (Hussain 2013b). Invariable, the large secular environmental organisations are referred to by Muslim environmentalists as 'mainstream' organisations, and the activists see themselves – and Islamic environmental organisations – as filling a special, necessary role in the environmental movement (Hussain 2013b; Khalid and Price 2012; Lymer 2013).

Conclusion

Testing Social Movement Theory with two Islamic Environmental Organisations demonstrates that contemporary social and religious movements, far from being neatly differentiated, in many respects share key movement specific features. WiN in particular displays marked similarity with New Social Movements, in so far as they align with Claus Offe's (1985: 828–829) characterisation of New Social Movements as having egalitarian or de-differentiated structures, valuing autonomy from institutional politics, and not relying on established socioeconomic or political codes to define membership. IFEES, with slightly less emphasis on autonomy and a more hierarchical organisational structure, perhaps shares more in common with Islamic movements. Both organisations meld aspects of the environmental movement with aspects of Islamic or religious movements. This indicates that there is either a spectrum upon which these organisations sit in relation to environmental and religious movements, or that there is perhaps a distinctive 'Islamic' environmental movement.

'Islamic' environmentalism in Great Britain demonstrates the possibility for Muslims to participate directly in grass-roots, civil society groups aimed at transforming British society, and to be involved in the political process through advocacy and direct action. It is significant that distinctively 'Islamic' environmental organisations have been formed by Muslims, for although the goals, action forms, and certain aspects of ideology are substantially similar to secular environmental organisations, Islamic environmental organisations, in grounding their ideology in Islamic teaching, philosophy, and spiritual practice, encourage the engagement of Muslims in an arena not often associated with Muslim (or religious) activism. Islamic Environmental Organisations and activists share in the religious language and codes of both Islamic religious movements and the broader environmental movement to varying degrees, and they express the desire for political and social change.

Where Islamic activism is, in the popular imaginary, too often associated with violent organisations, Islamic environmental activism in Great Britain proves that there are alternative political avenues by which Muslims can oppose social structures they find oppressive. Further, in doing so they stand alongside – both physically and symbolically – great numbers of non-Muslim activists who express the same discontents in substantially similar language.

Notes

1 The two broad strands of social movement theory can roughly be distinguished by the types of questions they seek to answer. In America, sociologists utilised the rational choice theory of economist Mancur Olson to develop a theory grounded in the inherent rationality of actors involved in social movements (Olson 1965). Resource Mobilisation theories examine how movements mobilise available resources, as well as the ways in which those resources are used and impact upon the successes and failures of social movements. RM theorists propose that the resources available to groups (McCarthy and Zald 1977; Olson 1965; Tilly 1978), the networks of actors in social movements (Diani 1990, 1992; McAdam 1982; Morris 1984), and the structure of political opportunities (Diani 1996; McAdam 1982; Tarrow 1989) are the most accurate predictors of collective action.

  In Europe, New Social Movement theory focused upon why social movements occur (Habermas 1981; Melucci 1989; see also Touraine 2002). NSM theory was influenced by a Marxist/Hegelian philosophy, and subsequent 'post-Marxist' theories (Crossley 2002: 10). NSM theory differentiates the so-called 'new' social movements of the 1960s and 1970s from 'old' social movements of the late nineteenth and early twentieth centuries. Where older movements were characterised as class-based struggles seeking economic and political power and redress, NSMs looked to reformulate the very structures of life and society, with protest occurring within 'sub-institutional, extra parliamentary' spaces (Habermas 1981: 33). As Habermas (1981: 33) states, 'the new conflicts are not sparked by problems of distribution, but concern the grammar of forms of life'.

2 These theorists are indebted to Alain Touraine's definition of what constitutes a 'post-industrial' society (Touraine 1971).

3 The German reads: 'Die Religion ... ist das Opium des Volks'.

4 Although Juergensmayer's (2005: 15) definition of civil society may be appropriate for this discussion, his view of religion's place in society is problematic. In asking whether or not religion contributes to civility he asserts, 'religion is more likely to have negative consequences for civility – that is, religion, more than not, tends to create conflict both within and between societies'. In characterising religion as polarising and a source of conflict, Juergensmayer effectively excludes religion from his interpretation of civil society. This chapter rejects the notion that religion is inherently a source of social conflict. In fact, Muslims involved in Islamic environmentalism demonstrably overcome exclusivist worldviews and work towards social justice.

5 This chapter uses M.A.S. Abdel Haleem's 2010 translation of the *Qur'ān* for all quotations from the *Qur'ān*.
6 For more on 'Eco' Mosques, see MADE in Europe's 'Green Up My Community' campaign: www.madeineurope.org.uk/volunteer/greenup.
7 *Ḥimā* is a designation given to conservation land, where this land may be used for community benefit and is owned by no-one. The use of this land can be designated, i.e. for conservation, or communal grazing. *Al-ḥarīm* is considered an 'inviolable' zone where use of the land is restricted or entirely prohibited. The *mustaḥib* is a community figure, in the early Islamic civilisations he was charged with inspecting the weights and measures in the marketplace and ensuring 'public health'. The functioning of *ḥimā* and *al-ḥarīm* lands came under his purview (Khalid 2009b: 6, 5).

Bibliography

Abdel Haleem, M.A.S. (trans.) (2010) *The Qur'an: A New Translation by M.A.S Abdel Haleem*. Oxford: Oxford University Press.
Abdul-Matin, I. (2010) *Green Deen: What Islam Teaches About Protecting the Planet*. San Francisco, CA: Berret-Koehler Publishers.
Abu-Hola, I. (2009) 'An Islamic Perspective on Environmental Education', *Education*, 130(2): 195–211.
Abu-Sway, M. (1998) *Towards an Islamic Jurisprudence of the Environment*. Formerly online, available at: http://homepages.iol.ie/~afifi/Articles/environment.htm.
Aouragh, M. and Alexander, A. (2011) 'The Egyptian Experience: Sense and Nonsense of the Internet Revolution', *International Journal of Communication*, 5: 1344–1358.
Bayat, A. (2005) 'Islamism and Social Movement Theory', *Third World Quarterly*, 26(6): 891–908.
Beck, U. (1995) *Ecological Politics in an Age of Risk*. Cambridge: Polity Press.
Blumer, H. (1939) 'Collective Behaviour', in R.E. Park (ed.) *Principles of Sociology*. New York: Barnes & Noble.
Crossley, N. (2002) *Making Sense of Social Movements*. Buckingham and Philadelphia, PA: Open University Press.
DeHanas, D.N. (2010) 'Broadcasting Green: Grassroots Environmentalism on Muslim Women's Radio', *The Sociological Review*, 57: 141–155.
Della Porta, D. and Diani, M. (1999) *Social Movements: An Introduction*. Oxford and Malden, MA: Blackwell Publishers Ltd.
Diani, M. (1990) 'The Networked Structure of the Italian Ecology Movement', *Social Science Information*, 29(5): 5–31.
Diani, M. (1992) 'Analysing Social Movement Networks', in M. Diani and R. Eyerman (eds) *Studying Collective Action*. London: Sage Publications.
Diani, M. (1993) 'Themes of Modernity in New Religious Movements and New Social Movements', *Social Science Information*, 32(1): 111–131.
Diani, M. (1996) 'Linking Mobilization Frames and Political Opportunity Structures: Insights from Regional Populism in Italy', *American Sociological Review*, 61(6): 1053–1069.
Eggert, N. and Giugni, M. (2012) 'Homogenizing 'Old' and 'New' Social Movements: A Comparison of Participants in May Day and Climate Change Demonstrations', *Mobilization*, 17(3): 335–348.

Friends of the Earth UK (2013) 'About Us: How Friends of the Earth is Funded', *Friends of the Earth: See Things Differently*. Formerly online, available at: www.foe.co.uk/what_we_do/about_us/friends_earth_funded.html.

Gilliat-Ray, S. and Bryant, M. (2011) 'Are British Muslims 'Green'? An Overview of Environmental Activism among Muslims in Britain', *Journal for the Study of Religion, Nature and Culture*, 5(3): 284–306.

Greenpeace (2013) *Greenpeace*. Formerly online, available at: www.greenpeace.org/usa/en/campaigns/.

Greenpeace UK (2013) *Greenpeace*. Formerly online, available at: www.greenpeace.org.uk/.

Habermas, J. (1981) 'New Social Movements', *Telos*, 49: 33–37.

Hannigan, J.A. (1991) 'Social Movement Theory and the Sociology of Religion: Toward a New Synthesis', *Sociological Analysis*, 52(4): 311–331.

Hannigan, J.A. (1993) 'New Social Movement Theory and the Sociology of Religion: Synergies and Syntheses', in W.H. Swatos (ed.) *A Future for Religion? New Paradigms for Social Analysis*. London: Sage Publications.

Hudson, W. (2007) 'Postsecular Civil Society', in H. James (ed.) *Civil Society, Religion and Global Governance: Paradigms of Power*. London and New York: Routledge, pp. 149–157.

Hussain, M. (2004) *Environmental Perspectives: Islam and Ecologism*. Formerly online, available at: http://wisdominnature.org.uk/Resources/Resources_documents/Islam_and_Ecologism.pdf.

Hussain, M. (2007) *Islam and Climate Change: Perspectives and Engagement*. Formerly online, available at: http://wisdominnature.org.uk/Resources/Resources_documents/CC_Islam_P_and_E.pdf.

Hussain, M., Khan, S., Daniju, W., Nisa, Z. (2010) *Islam and Climate Change*. London: Wisdom in Nature.

Hussain, M. (2013a) 'History of Wisdom in Nature and Islamic Environmentalism in the UK', *Wisdom in Nature*. Formerly online, available at: www.wisdominnature.org.uk/About%20Us/About_Us_docs/history.htm.

Hussain, M. (2013b) Interview by Rosemary Hancock (July 19).

iEngage (2013) "'Green' Campaign for Mosques and Communities', *iEngage*. Formerly online, available at: www.iengage.org.uk/news/2846-green-campaign-for-mosques-and-communities.

Inglehart, R. (1977) *The Silent Revolution*. Princeton, NJ: Princeton University Press.

James, H. (2007) 'Introduction: Civil Society, Religion and Global Governance – the Power and Persuasiveness of Civil Society', in H. James (ed.) *Civil Society, Religion and Global Governance: Paradigms of Power*. London and New York: Routledge, pp. 1–9.

Johnson, E.W. and Frickel, S. (2011) 'Ecological Threat and the Founding of the U.S. National Environmental Movement Organizations 1962–1998', *Social Problems*, 58(3): 305–329.

Juergensmeyer, M. (2005) 'Religious Ambivalence to Global Civil Society', in H. James (ed.) *Religion in Global Civil Society*. Oxford: Oxford University Press, pp. 3–22.

Kay, J. (1989) 'Human Dominion over Nature in the Hebrew Bible', *Annals of the Association of American Geographers*, 79(2): 214–232.

Khalid, F.M. (2002) 'Islam and the Environment', in *Encyclopedia of Global Environmental Change*. Chichester: John Wiley & Sons, pp. 332–339.

Khalid, F.M. (2005) 'Applying Islamic Environ Ethics', in R.C. Foltz (ed.) *Environmentalism in the Muslim World*. New York: Nova Science Publishers, pp. 87–111.

Khalid, F.M. (2008) 'The Heavy Burden of Waste', *EcoIslam*, 4(1).

Khalid, F.M. (2009a) 'Editorial: To Consume or Conserve', *EcoIslam*, 6(3).
Khalid, F.M. (2009b) 'Cultural Resources Management in Islam', *EcoIslam*, 6(5).
Khalid, F.M. (2010) 'Editorial: The Copenhagen Conundrum', *EcoIslam*, 7(3).
Khalid, F.M. and Price, D. (2012) Interview by Rosemary Hancock (April 23).
Khalid, F.M. and Price, D. (2013) Interview by Rosemary Hancock (July 20).
Khan, F. (2011) 'Water Ethics in Islam', *EcoIslam*, 8(4).
Lubis, A.R. (2007) 'Reviving a Lost Heritage: S.M. Mohamed Idris', *EcoIslam*, 3(6).
Lymer, E. (2013) Interview by Rosemary Hancock (July 16).
Mangunjaya, F. (2009) 'Indonesian Islamic School Revives Shariah Conservation Model', *EcoIslam*, 6(4).
Marx, K. (1967) *Deutsch-französische Jahrbücher*. Darmstadt: Wissenschaftliche Buchgesellschaft.
McAdam, D. (1982) *Political Process and the Development of Black Insurgency, 1930–1970*. Chicago, IL: University of Chicago Press.
McCarthy, J.D. and Zald, M.N. (1977) 'Resource Mobilization and Social Movements: A Partial Theory', *The American Journal of Sociology*, 82(6): 1212–1241.
Melucci, A. (1989) *Nomads of the Present: Social Movements and Individual Needs in Contemporary Society*. Philadelphia, PA: Temple University Press.
Morris, A.D. (1984) *The Origins of the Civil Rights Movement: Black Communities Organizing for Change*. New York: The Free Press.
Nasr, S.H. (1976) *Man and Nature: The Spiritual Crisis in Modern Man*. London: Unwin Paperbacks.
Nasr, S.H. (1996) *Religion and the Order of Nature*. New York: Oxford University Press.
Offe, C. (1985) 'New Social Movements: Challenging the Boundaries of Institutional Politics', *Social Research*, 52(4): 817–868.
Olson, M. (1965) *The Logic of Collective Action; Public Goods and the Theory of Groups*. Cambridge, MA: Harvard University Press.
Paltridge, B. (2006) *Discourse Analysis*. London and New York: Continuum Press.
Rootes, C. (2003a) 'Conclusion: Environmental Protest Transformed', in C. Rootes (ed.) *Environmental Protest in Western Europe*. Comparative Politics. Oxford and New York: Oxford University Press, pp. 234–257.
Rootes, C. (2003b) 'The Transformation of Environmental Activism: An Introduction', in C. Rootes (ed.) *Environmental Protest in Western Europe*. Comparative Politics. Oxford and New York: Oxford University Press, pp. 1–19.
Setia, A. (2007) 'The Inner Dimension of Going Green: Articulating an Islamic Deep-Ecology', *Islam and Science*, 5(2): 117–149.
Singerman, D. (2004) 'The Networked World of Islamist Social Movements', in Q. Wiktorowicz (ed.) *Islamic Activism: A Social Movement Approach*. Bloomington, IN: Indiana University Press, pp. 143–163.
Smelser, N.J. (1962) *Theory of Collective Behavior*. New York: The Free Press.
Snow, D.A. and Trom, D. (2002) 'The Case Study', in *Methods of Social Movement Research*. Minneapolis, MN: University of Minnesota Press, pp. 146–147.
Tarrow, S. (1989) *Democracy and Disorder*. Oxford: Oxford University Press.
Tilly, C. (1978) *From Mobilization to Revolution*. Reading, MA: Addison-Wesley Publishing Co.
Touraine, A. (1971) *The Post-industrial Society: Tomorrow's Social History: Classes, Conflicts and Culture in the Programmed Society*. New York: Random House.
Touraine, A. (2002) 'The Importance of Social Movements', *Social Movement Studies*, 1(1): 89–95.

Turner, R.H. and Killian, L.M. (1957) *Collective Behavior*. Englewood Cliffs, NJ: Prentice Hall Inc.
Wiktorowicz, Q. (2002) 'Islamic Activism and Social Movement Theory: A New Direction for Research', *Mediterranean Politics*, 7(3): 187–211.
Wiktorowicz, Q. (2004a) 'Conceptualizing Islamic Activism', *ISIM Newsletter*, 14: 34–35.
Wiktorowicz, Q. (2004b) 'Introduction: Islamic Activism and Social Movement Theory', in Q. Wiktorowicz (ed.) *Islamic Activism: A Social Movement Approach*. Bloomington, IN: Indiana University Press, pp. 1–33.
Wisdom in Nature (2011) 'An Islamic Ecological Activism: Uniting the Strands', *Wisdom in Nature Blog*. Formerly online, available at: http://wisdominnature.blogspot.com.au/2011/09/win-rep-talks-at-lambeth-palace-summary.html.
Wisdom in Nature (2012) 'The Challenges of Lessening Hierarchy: WIN Changes its Structure', *Wisdom in Nature Blog*. Formerly online, available at: http://wisdominnature.blogspot.co.uk/2012_09_01_archive.html.
Wisdom in Nature (2013a) 'Core Strands', *Wisdom in Nature*. Formerly online, available at: www.wisdominnature.org.uk/About%20Us/Core_strands/core_strands.htm.
Wisdom in Nature (2013b) 'Who Are We?', *Wisdom in Nature*. Formerly online, available at: www.wisdominnature.org.uk/About%20Us/who_are_we.htm.
Yearly, S. (2005) *Cultures of Environmentalism: Empirical Studies in Environmental Sociology*. New York: Palgrave Macmillan.

6 British Muslims and the anti-war movement

Timothy Peace

Introduction

On 15th February 2003 demonstrations were held around the world to oppose the invasion of Iraq, a global revolt considered to be the 'largest protest event in human history' (Walgrave and Rucht 2010). The demonstration held in London attracted an estimated 2 million people which dwarfed the previous mass rallies of British political history including the Chartists, the Suffragettes, and anti-Vietnam war protestors (Gillan *et al.* 2008). This anti-war movement 'generated not just the biggest demonstrations in British history but also an unprecedented outbreak of direct action, including the biggest wave of school walkouts' (Nineham 2013). Ten years on, it was claimed that this mass protest 'defined a generation', as for many it was the first time they had taken to the streets (Barkham 2013). Images from that day show a sea of people with various placards that were handed out. Alongside those prepared by the *Daily Mirror* newspaper and the Stop the War Coalition (StWC), the main organiser of the event, some of the most ubiquitous were those belonging to the Muslim Association of Britain (MAB). This is just one indication of the role that British Muslims played in both the organisation and participation of the anti-war march that day. Indeed, while it is impossible to garner exact figures, it is certain that this was also the largest mobilisation of British Muslims. Many of them had travelled from all over the country, often on specially organised coaches, in order to make their voice heard in the capital. Others participated in demonstrations in towns and cities up and down the country. Yet the involvement of British Muslims in the anti-war movement goes beyond their participation in that worldwide day of action. They were involved in the movement from the very founding of the StWC, at a time when the war in question was the invasion of Afghanistan. They also continued to be a part of the movement long after the invasion and occupation of Iraq had begun.

In this chapter I will trace the history of that involvement and in particular some of the key figures and activists who were involved. Data comes from interviews conducted in 2008 with these actors as well as secondary sources on the development of the anti-war movement. I will argue that the involvement of Muslims in the British anti-war movement acted as a springboard to the development of what we might call 'Muslim civil society' and also created opportunities for a new generation of Muslim leaders to emerge from the shadows of the first generation. Since 2003 we have witnessed increased politicisation and awareness regarding political participation amongst British Muslims. The chapter also highlights the varied modes of engagement with the anti-war movement, including progressive forms of political involvement and that of more conservative groups. Indeed, the movement provided a point of unity around which all Muslims could rally, irrespective of their ideological or sectarian differences. For Muslims to be embraced by the wider movement, barriers of mistrust and hesitancy had to be overcome. These tensions will be outlined and discussed as well as the reasons why certain Muslim figures were pushed to the forefront in order to display a 'united front' of Britons of diverse origins and backgrounds. Firstly however, it is necessary to put this activism in the context of earlier mobilisations of Muslims in Britain.

The Rushdie protests and the beginnings of British Muslim activism

The campaign to ban Salman Rushdie's book *The Satanic Verses* was the first example of a social movement that managed to mobilise British Muslims *en masse*. This is not to say that it was the first time Muslims had been involved in political protest. They had been involved in various forms of contentious politics such as industrial disputes or demonstrating against racism in society. However there was nothing 'Muslim specific' in these actions and the mobilising identity was more likely to be their status as either immigrants or ethnic minorities and the discrimination they faced as a result. Religious identities were simply not salient at the time. The Asian Youth Movements of the 1970s were keen to stress unity across the various South Asian religious groups but were essentially secular in character (Ramamurthy 2013). It was not until the 1980s that the first explicitly Muslim demands were made in the public sphere, this most commonly related to provisions based on religious needs such as providing halal food or prayer facilities. The formation of the Bradford Council for Mosques at the beginning of the decade had some early success in persuading the local government to enact policies that would reflect the specific needs of what we would now term the 'Muslim community'. Such concessions were not obtained merely through discussion or lobbying of local politicians. As documented by Philip Lewis (1994) in his groundbreaking book on the city, direct action was also employed in Bradford such as the 1983 boycott of schools and a demonstration outside the town hall to demand the provision of halal meat. Similar action was also taken in the wake of the 'Honeyford affair' when a local head teacher sparked controversy after he published an article in a right-wing journal in which he complained about the problems caused by large numbers of Asian children in his school and the influence of the 'race relations lobby'. Such mobilisations, which were not limited to Bradford, remained at a local level. The Rushdie affair changed all that.

The publication of *The Satanic Verses* in 1988 politicised a generation of Muslims in Britain. It contributed to the formation of a specific Muslim political identity (Meer 2010) and also provided the foundation for future mobilisation 'as Muslims' rather than a racialised minority such as Blacks, Asians, Pakistanis, etc. Bradford was again the focus of attention when a copy of Rushdie's novel was publicly burned in a square in front of the town hall on 14th January 1989 (Samad 1992). However, the mobilisation by British Muslims was national in character and managed to unite the various religious trends and political divisions that had hitherto been present amongst them. The United Kingdom Action Committee on Islamic Affairs (UKACIA) was set up in October 1988 as a national body to co-ordinate dissent and call for the book to be banned in Britain just as it had been in other countries such as India. A secondary aspect of this protest was the call for Rushdie to be put on trial for the offence of blasphemy. Indeed, the UKACIA even went to the House of Lords with their case but a previous ruling was upheld which stated that the English legal system only recognised blasphemy against Christianity, and in particular the Church of England (Weller 2009).

The high point of the co-ordinated protest by Muslims in Britain was the demonstration on 27th May 1989 in London, gathering an estimated 70,000 protestors. Hundreds of coaches took groups of Muslims down to the capital for the demonstration. The event could be described as a PR disaster. Demonstrators were photographed burning the British flag and effigies of Rushdie, some even carried portraits of the Iranian leader Khomeini. The methods of political protest seemed to be directly imported from the Indian sub-continent and demonstrated the importance of first generation migrants in their organisation. The protest turned violent and battles broke out between Muslim youths and the police as the march reached Westminster. The images from that day as well as those from the book burnings did irreparable damage to the perception of British Muslims in the eyes of the wider public. Unsurprisingly, none of their demands were ever met and their claims failed to resonate with the wider public who perceived this to be an attack on the freedom of expression from an illiberal minority. This prompted Kalim Siddiqui, founder and director of the Muslim Institute in London, to publish a 'Muslim Manifesto' in 1990 which proposed a Council of British Muslims. Two years later he created the Muslim Parliament, arguing that Muslims needed to form a separate political system. These initiatives remained marginal and beyond the mainstream of British Muslim opinion. In fact, it was not until March 1994 that then Home Secretary Michael Howard called on Muslim leaders (mostly those involved with the UKACIA) to establish a representative body. This eventually led to the creation of the Muslim Council of Britain (MCB) in 1997. However, the Rushdie protests actually retarded such a process because of the negative interpretation of events that was shared across the political spectrum. It did nevertheless prove that Muslims could be mobilised across the UK and also encouraged the formation of new national organisations such as the Islamic Society of Britain (ISB) that was set up in 1990.

British Muslim activism in the 1990s

The 1990–1991 Gulf War was the next event to mobilise the Muslim community in Britain although on a much smaller scale and without the vehemence and fervour that characterised the anti-Rushdie protests. Many Muslims opposed the intervention by Allied forces against Iraq, but more specifically, opposed the stationing of Western troops on Saudi Arabian soil close to Islam's most holiest sites. They also directed their anger at Saudi Arabia for allowing this to happen and some were bitter about what they perceived to be a lack of leadership the Saudis had shown during the Rushdie affair by not putting more pressure on the British government (Lewis 1994; Werbner 1994). Unlike the Rushdie affair, there was not a wide consensus amongst British Muslims regarding the war that was waged against Iraq in response to the invasion and annexation of Kuwait. However, what this event did have in common with the Rushdie protest is the general bemusement and misunderstanding from mainstream society with respect to those Muslims who opposed military intervention. Pnina Werbner, the anthropologist of Pakistanis in Britain, describes her reaction to the beliefs of a group in Manchester to the Gulf crisis:

> What struck me most forcefully, however, even in these early conversations with moderate non activists, was that once again, as in the Rushdie affair, British Pakistanis seemed to be setting themselves morally apart from British society, denying categorically what their fellow British nationals regarded as axiomatic moral imperatives: 'our boys' were in the Gulf, risking their lives, threatened by chemical warfare, poised to fight the fourth largest army in the world, to defend democratic values against a man who, at the very least, was a ruthless dictator who had invaded and taken over another country.
>
> (Werbner 1994: 213)

Muslim demands for the withdrawal of troops fell on deaf ears and this perceived lack of patriotism also led to attacks on Mosques and other forms of violence. For a number of second generation British Muslims, the Gulf War was their first experience of political activism. Anas Altikriti, whose family had fled Iraq in the early 1970s, was one such activist. He claims that people were wary about protesting against Operation Desert Storm because the reputation of the Muslim community had been badly damaged after the Rushdie affair. It was 'a badly managed campaign where Muslims came out looking worse than they did before'.[1] For this reason, it became more of a letter writing protest. The mainstream anti-war movement at the time was overwhelmingly made up of leftist activists who made no attempt to reach out to ethnic minorities. 'Black people against the war in the gulf' was set up by a small number of activists who felt the anti-war movement didn't reflect their concerns.[2]

Another significant episode that mobilised Muslims prior to 9/11 was the plight of the Bosnian Muslims during the war in the ex-Yugoslavia and in particular the British government's reluctance to intervene in the conflict. British Muslims who were aware of the atrocities suffered by their co-religionists in Bosnia became extremely concerned that not enough was being done by the international community to help and that it was even preventing the Bosnians from arming themselves. This galvanised the Muslim community to mobilise and attempts were made to lobby the UK government. The Muslim Parliament organized a demonstration outside the European Foreign Ministers Conference in London in July 1995 to demand an end to the arms embargo (Radcliffe 2004). Others travelled to the former Yugoslavia itself to work as aid volunteers. The 'Convoy of mercy' organised by British Muslims sent over 80 land convoys to the Balkans which transported medicines, medical equipment, clothes, books and aid workers. Much has been written on the radicalising effects of the Bosnian conflict on young Muslims in Britain, and some of those who travelled to Bosnia for ostensibly humanitarian reasons did end up fighting as *Mujahideen* (Wiktorowicz 2005; Husain 2007; Bhatt 2010). Indeed, there are interesting parallels with the Bosnian conflict and that which has engulfed Syria 20 years later. Nevertheless, most British Muslim activism regarding Bosnia remained non-violent and focused on providing aid.

September 11th and the formation Just Peace

It is difficult to underestimate the effect that the events of 11th September 2001 had on the British Muslim community. Amongst the older generation, the immediate reaction of many was to 'lay low and hope that it would all blow over'.[3] Whereas others decided to mobilise in order to 'defend what they saw as the civilised nature of their faith, to take a stand against their own extremists and to prevent the logic of revenge dictating an approach that would claim innocent Muslim lives with no connection to the original crime' (Birt 2005: 92). It is in this context that we can understand why many British Muslims later chose to join the anti-war movement. However, this involvement had rather humble beginnings. The Stop the War Coalition (StWC) was set up at a rally on 21st September 2001, just over 2 weeks before the start of 'Operation Enduring Freedom' in Afghanistan on 7th October 2001.[4] At the second meeting of the Coalition, attempts were made to organise various interest groups such as 'nurses against the war' or 'lawyers against the war.' This meeting was attended by Shahed Saleem who suggested creating a group that would mobilise Muslims against the war. They coalesced into a group of about 10 people including South African born activist Shahedah Vawda. It was Shahed and Shahedah who would take a leading role in this group of Muslims against the war and the two would later marry.[5] The group was named Just Peace and aimed to 'promote Muslim participation in movements that campaign for freedom from oppression and injustice'. It recruited many of its members from the City Circle, a network set up in 1999 for young Muslim professionals in London (Lewis 2007). The group regularly met up in order to mobilise the Muslim community for the anti-war movement and they were joined by secular groups such as the Palestinian Solidarity Campaign (Birt 2005). Shahed and Shahedah were also elected as members of the steering committee of the StWC.

Although set up as a group to encourage Muslim participation in the antiwar movement, its founders were keen for Just Peace to go beyond what they saw as a narrow interpretation of events held by the Muslim mainstream: that this was a war on Islam and that was the only justification for opposing the invasion of Afghanistan. Shahed felt it particularly compelling that there were so many people involved in StWC, not because of any affiliation to cultural or religious concerns, but merely because they thought it was wrong. He thought it would be good for Muslims to 'widen the scope of their campaign as it's not just about being Muslim, it's about principles. Opposition to the war should not be based simply on religion, race or ethnicity.'[6] In fact, Just Peace was a radical departure from traditional Muslim groups and organisations that 'tended to centre on the "Muslim condition" and were overtly, to a greater or lesser degree, religious. Just Peace was different in this regard – although its members practised their religion, it was not a "religious organisation" as such'.[7] It initially involved both Muslims and non-Muslims and made attempts to be as inclusive as possible. The group also did not label itself as a religious organisation and there was no religious agenda or ideology that underpinned what they were doing. Although they found that religion did need to be invoked when they were trying to persuade people to get active in the anti-war movement. A key theme that they utilised was the idea of justice:

> The announcement we made at the City Circle was from the angle of 'your religion tells you to stand up for justice.' So although we were motivated more from a Human Rights perspective, we knew that the principle of justice was important for believers, as indeed it is for any religion. So we used that to appeal to people and get them active.[8]

They asked religious leaders for help in order to provide some quotes and straplines for their leaflets. Providing religious justification was particularly important in the face of some opposition to their actions by Muslims who thought they should not be associating with non-Muslims. They also encouraged well known personalities from the Muslim community to speak at their events such as Ghayasuddin Siddiqui who by this time was leading the Muslim Parliament and was also involved with the StWC.

Just Peace retained a core group of about 10 people although some of their meetings did attract larger numbers. As the group remained small, they were able to decide on their actions via consensus at their weekly meetings. They organised public events and talks and encouraged Muslims to join the demonstrations that were being organised by the StWC. This would involve handing out leaflets outside mosques and generally putting the word out amongst the Muslim community through email newsletters which were subsequently forwarded on by various individuals. In this way they were able to influence Muslims beyond their own immediate social circle of London. They were, for example, pleasantly surprised to receive questions from Muslim groups in places as far afield as Wales.[9] The first major success of the group was the organisation of a collective breaking of the fast during a demonstration that took place during Ramadan on 18th November 2001. The protestors who were gathered in London's Trafalgar Square joined in with a collective *iftar* and members of Just Peace had organised the provision of dates and other food for this purpose as well as the call for prayer to be announced via loudspeakers. Muslim activists involved were moved by this gesture. It was seen as symbolising an important sign of unity and tolerance and encouraged others to join the anti-war movement. In fact, it must be pointed out that since the beginnings of the StWC, two keys slogans had been adopted which aimed to show support with the Muslim community – 'Defend civil liberties' (against anti-terrorism legislation) and 'Resist the racist backlash' (against the targeting of Muslims for reprisals).

As international political events developed, the StWC slowly started to shift its attention from the conflict in Afghanistan to the potential invasion of Iraq. Shahed Saleem recalls attending a meeting of the coalition in 2002 and seeing a banner saying 'Don't attack Iraq'. At the time he thought this 'seemed a bit far fetched' but weeks later it would become apparent that the administration of George W. Bush was seriously contemplating an invasion of Iraq. This factor also helped to mobilise more people to the cause, including many Muslims, who had by now become very visible at various anti-war protests. The members of Just Peace were keen for Muslims to get involved but not to separate themselves from the wider movement. As Shahedah Vawda explains:

> When we were preparing for a demonstration, one guy, who was actually a friend of mine, said 'all the Muslims should march together'. I said to him, 'I'm sorry but that's just defeating the whole purpose! The point is that we stand together in solidarity. It's about human rights and our common values. It's not about Muslims or Muslims in the West. That's what we're trying to move away from'.[10]

She felt that if they had gone out and marched 'as Muslims' this would have reinforced the stereotype of them not being a part of wider society. Through Just Peace they wanted to start a debate within their community about Muslims getting involved in the mainstream, about the problems of remaining insular, and how they could combat ideas of them not being considered as full citizens. These were debates that were already prevalent, particularly among Muslims who had been raised in Britain, but the issue of the Iraq war really brought them to the fore. However, the idea of Muslims as being 'different' was also promoted by leaders within the StWC. Shahedah felt like she was treated as some kind of celebrity during anti-war demonstrations as an articulate Muslim woman who also wore a headscarf. The middle class white women in the movement were 'quite taken with her' and some even expressed astonishment that she could 'speak English so well'.[11] She was also aware that as a Muslim women who covers her hair she was effectively being used by the coalition to send out a particular message, but she didn't mind. 'They wanted to get Muslim authenticity on board and the easiest way to achieve that was to put a Muslim woman with a headscarf on a stage.'[12]

The involvement of the Muslim Association of Britain (MAB)

For many, the involvement of Muslims in the anti-war movement is synonymous with the participation of the Muslim Association of Britain. This is puzzling when we consider that the organisation at that time was still quite new (founded in 1997) and yet to really establish itself on a national scale with a membership of no more than 400 (Phillips 2008). More importantly, it was highly unrepresentative of the Muslim community in Britain which is largely South Asian in origin. The MAB was set up by highly educated Arab individuals, many of whom had come to the UK to study in the 1970s and 1980s and ended up settling. As they felt largely unrepresented by existing Muslim groups, they decided to set up the MAB whose ideology is loosely based on the teachings of the Muslim Brotherhood (Bowen 2012). It is an affiliate of the Muslim Council of Britain (MCB) which would have been the obvious candidate for rallying Muslims to the anti-war cause as the most visible and representative national umbrella organisation. However, its role as primary interlocutor with the Labour government at the time put it in an awkward situation and immense pressure was applied to make the MCB toe the official line on the bombing of Afghanistan. Despite officially opposing the war, the MCB 'withdrew its support for the first anti-war march to placate the government, even though a number of its affiliates were involved, but, fearful of being outflanked, it publicly endorsed subsequent demonstrations' (Birt 2005: 96). The damage had already been done and organisations such as the MAB were well placed to exploit what was seen as a massive political misjudgement by the MCB by the majority of British Muslims. When the StWC was first formed, the MAB were invited to join as a member of the coalition but they declined. Yet they did take part on an individual basis in their demonstrations including the one mentioned above in November 2001 during Ramadan.

Throughout 2002 the anti-war movement grew as it became increasingly apparent that an invasion of Iraq was likely. The leadership of the StWC began to look for an organisation that could mobilise even larger numbers of Muslims on a nationwide scale for their protest marches. The MAB had organised a successful demonstration in April 2002 against the Israeli military operation in the Jenin refugee camp. Anas Altikriti, who was at the time their director of media and public relations, admits that the response to their call for a demonstration was overwhelming. When asked by the Metropolitan Police how many people they expected, he said 5000. The actual number turned out to be more than 20 times that amount.[13] The event attracted media interest and also that of the steering committee of the StWC who asked the MAB if they would become a partner and help to organise subsequent anti-war marches. Before responding to this invitation, the leaders of the MAB organised a meeting with those of Just Peace to ask for their opinion and information on those involved with the coalition. The response was positive and the MAB's young leadership was convinced that it was the right thing to do. This moment represented a passing of the baton as the MAB became the main organisation charged with mobilising Muslims. Just Peace activists were more than happy to allow this to happen as they had limited resources and felt that they had done as much as they could.[14] They considered that their initial objective to get Muslims to join the movement had been achieved and they continued to work with the StWC until the invasion of Iraq took place in March 2003.

The first joint demonstration organised by the StWC and the MAB took place on 28th September 2002 just before the start of the Labour Party Conference. There was some conflict around the framing of this action with the MAB insisting that Palestine needed to be the focus while the StWC preferred slogans to be solely against an attack on Iraq:

> The demonstration's slogan conveyed this pragmatic compromise, 'No war in Iraq, justice for Palestine.' Unable to agree completely on priorities, MAB decided that its leaflets would have 'Freedome for Palestine' above 'Stop the war in Iraq', while StWC's leaflets put the slogans in the opposite order. MAB had also wanted to call the joint demonstration the 'One million march' but accepted the StWC's objection to this, that a turnout of less than a million would have been humiliating.
>
> (Phillips 2008: 104)

In the end, the estimated turn out was half a million people making it by far the largest demonstration to date. It ended with a rally in London's Hyde Park with speeches from leading figures in the movement including the late Tony Benn. The scale of this protest gave the StWC huge momentum and encouraged other organisations to get involved such as the Campaign for Nuclear Disarmament (CND). Just over one month later, the European Social Forum (ESF) was held in Florence and a call was made to the citizens of Europe to 'start organising enormous anti-war demonstrations in every capital on February 15th' followed by a large protest held in the Tuscan city on 9th November 2002 (Verhulst 2010). Preparations were then started for the worldwide demonstration of 15th February 2003, of which the StWC in the UK played a leading role. The demonstration that took place in London was officially co-organised by the StWC, the CND and the MAB which now had a platform that was beyond its leaders wildest dreams. The fact that MAB spokesmen like Anas Altikriti and Azzam Tamimi were invited to address the sea of people in Hyde Park that day demonstrates the important role that they played in the organisation of this record breaking demonstration. The initial role of Just Peace was not forgotten as Shahedah Vawda was also given an opportunity to stand 'on the windswept stage to address a crowd so large she could not even see where it ended' (Brown 2003). She also took part in a televised debate with Tony Blair on 10th March along with other women who were opposed to the war.[15]

The difficulties of collective action

In the 'official' accounts of the anti-war movement produced by its leaders (Murray and German 2005; Nineham 2013), the participation of Muslims is recounted as mostly unproblematic. However, this glosses over a certain reticence that was apparent both within certain sections of the anti-war movement and internally amongst British Muslims themselves. When Just Peace began their efforts to bring Muslims into the anti-war movement they faced some resistance. Some felt it was wrong to be associating too closely with non-Muslims and by doing so 'you were taking up *their* cause rather than *ours*, which some saw as *haram*'.[16] This was a line that was being propagated by activists involved with groups like Hizb ut-Tahrir but there was also suspicion among those with less radical sympathies. For example, the MAB leadership had to work hard to persuade its members that 'collaboration with non-Muslim anti-war activists was halal (religiously permissible)' (Phillips 2008: 103). Part of the problem was that the StWC was known to be led by personalities associated with the radical left, in particular the Socialist Workers Party (SWP). This was part of the reason that the MAB refused to join the actual coalition, as it was known to be 'led by the Left' (Phillips 2008: 104) which was problematic for some. According to those in the MAB, the Muslim community needed to identify with something that it could trust: 'I couldn't bring out 200,000 Muslims to rally under the banner of trade unions, leftist, socialist or communist organisations.'[17]

This kind of mistrust was also present within some of the leftist groups that were part of StWC. There were anti-clerical factions which see religious organisations, particularly those with a more conservative bent such as the MAB, as reactionary and contrary to the aspirations of the working class. An example of such a group is the Alliance for Workers Liberty (AWL) which openly opposed the alliance with the MAB given that it was 'a right-wing organisation'.[18] Such opposition was quickly silenced by the leadership of the StWC, and its press officer Mike Marqusee claimed that 'those people who questioned the link with MAB were castigated as Islamophobes' (Gillan *et al.* 2008: 75). Such tactics are hardly surprising when we consider that some of the key figures in the StWC were also on the SWP's Central Committee, including the likes of Lindsey German, Chris Nineham and John Rees.[19] As a group that practices 'democratic centralism', a system of decision making in the revolutionary Marxist tradition, they were often criticised for promoting a veneer of equal participation, whilst effectively taking many key decisions behind closed doors. Shahed Saleem recounts that as an officer of the StWC he would attend their meetings where 'it seemed like the conversations that took place were a continuation of previous discussions they [SWP members] had been having. By having me there they could claim that they were being democratic but I didn't have that much input.'[20]

The involvement of the MAB was initially opposed by some members of the CND and they were also 'seen as too conservative by other Muslim groups' (Gillan et al. 2008: 67). Some regretted the fact that in order to work with the Muslim community, the StWC had 'decided to work with Islamists' and that they did not make any efforts to 'engage with the many secular groups that exist within the Muslim community' (Phillips 2008: 107). Similarly, journalistic accounts of the inherent ideological contradictions within the anti-war movement focus on the role of the MAB and its links to the Muslim Brotherhood (Cohen 2007). These critiques do however overlook the fact that the coalition's main goal was to rally as many as people as possible to its demonstrations rather than construct a coherent political project. They also conflate the participation of thousands of British Muslims in the demonstrations, most of whom would have no particular organisational affiliation, and the organisation which was tasked with mobilising them. The MAB leadership noted that most of those who volunteered to help them to organise the protests were not members of their organisation.[21] Its membership doubled as a result of its involvement in the anti-war movement but by the end of 2005 those who led this initiative lost control of the organisation and were later forced to set up a new group called the British Muslim Initiative (Phillips 2008).

Conclusion

The activists who were interviewed for this research were unanimous that participation in the anti-war movement led to a new found confidence within the Muslim community, particularly amongst those who were born and raised in Britain. 'What is noticeable about the post-September 11 response was the willingness of younger Muslims to form expedient alliances of dissent outside of their community, which was certainly not true of the Rushdie affair in 1989 or the Gulf War of 1991' (Birt 2005: 102). The idea of working and campaigning alongside people from other walks of life is no longer alien and Shahed Saleem was proud to play a part in 'leading Muslims out of the cold and away from blinkered thinking.'[22] The mistakes of the Rushdie affair were avoided as the second generation 'learned modes of protest' (Heath et al. 2013: 191) and adapted their methods of dissent to be more in tune with British political culture. It has been remarked that 'a new generation of skilled and media-savvy Muslims activists has emerged who regularly engage with journalists, policy makers, academics and activists from other faiths, in a self-conscious attempt to redress perceived biases in media coverage' (Bolognani and Statham 2013: 246). The generational shift that the anti-war movement promoted could only have positive effects for the perception of Muslims by the wider British public. Indeed, the overwhelmingly calm and sensible reaction to the London bombings of 2005, just two years after the huge anti-war march, impressed many and seemed to demonstrate the tolerance of wider society. This was also interpreted as a result of Muslims becoming more visible in the public sphere and increased interaction between them and other citizens. Shahedah Vawda thought that it was 'amazing how ordinary British people have tried to learn more about Islam and make an effort to show that they are not against all Muslims'.[23]

Despite the efforts to halt the war eventually being in vain, this mobilisation did propel a number of individuals to the forefront of what one might now term 'Muslim civil society'. A prominent example is Salma Yaqoob who founded 'Respect: The Unity Coalition' in early 2004. This political party would go on to play a leading role in getting Muslims involved in electoral politics and achieved some notable election victories (Peace 2013). Yaqoob served as a local councillor in Birmingham from 2006–2011 and narrowly missed out on becoming a Westminster MP in 2005 and 2010. Although she has now left the party, she is still a prominent figure in British public debates. Anas Altikriti, the driving force behind the involvement of the MAB in the StWC, was also briefly involved in Respect. He stood as one of their candidates in the 2004 European elections but then left to found the British Muslim Initiative and then the Cordoba Foundation. The path of Dr Ghayasuddin Siddiqui is symbolic of the changes in Muslim Civil Society since the Rushdie affair. In 1989 he was part of the British Muslim delegation in Iran that had asked Mohammad Khatami to act on Rushdie, which led to the notorious fatwa pronounced by Ayatollah Khomeini. He is now a trustee of British Muslims for Secular Democracy (BMSD) and campaigns against forced marriage, domestic violence and murder in the name of honour. The Muslim Institute, which he helped to form back in 1973, and at one time acted as a front for the Iranian Embassy in London, was re-founded in 2010 and now has a more progressive outlook publishing the quarterly magazine *Critical Muslim*. His son Asim Siddiqui was one of the founders of the City Circle which continues to provide Muslim professionals with 'a safe space for communities to self-critically discuss and debate issues that have concerned them'.[24] Just as the Rushdie affair led to the creation of a series of new Muslim organisations, the anti-war movement has provided the basis for the development of groups with more of a focus on wider society. For example, iENGAGE works towards enhancing the active engagement of British Muslim communities in national life, particularly in the fields of politics and the media and MADE in Europe is a movement of young people who want to see the Muslim community lead the fight against global poverty and injustice.[25] This trend of new Muslim Civil Society groups is likely to continue and they owe a debt of gratitude to those activists who became involved in the anti-war movement who demonstrated that Muslim activism could be about more than strictly religious issues.

Notes

1. Interview with Anas Altikriti.
2. Interview with Asad Rehman.
3. Interview with Anas Altikriti.
4. For information on the founding of the StWC see Murray and German (2005) and Gillan *et al.* (2008).
5. 'We love each other: Shahed Saleem & Shahedah Vawda', *The Guardian*, 15 March 2003. www.theguardian.com/lifeandstyle/2003/mar/15/weekend.craigtaylor.
6. Interview with Shahed Saleem.
7. Shahed Saleem quoted in Murray and German (2005: 59).
8. Interview with Shahedah Vawda.
9. Interview with Shahed Saleem.
10. Interview with Shahedah Vawda.
11. Ibid.
12. Ibid.
13. Interview with Anas Altikriti.
14. Interview with Shahed Saleem.
15. 'Prime Minister – the final countdown' was a studio debate chaired by the newsreader Sir Trevor McDonald, part of which can be viewed here: www.youtube.com/watch?v=MUW5OOQvv-U.
16. Interview with Shahed Saleem.
17. Interview with Anas Altikriti.
18. Interview with Sacha Ismail.
19. It should be noted that all these activists have since left the SWP.
20. Interview with Shahed Saleem.
21. Interview with Anas Altikriti.
22. Interview with Shahed Saleem.
23. Interview with Shahedah Vawda.
24. 'About us' www.thecitycircle.com/about-us.
25. See their respective websites http://iengage.uk.net/about-us/ and www.madeineurope.org.uk/about. iENGAGE is now known as MEND (Muslim Engagement and Development).

Bibliography

Barkham, P. (2003) 'Iraq War 10 Years On: Mass Protest That Defined a Generation', *The Guardian*, 15 February, available at: www.theguardian.com/world/2013/feb/15/iraq-war-mass-protest.

Bhatt, C. (2010) 'The 'British Jihad' and the Curves of Religious Violence', *Ethnic and Racial Studies*, 33(1): 39–59.

Birt, J. (2005) 'Lobbying and Marching: British Muslims and the State', in Abbas, T. (ed.) *Muslim Britain: Communities Under Pressure*. London: Zed Books.

Bolognani, M. and Statham, P. (2013) 'The Changing Public Face of Muslim Associations in Britain: Coming Together for Common 'Social' Goals?', *Ethnicities*, 13(2): 229–249.

Bowen, I. (2012) 'The Muslim Brotherhood in Britain' in E. Bakker and R. Meijer (eds) *The Muslim Brotherhood in Europe*. London: Hurst.

Brown, J.A. (2003) 'A Common Cause', *Emel*, Issue 1, available at: www.emel.com/article?id=1&a_id=1151.

Cohen, N. (2007) *What's Left? How Liberals Lost Their Way*. London: Harper Perennial.

Gillan et al. (2008) *Anti-War Activism: New Media and Protest in the Information Age*. Basingstoke: Palgrave Macmillan.
Heath, A. et al. (2013) *The Political Integration of Ethnic Minorities in Britain*. Oxford: Oxford University Press.
Husain, E. (2007) *The Islamist: Why I Joined Radical Islam in Britain, What I Saw Inside and Why I Left*. London: Penguin Books.
Lewis, P. (1994) *Islamic Britain: Religion, Politics, and Identity Among British Muslims*. London: I.B. Tauris.
Lewis, P. (2007) *Young, British and Muslim*. London: Continuum.
Meer, N. (2010) *Citizenship, Identity and the Politics of Multiculturalism: The Rise of Muslim Consciousness*. Basingstoke: Palgrave Macmillan.
Murray, A. and German, L. (2005) *Stop the War: The Story of Britain's Biggest Mass Movement*. London: Bookmarks.
Nineham, C. (2013) *The People V. Tony Blair: Politics, the Media and the Anti-war Movement*. London: Zero Books.
Peace, T. (2013) 'Muslims and Electoral Politics in Britain: The Case of Respect', in Nielsen, J. (ed.) *Muslims and Political Participation in Europe*. Edinburgh: Edinburgh University Press, pp. 426–454.
Phillips, R. (2008) 'Standing Together: The Muslim Association of Britain and the Anti-war Movement', *Race & Class*, 50(2): 101–113.
Radcliffe, L. (2004) 'A Muslim Lobby At Whitehall? Examining the Role of the Muslim Minority in British Foreign Policy Making', *Islam and Christian-Muslim Relations*, 15(3): 365–386.
Ramamurthy, A. (2013) *Black Star: Britain's Asian Youth Movements*. London: Pluto Press.
Samad, Y. (1992) 'Book Burning and Race Relations: Political Mobilization of Bradford Muslims', *New Community*, 18(4): 507–519.
Verhulst, J. (2010) 'February 15, 2003: The World Says No to War', in S. Walgrave and D. Rucht (eds) *The World Says No to War: Demonstrations Against the War on Iraq*. Minneapolis, MN: University of Minnesota Press.
Walgrave, S. and Rucht, D. (2010) 'Introduction', in S. Walgrave and D. Rucht (eds) *The World Says No to War: Demonstrations against the War on Iraq*. Minneapolis, MN: University of Minnesota Press.
Weller, P. (2009) *A Mirror for Our Times: The Rushdie Affair and the Future of Multiculturalism*. London: Continuum.
Werbner, P. (1994) 'Diaspora and Millennium: British Pakistani Global-local Fabulations of the Gulf War', in Ahmed and Donnan (eds) *Islam, Globalisation and Identity*. London: Routledge.
Wiktorowicz, Q. (2005) *Radical Islam Rising: Muslim Extremism in the West*. Lanham, MD: Rowman & Littlefield.

Part III
Exploring the political amongst young people

7 Diversity in political perspectives and engagement among young British Muslims

Asma Mustafa

Introduction

The growing concern about the influence of religious ideology on the political perspectives and practices of British Muslims has focused on the assumption that all Muslims follow and agree on the role of Islam in politics. Among other things, this supposition holds foreign policy as crucial to all Muslims; accuses Muslims of allegiance to their religion over their nation-state; and presumes the majority of Muslims believe in political violence as a means of gaining political goals and consequently it treats as questionable any form of political activism by young Muslims. Notwithstanding that, the previous decade has seen attempts by Muslims to defend their religion and religious identity against radical elements and their extremist political agenda. This chapter analyses the perception of young second generation British Muslims regarding political violence, foreign policy, citizenship and political engagement. The chapter highlights the diversity in religious interpretation of the 'political'; of variations in attitudes towards political violence and a progressive and varying degree of understanding of the role that Islam plays in politics. This does not undermine research on Muslim political participation, but emphasises the diversity in interpretation, attitudes and action among them.

There has been a constant spotlight on British Muslims and the political sphere. The 2005 7/7 terrorist London bombings and the 2013 murder of Drummer Lee Rigby in Woolwich have initiated debates surrounding British foreign policy (especially in the Middle East and North Africa) and the 'reasons' for violent extremism. The ongoing debate is exclusively focused on the role that Islam plays in the politicisation of British Muslims, rather than in their personal lives. Many young British Muslims use religious teachings, morals and values to inform their political perspectives and activities. Whether termed 'Islamist' politics, or political Islam, young Muslims are engaging in legitimate political activity, using a religious moral compass to guide them. This includes being highly critical of British foreign policy for example, and using legitimate political approaches to express their perspectives and views.

Methodology

Qualitative research approaches are chosen for varied reasons. For this research project they were chosen because they support sensitive engagement with respondents. This is especially important when discussing the complexity of identity and potentially insightful political attitudes. A key concern during the fieldwork was how to elicit responses from participants discussing intricate and intimate issues, especially when articulating views relating to identity and discussing methods of (at times violent) political engagement. During these engaging semi-structured interviews, a variety of creative sub-methods were incorporated in order to gather credible material. These innovative methods included auto-photography and word sorts to elicit concepts of identity, and photographic vignettes to capture concepts of political action.

The empirical research on young British Muslims was conducted across Britain. The main method of conducting the research was via semi-structured interviews with 67 second-generation British Muslims aged between 16 and 35. The sample was collected via snowball and then purposive sampling methods. The participants came from a variety of ethnic backgrounds. The snowball sample network points began in several places to ensure variation, and in engaging a large variety of gatekeepers from various backgrounds (e.g. people with theological differences, different social class backgrounds, etc.). The fieldwork took approximately 24 months to complete, in varying stages (January 2006–October 2007; June–July 2009).

During this research numerous research methods were used. Auto-photography was a tool used to assist respondents in discussing their self-identity. Auto-photography allowed respondents to take photographs which they then used during the interview to explain their identity. The interviews also included the use of 'word sorts' – small rectangular laminated cards with words on them that may or may not relate to identity. They included words that have little relation to ethnic, national and religious identity. The words by no means covered all words relating to national, ethnic and religious identity, but they at least assisted in eliciting identity-based respondent descriptions. To explore political activities, pictorial vignettes were utilised. Vignettes are short scenarios in either written or pictorial form, which are concrete examples of people or their behaviours, on which participants can offer comment or an opinion. Vignettes allow participants to define the situation in their own terms and explore how they would react, or have reacted, and why. Pictorial vignettes were used in this research in the form of photographs in order to explore political actions with the intention of extracting a response from the participants regarding that action.

Attitudes to political violence

One erroneous assumption is that all British Muslims who criticise British foreign policy are themselves disillusioned with the West, thus sympathising with the extremists and more likely to take part in violent political activity.

The accusation that Muslims support violence is regularly espoused by the Far-right or neo-conservatives such as Daniel Pipes:

> As has become evident of late, a vast number of Muslims, those living in Europe and the Americas no less than those elsewhere, harbour an intense hostility to the West. For most Muslims, this mix of envy and resentment remains a latent sentiment, but for some it acquires operational significance .... Their counterparts also live in the West, where they have a unique inclination not just to disrupt through violence but also to challenge the existing order.
>
> (Pipes 2002)

In Britain, politicians such as UKIP MEP Gerard Batten, who represents London and is a member of the party's executive, have also used similar rhetoric. In 2006 he commissioned a 'charter of Muslim understanding'. The document 'asks Muslims to sign a declaration rejecting violence and says that certain parts of the Qur'an that promote "violent physical Jihad" should be regarded as "inapplicable, invalid and non-Islamic"' (Mason 2014).

All British citizens should be expected to critique government policies and express their frustration, without being suspected of a violent disposition – it is similar to equating all heated football fans to violent football hooligans. The current trend in the media is to envelope peaceful, law abiding Muslim citizens with the tiny minority of violent extremists. Violent means of political activity are actually seen variably by the respondents in this research. Many young Muslim participants agree that even though violence can be effective in gaining media attention to an issue, it is also unproductive in changing government policy. There was a wide variety of opinions regarding political violence as a means – on one end of the spectrum there were respondents who felt that political violence is admissible as a response to state violence, specifically in the case of the Israeli/Palestinian conflict; and on the other end of the spectrum, there were those who felt it is completely unacceptable, in all circumstances

EMEL: The guy with the gun ... you'd think that was political given the circumstances of today's world, and yes he wants to achieve his objective in a way of doing it through violence ... he wants his message to get through, and his message is political, and this is his way of doing it ... it's oppositional, and I guess yes it is political, characterized as high politics.

SANA: It's used by both sides, we like to see the good and evil, always one right, one wrong, one person's freedom fighter, another's terrorist. It should be an option if they are defending the legitimate concerns of their country in defending their borders ... I don't have a problem with Hezbollah or Hamas, it's legitimate, they have clear-cut political demands and they have tried to engage with the political process, but their demands have been rebuffed. What I don't agree with is when civilians are murdered for the sake of achieving a political goal.

SAMIR: Violence is one means. It's a means of getting heard internationally, it is very effective ... I think that, in some ways, it's the only way because people aren't going to get heard and it's what drives them to be violent, they're not getting heard, and for that, it's justified for me. You know, these people [Palestinians], it's a little voice, nobody listens to them getting their houses trampled over or bulldozed over, so these people go to extreme measures because they've got no hope of doing anything about it, so that makes it justifiable for me.

DALAL: It really makes me so ashamed because these guys [violent Muslim extremists] are misinterpreting Islam, it's a complete contradiction and I just don't understand it, I can't get my head round where they got the justification (for political violence) ... it makes me really ashamed and sad that there's so much ignorance at the moment, and if people just picked up a good translation [of Qur'an] ... then they would see that Islam isn't about that and know that's wrong ...

The varied perspectives on political violence and its justification (or not) can and should be separated from the debate surrounding foreign policy. Muslims can both condemn the actions of extremists, while simultaneously highlighting the double-standards of British foreign policy in the Middle East, and how it can potentially exacerbate Muslim feelings of frustration towards the British government. The young British Muslim participants were clearly critical of British foreign policy, yet engaged in the political arena in non-violent ways. Unfortunately, there are a few individuals who make the jump from being frustrated by foreign policy to be motivated to take violent political action as a result. However, the larger proportion of British Muslims who believe that foreign policy is disproportionately unfair on Muslims, would never use political violence as a means to address any grievances. The perceived double standards in British foreign policy such as in the Israel/Palestine conflict, the invasion of Iraq, intervening in Libya but not in Syria are a few such examples that are brought up in political discussions among young politically aware Muslims.

BARA: I mean, no way am I saying it's right ... killing people is not right ... it says in the Qur'an– if you kill one person, it's like you've murdered the whole of mankind – that statement in the Qur'an shows how bad it is to do something which constitutes murder ... obviously there's a clause in between, and that's important, the clause is ... unless they've caused mischief in the land ... the saying goes that one person's terrorist is another person's freedom fighter ... situations like the Palestinian issue where, every day, you get bulldozers coming into people's houses; you get people being killed for no reason; by Israelis, and you wonder 'well, do the Palestinians have any other choice? Is violence the right answer?' Well, if someone's coming and attacking your home you have no choice but to defend yourselves and, if by defending yourselves you go up to what is a legitimate border, then that's fine. I don't see a problem with that because you have no choice, but then when you look at something like September 11th, when you look at something like the London bombings...is it fair to go into that country and then attack civilians? I wouldn't be able to justify that; I'd say 'no' ...

ASIF: ... the hypocrisy is something that I can get angry about a lot – I mean ... it's true, Islam/Muslims ... use violence and so have you, I mean if you look at the war in Iraq – there's Bush and Blair, both up there, doing God's work ...

There is in fact little evidence in the Qur'an regarding whether political violence is justified, sanctioned or condoned. There are those who would argue that the Qur'an encourages political violence in an attempt to gain political influence by force. However, the vast majority of Muslims do not interpret the verses in the Qur'an in this way, nor accept political violence as a legitimate method of gaining political means unless as a method of defence. As an example, in an interview with Shaykh Abdullah Al-Judai, a British Muslim scholar and expert in the field of *maqasid al Shari'ah* (the spirit or meaning behind the religious text) Al-Judai condemned the murder of Drummer Lee Rigby and the theory that he was a legitimate target due to his role as a combatant who had served in Afghanistan. Al-Judai argues that as British citizens the attackers had no right to take any action on foreign policy unless it was through the British legal system; second, that they had no right to take a life; and third that Drummer Lee Rigby was not a representative of the British armed forces but an employee like many others:

> The default state of any person's life is that it is sacred, particularly when it is subject to a covenant, or that of a Muslim. Regarding the concept of covenant, I already clarified that a person in these countries is in a natural state of covenant, i.e. the social or civil contract which requires him – in the eyes of Islam – to abide by the laws of the land. Suppose someone has a personal right – we are not talking about the right of the global nation (ummah) – is he entitled to enforce his right by his own hand, without going through the authorities? Of course not, as he would be in breach of that covenant which requires him to go through the proper legal channels to solve any dispute. Even if he is ultimately wronged, he cannot just take his right ... this action does not conform to any Islamic legal concept and cannot be justified by Islam in any way whatsoever. That soldier was a simple worker like anyone working in any institution.
> (Al-Judai 2013: 44–45)

In actual fact, the young British Muslims interviewed during the research referred to the Qur'an mainly when discussing historical scenarios where violence was justified – usually in cases of self-defence; rather than using the Qur'an as a justification for enacting violence or vengeance in modern society.

The contexts in which political violence can be used are difficult to sanction in Islam because the rules are very specific.

MEKKI: We as Muslims, living in Britain especially in an open society, it is totally unjust (to use violence) and Islam does not encourage or say that you should do these things, like kidnap other people or terrorism or arrest people, kill people -it is totally wrong.

USAYD: You can't justify the loss of human life, I don't know who the narrator was, but that the loss of one person is the loss of mankind, it doesn't specify Muslim or non-Muslim ... I do feel hurt, there is emotion, for innocent people, for the loss of innocent life, whether it's an Israeli bomb or a Palestinian suicide bomber ... you can't justify the loss of human life, no matter who.

The evidence from this research highlights that any justifications for political violence lies less in theological evidence, but in violence as a method of political communication. Though it is not condoned, nor accepted as a method of political engagement by most Muslims, political violence is a political action nevertheless. Unfortunately, political violence garners much media attention when perused, and as a method of political communication, political violence speaks much louder and gains far more global prominence than peaceful means.

Identity politics

There have been several issues that have encouraged the focus on British Muslim identity during the last decade – their ethnic and religious visibility, the terror threat from extremist Muslims and the perceived discrepancy between Muslims' religious values and British nationality has resulted in an on-going concentration on the identity of this growing group of British Muslims. The socialisation of second-generation British Muslims since 2001 has happened in an arena where their faith, religious observance and practice are severely critiqued – in the tabloid media, policy circles and among the political elite. This has inevitably led to questions being asked both among Muslims and by mainstream academics and policy makers regarding integration, citizenship and belonging. British Muslims are regularly challenged with the accusation that their religion and national identity are incompatible:

> Muslims not only despise Western secular values as decadent, materialistic, corrupt and immoral ... for Muslims, the whole of human life must represent a submission to God. This means that they feel a duty to Islamicise the values of the surrounding culture ... The sheer weight of numbers, plus the refusal to assimilate to Western values, makes this an unprecedented crisis for Western liberalism. The crisis is forcing it to confront the fundamental questions of what constitutes a country, national identity and the very nature of a liberal society.
>
> (Phillips 2002)

At a Q&A session at the Scottish Parliament in April 2012, a Muslim MSP was asked whether he felt more Scottish or Muslim – a variation on the question which British Muslims are asked on a regular basis, pitching nationality against religion. His answer was a suave take on the responses that British Muslims repeatedly use: 'If I asked you which you preferred, your brown hair or green eyes, how would you answer? They are both a part of who I am' the MSP replied[1]. Research also highlights that British Muslims identify strongly with their nation state (Gallup 2009: 21–24; Wind-cowie and Gregory 2011: 39–40; CLG 2010: 40).

> The article claims that ... Muslims and South Asians are almost as likely as whites to identify themselves as British. In addition, factors such as socio-economic difficulties and ethnically and religiously segregated networks that supposedly contribute to Muslim and South Asian alienation have been shown to be insignificant ... and despite retaining ethnic and religious social and political networks, Muslims and South Asians have also actively built integrated networks and consider themselves part of the larger British community.
>
> (Maxwell 2006: 749)

This obsession with choosing one identity facet over another can be a very contentious issue at a time when far-right discourse argues that Muslim citizens cannot and will not be European, British, Scottish and so on. This far-right discourse on Islam and Muslims in Europe (see Allen 2010; Bartlett and Littler 2011) accuses Muslims of a lack of integration/assimilation; as well as the perceived failure of multiculturalism. Prime Minister David Cameron's speech on 5 February 2011 stating that multicultural state policies have failed came at the end of a string of world leaders echoing similar sentiments (German Chancellor Angela Merkel in October 2010, former Australian Prime Minister John Howard in 2010 and former French Prime Minister Nicolas Sarkozy in 2011), most of whom were referring to Muslims within their respective countries.

At the core of the above discussions is the concept of citizenship. Citizenship is imperative because it underscores the affiliation between citizens and their nation-state. In our media focused world, citizenship is encapsulated as an emotional as well as a legal attachment to the state. Citizens who are not perceived as conforming to this notion of citizenship are branded as foreign, 'other' or at worst, traitors. The academic understanding of citizenship is far more nuanced (Kymlicka and Norman 2000; Cohen 1999), mainly composed of three overlapping concepts: citizenship as a legal status, enshrining political, social and civil rights; citizenship as a political status, encouraging the active engagement of citizens in its democratic process; and finally citizenship as an identity, encouraging a sense of emotional belonging and national identity. This identity 'type' of citizenship is the one most focused on by commentators, as debates surrounding cohesion and integration are debated.

Most of the young British Muslims interviewed during this research follow religiously contextual interpretations and understandings of citizenship. An example of such interpretations is the response of the deputy head of the European Council for Fatwa and Research, Sheikh Faysal Mawlawi. When asked about citizenship on Islam Online, he said:

> A Muslim can affiliate to a non-Muslim country and he or she can also give his or her loyalty to such a country. This is rooted in the *Sunnah* of the Prophet (peace and blessings be upon him) ... The religious duties required from a Muslim living in a non-Muslim country ... are to live with other people by Islamic morals, to cooperate with them in whatever is necessary or permissible, to deal with them justly, even if it is against himself, to comply with the obligations he undertakes in a way that does not contradict his religious freedom and duties. A Muslim also must not betray the society where he lives or the country to which he belongs. Betrayal is never permissible.
>
> (Mawlawi 2012)

The Cambridge University academic Professor T.J Winter writes:

> Islam, therefore, supplies arguments for loyalty. Not because it regards the present state of affairs as ideal (a view commended by no-one) but because it recognises that it is the point from which one needs to begin working towards the ideal, an ideal which will itself be reshaped by the powerful instruments of *ijtihad*. The fundamental objects, *maqasid*, of the *Shari'ah* are the right to life, mind, religion, lineage, and honour, and these are respected in the legal codes of the contemporary West. We may even venture to note that they appear to be better maintained here than in the ham-fisted attempts at creating *Shari'ah* states that we see in several corners of the Muslim world.
>
> (Winter 2003: 20)

It is noticeable on public occasions that Muslims engage in a shared sense of Britishness. Observing the numbers of Muslims who turned out for the Queen's jubilee celebrations in London in 2012, who attended and participated in the London Olympics and who voiced elation at the birth of Prince George, one can anecdotally say that the public affection and public engagement of Muslims in such moments of national pride are a manifestation of their civic loyalty and belonging. Of course we should not judge such actions as the norm to which all British minorities are monitored or judged, but the images seen on television, voices heard on the radio and comments read online are an indication of the sense of shared national identity that many British Muslims identify with. This form of national affection is the third 'type' of citizenship, one based on an emotional attachment to the nation state.

Diversity in political perspectives 149

ADAM: What makes me feel British [is the] British are huge on the social justice issues, the morals the principles the free will of society. Those are the core issues and the fact that it accommodates people such as myself and make them part of the wider society and that's what makes me feel more British or English than being non English.

BILAL: I was born in Britain, I've always lived here and I think there is no conflict between being British and being Muslim together ...

FARAH: If you were just to ask me about my nationality or how I identify myself it would be British Muslim with a Kashmiri Asian background

IMAN: I'm not a patriotic person, but I'm very proud of being British. For me the idea of being British is different from being patriotic. I don't agree with the wars, with the policies that are coming out in the country .... I'm not about hail Britain or hail England ... I'm proud of the fact that I'm British, it makes me a unique individual, because I'm British and Muslim and have ancestral roots in Bangladesh.

However, not all British Muslims engage with an emotive form of citizenship. A small group perceive their civic identity in purely instrumentalist terms. These respondents have a practical perception of their citizenship; it is observed as a legal status, consisting of a passport, obeying the state laws and a geographical status. They have little affection for being British. For some respondents, they go further by showing antagonism towards their civic identity. In these cases, citizenship is still legally abided by, yet engaged in a purely rational and relational sense, with little emotive or emotional attachment to a shared national identity.

LEYLA: British doesn't mean much, just that I have a British passport and that I live in Britain.

UTHMAN: Being British means that I can do whatever I want as long as it's within the law and not be questioned about it – but in fact, it's not the way, people question why is he dressed like that, what's he hiding under that jacket, what's he got underneath the hat ... I've had kids ask me have I got a gun underneath the turban or hat ...

JAMILA: My Islam makes me a good citizen, my humanity from Islam makes me want to be good to people around me, and yes I like living here and Britain is tolerable to Muslims, but in terms of my identity, it's not the hugest thing.

The sense of Britain as a 'home' is less relevant to this minority of British Muslims, as they see their citizenship in a rational or instrumental sense. They sometimes feel foreign everywhere else in the world, and Britain is all they know and associate with as a place of residence, yet not as an affectionate homeland. The religious interpretation that they hold as crucial to their understanding of citizenship lies in the concept of the 'ummah' or global Muslim community as beyond national ascriptions and borders. This allegiance to Islam and Muslims is beyond national borders, thus above British citizenship – at lease emotionally if not in actual practice.

SA'IL: People used to ask me are you Pakistani or British, I used to say British. Muslim never came up in those days. Over the years, I've begun to realize that life is more than just nationality.

The majority of second generation British Muslim respondents in this study felt strongly about their British national identity and its compatibility with their religious identity. They felt that both identity facets brought value to their lives, and no respondents admitted an experience where these identities where in conflict. Identity is a flexible, fluid and multifaceted aspect of life. It is not concrete and it is not always consistent. It may change through time, and it may be reassessed and re-evaluated. Being British was meaningful to most respondents – values, socialisation and expectations are important. At the same time, many young British Muslims felt a strong connection beyond borders – some with people of many diverse backgrounds and cultures and some were far more attached to the concept of the ummah and global Muslims.

Voting

Continuing with the discussion, the claim that all Muslims engage in politics specifically with a Muslim 'agenda' is often proposed with little evidence. The role of Islam in politics varies among young British Muslims, and is most clearly noticed in political activities such as voting, demonstrating and boycotting. The majority of political participation engaged in by the young Muslim participants was peaceful; to be a Muslim political activist does not mean to hold an extremist political agenda, but a care for this society, and the well-being of our fellow citizens, as seen when exploring reasons that young Muslims vote. Research has highlighted that British Muslims vote at a similar rate or higher than other British voters (Anwar 2001; Saggar 1998; Fieldhouse and Cutts 2006; Fieldhouse and Cutts 2007). Most of the young Muslim respondents from this research felt extremely passionate about elections and the right to vote. They say it's a privilege, that it's a right that should be appreciated and that everyone should vote.

SUHAIL: I think it's very important to vote, and it's really important and we've got a problem only two in ten young people vote at general elections. I think it's a right which you should exercise, your government is accountable to yourself by your vote, your vote has a lot of value and it's important to recognize its value and shape up the future of law which will affect you and policies and initiatives that will directly…yes I always vote.
BANAN: Well the last general election was the first time I was eligible to vote, I'd turned 18, so it was quite a romantic action, I'd always wanted to vote…reading about the suffragettes, and how they died getting us the

Diversity in political perspectives 151

vote that made me want to go out and exercise my democratic right. Young British Muslims do distrust political parties and individual politicians, as wider society does (Pattie *et al.* 2004) which is healthy in a democracy, but they also feel strongly about their right to vote, and that it is their civic duty to do so. However, there were a small number of participants who regularly avoided voting, some of whom believed that voting is unimportant, some believed democracy a fallacy and some believed voting in a non-Muslim nation state to be impermissible in Islam.

SAIL: I don't vote. I think its haram to vote in this society. I don't think voting as a whole is a bad thing. Voting within this political system I don't do, because I think it is a haram issue. But not in an Islamic society, or at university- you know like voting for an amir and things like that, I have no issues with. In terms of voting for a political party in this country I think its haram and I wouldn't do.

TUFAYL: Because now, whereas before I thought it was pointless, now it's a creedal issue for me...on a creedal level I believe that this act is tantamount to telling somebody in this country 'you, as a man, can legislate and make the law', when I believe that the only one that can do that is Allah.

While voting signalled to the government how citizens feel regarding state policies; these young British Muslims felt that signalling discontent to international governments, corporations and individuals to be more difficult, thus used boycotting of goods as a method to do so. The respondents don't always boycott; they make political choices based on monetary value, effectiveness of a given action, its potential usefulness, and so on. They are aware that boycotting is not always effective, nor is buying fair trade a solution. However, they believe that state-sponsored boycotting together with individual boycotting is more effective than individual boycotting alone. Boycotting Marks & Spencer, Proctor and Gamble, Starbucks, and Nestlé, were the most popular individual boycotts, while the boycotting of Danish goods was the most popular state boycott.

There were choices to boycott certain brands or products based on religious identity. Any products or companies who are rumoured or deemed to be pro-Israeli are boycotted in an attempt to support the Palestinian cause. These views as stated by the respondents are based on hear-say, with no participants able to provide evidence that these companies actively support the state of Israel.

LEYLA: I do boycott products, I do think it is effective, I have boycotted products. I boycott Nestlé because I heard they give money to Israel and they [Israel Defence Forces] kill innocent children. Same reason I boycott Starbucks because I can get a cappuccino anywhere and I can live without eating a KitKat.

SALMA: I boycott M&S because they put money towards weaponry and mass destructions, they support Israel, I don't like that either.

However, there are also young British Muslims who feel that not only is boycotting irrational and useless, but framed in a dishonest way through rumours, myths and religious agendas. The debate surrounding the most effective way to take political action is ongoing, and is by no means a unanimous opinion among these young British Muslims. The varied forms of 'effectiveness' did have a role to play in the choices the respondents made when participating in the political sphere. Effectiveness had a role in motivating these young people to choose one political action over another; however, effectiveness is relative – it does not necessarily mean policy change. For example, demonstrations are very popular among the group; however, their effectiveness lies not in policy change, but in expressive and signalling mechanisms such as showing support, media emphasis, and signalling concerns to a wider audience; whereas petitions were popular simply for their convenience, and other than that they were criticised as ineffective. This is also obvious in the debate on whether media and communication methods are political activities or not.

During the research, young Muslims discussed the political nature of the media and communication, and how under certain contexts, their activities are considered as political one – or not. The world of media and communications has vastly changed our world. It has increased the speed at which information is passed on, and the way in which political news has become globalised. Media and communication formats as a form of political engagement may have been considered as unconventional in the past, but have since begun to eclipse those that were once more popular forms of political actions. Many of the young Muslim respondents felt that those who produce and make political messages via media and communication avenues are taking a political action – this includes writing a blog, uploading a video on YouTube, producing a TV documentary or programmes, and making a music CD. However, the respondents who listened to, tuned in to, and bought these items were not necessarily considered to be conducting a political action.

UMAMA: I mean, like stuff on the internet as well, that could be quite political – you know, how like, for instance David Cameron's got his own blog now and stuff like that – I've actually read it, it's so funny – just like blogs in general ... a lot of some really famous Iraqi blogs, some really good Saudi blogs. I think blogs ... become the new ... form of political action.

RASHID: I think you need to examine anything and everything that you can utilize and move forward, put videos on YouTube, etc. can be just as effective as getting arrested.

JAMILA: The most effective form of political change is talking to the masses, planning talks all over the place, they affect people's views. I work on the Islam Channel, talking can influence people, their views, why they have those views, press releases, conferences, radio as a means of gaining political understating.

UMAMA: ... even music, like that guy who's like on the front cover of Q – I've forgot his name – but he's ... like he's just brought out an album called

'Jihad blah, blah, blah' and I guess his music is really political. There's loads of political music, even like rappers these days – what they're rapping about – that's really political.

There seems to be a need for clarification in this new arena of communication and political engagement. It is clear that those who write blogs and produce music with a political context are using modes of political participation. However, those who place a political petition or link to their Facebook site or purchase a CD with political lyrics are less clearly politically engaging according to a traditional understanding of political activity. This all underlines that media and communication formats should be considered as evolving, useful and popular methods of political engagement.

The British Muslim young people interviewed for this research engaged in politics for a wide variety of reasons. Very few of the respondents engaged in 'Muslim' only issues – campaigning against a niqab ban is a matter that non-Muslim human rights activists are also grappling with; participating in anti-Iraq-war protests were popular with British people across a spectrum of political platforms and so on. The motivations behind the political engagement of young British Muslims also varied considerably depending on the political activity, whereas boycotting Israeli products made in settlement areas was motivated by religious and ethical values; voting in European, national and local elections was perceived as very much a national civic responsibility, significant not only for the success of the state, but also a consideration for the welfare of society and of our fellow citizens.

Conclusion

The presumption that Muslims all hold similar values and perceptions regarding the political sphere is far from reality. Some Muslims supported the intervention in Iraq, while most did not. Similarly, some support British military action against the Assad regime in Syria, while others disagree. British Muslims, just as other citizens, have varied perspectives and judgements to make, all observed through differing religious and civic lenses. While many Muslims cannot justify political violence, others will validate such actions under certain circumstances, which in and of themselves will vary. British Muslims also perceive their citizenship in a multitude of ways, recognizing the existence of a plurality of social identities and engaging with their civic rights; while others treat their Britishness as a given national ascription, without emotional attachment. This research has highlighted the nuanced differences in religious identification and practice found among Muslims. The perpetual assumption that all Muslims have and hold the same values, choices, and preferences is mistaken.

Ultimately Islam as a faith does not support a specific political framework even though it inspires certain political ideals and norms. The way these are interpreted by Muslims is wide-ranging – some are reactionary, literary and radical in their perspective; others are pragmatic and more nuanced. At the heart of Islam lies the Qur'an, surrounded by other textual sources including Hadiths, historical narrative in the seerah and further legal rulings over time through the Shari'ah – the interpretation varies not only among scholars, but across time and geographical space. Muslims are hugely diverse in many ways, including their perspectives of politics, evidenced by the varied opinions on British foreign policy. It is rather unfortunate that the debate has focused solely on radical extremism and thus shifted attention away from the vision of other responsible young British Muslims and their meaningful political participation. This debate needs to be refocused on the majority of British Muslim citizens who are politically active and aspire to a civic method of engagement.

Note

1 A special event organized at the Scottish Parliament in April 2012 as part of the academic conference 'Muslims and Political Participation in Britain' hosted by the Alwaleed Centre, University of Edinburgh.

Bibliography

Al-Judai, A. (2013) 'An Interview With Shaykh Abdullah Al-Judai', *The Mena Report*, 6(1).
Allen, C. (2010) *Islamophobia*. Aldershot: Ashgate.
Anwar, M. (2001) 'The Participation of Ethnic Minorities in British Politics', *Journal of Ethnic and Migration Studies*, 27: 533–549.
Bartlett, J. and Littler, M. (2011) *Inside the EDL: Populist Politics in a Digital Age*. London: Demos.
CLG (2010) *Attitudes, Values and Perceptions: Muslims and the General Population in 2007–2008*. London: Communities and Local Government.
Cohen, J.L. (1999) 'Changing Paradigms of Citizenship and the Exclusiveness of the Demos', *International Sociology*, 14(3): 245–268.
Gallup Coexist Index (2009) *A Global Study of Interfaith Relations*. London: Gallup.
Fieldhouse, E. and Cutts, D. (2006) *Voter Engagement in British South Asian Communities At the 2001 General Election*. London: Joseph Rowntree Foundation.
Fieldhouse, E. and Cutts, D. (2007) *Electoral Participation of South Asian Communities in England and Wales*. London: Joseph Rowntree Foundation.
Gingrich, N. (2011) In Islamic Law, Gingrich Sees a Mortal Threat to U.S. New York Times, December, available at: www.nytimes.com/2011/12/22/us/politics/in-shariah-gingrich-sees-mortal-threat-to-us.html?pagewanted=1&_r=0.
Kymlicka, W. and Norman, W. (2000) *Citizenship in Diverse Societies*. Oxford: Oxford University Press.
Mason, R. (2014) 'Ukip MEP Says British Muslims Should Sign Charter Rejecting Violence', *The Guardian*, available at: www.theguardian.com/politics/2014/feb/04/ukip-mep-gerard-batten-muslims-sign-charter-rejecting-violence.
Mawlawi, F. (2012) 'Citizenship of Muslims in Europe', *On Islam*, available at: www.onislam.net/english/shariah/contemporary-issues/interfaith-intercivilisational-and-intercultural/416338.html.

Maxwell, R. (2006) 'Muslims, South Asians and the British Mainstream: A National identity Crisis?', *West European Politics*, 29(4): 736–756.
Pattie, C., Seyd, P. and Whiteley, P. (2004) *Citizenship in Britain: Values and Democracy.* Cambridge: Cambridge University Press.
Phillips, M. (2002) 'How the West Was Lost', *The Spectator*, available at: http://archive.spectator.co.uk/article/11th-may-2002/14/how-the-west-was-lost.
Pipes, D. (2002) *Faces of American Islam*. Available at: www.danielpipes.org/441/faces-of-american-islam-muslim-immigration.
Saggar, S. (1998) *The General Election 1997: Ethnic Minorities and Electoral Politics.* London: Commission for Racial Equality.
Sheikh Faysal Mawlawi (2010) *The Ruling on Political Participation in the West.* Available at: www.islamonline.net/servlet/Satellite?c=Article_C&pagename=Zone-English-Living_Shariah%2FLSELayout&cid=1248188089986.
Wind-cowie, M. and Gregory, T. (2011) *A Place for Pride*. London: Demos.
Winter, T. (2003) 'Muslim Loyalty and Belonging: Some Reflections on the Psychosocial Background', in M. Seddon, D. Hussain and N. Malik (eds) *British Muslims: Loyalty and Belonging*. Leicester: Islamic Foundation.

8 Facebook groups as potential political publics?
Exploring ideas of the political amongst young British Muslim Facebook users

Brooke Storer-Church

Introduction

In contemporary Britain, where public debates persist about the strengths and weaknesses of diversity, its recognition and its implications for political participation and practices, Muslims have gained particular attention, subject to suggestions that they are somehow illiberal or incompatible with modern democratic British society (Abbas 2005; Lewis 2002, 2007; Modood 2005). Despite those suggestions, Muslims have sought to engage directly with government and wider society at various levels; for example: running for office, forming Muslim-interest organisations like the Muslim Council of Britain (MCB) or British Muslims for Secular Democracy (BMSD), and creating Muslim-driven media, like *Q-News* or *Muslim News*. Interest and involvement in the political process amongst *young* British Muslims, however, has been observed as problematically low; problematic insofar as the perceived lack of interest is viewed as causally related to tendencies towards violent or extremist behaviour (Home Office 2005). But, if a more general decline in political engagement is considered, then apathy with the political process among younger populations is not particularly noteworthy (O'Toole and Gale 2011).

This chapter suggests two aspects of the young British Muslim population that make it a valuable case for exploring ideas of the political more generally as well as evolving (and potentially political) uses of Internet-based social media applications. For one, as young people, they represent a cohort whose particular understandings of the political have typically been subsumed within and ignored by political participation literature which often adopts narrow, quantitative, survey-driven approaches and traditional formulations of political engagement (O'Toole 2003). And two, as Muslims, they are part of a group which has experienced a particular relationship with the Internet, as it has been suggested that the Internet has transformed individual Muslims' relationships with Islam through greater access to information sources as well as to complementary and oppositional interpretations of Islam from others around the world (Anderson 2003; Bunt 2009; Mandaville 2001; Piela 2010). As such, there may be distinctively 'youthful' understandings of the political which can be recovered from an exploration into young British Muslims'

Facebook groups as political publics? 157

ideas of politics and political action, or there may be particular conceptions of the political which are derived from, challenged by or ambivalent towards the proliferation of Internet use and the accesses afforded by that use; perhaps both. Regardless, a link can and has been drawn between new social media specifically and new forms of political action. New social media have both enabled increased access to the means of message creation and contributed to some form of 'new politics' as witnessed through their use in both the Arab Spring uprisings and the English Summer Riots of August 2011 (Morrell et al. 2011; Howard et al. 2011). Thus, the growing relevance of Internet technologies to group-based claims-making and the adoption of new social media by various social movements, suggest a need to explore the ways users conceive of such media and how their usage squares with their ideas of the political.

Theoretical grounding

My analysis has been guided by recent academic literature regarding young people's conceptions of 'the political' and suggestions that new understandings (Poster 1997) or 'grammars' (O'Toole and Gale 2009) of the political are necessary both to make sense of young people's experiences and to create greater understanding of contemporary behaviours which sit outside the norm of traditional politics or political areas but can still be understood as efforts to substantiate citizenship, increase one's individual or collective voice or affect change within society.

Examining young Muslims within this context can prove valuable as they may provide insight into purported increases of political apathy amongst British young people, especially minority ethic youth (Marsh et al. 2007). Marsh et al. (2007) cite several recent studies supporting these trends, including one in which it was concluded that the 'Millenial Generation', defined by Pirie and Worcester (1998; cited in Marsh et al. 2007) as those people who reached the age of twenty-one around the turn of the millennium, is an 'apolitical generation' (Marsh et al. 2007: 2). Public debate regarding the particular disengagement of young British Muslims has increased in tandem with the 2001 disturbances in Bradford, Burnley and Oldham, and repercussions from the 9/11 attacks and the London bombings in July 2005, with official reports identifying such disengagement a 'a key background factor contributing to the events' (O'Toole and Gale 2009: 144). Yet, more recent literature suggests that young Muslims are not politically disengaged, but instead engaging in ways which spill over traditional conceptions of political participation and, therefore, may go unseen (Marsh et al. 2007; O'Toole and Gale 2010; O'Toole and Gale 2011).

Some of those more creative or individualised modes of action can be witnessed online as young Muslims have increasingly taken to the Internet as a mode of communication, a means of accessing religious information, and as a gathering place for identity-based claims-making debate and discussion (Bunt 2009; Mandaville 2001; Michael 2012; Piela 2010; Sands 2010). At this point, the intersection between the Internet and political activity comes into view (Christensen 2011; Feezell *et al.* 2009; Kushin and Kitchener 2009; Marichal 2010). While recent studies examining that intersection address a variety of concerns, from the quality of political communication within online sites (Kushin and Kitchener 2009) to the effectiveness of online activism and 'slacktivist' critiques (Christensen 2011) and the relationship between online and offline political participation (Feezell *et al.* 2009), they tend to use 'the political' uncritically. In fact, none of the studies referenced define what they mean as 'the political'. Instead, they utilise the term in its traditional capacity: to refer to governance structures, electoral behaviour and campaign activities. The forthcoming analysis, however, takes a slightly different tack: simultaneously recognising those more traditional conceptualisations of the political in order to explore respondents' own ideas while also striving to unearth the ways in which respondents' usage and understandings of *Facebook* Groups may suggest newer or more innovative repertoires of action which have not yet received much attention in academic literature (O'Toole and Gale 2011: 67). As recommended by Back *et al.* (2009) and O'Toole (2003), opening the analysis to respondents' own understandings of the political is here intended to foster a more nuanced account of the ways in which young British Muslims are engaging with certain online groups.

Data collection

Fieldwork was conducted for approximately eight months, between January and August 2010. At the start, two pilot interviews were conducted to collect some feedback about the intended interview schedule. While it included some questions about respondents' online behaviours, it did not specifically ask about *Facebook*. The piloting process, however, suggested that *Facebook* may be a valuable repository of potential respondents and observations because both respondents spoke at length about using *Facebook* to discuss public representations of Muslims and other identity-related concerns with others. As a result of those pilot interviews, I chose to visit *Facebook* Groups to recruit participants and observe the types of discussions taking place there.

There were a handful of *Facebook* Groups from which respondents came. They were *Muslim Defence League (MDL)*, *United Shades of Britain (Muslims and Non-Muslims Who Oppose Extremism)*, *United against Religious Discrimination*, *Bristol Muslims*, *The Young Muslims UK*, and *British Muslims*; the majority of respondents are represented by the first three Groups. While some of these Groups had been in existence for several years and were formed as extensions of formal youth organisations (e.g. *The Young Muslims UK*), others had formed at the start of my fieldwork as a direct result of specific events. For example, both *United Shades of Britain* and the *Muslim Defence League* Groups were founded at the start of 2010 in response to the proposed Islam4UK marches through Wooton Basset. In an effort to differentiate themselves from more extreme or violent individuals, several young

British Muslims and non-Muslims established *United Shades of Britain* (*USoB*) to create a space which could challenge negative portrayals of Muslims and nurture more positive interactions and images. The *Muslim Defence League* emerged from *USoB* to focus specifically on opposing Islamophobia and countering misinformation about Islam. A common thread through all Groups from which respondents were solicited was that they focused on challenging negative portrayals of British Muslims, whether through direct confrontation of those negative representations, creation of more positive images or some combination of both. Since I was interested to query the ways in which young British Muslims might use online environments to create or recreate public representations of Muslims, these Groups were viewed as appropriate and adequate avenues for reaching such respondents.

From these Groups, I confirmed twenty-five participants, nineteen to thirty years old, who were born in Britain and self-identified as Muslim. The sample consisted of ten men and fifteen women with ethnic backgrounds ranging from Pakistani to Bangladeshi to Iraqi to White British; the largest ethnic background represented was Pakistani with thirteen respondents identifying themselves as such. There were fourteen students and eleven non-students. The de-territorialisation of virtual communities allowed for participants to be located anywhere geographically. As such, I was able to include in the sample people who lived in many different parts of Britain.

It must be acknowledged that the sample is a small, self-selected sample and, therefore, presents both limitations to its generalisability and to the diversity of representatives within the sample. For example, while it was possible to sample both students and non-students within Groups, many of the non-students had previously completed some form of further or higher education and, therefore, may demonstrate some demographic similarities to the current students in the sample. In sampling respondents through *Facebook Groups*, it was necessary to balance my interest in gathering as many willing participants as possible with my interest in some obtaining some diversity within the sample. Though the demographic details, both known and unknown, limit the sample's applicability and negate its representativeness, those limitations are argued to be acceptable within the parameters of case study research such as this, which does not seek to collect a representative sample but, instead, strives to collect data that can speak to particular theoretical concerns and particular, time-bound phenomenon.

In terms of collecting data, a variety of means were used, both synchronous and asynchronous methods (Bryman 2004: 470). These methods included online and offline interviews, open-ended questionnaires and one instance of instant messaging. I conducted eleven face-to-face semi-structured interviews, collected ten open-ended questionnaires, held three computer-based interviews through Skype software and conducted one interview with the help of MSN Instant Messenger. While a significant level of structure was needed in order to allow for comparisons across the sample, participants were given freedom to add additional talking points into both spoken and written interviews so that participants could share their experiences and I could explore the meanings of relevant terms (Kazmer and Xie 2008).

Facebook as a social action tool

With respect to both extending communicative capabilities and expanding the scope of political concern and action, the Internet provides a space for like-minded individuals to coalesce around common issues or interests (Häyhtiö and Rinne 2007). To that end, websites have emerged which act as gathering places for various groups and collectives: ranging from more light-hearted interests such as dog ownership (www.dailypuppy.com) or popular music fan pages (for example, www.justinbiebermusic.com) to issues of discrimination and social justice (www.onlinesocialjustice.com). There is an extensive list of Islam-related websites. For example, there are sites with wide appeal such as *Islam Online* (www.islamonline.com), which claims to be the 'leading and original Islamic portal on the Internet…the number one source for Islamic content in the Islamic world,' and other smaller, more personal sites such as *The Hijablog* and *Unique Muslimah* blogs which several respondents mentioned following. There are also watchdog sites that critique mass media behaviour, particularly coverage of Muslims. *Loonwatch* (www.loonwatch.com) is one such site, describing itself as 'a blogzine run by a motley group of hate-allergic bloggers to monitor and expose the web's plethora of anti-Muslim loons, wackos, and conspiracy theorists,' while *Islamophobia Watch* (www.islamophobia-watch.com) sets out to 'document material in the public domain which advocates a fear and hatred of the Muslim people of the world and Islam as a religion.'

Of course, not all sites are focused on anti-Muslim sentiments. There are plenty of Muslim friendship and dating websites (a long list of which can be found at www.muslimmarriagelist.com) and other social networking sites which provide meeting places for those Muslims (and non-Muslims) with particular interests in issues which may be local, national or global in scope. The presence of social networking sites (SNSs) on the Internet has been growing over the past decade. Some examples of popular SNSs are *MySpace, LinkedIn, Bebo*, and arguably the most popular site, *Facebook*.[1] Social networking sites are defined by boyd[2] and Ellison as:

> Web-based services that allow individuals to (1) construct a public or semi-public profile within a bounded system, (2) articulate a list of other users with whom they share a connection, and (3) view and traverse their list of connections and those made by others within the system.
>
> (2007)

Despite the emergence of a variety of cultures around these sites, most of them function to support existing social networks, while some go beyond that to 'help strangers connect based on shared interests, political views or activities' (boyd and Ellison 2007). It is this latter phenomenon which is of interest here as *Facebook* has become well known for its Groups function, which allows users to gather collectively around particular interests, events or political aims without any pre-existing network or group needed.[3] Despite the availability of statistics regarding membership and trafficking figures, *Facebook* currently provides no statistics regarding the number of Groups within its site.[4] The website *All Facebook* claimed in early 2010 that there were 620 million Group pages (O'Neill 2010). Its method was to search Google for all *Facebook* Groups as Google now indexes all public Groups for its search engine. Conducting a similar search in August 2013 yields a total of 993,000 Groups.[5]

Despite their increasing popularity, sociological scholarship regarding the ways in which SNSs, and *Facebook* in particular, may constitute online publics is still in its infancy. That is, the ways in which these sites may provide platforms for the expression of, debate over and re-articulation of group identities or other collective concerns has yet to be well explored because the various capabilities of social media are still coming to light. Research on social networking sites has evolved over the last ten years and tends to investigate self-presentation and identity performance (Papacharissi 2009). Previous studies tend to view use of SNSs as functions of 'social searching', or finding information about offline acquaintances, rather than 'social browsing', or using the site to develop new acquaintances and connections (Joinson 2008; Lampe *et. al.* 2006). In support of that point, boyd and Ellison (2007) argue that users of most social networking sites are not looking to meet new people and are instead interested in maintaining contact with existing friends and groups. Arguments like these can be located within literature that adopts traditional conceptualisations of virtual environments in which online relationships and interactions are mere extensions of previously established offline ones, yet other work is emerging which diverges from those traditions, arguing that virtual environments can and do foster unique and innovative interactivity which can be independent of offline relationships (see, for example, Zhao 2006). This chapter contributes to that emerging body of work which examines the uses to which young Muslims put *Facebook*, specifically, and ways in which their use of that site may be understood through both traditional and more innovative conceptualisations of 'the political'.

Young British Muslims' use of *Facebook* groups

In this section, I will discuss respondents' general use of the site as evidenced through their own words, including frequency of use and the reasons for it. However, in examining that use, what will become clear is that much of respondents' interest in browsing various Groups relates to their Muslim identities: to perceptions of Muslims, to posts about Muslims, or to relevant links or stories about Muslims. The extent to which respondents' use of *Facebook* reflects their desire to assert, debate, or define public senses of British Muslim identity will be emphasised where appropriate.

Connecting and disconnecting

In line with boyd and Ellison's (2007) argument that users of social networking sites are primarily interested in maintaining contact with their existing social network, several respondents claimed that their main reason for using *Facebook* was to keep in touch with family and friends. Nazia's comment were typical of this tendency:

> [I use it] to keep in contact with friends and family as well as work usage in terms of university ... if we have group work, it's easier to communicate over *Facebook* as sometimes it's hard for a group meeting live.

While all respondents used *Facebook* to some degree in this way, several respondents talked about other reasons for using it. Sam spoke about *Facebook*'s ability to relieve some of the isolation she feels living as an Asian in a non-Asian community:

> Because I don't live in a predominantly Asian area so the *Facebook* page lets me think that I'm not the only Asian person that thinks this way. If they think the same as me and they enlighten me with information and the truth about something. I said before about having conversations, that's what you need to seek the truth. You need to communicate.
> [Brooke: So in that way *Facebook* allows you to connect with people you wouldn't otherwise have access to?]
> Yeah, definitely.

For Sam, *Facebook* adds a degree of communicative connection to others who share her viewpoints. These others are not necessarily people who are already familiar to Sam so that connecting with them constitutes 'social browsing', or making new connections (Lampe *et al.* 2006). Similarly, Layla spoke about the ways in which *Facebook* allows her to feel connected to other people regardless of whether she has met them before or where they may be located geographically. Such a physical dislocation is mirrored in what she saw as a disconnection from physical identity markers:

> *Facebook* is one of my main interactions with the outside world. It's an emerging thing that a lot of people they can be sitting in one room anywhere in the world and they can be typing out their feelings to a wider community. One of the unique things about *Facebook* is that that woman who was writing her feelings could be head-to-toe dressed in black and completely covered and everything but she is saying her thoughts and her feelings to the world and she's communicating them and no one knows that she's this woman. Everyone is just reading her thoughts and that's one good thing about *Facebook*.

Here, Layla shares her view that the physical or visible sharing of one's identity (e.g. through Islamic dress) can impede the sharing of one's thoughts and ideas. *Facebook*, as a virtual environment in which one's physical identity is not necessarily visible to others, is seen as enabling a freedom from that identity, or at least from the perceptions of that identity that others may have. This perspective is articulated in academic arguments (e.g. Bolster 1996; McKenna *et al.* 2002) which claim that virtual environments allow for the removal of obstacles such as stigmatised appearances, thereby 'liberating expression via anonymity' (Papacharissi 2009: 200) and supported by more general social psychological literature regarding the ways in which the Internet has transformed the 'traditional conditions of identity production' in which that disembodiment combines with anonymity resulting in a blank slate upon which individuals may transcend corporeal constraints and create a new self (Zhao *et al.* 2008: 1817).[6]

Anonymity from identity was not the only type of freedom mentioned. Ruby spoke of free access and the ability to create messages of her own as contributing to her use of *Facebook*:

> *Facebook* has become a worldwide phenomenon, what we say affects or rather is absorbed by others and it's hard to deny that this doesn't have an impact. Censorship is in our own hands and this is a massive factor. This means we can say, show or think what we want, although it's 'monitored' it offers A LOT of freedom to its users.

That ability to create messages of one's own, whether positive or negative, emerged in many of the respondents' views. They saw *Facebook*'s open policy as leading to a diversity of users. Despite evidence which suggests that the Internet presents conditions which are conducive to selective exposure to media content and that users gravitate to political perspectives which are comparable to their own, some research has been done which suggests that there is potential for users to engage with opposing viewpoints in online discussions (Kushin and Kitchener 2009). Through content analysis of posts made in a *Facebook* Group discussing state-sanctioned torture, Kushin and Kitchener demonstrate that, while the majority of posts were in support of the group's overall position, there was a significant minority of oppositional posters (seventeen per cent), the presence of which reflects 'the capability of social networks to afford persons of different perspectives the ability to coalesce and engage in political debate' (2009: 11).

Engaging with similar and dissimilar views

The ability to engage both with like and unlike-minded people was a draw for several respondents. It was generally felt that a diversity of views afforded participants the ability to learn about others who live or think differently. This was seen as a positive aspect and one reflecting *Facebook*'s openness. For instance, creating a space in which opposing views would be welcomed was the drive behind the formation of *United Shades of Britain* Group. Here, one of the group administrators, J, explains that the presence of oppositional viewpoints was taken as an opportunity to debate:

> There are people that will try to be unnecessarily controversial but you can't forbid them from having their views because they'll become even more radical or extreme. So if you give them an outlet and you say, look, how about this, this counter-argument, there can be some sort of discussion or debate, instead of either you believe in this or you can't get on to the Group.

Despite the acknowledgement by some of negative aspects of that openness, typified by encounters with individuals perceived to be misinformed or prejudicial of Muslims or Islam, a common thread through both positive and negative perspectives was that *Facebook* afforded the opportunity for education; for engaging in a conversation with a wide variety of people; for reinforcing one's own views or for adjusting those views in light of others' arguments. Thomas claims his impetus to correct misinformation about Islam is the driving force in his *Facebook* usage and applies both to Muslims and non-Muslims. He explains that he uses it:

> To help educate the misinformed. There is much ignorance within the Muslim community, as to what Islam is really about, never mind the wider society as well! Networking, connecting with other like-minded people who want to see a brighter, more spiritual future. The *Facebook* Groups are used for educational purposes and dialogue too.

It is important to note that respondents' efforts to correct misinformation were not necessarily directed only at non-Muslims. *Facebook* Groups have also been used as platforms upon which Muslims may debate with other Muslims over various Islamic interpretations or ideas about being Muslim, functioning as one field within the broader cyber-environment through which Muslims engage one another and articulate alternative narratives of belonging (cf. Anderson 2003; Mandaville 2001, 2002; Michael 2012). Here, one respondent talks about the ways in which Groups host debate amongst Muslims, as well as how those discussions can lend themselves to reinforcing notions of belonging within British society:

> There are some misconceptions that some non-Muslims have, and Muslims have, too. I mean, you might have seen, there was a whole thread on the distinction between what secularism is and what the caliphate is, because there are Muslims out there that believe in that but I don't necessarily believe in that. That's politically motivated because those that believe in the caliphate believe it's a religious obligation but it's a political system, so in that case, you can argue both ways. You can say it's not a

religious obligation and neither is it an effective political system in today's modern Britain…I think one of the things that will change the minds of non-Muslims and Muslims is promoting the idea that we want to live together and see our values as British values.

This respondent explains that he sees his primary concern in engaging in dialogue on *Facebook* as 'changing people's political ideas basically from caliphate to a secular democracy rather than any particular political party or anything'.

In wanting to persuade other Muslims and debate the terms by which they define their Muslim obligations, behaviours and identities, he reflects one way in which *Facebook* Groups can provide a sort of middle ground between public discourse about Muslims which is far removed from individuals' daily lives and the face-to-face personal relationships which shape individual senses of being Muslim. In this way, these online Groups encourage expansive senses of community noted by Mandaville (2001, 2002) as marked by critical engagement with Islam and the 'recognition of disparate Muslim voices and alternative articulations' (Sands 2010: 140). As a result of that engagement with alternative views and voices, it can also be said that these *Facebook* Groups resemble Anderson's (2003) notion of online Islamic public spheres which allow individual Muslims to experience alternative interpretations of Islam through greater, individualised access to information, as well as exercise greater agency in defining the terms of their identities, experiences and representations. Activities such as these in which *Facebook* Group members participate can be seen as part of a broader expanse of Internet-based reflexive styles of engagement through which individuals may 'express their own ideas, gather support for their own interests, and deal with their own worries and concerns' (Häyhtiö and Rinne 2007: 346; see also Bennett 2004).

Sid describes a similar motivation for using *Facebook* Groups, using them primarily for the purpose of correcting anti-Muslim comments or ideas. When asked why he chooses to use *Facebook*, he answered:

> One hundred and ten per cent to answer to anti-Islamic comments. I never comment personally on people or what they're like. I don't involve myself in this sort of politics where they say, we're lefties, you're righties. All I do is respond to these anti-Islamic posts and maybe sometimes I'll have a bit of banter with some of these guys, like oh yeah, all of us Muslims wants to blow everyone up, but I'm absolutely joking and make sure that everyone knows I'm joking.
>
> [Brooke: When you are responding to these anti-Islamic posts, what are you saying in general? Is it to argue with them or inform them or?]
>
> I've never sort of claimed myself to be a scholar, but I have a deep interest in Islam. I'm not someone who just goes on Google, finds a couple of anti-Islamic or pro-Islamic sites and copies and pastes it. I literally do it just to let people know, okay you think that's the idea of Islam, why don't you explain this to me then?

Sid spoke of watching various Group discussions without contributing until a specifically negative or misinformed comment was posted, at which point he participated by posting a response in the form of a direct Islamic quotation or citation from the Qu'ran. This sort of interaction between previously unacquainted people is not substantiated by existing *Facebook* studies, nor by more general work on social-networking sites which argue them to be reflections of offline social networks (e.g. boyd and Ellison 2007; Joinson 2008; Lampe *et al.* 2006), but is beginning to feature in analyses which look into the Group features of *Facebook* or the ways in which *Facebook* provides public, political forums for identity concerns (e.g. Kushin and Kitchener 2009; Michael 2012). It was observed during the course of fieldwork that many of the respondents participate in *Facebook* Groups which represent a particular interest of theirs, but in which they have had little or no contact with other members prior to joining the Group. In those instances, the Group itself is the shared connection. Aliyah talks about the value she finds in being able to interact with people who feel or think the same way about things as she does:

> I read [Group] discussion boards on a daily basis but only contribute on an ad hoc basis. I find it interesting to read what like-minded people have to say on issues such as race and religion. I also find it reassuring when I see that not all people hold negative opinions of Muslims.

While Aliyah may not be familiar with or know individual members, Groups such as the ones she discusses afford her a mirroring of her own thoughts and identity as a British Muslim. Conversations she observes and participates in reinforce the sense of British Muslim identity she has cultivated through personal relationships and practices and assuage her fears over negative perceptions of Muslims. This sort of interaction within Groups, though, was not unique to Aliyah. While Aliyah browses Groups to find like-minded views and posts her own thoughts sporadically, Zahra is committed to a more active promotion of her ideas and experiences of being Muslim and so involves herself more heavily in Group discussions:

> I use *Facebook* primarily to promote my Islamic and political ideas and views. I tend to contribute considerably to discussions in various Groups and I also regularly make comments on postings made by others. I participate on pretty much a daily basis, varying from an hour or two a day to occasionally several hours a day ... I hope to influence people's views and thinking processes – to raise issues, perspectives and questions they may not have considered before and alternative solutions.

In attempting to influence others' different viewpoints, Zahra expresses her own agency to affect the way Muslims are viewed by others and to shape discussions about Muslims in her own terms (Anderson 2003; Mandaville 2001, 2002). Zahra is able to do this in Groups with which she feels an affinity as well as Groups with which she feels she is in opposition. Respondents spoke of joining many different Groups, but most of them spoke of joining those which reflected some aspect of their own lives or interests. For example, several students with whom I spoke joined university-based Islamic Society *Facebook* Groups. Yet there were other respondents, such as Zahra, Abdullah and Alana, who took the initiative to join Groups with whom they felt they lacked common ground, e.g. the English Defence League (EDL) *Facebook* Group, which was viewed by nearly all respondents as being ostensibly anti-Muslim. Here, Abdullah and Alana elaborate on using *Facebook* in this way:

> I recently joined several EDL groups on *Facebook* and I tried to engage with them, and discuss with them, and debate and show them things about Islam and Muslims they didn't know but I felt I made little progress because their anti-Muslim views were so entrenched.
>
> (Abdullah)

> ... if there's a Group that makes me really angry ... I once, there was a Group 'Fuck Islam', they still exist, and I read something that someone wrote that made me so angry. I mean, fair enough if you don't believe in religion, but then don't say it's stupid just because you don't believe in it. I don't believe in a lot of things, but that doesn't make it stupid ... I joined the Group, wrote what I needed to and then left the Group ... I join Groups when they really get to me.
>
> (Alana)

The efforts of Abdullah and Alana to expose themselves to alternative points of view resonate with some Internet features highlighted by Norris (2002) in her exploration of the bridging and bonding aspects of online communities. Norris argues that, while certain features such as their 'fragmented hyperpluralism' 'should encourage interaction and exchange within social groups sharing similar beliefs and values,' degrees of anonymity afforded by text-based communication allow for certain social divides to be bridged (2002: 4–5); though, importantly, such anonymity may also increase divides or the propensity for abuse, as discussed at the start of this thesis. Despite such possibilities, Norris (2002) contributes an important point with regards to the ways in which participation in online communities such as these *Facebook* Groups may both deepen users' experiences of community (i.e. reinforcing existing beliefs and social networks) and widen users' experiences (i.e. connecting users to others with different backgrounds or beliefs).

Discussion

While nearly all respondents admitted to using *Facebook* in Norris' (2002) sense of deepening community, the majority of them also spoke of using it to widen that sense of community: as a platform for educating others about Islam or Muslims; to engage with others holding alternative viewpoints; to correct misconceptions about Muslims. Respondents often focused their *Facebook* use to specific Groups when talking about the ways they might engage with others on Muslim-related issues, as evidenced already in the comments from Zahra, Abdullah and Alana. Groups function as collections of *Facebook* users who wish to express solidarity with some idea, issue or event. In the case of these respondents, the idea or issue around which they choose to mobilise is British Muslim identity and its definition, meanings and representation. They participate in Groups which provide them with space to assert, debate, or define public senses of British Muslim identity through their own senses of that identity. Respondents' own words about the reasons for participating in Groups illustrate the capacity of those Groups to provide interest points around which members coalesce to combine agency and action. Respondents' descriptions of their own regular interactions within Groups reflect use of them as identity platforms, instilling respondents with greater agency to address misconceptions about Muslims, to express their own senses of Muslim identity, and to participate in dialogue over the terms of that identity with both like and unlike-minded people.

Importantly, observable discussions were not only between Muslims and non-Muslims, but also between Muslims themselves as they strove to debate varying interpretations of Islamic prescription or debate their individual views about Muslims' presence in Britain. *Facebook* Groups thus provide a middle ground of sorts between public discourses about Muslims and the face-to-face, intimate relationships that shape private senses of being Muslim. Thus, the *Facebook* Groups under investigation can be likened to Catherine Squires' (2002) and Nancy Fraser's (1990, 1997) notions of counter or subaltern publics, affording respondents spaces in which their voices, marginalised from the dominant public sphere and mass media, can be exercised and heard by others. Responses regarding the effects that *Facebook* Groups could have in countering negative views of Muslims, however, were varied, ranging from confident and hopeful to pessimistic. Despite that range, the majority of respondents actively and regularly use Groups to either observe or address both benign and more problematic views. It was observed that *Facebook* Groups in particular provide a point around which respondents can gather, debate and discuss the terms of British Muslim identity and representation, as well as participate in collective action as documented through several campaigns.

Through these observations, I argue that the *Facebook* Groups under investigation here may enable a transversing of traditional and imagined boundaries between public and private spheres by embedding civic engagement and political exercises more deeply in everyday life (Bakardjieva 2009: 102); in the ways they function as spaces for talk, deed and interaction which engage members in issues of concern to them and encourage senses of community and belonging through interactions within that space. The ways in which such Groups can provide arenas for the expression, redressing, or reframing of both complementary and conflictual views suggests an agonistic potential which Chantal Mouffe (2005) argues is vital to functioning democratic societies. On a more personal level, such spaces for the articulation of views and ideas resonates with the focus on self-actualisation of both Anthony Giddens' (1991) 'life politics' and, more recently, Häyhtiö and Rinne's notion of 'reflexive politics', which sees individuals as the primary political unit, 'intertwined in many personal ongoing projects that reflect the subjective self-image' of those individuals (2007: 339).

My analysis has been concerned with the expressed use of *Facebook* Groups as gateways to and platforms for British Muslim identity politics. While much of the activities within those Groups is talk-based and can be seen through the lens of 'microactivism' (Marichal 2010), instances were observed in which that talk-based online action translated into offline activism. For example, the *United Shades of Britain* and *Muslim Defence League* Groups drove a coordinated campaign against an *English Defense League* (EDL) protest scheduled to take place in Dudley in April 2010. Through a barrage of posts, repeated emails and the organisation and communication of transportation for interested participants, the Groups were able to participate in a larger effort by *Unite Against Facism* and Dudley's trade councils to organise citizens in protest against the EDL demonstration (Smith 2010).

Another example of the way in which these Groups may be used to orchestrate collective action can be located in the more regular uses to which they are put: as discussion and poster boards upon which can be found links to news stories, services, e-petitions, blogs and other *Facebook* Groups which match the interests of members (or the expressed interest and intentions of the Group itself). Links to news items posted on several of the Groups were observed as tending to focus on anti-Muslim sentiments, government spending, British foreign policy towards the Middle East, and racism or issues of social justice more generally. Similarly, links to blogs and other *Facebook* Groups posted on Group Walls tended to lead to sites which focused on some aspect of Muslim identity or experience in Britain or the wider world, e.g. *London Muslim* blog. There were also links posted to e-petitions in support of various humanitarian concerns like human trafficking or the extradition of falsely-imprisoned Muslims elsewhere, as well as occasional links to Muslim-related services like MAMA (Measuring Anti-Muslim Attacks), a service which reports and maps anti-Muslim attacks in an effort to minimise the continuation of racial and religious hatred.[7]

The uses to which these Groups have been put are indicative of the ways in which the Internet is expanding repertoires of collective action (Van Laer and Van Aelst 2009: 231). Not only have these Groups been used to support more traditional social movement protest actions, like organising and mobilising street protests, but also they have been used to promote online modes of action, like sharing links to e-petitions or generating campaigns for email writing. While these last two examples are typical of Internet adoption into traditional actions and not necessarily indicative of Internet-innovated actions like virtual sit-ins or site hacking, such dependence upon Internet technology for its organisational and communicative capacities suggests ways in which the Internet is contributing to and expanding traditional repertoires of collective action. But it is also providing a space in which modern and postmodern subjectivities may be developed through the expression and exercise of a reflexive, political self-project; participation in these *Facebook* Groups may be seen as part of the making and remaking of the self-image of individuals, now seen as the primary political unit (Häyhtiö and Rinne 2007: 339). These examples demonstrate the ways in which *Facebook* Groups provide spaces in which 'microactivism' (Marichal 2010) can be witnessed, in which aspects of 'subactivism' (Bakardjieva 2009) or the greater meshing of politics and everyday practices and experiences is actualised, and in which services or information relevant to users can be provided (Siapera 2005). They also function as spaces in which issues which are viewed as essential and formative to individuals can be addressed. These instantiations illustrate some of the ways in which these social-networking Groups may be considered political; as spaces for discussion, debate and action concerning the simultaneously personal and political identity-based issues which stand as the focus of many of these Groups.

Notes

1 *MySpace*: founded 2003; users aged 13 and over; 130,000,000 registered users. *LinkedIn*: founded 2003; users aged 18 and over; 80,000,000 r.u. *Bebo*: founded 2005; users aged 13 and older; 117,000,000 r.u. *Facebook*: founded 2004; users aged 13 and over; 800,000,000 r.u. These figures are taken from market research conducted by *Alexa.com* and listed on *Wikipedia*: http://en.wikipedia.org/wiki/List_of_social_networking_websites, last accessed 20 December 2011. *Facebook* member figures have been updated to reflect current statistics available on own website. boyd and Ellison (2007) claim that there is still no reliable data on how many people use SNSs beyond market research, which suggests they are growing in popularity at a rapid rate.
2 danah boyd chooses to 'leave the capitalisation out' of her name and so, with respect to her choice, her name is preserved as such regardless of where used. A fuller explanation of her choice can be found on her website at www.danah.org/name.html.
3 See also Feezell *et al.* (2009) for a description of the Groups feature. At the time of my fieldwork, Groups were unrestricted and the largest Group involved in this project had membership in excess of 13,000 members (*United Shades of Britain*). However, starting in the winter of 2011, *Facebook* began limiting Group membership numbers and requiring collectives with more than five hundred members to form Fan Pages instead.
4 Official *Facebook* statistics are available at www.facebook.com/press/info.php?statistics.
5 The discrepancy between the 2010 figure and the 2013 figure may have to do with *Facebook*'s restructuring of Groups. The restructuring took place after fieldwork concluded and resulted in many Groups disappearing from *Facebook*'s pages. To search for current figures on public *Facebook* Groups via Google, enter 'url: Facebook.com/group.php' into the search window. This technique was cited as most

accurate by the team at *All Facebook* in lieu of any official statistics from *Facebook* itself, but only reflects Groups which have been categorised as 'public' by their creators.

6 Such academic arguments typically reside in literature concerned with anonymous online environments, like multi-user dungeons or chat rooms (Zhao *et al.* 2008). Although Layla imagines other users' abilities to escape their identities through their *Facebook* use, *Facebook* has been called a 'nonymous' environment; one in which online interactions are largely based on offline, anchored relationships (Zhao *et al.* 2008: 1819–1820). As such, identity 'escape' is more difficult. It is important to note, however, that Zhao *et al.*'s (2008) interest in *Facebook* as 'nonymous' relies on the institutional affiliation which was mandatory for *Facebook* membership at the time of their study. That constraint no longer exists as *Facebook* opened membership to any email address in September 2006 (http://newsroom.fb.com/content/default.aspx?newsAreaId=20), though lack of institutional affiliation should not be mistaken for anonymity since users are still required to verify real names and email addresses to establish a profile.

7 'Tell Mama: Measuring Anti Muslim Attacks' (http://tellmamauk.org) is a public service website which measures and monitors anti-Muslim incidents, as well as provides resources, contact links and information for public use. Its stated intention is to collect the diversity of reported attacks to better understand religious prejudice and discrimination in order to better tackle anti-Muslim feelings.

Bibliography

Abbas, T. (2005) 'British South Asian Muslims: State and Multicultural Society', in T. Abbas (ed.) *Muslim Britain: Communities Under Pressure*. London and New York: Zed Books, pp. 3–17.

Anderson, J.W. (2003) 'New Media, New Publics: Reconfiguring the Public Sphere of Islam', *Social Research*, 70(3): 887–906.

Back, L., Keith, M., Khan, A., Shukra, K. and Solomos, J. (2009) 'Islam and the New Political Landscape: Faith Communities, Political Participation and Social Change', *Theory, Culture and Society*, 26(4): 1–23.

Bakardjieva, M. (2009) 'Subactivism: Lifeworld and Politics in the Age of the Internet', *The Information Society: An International Journal*, 25(2): 91–104.

Bennett, W.L. (2004) 'Communicating Global Activism: Strengths and Vulnerabilities of Networked Politics', in W. van de Donk, B.D. Loader, P.G. Nixon and D. Rucht (eds) *Cyberprotest: New Media, Citizens and Social Movements*. London: Routledge, pp. 123–146.

boyd, d. and Ellison, N.B. (2007) 'Social Network Sites: Definition, History and Scholarship', *Journal of Computer-Mediated Communication*, 13(1). Available at: http://jcmc.indiana.edu/vol13/issue1/boyd.ellison.html (accessed 31 November 2011).

Bryman, A. (2004) *Social Research Methods*, 2nd edn. Oxford: Oxford University Press.

Bunt, G.R. (2009) *iMuslims: Rewiring the House of Islam*. London: Hurst & Company.

Christensen, H.S. (2011) 'Political Activities on the Internet: Slacktivism or Political Participation by Other Means?', *First Monday*, 6(2), February.

Feezell, J.T., Conroy, M., and Guerrero, M. (2009) 'Facebook is … Fostering Political Engagement: A Study of Online Social Networking Groups and Offline Participation'. Paper presented at the *American Political Science Association* meeting, Toronto, Canada, September. Available at: http://papers.ssrn.com/sol3/papers.cfm?abstract_id=1451456 (accessed 23 January 2012).

Fraser, N. (1990) 'Rethinking the Public Sphere: A Contribution to the Critique of Actually Existing Democracy', *Social Text*, 25/26: 56–80.
Fraser, N. (1997) *Justice Interruptus: Critical Reflections on the 'Postsocialist' Condition*. New York and London: Routledge.
Giddens, A. (1991) *Modernity and Self-identity*. London: Polity Press.
Häyhtiö, T. and Rinne, J. (2007) 'Hard Rock Hallellujah! Empowering Reflexive Political Action on the Internet', *Journal for Cultural Research*, 11(4): 337–358.
Home Office (2005) 'Preventing Extremism Together: Working Groups', in *Working Together to Prevent Extremism*. London: Home Office.
Howard, P.N., Duffy, A., Freelon, D., Hussain, M., Mari, W. and Mazaid, M. (2011) 'Opening Closed Regimes: What Was the Role of Social Media During the Arab Spring?', Working Paper 2011.1, Project on Information Technology and Political Islam, University of Washington. Available at: http://pitpi.org/index.php/2011/09/11/opening-closed-regimes-what-was-the-role-of-social-media-during-the-arab-spring/ (accessed 21 November 2011).
Joinson, A.N. (2008) 'Looking At, Looking Up or Keeping Up With People? Motives and Uses of Facebook', in *Proceeding of the twenty-sixth annual SIGCHI conference on human factors in computing systems*. New York: ACM Press, pp. 1027–1036. Available at: http://dl.acm.org/citation.cfm?id=1357213 (accessed 4 December 2011).
Kasmer, M., and Xie, B. (2008) 'Qualitative Interviewing in Internet Studies: Playing With the Media, Playing With the Method', *Information, Communication and Society*, 11(2): 257–278.
Kushin, M.J. and Kitchener, K. (2009) 'Getting Political on Social Network Sites: Exploring Online Political Discourse on Facebook', *First Monday*, 14(11), November.
Lampe, C., Ellison, N. and Steinfield, C. (2006) 'A Face(book) in the crowd: Social Searching Vs. Social Browsing', in *Proceedings of 2006 20th Anniversary Conference on Computer Supporter Cooperative Work*. New York: ACM Press, pp. 167–170. Available at: http://dl.acm.org/citation.cfm?id=1180901 (accessed 4 December 2011).
Lewis, P. (2002) *Islamic Britain: Religion, Politics and Identity Among British Muslims*. New York: I.B. Tauris & Co.
Lewis, P. (2007) *Young, British and Muslim*. London: Continuum.
Mandaville, P. (2001) *Transnational Muslim Politics: Reimagining the Umma*. New York: Routledge.
Marichal, J. (2010) 'Political Facebook Groups: Micro-Activism and the Digital Front Stage'. Paper given at the Internet, Politics, Policy 2010: An Impact Assessment conference, University of Oxford, September. Available at: http://microsites.oii.ox.ac.uk/ipp2010/programme/115 (accessed 26 January 2012).
Marsh, D., O'Toole, T. and Jones, S. (2007) *Young People and Politics in the UK: Apathy or Alienation?* Basingstoke: Palgrave Macmillan.
Michael, L. (2012) 'Frames, Forums and Facebook: Interpreting British Muslim Understandings of Post-7/7 Militarist Media Narratives', in A. Karatzogianni (ed.) *Violence and War in Culture and the Media: Five Disciplinary Lenses*. London: Routledge, pp. 148–162.
Modood, T. (2005) *Multicultural Politics: Racism, Ethnicity and Muslims in Britain*. Minneapolis, MN: University of Minnesota Press.
Morrell, G., Scott, S., McNeish, D. and Webster, S. (2011) 'The August Riots in England: Understanding the Involvement of Young People'. A Report prepared for the Cabinet Office by the National Centre for Social Research. Available at: www.ca

binetoffice.gov.uk/sites/default/files/resources/The%20August%20Riots%20in%20 England%20%28pdf,%201mb%29.pdf (accessed 7 November 2011).
Mouffe, C. (2005) *On the Political*. Abingdon: Routledge.
Norris, P. (2002) 'The Bridging and Bonding Role of Online Communities', *The Harvard International Journal of Press/Politics*, 7(3): 3–13.
O'Neill, N. (2010) 'Google Now Indexes 620 Million Facebook Groups', *AllFacebook. com*, available at: www.allFacebook.com/google-now-indexes-620-million-Facebook-groups-2010-02 (accessed 12 January 2012).
O'Toole, T. (2003) 'Engaging With Young People's Conceptions of the Political', *Children's Geographies*, 1: 71–90.
O'Toole, T. and Gale, R. (2009) 'Young People and Faith Activism: British Muslim Youth, Glocalisation and the Umma', in A. Dinham, R. Furbey and V. Lowndes (eds) *Faith in the Public Realm: Controversies, policies and practices*. Bristol: Policy Press, pp. 143–162.
O'Toole, T. and Gale, R. (2010) 'Contemporary Grammars of Political Action Among Ethnic Minority Young Activists', *Ethnic and Racial Studies*, 33(1): 126–143.
O'Toole, T. and Gale, R. (2011) 'Grammars of Political Action Among Urban Muslim Youth', in M. Micheletti and A.S. McFarland (eds) *Creative Participation: Responsibility-taking in the Political World*. Boulder, CO and London: Paradigm Publishers, pp. 67–81.
Papacharissi, Z. (2009) 'The Virtual Geographies of Social Networks: A Comparative Analysis of Facebook, LinkedIn and ASmallWorld', *New Media Society*, 11: 199–220.
Piela, A. (2010) 'Muslim Women's Online Discussions of Gender Relations in Islam', *Journal of Muslim Minority Affairs*, 30(3): 425–435.
Poster, M. (1997) 'Cyberdemocracy: The Internet and the Public Sphere', in D. Holmes (ed.) *Virtual Politics: Identity and Community in Cyberspace*. London: Sage Publications, pp. 212–211.
Sands, K.Z. (2010) 'Muslims, Identity and Multimodal Communication on the Internet', *Contemporary Islam*, 4: 139–155.
Siapera, E. (2005) 'Minority Activism on the Web: Between Deliberative Democracy and Multiculturalism', *Journal of Ethnic and Migration Studies*, 32(3): 499–519.
Smith, V. (2010) 'Vibrant and Defiant Protest Against EDL in Dudley', *Socialist Worker Online*, available at: http://socialistworker.co.uk/art.php?id=20841 (accessed 16 February 2012).
Squires, C. (2002) 'Rethinking the Black Public Sphere: An Alternative Vocabulary for Multiple Public Sphere', *Communication Theory*, 12(4) (November): 446–468.
Tapscott, D. (2009) *Grown Up Digital: How the Net Generation is Changing Your World*. New York: McGraw-Hill.
Van Laer, J. and Van Aelst, P. (2009) 'Cyber-protest and Civil Society: The Internet and Action Repertoires in Social Movements', in Y. Jewkes and M. Yar (eds) *Handbook on Internet Crime*. Portland, OR: Willan Publishing, pp. 230–254.
Zhao, S. (2006) 'The Internet and the Transformation of the Reality of Everyday Life: Towards a New Analytic Stance in Sociology', *Sociological Inquiry*, 76(4): 458–474.
Zhao, S., Grasmuch, S. and Martin, J. (2008) 'Identity Construction on Facebook: Digital Empowerment in Anchored Relationships', *Computers in Human Behavior*, 24(5): 1816–1836.

9 From crisis to opportunity – 9/11 and the progress of British Muslim political engagement

Khadijah Elshayyal

Introduction

The attacks of September 11th 2001 had a profound and lasting impact on British political life, most pertinently in relation to Britain's Muslim communities. Rapid alterations took place in the global and domestic arenas in reaction to the terrorist attacks of September 11th. The 'war on terror' launched by the USA and her allies was to dramatically change international politics. In the UK, the need for securitisation presented urgent challenges for both the government and Muslim community organisations. The government felt the pressing need to act immediately against the threat of modern terrorism, and Muslim organisations were thrown into the task of denouncing it, while at the same time defending their communities against the hostility of a racist backlash, and engaging with the government on both domestic and international issues of concern. In this chapter, I look at how the period 2001–2005 proved to be a watershed for the development of British Muslim identity politics, arguing that despite the immense pressures, tangible progress was made particularly by younger generations in British Muslim community organising.

This period is characterised by a sharp increase in the level of Muslim political agency and the intensity of community organising. Much of this increase came about as a direct response to the rapid alterations which were taking place in the global and national arenas in reaction to the 9/11 attacks. The introduction of new anti-terror laws and the style, discourse and thinking behind the resulting 'war on terror' provoked concerns in many quarters about silencing, restricting and/or channelling of expression and dissent.

These presented Muslim community representatives and the government with fresh challenges that resulted in a defining moment in their relationship, leading to a somewhat cool and more cautious attitude between them. At the same time, there was an essentially reactive drive among Muslims to state clearly their positions on matters which they felt they were being misunderstood and seriously misjudged on – including the denouncement of terrorism and violence, issues of loyalty and citizenship, and the notion of separate cultures and the irreconcilability of Islam with western democracy – often characterised as a 'clash of civilisations' (Huntington 1996). The latter concept, as I will show later on in this chapter, became increasingly utilised as a tool by the far-right and others to justify an emergent 'clean-faced', pseudo-respectable form of Islamophobia.

This period saw a growth in second and third generation Muslim involvement within broad-based social and political coalitions (such as the anti-war movement), as well as the emergence and development of various new and more creative modes of Muslim self-expression to join pre-existing ones. It also witnessed a refreshed, more nuanced approach to reasoning that was used by Muslims to argue for their causes in the public-political domain, in particular the old issue of a legal response to religious discrimination and incitement to religious hatred.

I will first outline notable aspects of British Muslim political consciousness in the few years prior to the attacks of 9/11. This will help me to draw out exactly how this juncture represents a turning point and the role that freedom of expression and civil liberties played in these changes. I will look at the reactions to 9/11 across government and Muslim advocacy groups and then discuss the changes that took place during the four years between 9/11 and the summer of 2005 under four main headings: new security legislation and the language of securitisation, relations between the government and the Muslim Council of Britain (MCB), developments in the far-right and Islamophobia, and innovation in self-expression among young British Muslims. I will analyse what the various developments under each of these four themes meant for Muslim groups, and also what they meant for the government's relations with them as well as British Muslim political consciousness in general. This analysis will include a consideration of the policy developments related to each of these respective themes.

British Islam at the turn of the millennium

In the years running up to the new millennium, British Muslim public and political life was developing to become both outgoing and highly confident. The intense efforts at institution building that took place during the 1990s paid off by creating a generation of young, politically conscious and religiously committed British Muslims who viewed their Islamic identity and its primacy in their lives not only as something to protect and preserve, but also to positively promote.

As I have discussed elsewhere (Elshayyal 2013), religio-political activism in the wake of the Rushdie affair (1988/9) had attracted the interest and subsequently, consolidated the influence of Islamic movements from around the Muslim world on the Muslim communities of the UK. One impact of this was that young British Muslims found that they now had easier access to a whole range of different political interests and perspectives – each was keen to widen its sphere of influence as far as possible. For many young Muslims in this generation there was something of a collective discovery that their

'Muslim identity' could be represented by a whole range of different political interests and perspectives. Youth and student groups, spurred on by this growing 'Muslim-consciousness' (Meer 2010), vied with one another to win a following amongst the second and third generations who had grown up without the kinds of psychological and practical struggles that their parents had faced. Whereas the newly arrived first generation had been preoccupied with laying down foundations for their families' basic needs, their children enjoyed a far greater degree of confidence and capability to assert what was distinctive about their own identities rather than trying hard to blend in with wider society.

The new 'primarily Muslim' religious identity that had been fostered by the events of the Rushdie affair was carried with pride by many of the community's young people. Visible manifestations of this included a steady increase in those who preferred to wear traditional religious or cultural dress. While such a development is clearly difficult to measure since no statistics directly measuring such a fluid aspect of individual choice as clothing can be obtained, anecdotal evidence sourced from articles and accounts written about this period are useful in giving an idea of how much the 1990s were a period of religious discovery and self-assertion for young British Muslims.[1] And while the socio-economic status of many Muslim communities remained relatively low, significant numbers of young Muslims had nonetheless enjoyed access to good education, often better than that of their parents. Their entry into universities and the professions injected greater levels of confidence within their communities, not to mention diversity of opinion, aptitude and expertise.

Strides had been made in political representation too, and the number of Muslims entering local politics was on the increase. While the statistics for Muslims in local politics can only be approximated from more general statistics on race and ethnicity in the field, they are definitely indicative of a steady, if limited, rise during this period (Anwar 2005), although as Hussain (2004) notes, this was largely due to individual endeavours rather than group participation or mass-organising. Indeed, where there were attempts at group participation in politics, such as the Islamic Party of Britain[2] and the Muslim Parliament, results were poor and projects were short-lived and limited in their reach.

In terms of public self-image, and how Muslim communities saw themselves reflected in the mainstream, it was not uncommon to find a deep suspicion and mistrust of the portrayal of Islam and Muslims in the media ingrained in the collective psyche of many in the Muslim community. A large part of this can be put down to memories of the Rushdie affair, which were still fresh (Elshayyal 2013), but also goes back much further in the past.[3] Both print and broadcast media were frequently portrayed as a form of enemy, who had ulterior vested interests in projecting a negative image of the Muslim community to their wider audiences. Such an understanding fed neatly into a polarised postcolonial perspective of 'The West versus Islam' which featured Islam and Muslims as downtrodden and mistreated by an exploitative, and godless, anti-Islamic 'West' (Akhtar 1989).

Small- to medium-scale community organising and ad hoc official representation among Britain's Muslims dates back at least to the late 19th and early 20th centuries (Halliday 2010; Ansari 2004; Lawless 1995). However, it was the Rushdie affair which really ignited concerted efforts to centrally organise and coordinate the various Muslim communities that had made their home across the UK. Yet even then, the role of coordination was claimed by more than one body, sometimes with competing or conflicting approaches – partly due to differences in personalities, traditions, as well as the practical (yet significant) consideration of different sources of foreign funding (Malik 2009: 123).

By the mid-1990s progress had been made in streamlining representation efforts by the National Interim Council for Muslim Unity (NICMU) which sought to lay the foundations for a body that could fulfil both a unifying and a representative role for the vast multitude of groups and interests of British Muslims. This concept was encouraged by successive governments (Ansari 2004: 364), who envisaged future coordination with Muslim representatives to follow a similar format to its relations with the well established Board of Deputies of British Jews.

In 1997, the MCB was born as a culmination of the NICMU's work, and soon enjoyed public endorsement from the Blair government. Up until 2001, its relationship with the government was cordial and cooperative, with ministers regularly attending its events and key campaigns making tangible headway (Sherif 2011). By September 2001, the MCB had reached the unique position among Muslim organisations in the UK of bringing together a broad spectrum of affiliate groups – in terms of geographical location, cultural backgrounds and theological perspectives. Despite its own more ambitious claims, it nonetheless could only represent its members who constituted the small percentage of Britain's wider Muslim population who were involved in any local, regional or national organisation. Still, the breadth and depth of its reach was as yet unrivalled by any other Muslim representative group, and so by the end of the 20th century, the MCB had become *the* port of call for anyone from the government, media and policy sectors who wished to engage with British Muslims on an official level. For this reason, in the second section of this chapter and beyond, I will use the MCB as my starting point when considering the official Muslim response to 9/11. By the end of the chapter, I will have demonstrated how the landscape of British Muslim representation changed and diversified remarkably during the period under discussion, not least in the number of new initiatives to speak for and represent British Muslims, many of which had been spearheaded by the younger generations.

By the turn of the millennium, Britain was sheltering a whole host of different political refugees from the Muslim world, who were attracting followers from among the country's own Muslim population. For better or for worse, the UK's perceived leniency when it came to allowances for political asylum seekers made it a popular destination for those Islamic political activists who were exiles or fugitives from oppressive regimes in their home countries. Many would cite the UK's scope for freedom of expression as well as its historic reputation for sheltering 'foreign dissidents, from Karl Marx to Victor Hugo'.[4] The UK's position as a 'destination of choice' was no doubt enhanced by its geography. In terms of distance, it easier to travel to from their home countries in the Muslim world (as compared with North America for instance), the UK also had the benefit of easier access to mainland Europe, as well as the fact that the English language itself is widely spoken as a second language. In addition, Britain's imperial past may well have fed into a sense of entitlement among political agitators seeking asylum, insofar as their utilising the UK as a haven amounted to 'taking back' from a former empire which had previously exploited and dominated their homelands.

The influence of international political dissidents was not limited to those who were resident in the UK – leading personalities from a spectrum of Islamist movements operating abroad were regularly hosted to speak at events in the UK. Such gatherings were used not only to spread their ideas and drum up support in the UK, but also to fundraise for these political movements.[5] Hailing from countries such as Algeria, Bangladesh, Egypt, the Sudan, Pakistan and Syria, the UK provided opportunities for speeches and fundraising activities that were rather more difficult for these movements to arrange within those home countries that were the objects of their struggles.

International events such as the first Gulf War (Iraq's invasion of Kuwait in 1990, and the subsequent US invasion of Iraq) and later the conflict in the former Yugoslavia and the tragic events in Bosnia, all served to rally together a sense of communal or 'associational' identity (Modood 1997), especially among Muslim youth. Somewhat linked to this was the display by many Muslim organisations in their discourse and activities of a confident (perhaps overconfident) and unguarded sense of openness that was raw, fresh and even acutely naïve in its choice of language and emphasis. Among the mainstream groups within the community there was sometimes a sense of pride taken in harbouring the desire to bring Islamic rule to the UK. In the main part, it was hoped to achieve such ambitions through peaceful *da'wa* (the evangelical call to Islam), however there was some talk among the most extreme of more violent means, although how seriously such talk was intended is a matter of debate, which I will come to shortly.

More moderate thinkers within this strain spoke of a Britain that was 'in search of a vision and a direction' and to which its Muslim citizens bore the responsibility of offering guidance.[6] On this basis, they emphasised the importance of civic participation. However, this was often accompanied with the qualification that responsible citizenship would further the cause of *da'wa*, and that community service was a means through which Islamically inspired social values could be disseminated through to wider society. By highlighting this aspect, I am not suggesting that this attitude towards social participation was inherently disingenuous or insidious; however, it is telling that these sorts of justifications were so readily used. As I shall demonstrate later on in this chapter, the experience of building broad political partnerships post-9/11 catalysed a change in approaches to civic participation, such that it became more open, more pragmatic and less conditional upon religiously-grounded caveats and justifications.

On the more extreme end of the scale, the British arm of Hizb ut Tahrir (HT), an Islamic political party with its roots in the Middle East, provides one window into perspectives among radical Muslims during this period (Elshayyal 2013). During the 1990s its activities regularly grabbed the headlines for their dramatic and confrontational nature (Hamid 2007). HT provoked anxiety and outrage in equal measures as it called for the 'supremacy' of Islam and preaching separatism to its followers, in addition to indulging regularly in antisemitism and clashes with gay and Jewish groups on university campuses. Probably its most highly publicised activity during this period was an international 'Khilafa Conference' that was organised in August 1994 at the Wembley Arena in London. The event courted plenty of controversy before it even happened. Bright, luminous publicity stickers were posted in high streets and public places, boasting of: 'Khilafa – coming soon, to a country near you' (Husain 2007: 134–138, *Q News* 12th August 1994). Invited speakers included individuals who were linked with the organisation from various Arab and Muslim countries. The conference organisers spoke of bold ambitions to 'fly the flag of Islam above Number 10 Downing Street' and there was even a call for the assassination of Prime Minister John Major from the leader of HT (Hamid 2007: 145). However although organisers anticipated 8–10,000 attendees and an enthusiastic reception (*The Guardian* and *The Independent* 4th August 1994), the conference did not meet these expectations, with a much more modest audience turning up and barely any tangible impact beyond the few alarmist newspaper headlines that were generated. The comparison of HT-type views with those that were expressed in more moderate, mainstream settings is stark. Yet in many instances, they both relied to some degree on the notion of Islamic religious and cultural primacy, juxtaposing it with some notion of western decadence.

As a final example, I will look at a case among groups with more *salafi* (literalist) and *jihadi* leanings.[7] Jonathan Birt (2009: 107–109) sheds light on a mood of isolationism in which self-identification was constituted in opposition not only to 'the West', but also their own communities, both locally and as an *ummah*. All of these groups were seen to be misguided in various ways – whether through godlessness, or through 'associating with' or 'following' the godless West. Central to this way of thinking was the notion of '*al wala wal bara*'; a concept with roots in early Islamic thought which roughly translates as 'loyalty and disassociation'. Many *salafis* and *jihadists* would use this as a mantra to justify an exclusivist and self-righteous world view whereby their own remaining on the 'straight and narrow' was inextricably linked with a vehement denouncement of those around them for their misguidance – whether wilful or erroneous. So at a meeting of a typical *jihadi* study-group, Birt reports of a mentor urging attendees to 'cut your ties from the people of *shirk* (polytheism), because you can't cut your ties from *shirk* except that you cut your ties from the people of *shirk*'. He then goes on to elaborate on the grave differences between 'believers' and *kuffar* (unbelievers), including the direct link, as he sees it, between faith and an obligation of *jihad*; in addition to emphasising the 'need' for true Muslims to migrate to the Muslim world, to *dar al Islam* and away from *dar al kufr*,[8] since doing so was an appropriate and necessary demonstration of their loyalty to the faith and their disassociation from disbelief and decadence.

The language and approach that was used by these types of groups is chilling and would certainly raise alarm bells in today's securitised post-9/11 Britain. Talk of an obligation of *jihad* and of disassociation from non-believers would hardly be permitted to take place openly in mosques, nor would these sorts of conversations happen in open gatherings that members of the public could freely join. When considered with the benefit of hindsight acquired over the past decade, this sort of approach may well give impressions of an aggressive or threatening desire to violently dominate Britain and impose Islamic ideals on culture, politics and society in general. However, it is important to resist forming an instant teleological judgement of these groups and to consider the period and context in question. As Birt (2009) and Ronson (2007) point out, the mainstream of the Muslim community rarely took such groups seriously and preferred instead to ignore or sideline them. For many, (Muslims and non Muslims), these types of characters were nothing more than 'affable fools' (Hamid 2007: 148), rather than an urgent threat. At the same time, these groups in actuality had very little to hide – in essence many of them were talk-shops; gathering together disgruntled Muslim youth who faced common grievances or who were dealing with similar challenges in life. Often these included day-to-day issues such as difficulties in education or finding work, providing for their families or simply 'fitting in' with their peers. Overlapping with or running alongside these were the challenges of practising their faith, reconciling their Britishness with their cultures of origin and dealing with experiences (whether real or perceived) of discrimination and injustice – such as Islamophobia or cases of unequal legal treatment, as well as frustration at aspects of British foreign policy that were interpreted as being anti-Islamic.

In summary, the young British Muslim 'scene' by the turn of the 21st century was one of increasing diversity, confidence and growing sophistication in the nature and style of its political participation. However, many within the Muslim communities retained a strong element of naïveté regarding the true nature and meaning of citizenship and civic participation.

Muslims, civil liberties and securitisation in a post-9/11 Britain

9/11 has come to be seen as a historic watershed moment in so many different respects, the world over; but extremely acutely so for the Muslim communities of western countries. British Muslims are a case in point, and the 'before' and 'after' comparisons that can be made are innumerable. From the outset, a deep sensitivity was attached to the attacks – both as a reaction to their very happening, and in response to the association (whether covert or explicit) that was widely made between them and the Muslim faith. I will look at how this turning point came about in each of three areas: government, Muslim representative organisations and Muslim 'grass roots' – meaning 'ordinary' Muslim individuals and smaller/local groupings. I will then discuss the impact of the changes in discourse and communication that were precipitated by the events of 9/11 under four main categories: Islamophobia, security, government–community relations and innovation in self-expression within British Muslim communities.

For the government, the most immediate and pressing concern was naturally that of national security. The attacks were of such a large and unprecedented magnitude, that an immediate response was called for, and considering that the motives[9] for the attacks were traced back to international Muslim terror networks, the potential threat to British national security was clear and pressing. At the same time, the fact that the link was with *Muslim* terror networks meant that government had to deal with the impact of the attacks on community relations, and most specifically, to minimise the impacts of the backlash against Britain's Muslims through the racism, discrimination, or 'revenge attacks' that took place across the country (MCB 2002a: 29–37; FAIR 2005),[10] to reassure Britain's Muslims by emphasising unity, shared values and especially a shared abhorrence of terrorism, violence and victimisation.[11]

In addition to an introduction of anti-terrorism legislation, Blair's Labour government advanced decisive policies at home and abroad to ensure that it was seen to be in control in dealing with the new terror threat. These included a more hard-line approach in matters of immigration – for instance through the introduction of compulsory citizenship tests. This attitude was also manifested in foreign policy, emphasising Britain's 'special relationship' with the USA and the shared interest in combating international terrorism – both through increased security measures as well as going to war in Afghanistan.

Government-MCB relations

On the home front, the government took steps to indicate its commitment to containing and minimising the terrorist threat, and significantly, stability and cohesion within and among the country's communities, in particular with regard to Britain's Muslims (Blair 2001a, 2001b). Meeting with MCB representatives, Blair declared that racism and revenge-type attacks on Muslims 'have no proper place in our country' and similarly, remarked upon the shared heritage between Islam and Christianity, in an effort to inject positivity into a mood that was weighed down by feelings of anger, suspicion and vulnerability.[12]

Together, these remarks represent an affirmative drive on the government's part to speak to Muslims in the UK, and also internationally. However, when considered alongside the evermore stringent and heavy handed legal strand of the Government's post-9/11 response, it is difficult not to suspect that the associated motives must have contained some element of instrumentalism.

Perhaps it was thought that the ongoing introduction of restrictive and highly controversial anti-terror laws coupled with the pursuit of an unpopular foreign policy approach could be sweetened with efforts to reassure British Muslims and underline their (at least nominal) inclusion in the evolving national conversation on security, citizenship and cohesion.

As for Muslim organisations, there was a near-unanimous immediate reaction of swift and unequivocal condemnation.[13] Press releases and a dense, consistent flow of media writings and appearances were the hallmark efforts of all Muslim advocacy groups and representatives, most notably the MCB. On a community level, positive responses to 9/11 were developed. For example, the annual Islam Awareness Week for November 2001 had as its theme 'Islam for Peace and Justice' and held events across the country with the aim of dispelling the abundant tabloid myths of an inherently violent Islam as well as tackling questions on the nature of a just and commensurate response to the attacks.[14]

The War on Terror was overwhelmingly opposed by British Muslims. But many young people were uneasy with the slow pace with which the MCB's position on this developed (Abbas 2005). Instead, many young Muslims engaged with grassroots community groups, for instance, the Muslim Association of Britain, which subsequently joined the newly-formed Stop the War Coalition (StWC), as did a number of other local and regional Muslim groups (Birt 2005).

The rising far-right and religious hatred legislation

Another noteworthy change which came about during this period was a renewed and highly focused bout of activity from the Islamophobic far-right. Racists and the far-right were able to play on genuine fears and paranoia in the wake of 9/11, and build up hostility that was directed squarely at Islam and Muslims in the UK. The British National Party (BNP) launched a 'Campaign Against Islam' (Goodwin 2010a),[15] focusing its efforts particularly in areas of the country which housed large Muslim communities. On the back of recent race riots that had taken place in the Northern towns of Burnley and Oldham during the summer of 2001, coupled with the fallout from 9/11, these campaigns made use of a number of widespread stereotypes regarding violence, intolerance and the subjugation of women, among others, and sought to warn the public of the perils of the impending 'Islamification' of Britain, and the need to stop it in its tracks.

Chris Allen has demonstrated how the arguments employed in the party's literature and campaign material were built on remarkably shaky and highly skewed foundations (Allen 2005). Indeed, judging by the sheer incredulity of the numerous implausible accusations that were made, it seems that the BNP was intent on transferring the blame for each and every social ill or irritation that the 'indigenous Anglo-Saxon white working classes'[16] suffered from, onto the shoulders of Britain's Muslims. Campaign leaflets distributed by the BNP during this period depicted Islam as an acronym: ISLAM = Intolerance, Slaughter, Looting, Arson, Molestation of Women, reinforcing the message that the faith itself was centrally linked to despicable social ills and criminality (Allen 2010). Although politicians and public figures of every shade did denounce and distance themselves from this bold new trend in the far-right political agenda (*The Guardian* 17th July 2004), much of it remained technically legal, and this reality highlighted anew the old problem of how to deal with prejudice and discrimination when it was targeted at groups that were identified by their religion, or where, as Kay Goodall (2007) describes it, 'religion is used as a surrogate for racism'.

While the BNP's anti-Islam campaign was ongoing, activity was stepped up during election time, and targeted areas with large Muslim populations and where segregation was a problem. The language that was used exploited a gap in anti-discrimination legislation which at that point (the council elections in 2002, European, London Mayoral and council elections in 2004 and the General Election in 2005) did not yet outlaw incitement to hatred on the basis of religion. Publicity material – both printed and online – was careful to criticise Islam and Muslims as a religion, and culture, rather than in a racial way (Goodall 2007: 93–4).[17] It also defined the party as defending Britain's 'heritage', its 'Christian values' and guarding against their dilution – partly through immigration and partly through its incorporation of immigrants (in particular Muslims) into society through access to resources. Another tactic employed by the BNP was to showcase its 'ethnic' membership, in a bid to shake off its racist image, while simultaneously attack Islam and Muslims. This included featuring a turban-wearing Sikh man in its 2004 election broadcast and fielding Jewish and mixed-race candidates (Goodwin 2010b).[18]

This new wave of open Islamophobia generated renewed debates on whether the existence of this loophole in equalities legislation could continue to be justified. It also prompted discussions on the arguably fine line between calls for the criminalisation of incitement to religious hatred, and instituting what could be construed as a new form of blasphemy law whereby criticism of any religion or its texts could be penalised, and free speech restricted as a result (Goodall 2007). Lobbying from the MCB (2002b) and other Muslim bodies (FAIR 2002)[19] emphasised the impacts of religious hatred, and was bolstered by recommendations that had been made throughout this period from organisations such as the Runnymede Trust's Commission on British Muslims and Islamophobia – which published in 2004 a report to review and discuss progress and developments since its previous (1997) ground-breaking report on Islamophobia (CBMI 2004: 75). The 2004 report made specific recommendations for a whole range of government departments to adopt as a way of tackling Islamophobia. Importantly, it made detailed recommendations regarding the need to 'make discrimination on religious grounds unlawful', noting that while EU laws had brought this about in the area of employment, 'the government's continuing failure to deal robustly (on all levels) with this matter remains a matter of great concern' (CBMI 2004).

The government made several attempts to pass a law during this period dealing with religious hatred, but these were regularly opposed and voted out by the House of Lords. Nonetheless, a Select Committee was set up to look into the matter and by the 2005 General Election, the government made a firm manifesto commitment that it would: 'give people of all faiths the same protection against incitement to hatred on the basis of their religion. We will legislate to outlaw it and will continue the dialogue we have started with faith groups from all backgrounds about how best to balance protection, tolerance and free speech' (Labour Party 2005: 111–112). A law was eventually passed in 2006, and although this falls just outside of the time-frame under consideration in this chapter, I shall discuss it briefly, since its enactment can be attributed in a large part to the post-9/11 discussions that took place on the matter.

The Racial and Religious Hatred Act 2006 weathered significant resistance and controversy from diverse quarters. Outside of parliament, a host of actors, comedians, writers and artists opposed the law, seeing it as a threat to freedom of expression and artistic freedoms, including the space to be able to laugh at religion, religious dogma and establishment. The civil liberties group, Liberty, while acknowledging the need to protect minority groups, argued that freedom of speech was a value far more worthy of preservation. Moreover, it argued (along with the Discrimination Law Association, and many others) that the legislation, as proposed by the government, was not much more than an effort to 'placate' Muslims communities, in particular the MCB, who were aggrieved by foreign policy and relentless draconian anti-terrorism measures at home (Meer 2010: 163–4). Within parliament there was a large voting rebellion by Labour backbenchers and strong opposition from the Conservatives, Liberal Democrats and many in the House of Lords. As a consequence, the final piece of legislation was passed with two amendments introduced by the Lords. These changes stipulated that the law should only criminalise 'A person who uses threatening words or behaviour, or displays any written material which is threatening... if he intends thereby to stir up religious hatred' (HM Government 2006: Part 3A), thus limiting its application so that it could not cover words that were 'merely' abusive or insulting; in addition to making it a requirement for there to be an actual intention to stir up hatred, rather than simply a possibility.

It was this last requirement of intent that proved to disappoint supporters of the law. With the requirement of intent clearly stipulated, it meant that in cases where defendants denied intent, prosecutors would be faced with the almost impossible task of proving it. This, as Goodall (2007: 113) points out, renders the new legislation 'almost unenforceable', since while 'extremist clerics who confess their intentions may be caught ... racist activists will have little trouble adapting their rhetoric' to avoid falling foul of the intent clause. The MCB expressed its dismay at this development, arguing that it had now created 'a hierarchy of rights among British citizens' (MCB 1st February 2006).

The government's clear and firm intention by 2005 to pass a law on religious hatred, despite the fierce controversy that it drew, represents how much had changed during this period in its policy relations with the Muslim community. Back in 1997, Home Secretary Jack Straw had been unwilling to consider any such legislation (*The Daily Telegraph* 23rd October 1997), yet by 2005 his party was on its third attempt to pass religious hatred legislation and was prepared to suffer extensive criticism *and* one of its most humiliating Commons defeats, in order to have it enacted. When considered in context, this new commitment must have been prompted by factors that were not present in 1997 – and, as was suggested at the time by the government's critics in parliament, a desire to appease otherwise disgruntled Muslim communities seems a convincing explanation (Goodall 2007: 91). Nonetheless, it also represents progress in the maturing government-community political conversation, as the lobbying by the MCB and Muslim pressure groups was lodged squarely in the language of equalities legislation (FAIR 2002 and MCB 2005) and all but discarded entirely the argument from blasphemy that was so often rehearsed during and after the Rushdie affair. As such, the MCB was able to confidently present its case alongside other interest-groups, as their support for the law shared common foundations. For example, in January 2005 it held a meeting at the House of Commons jointly with the Commission for Racial Equality, the British Humanist Association and Justice on 'The Need to Protect Faith Communities from Incitement to Hatred' (MCB 2005).

In addition to the developments in the area of religious discrimination, another reaction to the rise of the far-right was in the field of immigration and the integration of immigrants and minority groups. As I have mentioned, the main parties were regularly at pains to denounce and isolate the BNP. However, the BNP's very act of raising such issues, coupled with the constant (often media-fuelled) public concerns around security (Richardson 2010), meant that the main political players were forced to tackle them in their own political agendas – if only as a matter of political expediency, to retain voters who were being attracted to the BNP, and to allay public fears regarding immigration and security (Eatwell 2010: 213–220). What this meant was that while there was a politics of reconciliation towards minorities in matters relating to tackling discrimination and racism, there was on the other hand a growth in 'tough talk' on immigration – especially so when it came to immigrants from outside the European Union.

In real terms, this trend impacted on Muslim communities more strongly than other minority communities. Legislation tightening the conditions required for immigrants to obtain citizenship called for applicants to learn to speak English to a minimum standard and to pass a test on 'Life in the UK'. Other legislation made seeking asylum a far more rigorous process, making detention and deportation very real outcomes of asylum seeking attempts for those who could not provide watertight evidence to support their cases.

Proactive self-expression – through politics, civil society and creativity

A final development worth noting is the growth of momentum in the field of diverse and creative forms of expression within Britain's Muslim communities during this period. I have already discussed the significant political leap that was taken by several Muslim groups by entering into partnerships with left wing organisations to voice their opposition to the war. It is arguable that this move was made more out of circumstance than any preferred choice, since it came about only after the MCB failed to move swiftly and decisively in leading a Muslim opposition to the war. Nonetheless, as pragmatic a deal as it was, it was entered into wholeheartedly, and this move in itself represented a capacity among young British Muslims to explore new avenues for self-expression and making themselves heard (Phillips 2008). At the start of this chapter, I observed how British Islam of the 1990s was somewhat hindered in its reach and its progress by an underdeveloped sense of citizenship, and a rather overrated sense of self-mission. By the early 2000s, this mindset was changing at a steadily growing pace.

The Muslim Association of Britain (MAB) had positioned itself as a key partner in the British anti-war movement, playing a central role in organising for the epic demonstration of February 2003 that took place on the eve of the invasion of Iraq. Its alliance with the left was not without criticism – both from more extreme Muslim groups such as HT, and the liberal, pro-war left (Cohen 2007; Anthony 2007). However, the support it enjoyed was widespread, and the partnership provided invaluable learning experiences and networking opportunities for Muslim anti-war activists and groups. For example, this intensive participation in mainstream political movements paved the way for Muslim anti-war personalities standing as candidates for the recently formed Respect Party during the 2004 European, council and London mayoral elections (Peace 2013). These included Anas Altikriti, himself a former President of the MAB, and Salma Yaqoob who cut her political teeth as a founder and leader of the StWC in Birmingham in 2001, as well as Yvonne Ridley, a former *Sunday Express* reporter who had been held captive by the Taliban and subsequently converted to Islam. The experience of working with the Left served to broaden the political experience of many within the Muslim community, in addition to accelerating the pace at which their level of mainstream political engagement intensified.

The burgeoning of Muslim self-expression was not limited to politics and foreign affairs. This period also witnessed a growth in Muslim press and media. *Q News* – originally founded in the early 1990s as a Muslim community newspaper with local preoccupations and a limited circulation, had reinvented itself as a glossy magazine. Post-9/11 Britain was an optimal environment within which it could flourish – and it did, with impressive (albeit irregular) issues covering wide-ranging, topical and controversial subjects.[20] *The Muslim Paper, The Muslim Weekly* and the *London Muslim* were altogether new newspaper initiatives born during this period, each devoting large sections of their publications to politics and Muslim identity issues – yet also making space for art, culture, sport and finance. The year 2003 saw the launch of *emel*, a Muslim lifestyle magazine which sought to provide an upbeat yet honest perspective into British Islam by providing 'a window into the Muslim community away from the clichés' (Wavell 2005). In the area of new media, websites and blogs grew at a phenomenal rate, being used especially by younger Muslims to express themselves and make connections and networks in ways that weren't possible before. Some are worth particular mention due to their longevity and continuous development since this period, proving their utility of purpose and relevance. These include www.salaam.co.uk – which was devoted to documenting wide-ranging information and data on British Muslim history as well as providing magazine-type features and directories of services, mosques and jobs; and www.deenport.com, a multi-faceted internet portal bringing together discussion forums, blogs, articles and artwork. Both of these sites were first set up in 2003 and have served as a point of expression, conversation and information on British Muslim communities for the individuals who run them as well as their users.

On the more creative side, this period also witnessed a bolder proliferation and experimentation with traditional *nasheeds*.[21] A notable example is the release in 2003 of the British artist Sami Yusuf's first album. Yusuf's songs blended authentic English with authentic Arabic, eastern music with western, and importantly, shifted away from the direct religious preaching-style which had traditionally been the norm. Instead, he offered a blend of spirituality and social justice themes, a style which proved accessible and appealing to a very wide audience. The idea of a young, indigenous British Muslim identity that was comfortable with its heritage and history as well as confident about its future was also something that Yusuf was keen to promote. To quote him:

> I feel as though (my fans) see me as representing them, not Osama Bin Laden ... A lot of young guys are going through an identity crisis and I think that's where people like me come in and say you can be British, you can be Muslim, you can be hip, you can be having fun – its not either or.
> (*Arab News* 19th August 2007)

Yusuf's work has been credited not only with triggering a 'revolution in Islamic pop', but also with playing an immensely positive international ambassadorial role for Britain, for instance, he has been invited on more than one occasion by the British Council and the Foreign Office to feature at their events (Rahman 2006).

Other initiatives included *Living Islam* – a large four day summer country residential event for families which was first organised by the Islamic Society of Britain in 2003 incorporating arts, culture, speeches and debates as well as children's activities and entertainment. In July 2005, a weekend Islam Expo was organised by many of the personalities who had spearheaded the MAB-StWC alliance. Showcasing Islamic contributions to art, culture, science and civilisation, politics was nonetheless central to this event's programme, which boasted participation from political figures across the spectrum, but in particular, the patronage of the then London Mayor, Ken Livingstone. Interesting parallels have been drawn between this event and the European Social Forum which was held prior to it, in London, in 2004 (See Peace in this volume). Both used Alexandra Palace in North London as their venue, and both events followed very similar formats, suggesting a direct link between the Muslim-Left alliance and the nature and direction in which aspects of Muslim civic engagement had developed. Finally, in the field of media and research, Anas Altikriti, a veteran anti-war leader and a former Respect Party candidate in elections to the European Parliament, established the Cordoba Foundation, a research and public relations organisation with the aim of promoting dialogue and peaceful coexistence between cultures through research, facilitation and advisory roles.[22]

Conclusion

All of these developments paint the picture of a sharper, more complex landscape in British Muslim identity politics that had developed by 2005, owing a great deal of its development to factors related to the events of 9/11 and reactions to it. Indeed, if it can ever be said that the impact of 9/11 gifted British Islam(s) with anything, then perhaps it could be that this was it: a deepened sense of humility, bringing with it a more accurate understanding of their exact place in the wider scheme of things. The magnitude and suddenness of the 9/11 attacks and the overwhelming nature of the world's reactions to it meant that Muslims really had to 'think on their feet' – to be able to deal with the immediate shock, question their feelings and identity, affirm it, defend it and make their views on the War on Terror known – all practically simultaneously.

This four year period was one of momentous change and development for British Muslim identity politics. 9/11 threw open a large public window into British Muslim communities, creating an atmosphere of pressure, urgency and self-defence. Faced with pressing security concerns, the government strove to address them, but found it difficult to maintain a balance between fulfilling its foreign policy commitments and winning the loyalty of a Muslim community which sought political even-handedness both at home *and* abroad. For community organisation and representation – this definitely came of age in the crucible of post-9/11 politics, pushing for age-old Muslim issues such as the criminalisation of religious hatred in a more contextual, mature and inclusive manner than before. Islamophobia and its manipulation by the rising far-right prompted serious government attention to this matter, as well as to the restriction of immigration and a more stringent approach to the integration of minority communities and newcomers to the country. Finally, a host of factors, in particular the decision, especially by young Muslims, to enthusiastically participate in mainstream political activity alongside other interest groups sparked real development, change and diversification within the British Muslim political landscape, which, when compared with that of the 1990s, shows just how far British Muslim politics has travelled over this period.

Notes

1 For instance, Jonathan Birt reports on the preferred dress of a local salafi meeting-group of young men. I quote: 'Some members of the group had developed a

"look": Pakistani-style *shalwar kameez* in camouflage, an Afghan hat alongside the obligatory Doctor Martin boots or Nike trainers. This was recognized among local Muslims as the "jihadi" style.' See Birt 2009: 106. Also cf. Imtiaz 2011, esp. pp. 64–76, which recounts his own personal experiences of activism in British Muslim youth organisations [specifically FOSIS and YMUK], and highlights the intricacies of inter-group rivalries and debates during the 1990s: 'I think most of these inter-group debates, if we were to talk about them with non-Muslims, they'd think we've lost it. We have a highly developed internal or private language ... between ourselves, and a hardly-developed public language'.

2 Ibid. and the IPB website www.islamicparty.com (accessed 8th October 2010).
3 For a window into British historical perceptions of Islam and Muslims cf. works by Nabil Matar, e.g. Matar 2010, where he shows how Muslims and Islam typically suffered prejudice and negative stereotypes in their portrayals in literature and theology, while actual interactions by diplomats and traders with Muslims led to less hostile, and more tolerant perspectives of Muslims and Muslim cultures.
4 'Shutting the Door in the Face of Islam's Bogeymen', *The Guardian* 27th May 1995.
5 'Militants in the Line-up for Conference Season', *The Guardian* 5th August 1995.
6 *The Muslim News* 24th November 1995, reporting on speeches at Islamic Convention held in September 1995 at the London Arena by the Islamic Society of Britain.
7 I use both of these terms as they would generally be used in day to day parlance. The *salafi* trend referring to a preoccupation with a strict and often puritanically literalist interpretation of original sources and texts, coupled with a deep suspicion of any 'innovation' in religion. The *jihadi* trend, which often attracts sympathisers from *salafi* circles, is broadly descriptive of a support for violence/armed fighting in the name of Islam – during this period, still very much confined to the international (rather than domestic) arena.
8 Arabic for 'realm of Islam' and 'realm of disbelief', respectively.
9 At this very early stage, still only apparent motives, as evidence of the perpetrators had not yet been uncovered.
10 Other reports documenting the kind of anti-Muslim hostility that took place in the wake of 9/11 include 'September 11 and its Aftermath' at www.salaam.co.uk/theme ofthemonth/september03_index.php?l=34 (accessed 16th May 2010).
11 This sort of gesture became a regular feature of government-community conversation, used by Tony Blair and other prominent politicians both domestically and internationally. Stephen Lyon (2005) describes it as 'the rise of universal values'.
12 'Muslims and Christians Share Values – Blair', *BBC Website*, 27/09/01 http://news.bbc.co.uk/1/hi/uk_politics/1567187.stm (accessed 19th October 2010); 'Blair condemns Racist Attacks – PM Stresses Shared Heritage', *The Guardian*, 28/09/01.
13 The only exceptions to this were extremist elements such as al-Muhajiroun who (often provocatively) expressed praise and approval of the attacks, and eventually held an 'anniversary' event celebrating the 'Magnificent 19', a reference to the 19 hijackers who carried out the three attacks on 9/11. See 'Rallies Will Highlight "Magnificent 19" of Sept 11' in *The Daily Telegraph* (10th September 2003), http://www.telegraph.co.uk/news/uknews/1441070/Rallies-will-highlight-Magnificent-19-of-Sept-11.html (accessed on 27th May 2010). Also Akhtar (2005: 164). However, even these were lone, marginal voices that were given very little serious attention by the mainstream within Muslim communities.
14 Cf. Islam Awareness Week website page for 2001: www.iaw.org.uk/previous/2001 (accessed 8th October 2010).
15 According to Goodwin (2010a), this campaign was launched 'in the hours following the terrorist attacks of September 11th 2001'.

16 The BNP under the leadership of Nick Griffin has been at pains to portray itself as respectable, patriotic and wholly un-racist. In doing so, it describes its struggle as that of the native, or indigenous white population of the British Isles, whose culture, language, religion and other norms are being threatened by immigration and multiculturalism. In the words of Griffin (2010): 'Towns and cities all over our beautiful country now resemble parts of Africa or Asia. British people have become a minority in many areas already, and within a few decades, we will become a minority across the country as a whole.'
17 Here Goodall documents (now purged) online statements from the BNP website where party leader Nick Griffin provides guidance for contributors. To quote directly: 'Emotive words, however justified they may be, must be avoided. Truth hurts, so words like 'alien', 'vermin', 'gang' instead of 'group', and such like must be avoided. A white rapist may be described as a 'beast' or an 'animal', but a black one must be merely a 'criminal'.
18 The broadcast itself can be viewed at www.youtube.com/watch?v=2epLm34iNok (accessed 30th July 2013).
19 FAIR (2002) emphatically makes the case for policy changes to criminalise incitement against religious identity, along with discrimination on the grounds of religion.
20 Archive at www.q-news.com/buy-UK.htm (accessed 19th November 2010).
21 *Nasheed* is an Arabic word for 'song', popularly used to refer to Muslim religious/ devotional singing.
22 The Cordoba Foundation – About Us: www.thecordobafoundation.com/about_us. php (accessed 21st November 2010).

Bibliography

Abbas, T. (2005) 'British South Asian Muslims: Before and After 9/11', in T. Abbas (ed.) *Muslim Britain: Communities Under Pressure*. London: Zed Books, pp. 3–17.
Akhtar, P. (2005) '"(Re)turn to Religion' and Radical Islam', in T. Abbas (ed.) *Muslim Britain: Communities Under Pressure*. London: Zed Books, pp. 164–176.
Akhtar, S. (1989) *Be Careful With Muhammad!* London: Bellew Publishers.
Allen, C. (2010) *Islamophobia*. Aldershot: Ashgate.
Allen, C. (2005) 'From Race to Religion: The New Face of Discrimination', in T. Abbas (ed.) *Muslim Britain: Communities Under Pressure*. London: Zed Books, pp. 49–65.
Ansari, H. (2004) *The Infidel Within*. London: Hurst.
Anthony, A. (2007) *The Fallout: How a Guilty Liberal Lost His Innocence*. London: Jonathan Cape.
Anwar, M. (2005) 'Issues, Policy and Practice', in T. Abbas (ed.) *Muslim Britain: Communities Under Pressure*. London: Zed Books, pp. 31–46.
Atkinson, R. (2006) 'Every Joke Has a Victim', speech delivered at House of Commons, transcript available at: www.guardian.co.uk/politics/2006/jan/30/immigrationp olicy.religion (accessed 30th July 2013).
Birt, J. (2009) 'The Radical Nineties Revisited: Jihadi Discourses in Britain', in M. Al-Rasheed and M. Shterin (eds) *Dying for Faith: Religiously Motivated Violence in the Contemporary World*. London: I.B. Tauris, pp. 105–110.
Birt, J. (2005) 'Lobbying and Marching: British Muslims and the State', in T. Abbas (ed.) *Muslim Britain: Communities under pressure*. London: Zed Books, pp. 92–106.
Blair, T. (2001a) Statement in House of Commons on 12th September 2001. Full text available at: www.guardian.co.uk/politics/2001/sep/12/politicalnews.september111 (accessed 30th July 2013).

Blair, T. (2001b) Speech to House of Commons on 14th September 2001. Full text available at: www.guardian.co.uk/politics/2001/sep/14/houseofcommons.uk1 (accessed 30th July 2013).
Bodi, F. (2001) 'Opportunistic Cronies', *The Guardian*, 13th November.
Cohen, N. (2007) *What's Left: How Liberals Lost Their Way*. London: Fourth Estate.
Commission on British Muslims and Islamophobia (CBMI) (2004) *Islamophobia: Issues, Challenges and Action*. London: Runnymede Trust.
Eatwell, R. (2010) 'Responses to the Extreme Right in Britain', in R. Eatwell and M.J. Goodwin (eds) *The New Extremism in 21st Century Britain*. Abingdon: Routledge, pp. 213–220.
Elshayyal, K. (2013) *Muslim Identity Politics in the UK, 1960–2010: Development, Challenges, and the Future as Illustrated by 'The Fate' of Freedom of Expression*, unpublished PhD thesis.
FAIR (2005) A Log of Islamophobic Incidents in the UK as Reported to the Forum Against Islamophobia and Racism (FAIR) Between 11th September 2001 and 18th January 2005, available at: www.fairuk.org/research/FAIRuk-ResearchData-IslamophobicIncidentLog.pdf (accessed 30th July 2013).
FAIR (2002) 'The Religious Offences Bill 2002: A Response'.
Goodall, K. (2007) 'Incitement to Religious Hatred: All Talk and No Substance?', *Modern Law Review*, 70(1).
Goodwin, M.J. (2010a) 'The BNP and Islam' at the election blog of the University of Nottingham's School of Politics and International Relations, available at: http://electionblog2010.blogspot.com/2010/04/bnp-and-islam.html (accessed 30th July 2013).
Goodwin, M.J. (2010b) 'In Search of the Winning Formula: Nick Griffin and the 'Modernization' of the British National Party', in R. Eatwell and M.J. Goodwin (eds) *The New Extremism in 21st Century Britain*. Abingdon: Routledge, pp. 167–190.
Griffin, N. (2010) 'A Message From BNP Leader Nick Griffin', available at: www.bnp.org.uk/introduction (accessed 30th July 2013).
Halliday, F. (2010) *Britain's Frst Muslims: Portrait of an Arab Community*. London: I. B. Tauris.
Hamid, S. (2007) 'Islamic Political Radicalism in Britain: The Case of Hizb-ut-Tahrir', in T. Abbas (ed.) *Islamic Political Radicalism: A European Perspective*. Edinburgh: Edinburgh University Press, pp. 145–159.
HM Government (2006) 'Part 3A: 'Acts Intended to Stir up Religious Hatred' in Schedule: Hatred Against Persons on Religious Grounds', *Racial and Religious Hatred Act 2006*.
Husain, E. (2007) *The Islamist*. London: Penguin.
Hussain, D. (2004) 'Councillors and Caliphs: Muslim Political Participation in Britain', in M.S. Seddon, D. Hussain and N. Malik (eds) *British Muslims Between Assimilation and Segregation*. Leicester: Islamic Foundation.
Huntington, S.P. (1996) *The Clash of Civilizations and the Remaking of World Order*. New York: Simon and Schuster.
Imtiaz, A. (2011) 'A Marcher's Song', in his anthology *Wandering Lonely in a Crowd*. Leicester: Kube.
Labour Party Manifesto (2005) 'Forward Not Back'.
Lawless, R. (1995) *From Taizz to Tyneside*. Exeter: University of Exeter Press.
Lyon, S. (2005) 'The Shadow of September 11: Multiculturalism and Identity', in T. Abbas (ed.) *Muslim Britain: Communities Under Pressure*. London: Zed Books, pp. 79–84.

Malik, K. (2009) *From Fatwa to Jihad: The Rushdie Affair and Its Legacy*. London: Atlantic Books.
Matar, N. (2010) 'Britons and Muslims in the Early Modern Period: From Prejudice to (a Theory of) Toleration', in M. Malik (ed.) *Anti-Muslim Prejudice: Past and Present*. Abingdon: Routledge, pp. 7–25.
Meer, N. (2010) *Citizenship, Identity, and the Politics of Multiculturalism*. Basingstoke: Palgrave Macmillan.
Modood, T. (1997) '"Difference', Cultural Racism and Anti-Racism', in T. Modood and P. Werbner (eds) *Debating Cultural Hybridity: Multicultural Identities and the Politics of Anti-racism*. Atlantic Highlands, NJ: Zed Books.
Muslim Council of Britain (2002a) *The Quest for Sanity*. London: MCB.
Muslim Council of Britain (2002b) 'Muslims Laud Tony Blair's Stand on Faith Schools, But Concerned Over Rise in Islamophobia', *MCB Press Release*, 20th May, available at: www.mcb.org.uk/media/pr/200502.htm (accessed 26th July 2013).
Muslim Council of Britain (2005) 'MCB Calls For an End to Misrepresentation of Proposed Incitement Law', *MCB Press Release*, 13 January, available at: www.mcb.org.uk/media/presstext.php?ann_id=128 (accessed 26th July 2013).
Muslim Council of Britain (2006) 'Religious Hatred Law Perpetuates Inequality After Commons Vote', *MCB Press Release*, 1st February, available at: www.mcb.org.uk/media/presstext.php?ann_id=186 (accessed 26th July 2013).
Peace, T. (2013) 'All I'm Asking, is for a Little Respect: Assessing the Performance of Britain's Most Successful Radical Left Party', *Parliamentary Affairs*, 66(2): 405–424.
Phillips, R. (2008) 'Standing Together: The Muslim Association of Britain and the Anti-war Movement', *Race and Class*, 50(2): 101–113.
Rahman, S. (2006) 'The Biggest Star in the Middle East is a Brit', *The Guardian*, 27th April.
Richardson, J.E. (2004) *(Mis)representing Islam: The Racism and Rhetoric of British Broadsheet Newspapers*. Amsterdam: John Benjamins Pub. Co.
Richardson, J.E. (2010) '"Get Shot the Lot of Them": Election Reporting of Muslims in British Newspapers', in M. Malik (ed.) *Anti-Muslim Prejudice: Past and Present*. Abingdon: Routledge, pp. 146–168.
Ronson, J. (2007) 'My Night of Jihad', *The Guardian Comment is Free*, 30th April, available at: www.guardian.co.uk/commentisfree/2007/apr/30/mynightofjihad (accessed 26th July 2013).
Sherif, J. (2011) 'A Census Chronicle – Reflections on the Campaign for a Religion Question in the 2001 Census for England and Wales', *Journal of Beliefs and Values*, 32(1): 1–18.
Taylor, M. (2004) 'BNP Leaders May Face Charges After TV Exposé of Racism', *The Guardian*, 15th July.
The Cordoba Foundation (n.d.) 'About Us', available at: www.thecordobafoundation.com/about_us.php (accessed 21st July 2013).
Wavell, S. (2005) 'Putting a Good Glossy on the Muslim Lifestyle', *The Sunday Times*, 9th October.

Part IV
Representation

10 The Muslim Council of Britain and its engagement with the British political establishment

Ekaterina Braginskaia

Introduction

This chapter examines the Muslim Council of Britain's participation in British politics and its engagement with the changing nature of state-religion relations under the different governments in 1997–2013. The Muslim Council of Britain (MCB) has found itself at the heart of discussions on Muslim minority representation, while its own role and ability to serve as an authoritative voice of British Muslims has not gone unchallenged. Although unable to escape some of its negative labels, it remained true to its objective of lobbying the government on behalf of its affiliates and raising awareness on Islamophobia. Based on the research conducted in 2011–2012 and updated in light of the recent policy changes under the Coalition government and the aftermath of attacks on the mosques in West Midlands in 2013, the chapter revisits some of the debates on the MCB and its involvement in British politics. It suggests that while the level of the criticisms of the MCB has increased, its own discourse of engagement has become more nuanced.

The changing nature of engagement will be analysed in light of opportunities and constraints of state-religion relations under the New Labour administrations and the Coalition government. I suggest that the level of cooperation between the MCB spokesmen and politicians was largely influenced by a series of shifts in state approaches to engaging with religion in general and the Muslim faith in particular. Matched expectations and good personal relations have also played a key role in shaping the level of interaction between the MCB and senior politicians. To trace a series of ups and downs in the MCB's engagement in British politics, I will explore some of the written and verbal communication between the MCB senior representatives and key politicians, including Tony Blair and Jack Straw, Ruth Kelly and Hazel Blears, Sayeeda Warsi and Eric Pickles. The chapter will also examine how the MCB tried to adapt to the changing landscape of state-Muslim relations by diversifying its own engagement with a variety of actors through wider political networks and interfaith activities.

Muslim collective representation and the creation of the MCB

The MCB was formed in 1997 as a voluntary umbrella organisation engaged in representing Muslim collective interests in British politics and voicing Muslim concerns of social exclusion and Islamophobia. The Rushdie affair (1988–9) fuelled debates in the media on the freedom of speech and religious rights, highlighting 'the strengths and weaknesses of a Muslim community leadership grounded in grassroots networks and associations.' (Cesari and McLoughlin 2005: 59).

The MCB has remained a controversial institution which continued to divide opinions. Some scholars questioned its Islamist legacies and a somewhat disproportionate number of affiliated institutions dominated by traditional mosque structures (Amin 2011; Pedziwiatr 2007: 271). Others maintained that despite its shortcomings it was still considered one of the most 'reasonable voices' for the government to engage with (Interview 5). Before examining the MCB's relations with New Labour and the Coalition, it is important to note that its creation was facilitated by a series of political opportunities and matched expectations on the need for Muslim representation on the national level. A delicate interplay between national-level representation and local-based community agenda would prove to be a key factor in the Council's interaction with the British political establishment.

The MCB was a result of a consultative process which revealed a strong need for moderate, professional spokesmen to articulate Muslim interests in an institutionally accepted way.[1] The growing violence of the Rushdie events and the initial lack of community leaders to engage with the Conservative Government of the day provided an opportunity for more eloquent and organised individuals to speak on behalf of the community. A group of individuals, inspired by South-Asian Deobandi teachings and Islamist ideology of Muslim Brotherhood rallied to the call to defend Muslim interests and create a national umbrella body. This signalled a transition of Muslim local interests to the national arena (Kepel 1997: 136).

The coming together of senior Muslim figures was welcomed by the Conservatives. Michael Howard, the former Home Secretary, had called on Muslim groups to unite and speak with one voice to have a stronger impact on the government. A meeting of the two pressures, one from below and one from above was aptly summarised by Archer (2009: 335) who suggested that the 'Muslim Council of Britain was a product of the Rushdie affair, but the Conservative Home Secretary at the time ... was ... its midwife.' In 1997 the MCB became the *de facto* spokesmen for British Muslims vis-à-vis the government and the media (Vidino 2011). This coincided with New Labour taking power the same year.

The MCB's engagement with New Labour: mainstreaming faith

The MCB's engagement with New Labour between 1997 and 2005 was traditionally characterised as a honeymoon period of cooperation between senior-level politicians and the Council. The research suggests that a strong sense of cooperation was made possible because of the initial alignment between the government's agenda on faith and integration and the MCB's lobbying efforts to protect Muslim rights.[2] A match in expectations was twofold. The first involved a desire to recognise faith as a strong identity marker. The second focused on the importance of Muslim collective representation through an officially-recognised faith organisation.

New Labour's approach to mainstreaming faith in governance and creating a greater sense of unity between different faith communities is well-documented.[3] During its first years in power, Tony Blair's government took a series of steps to improve its relations with Muslim communities by widening the scope of protective legislations on race and ethnicity and including religion in the debates on British national identity. The greater 'receptivity to faith' (Birt 2006) was partly dictated by New Labour's ideology, partly by Blair's personal religious views and convictions. The government set up Faith Community Liaison Group to consult different departments 'for the effective long-term involvement of the faith communities' perspectives and needs in policy development across government' (Hansard 2003).

New Labour's willingness to give faith communities a stronger recognition in the public sphere can also be attributed to its 'communitarian' preferences which emphasised 'social cohesion … over the resolution of conflict between competing interest groups' (Birt 2006: 691–692). In his speech on faith in politics, Blair (2001) stressed the importance of major faith traditions 'in supporting and propagating values which bind us together as a nation.' The desire to create a public space where civic religion would heal the scars of ethnic and racial tensions resulted in what some scholars called a neoliberal incorporation of 'community organisations into partnership structures' (Glynn 2009: 5). The focus shifted from recognising racial differences to celebrating cultural diversity and promoting peaceful coexistence of faith communities (Peach 2005).

The research supports a widely-held view that the Blair government 'has brought up faith as a fairly central policy issue' (Interview 5). Moreover, an emphasis on the value of multi-faith society provided a positive drive towards recognising the religious dimension of Muslim identity. New Labour's ideology on faith, social cohesion and communitarianism provided a powerful incentive for the creation of the 'interfaith industry where you … get funded for interfaith activity' and benefit from 'state patronage' (Interview 6). It permeated political discourse on community cohesion and integration and became a common language between the government and the MCB.

The Council's engagement with New Labour was facilitated by the government's somewhat corporatist attempts to mainstream faith in the public sphere. Rather than engaging with a variety of voices, early policies under New Labour aimed at empowering particular organisations to represent different faiths.[4] The Review undertaken by the Department for Communities and Local Government acknowledged the present use of a 'decentralised model' (Communities and Local Government 2004: 75). However, it also announced the government's drive to develop a more central role to support faith communities (ibid.). A key recommendation included ensuring that 'faith-based organisations [would] not face unnecessary additional barriers when applying for funding under Government programmes' (ibid.: 77). Previously, the state was removed from engaging in faith issues and the Church of England was 'working as an interlocutor for other faiths' (Interview 6). This model was replaced by Labour's multi-faith approach of the 1990s (ibid.).

It would appear that whenever there was a match between the state's approach to faith and the MCB's own agenda of promoting Muslim interests, the level of cooperation was high. New Labour's singling out of the MCB as a key interlocutor to speak on behalf of Muslim citizens may have been atypical for the British context. And yet, it paved the way for a closer engagement between the MCB and government ministers. The newly-found emphasis on religious equality provided the MCB with an opportunity to represent the needs of the Muslim community as a singular category on the grounds of parity with other faith groups, rather than within the previously-used ethnic and racial labels. For example, in the words of one interviewee:

> For democracy to work and to cater for everybody effectively, you need to have that intermediary or representative voice for any group of people who have a common agenda or interest.
> (Interview 9)

The MCB has positioned itself as a representative voice of the Muslim faith. A series of informal meetings took place between the MCB and different government departments, while reports of the 'Whitehall encounters' became a regular feature of the MCB's newsletters. The government welcomed the MCB's input in counteracting Islamophobia, preventing extremism and facilitating interfaith activities. The MCB praised the government for keeping its election promises to establish Muslim faith schools, introduce NHS chaplains and make 'provisions of a funded Muslim advisor for the Prison Service' (Muslim Council of Britain 1998).

Members of the MCB's committees were invited to the Foreign Office to discuss policies and were consulted by the Treasury and the Department of Health on Muslim participation in eradicating poverty (Muslim Council of Britain 2001: 9). Iqbal Sacranie, the MCB's Secretary General, spoke of 'the regular bilateral meetings with the Secretary of State for all major Government departments' as an 'opportunity to raise issues of concern at the very highest level of government machinery' (Muslim Weekly 2004). Regular consultations helped endorse the MCB as the government's key partner. The 'insider' status enabled the MCB leaders to lobby the government to promote Muslim religious and social concerns in public debates and address the issues of Islamophobia and marginalisation of Muslim communities.[5] The MCB saw itself as a 'voice of Muslim organisations, mosques, charities – a coalition of

Muslim organisations' with a particular mandate to 'enhance the image and perception of Muslims and Islam as a whole' (Interview 9).

The MCB's campaign for a religious question to be included in the 2001 Census was arguably one of the most fruitful moments of cooperation between the MCB, senior politicians and other faith groups. Coupled with favourable opportunities created by inter-religious alliances and personal connections, the campaign marked an important milestone in lobbying the government to improve religious provisions for Muslim communities. In its efforts to include a category of religion in the 2001 Census, the MCB took active part in consulting the government, wrote letters and issued joint press releases with other religious groups. While the efforts of the MCB's leadership cannot be underestimated, some of the success of the campaign was also partly down to Labour's own receptivity to matters of faith. For Jamil Sherif (2003: 2), the MCB's representative on the Religious Affiliation Group, this campaign 'marked the emergence of a new faith constituency.' Instead of 'characterising people by what they looked like – their race or ethnicity – allegiance to moral and ethical values [became] more important in some contexts' (ibid.).[6]

The success of the MCB's campaign can be attributed not only to the MCB's own persistent efforts and rhetoric, but also to good personal connections and shared perspectives on religion between senior government figures and the MCB. The Council made an explicit link between acknowledging Muslim religious presence and 'pav[ing] the way for proper provision of public services in areas such as education, health, housing and employment' (Muslim Council of Britain 2000). In his speech during the Prime Minister's reception, Iqbal Saranie (1999) made a powerful plea to include religion to show policymakers how many Muslims in Britain suffer from 'the high rates of educational underachievement, the crippling levels of unemployment, and the suffocating social exclusion.'

The importance of personal connections became apparent once the Census (Amendment) Bill was to pass through both Houses of Parliament. Sacranie wrote to Blair urging him for 'direct intervention ... to ensure that a few hours of Parliamentary time is given to this important Bill' (cit. in Sherif 2011: 10). Further opportunities to make the Bill pass were provided by the interfaith cooperation between different leaders of Muslim, Jewish, Christian and Sikh communities. By working together with different faiths and creating a particular narrative of how the question of religion was introduced in the Census, the MCB successfully lobbied the government to achieve greater recognition of British Muslims as a faith community.

New Labour's disengagement from the MCB: securitising Muslim faith

A turning point in the MCB's engagement with the government came in 2005, following the London bombings in July that year. The aftermath of 7/7 imposed a considerable constraint on Labour's cooperation with the MCB.

There were previous disagreements over foreign policy, particularly after 9/11 and the invasion of Iraq. However, terrorist attacks closer to home have contributed to the increased securitisation of the government's engagement with Muslim communities.

The government's response to home-grown terrorism was the establishment of the Prevent Violent Extremism ('Prevent') agenda within a wider counter-terrorism CONTEST strategy. The aim of 'Prevent' was 'to stop radicalisation, reduce support for terrorism and violent extremism and discourage people from becoming terrorists' (HM Government 2009: 14). The extent to which different government departments were consistent in formulating and delivering provisions under Prevent remains debatable.[7] However, security concerns increased government pressure on the MCB not only to facilitate relations with Muslim communities, but also to 'deliver a law-abiding, loyal ethnic minority' (Bunting 2010).

The MCB and the Blair administration shared expectations on mainstreaming faith. However, their perspectives on how to deal with extremism resulted in strong disagreement over the extent to which 'faith' was at the centre of the problem. The interview data indicates that some members of Muslim communities felt that the government wanted the MCB to denounce terrorist activities and 'accept that this was a religious problem, an Islamic problem ... that these terrorists are Muslims' and that the Muslim communities 'have not done enough to stop their rise' (Interview 5).

The difference in expectations revealed how a securitised dimension of faith had created a considerable obstacle for the MCB's cooperation with the government and the government's engagement with the MCB. The lack of agreement on combating terrorism marked an end to the government's experiment of engaging with a single Muslim umbrella organisation. The MCB leaders were still consulted on a number of issues, including the 'Prevent' agenda. However, there were signs they were no longer treated as the leading spokesmen for Muslim communities. In a short period of time, a close cooperation between the MCB and the government changed into a relationship increasingly underlined by disagreement. A clear consequence of the government's disapproval of the MCB was a gradual process of distancing itself from the institution on matters of integration and cohesion.

In July 2005, senior members of the MCB were still invited to a roundtable meeting chaired by the Prime Minister to announce the formation of the 'Preventing Extremism Together' Working Groups (Sacranie 2006). A year later the MCB was already excluded from taking part in consultations led by the Commission on Integration and Cohesion. While the MCB welcomed 'the inclusion of a commissioner representing the Hindu Forum of Britain', it felt 'puzzled by the absence of a representative from the Muslim community's largest umbrella body' (Muslim Council of Britain 2007).

The findings of the Commission had two implications for the MCB-government engagement. First, the Report criticised the previous patterns of engagement with older community leaders who were labelled as 'self-styled and appointed and ultimately not strongly representative' (Commission on Integration and Cohesion 2007: 40). Second, it suggested that Labour's initial focus on faith communities was too narrow and instead of contributing to social cohesion it had contributed to further social segregation. While it praised the interfaith work and recognised that '[f]aith groups and leaders can play a vital part in promoting harmony and understanding between faiths' it also noted that there was a 'tendency to emphasis religious identities to the exclusion of other identities' (ibid.: 50).

The MCB's earlier refusal to attend a Holocaust Memorial Day (HMD) in 2006 played an important role in Labour's ministers distancing themselves from the Council. The MCB maintained that its initial refusal to attend the commemoration was motivated by conviction that it should have been called a 'Genocide Memorial Day' which would mean making 'no distinction between genocides undertaken against people of other religions and ethnicity' (Bunglawala 2005). Although the MCB's affiliates were split on the issue, the final decision to continue the boycott had a damaging effect on its relations with the government.

Whether the government was following its own conviction, or was responding to the pressure from the media and right-wing think-tanks, the MCB's decision to boycott the HMD in 2006 was taken as a further proof that the MCB was no longer 'fit to engage with' (Interview 9). As a result of a securitised classification of political and apolitical Muslim groups, the government embarked on working with other Muslims groups, such as the Sufi Council and the British Muslim Forum. The later years under New Labour were to show that these efforts did not yield the desired result either. However, these were the first steps the government took to diversify its engagement with Muslim organisations, recognising the need 'to engage with Muslims in plural ways' (Interview 2).

Personal relations have played an important role in the MCB's negotiations with the government in the early period of the Labour administration. This was to change once Ruth Kelly and Hazel Blears were in charge of Communities and Local Government affairs. A series of rather confrontational exchanges demonstrated the extent to which personal relations have deteriorated in the period leading to the government's disengagement from the MCB. For example, while Hazel Blears was the Minister of State, she defended a use of counter-terrorist powers against Muslim communities on the grounds of the threat from 'people associated with an extreme form of Islam' (House of Commons 2005: 46). The MCB noted that 'the characterisation of British Muslims as a "problem community" in much of ... the media and through statements made by government and police officials have contributed to an undoubtedly growing anti-Muslim climate in the UK' (Muslim Council of Britain 2005).

A brief analysis of Ruth Kelly's speech on 11 October 2006 and the MCB's response to it on 14 October 2006 illustrate the extent to which personal relations had broken down. The speech entitled 'Britain: our values, our responsibilities' was aimed at engaging a wide range of Muslim organisations to work with the government to tackle extremism. Although the MCB was also invited, its leaders reported to be unable to attend due to a previously organised meeting with Home Secretary John Reid the same day. Kelly reconfirmed a change in government policy in tackling extremism. However, on a closer inspection she also offered an explanation as to why the government decided to scale down its engagement with the MCB.

Highlighting successful joint ventures between the government and Muslim communities, she first emphasised the government's contribution to 'protect people from discrimination on the basis of faith at work and in their day to day lives' (Kelly 2006). She recalled that it was New Labour which had supported Muslim efforts to pass the Religious Hatred legislation in 2006 and went on to criticise the MCB's unwillingness to attend the HMD. No specific organisations were mentioned in the speech. However, such words like 'some people who don't feel it right to join in the commemorations of HMD even though it has helped raise awareness not just of the Jewish holocaust, but also more contemporary atrocities like the Rwanda genocide' (ibid.) arguably were directed mainly at the MCB. The speech called for 'a fundamental rebalancing of ... relationship with Muslim organisations' (ibid.). This marked a key shift from the corporatist-style cooperation with one official interlocutor towards increased diversification of the government engagement with a variety of Muslim organisations:

> I am clear that our strategy of funding and engagement must shift significantly towards those organisations that are taking a proactive leadership role in tackling extremism and defending our shared values.
>
> (Ibid.)

The MCB replied with a detailed letter written by Muhammad Abdul Bari, the MCB's Secretary General from 2006 to 2010, aimed at rebuking some of the accusations. It reconfirmed the MCB's commitment to combat extremism by citing instances when it spoke strongly against terrorism following 9/11 and 7/7. The overall tone of the letter was balanced and non-confrontational. However, its frustration was made clear by finding it 'most patronising to be lectured in this way' (Bari 2006). The MCB challenged the government on the issue of equal and fair treatment of Muslim communities. It merged its own concerns of being 'sidelined' by the government with the 'ministerial statements stigmatising' Muslim communities (Ibid.).

It hinted that by disengaging from them, the government would damage its relations with Muslim communities. By positioning itself as 'a responsible representative organisation', it wished to reassure the government that it 'reflect[ed] the views of its constituents fairly' and if those views were 'unpalatable to the government of the day, so be it' (Ibid.). While acknowledging the government's right to 'speak to a wide range of Muslim organisations', the MCB questioned the strategy of rewarding with public funds 'only those' who supported the government (Ibid.). The letter also warned of the need to 'distinguish the mainstream, democratically-constituted Muslim bodies from the mavericks' (Ibid.).

These statements reveal the issues which contributed to the growing tensions between the government and the MCB. However, there was also a sense of betrayed expectations which illustrated the extent to which informal relations had deteriorated. As relations soured, the MCB became more critical of the government's treatment of Muslims. For example, in his critique of the 'Prevent' agenda, Sacranie (2006) referred to the Muslim community as a patient suffering from unjust treatment. A final suspension of relations came in 2009 when Daud Abdullah, the MCB's Deputy Secretary General signed the 'Istanbul Declaration.'[8] One interviewee provided a sober assessment by saying that 'first, the MCB fell into a trap of being too close to the Labour Party and second, they managed to fall out with them as well' (Interview 11).

Personal connections would become important once again towards the end of the Labour administration as there was a gradual improvement in the MCB's relations with the government. In 2010 Farooq Murad was elected as the MCB's new Secretary General and John Denham became a new minister for Communities and Local Government. There were signs that the MCB was still considered as an important Muslim voice. While the MCB showed its support for British forces abroad and its determination to build better relations with the Jewish community through interfaith dialogue and by ending its boycott of the HMD, Labour ministers demonstrated willingness to re-engage with the MCB.

The MCB and the Coalition: pluralising faith

When the Coalition government took office in 2010, its engagement with Muslim communities was in some ways reminiscent of the New Labour administration in its final years, particularly on the issues of security and anti-Muslim crime. The MCB's cooperation with key politicians under the Coalition was also subject to a similar combination of opportunities and constraints, namely the presence of a shared agenda and the existence or lack of good personal relations. However, it was also complicated by the Coalition's increased diversification of interfaith partnerships and its firm policy of non-engagement with what it considered to be 'Islamist' organisations (HM Government 2011).

The issue of faith remained central to the government's engagement with Muslim communities. However, the way it was conceptualised under the Coalition differed from that of New Labour. The nature of divergence was two-fold. The first aspect involved the Coalition's greater reliance on the Church of England and the Near Neighbours Fund as 'a conducive channel for interfaith' and distribution of funding (Interview 10). The second shift was a re-introduction of local-level initiatives. These developments were seen as 'a return to the status ante of the early 1990s' (Ibid.). Before discussing the ways in which the MCB tried to navigate the changed political landscape, it is important to outline the nature of state-religion relations under the Coalition.

The government's engagement with faith-based organisations was delegated to the Faith Engagement team under the leadership of Sayeeda Warsi in the Department for Communities and Local Government. The Department was entrusted to provide 'expertise for colleagues across Whitehall, facilitating productive contacts between faith representatives and civil servants on policy areas' (Hawkins 2013). It primarily engaged in 'defending the value of religious belief' and 'working with communities and colleagues in other Departments to tackle religious hate crime and support its victims' (Ibid.). There was also an increased focus on interfaith dialogue and cooperation between different faith communities, particularly on the local level.

In their research on Muslim representation, O'Toole et al. (2013) emphasised a link between the Coalition's approach to faith and the Big Society's renewed interest in interfaith work. While the programme was administered in close cooperation with the Church of England, a key change was a shift from delivering individual faith-based projects to building interfaith partnerships. My research also suggested that while cooperation between different faiths was nothing new, a stronger engagement between different faith organisations supported by increased funding was seen as an important step to break the barriers between different communities.

Another aspect of the Coalition's engagement with faith was its ideological departure from New Labour's corporatist approach and a renewed preference for a local, decentralised approach. Centrally-controlled practices favoured by New Labour gave way to the Big Society's support for localities and civil society initiatives. A clear illustration of the Coalition's strategy of empowering local authorities was introduced in the paper outlining the government's integration strategy:

> Integration is achieved when neighbourhoods, families and individuals come together on issues which matter to them, and so we are committed to rebalancing activity from centrally-led to locally-led action and from the public to the voluntary and private sectors.
> (Communities and Local Government 2012: 2)

As was noted by one respondent, the Coalition government did not believe in 'engaging with people through representative organisations ... so it ignore[d] any kind of institutionalised attempt to engage with the Muslim community' (Interview 11). Muslims were increasingly seen as citizens, who have the same access to members of parliament and do not require any particular organisation to represent them (Ibid.). A similar view was expressed by a member of the House of Lords, who noted that unlike France or Germany, in Britain 'we don't understand representation in terms of corporate structures' (Interview 10). New Labour's desire to set up regular formal meetings with Muslim organisations may have been beneficial for the MCB's efforts to position itself as a leading community voice. The Coalition's preference for a more individual approach based on a variety of partners has pluralised the nature of state-Muslim relations. Consequently, the MCB found itself increasingly in the situation where it had to diversify its own network of partners.

The MCB took a number of steps to lobby the government and articulate Muslim claims by using the shared channels of civic engagement. Although this may have revealed the extent to which the MCB was no longer in direct contact with the government, it provided an opportunity to build alliances with other political actors. In his address to the MCB's General Assembly, Murad (2012) emphasised the need to 'build meaningful bridges' to overcome 'ignorance and mistrust and exploitation by certain groups and individuals for their self-interest.' He also urged the MCB's affiliates to 'strategise and choose where to place our voice' (Ibid.). Therefore, the MCB has become increasingly sensitive to the changing landscape of state-Muslim relations and sought to adapt its own discourse to new rules of pluralist representation.

Close cooperation with the Church of England helped unlock government funding through the Near Neighbours programme. Additionally, the MCB continued to build bridges with other faiths, particularly through its leaders' personal contacts, as was exemplified by annual public events such as Interfaith Harmony Week at the House of Lords. Speaking at the UN World Interfaith Harmony Week, Murad emphasised the MCB's commitment to 'working together with all faith communities ... on the common values of peace and harmony' (Muslim Council of Britain 2012a).

Increased engagement with Muslim peers created an opportunity to attract attention to the challenges of Islamophobia. Moreover, active participation in these high-level events showed that the MCB was still invited to the Parliament and was not completely ignored by the British political establishment. In his article on the British government's engagement with Muslim organisations, Bari (2012) highlighted a rather controversial nature of the government's alleged disengagement from the MCB by noting that 'while senior Muslim leaders continue to attend and speak at events in Parliament, the official position is that there is no "formal" dealing with the bodies that organise them'.

The MCB's press department has continuously emphasised the Council's active participation in British politics. In November 2012, the MCB hosted the Eid Reception in Whitehall to celebrate the Muslim festival. It was important for the MCB that the event was attended by politicians, interfaith leaders and business representatives (Muslim Council of Britain 2012b). Manzila Uddin was quoted congratulating the MCB on 'ensuring that the Muslim community is part and parcel of British society' (ibid.). A more recent example was the reception at the World Islamic Forum in London, held at the House of Lords in November 2013. Similarly, the MCB's press release drew attention to high-level guests and the MCB's contribution to the event. Focusing on the importance of 'addressing poverty in the third world countries ... and building a just, peaceful and cohesive society' Murad highlighted that the same concerns were 'at the heart of the vision of the Muslim Council of Britain' (Muslim Council of Britain 2013b).

Another way in which the MCB has developed its relations with the British political establishment was its ongoing cooperation with left-wing politicians. While explaining its efforts to build new alliances, Bari (2007) noted that 'ignoring the politically motivated discourse from Whitehall and Westminster village we have decided to invest our time and efforts in cultivating more friends within civil society and strengthening our existing links with the community at large.' In 2007, the MCB had already worked to improve its links with London local authorities and the Mayor, as well as the National Union of Students and the National Youth Agency.

Under the coalition, the MCB's cooperation with left-wing politicians was reinforced by shared opposition to some of the measures proposed by the Conservative members of the Coalition. In the past, the MCB leaders made an alliance with the Trade Union Congress (TUC) and were encouraged by its support. In 2011, the MCB continued to work closely with the Left and signed a petition against David Cameron's statement on multiculturalism. The 'Statement on David Cameron's multicultural speech' was launched by Labour MPs Peter Hain, Jeremy Corbyn and Ken Livingstone and expressed criticism of the Coalition's sliding back into the Thatcher's rhetoric of 'enemy within' (SWP Online 2011). The MCB shared their concerns that 'people with a different religion, culture or skin colour [would] be scapegoated and treated as inferior' (ibid.).

A key flaw in the MCB's participation in British politics was its poor engagement with the Conservative Party. This would become all the more apparent once Conservative politicians were in charge of the Department for Communities and Local Government. The Interim Report on the MCB delivered by the Conservative Party's Group on National and International Security (2007) revealed that their relations had already become strained in the aftermath of 7/7. The MCB's leadership may have dismissed the report as failed attempts by neo-Conservative think-tanks and 'Islam-bashers [to] drive a wedge between Muslims and the rest of the nation' (Bari 2007). However, the war of words revealed the lack of positive personal contacts and ideological differences which proved difficult to shift under the Coalition.

Recently, the MCB tried to bridge the gap with the Conservative Party by emphasising its organisational diversity and openness to different political perspectives. Calling for inclusive politics, Bari (2012) argued that although many Muslims were 'traditionally Labour supporters' they were 'fast-learning the nuances and reality of British politics' which was illustrated by the creation of Conservative Muslim Forum. He also noted that:

> [A]lthough Muslims are still under-represented in the Westminster village, we now have this presence in the Conservative Party and among the Liberal Democrats, too, as well as Labour. This is a natural progression: we – as a 'community of communities' – are maturing.
>
> (Ibid.)

The MCB's own engagement with the Coalition government and its Conservative ministers has also become more nuanced. While there was no formal interaction between the governments' leading figures and the MCB leaders, engagement took the form of informal relations between the MCB and the Department for Communities and Local Government. A brief analysis of the MCB's engagement with Sayeeda Warsi, Minister of State for Faith and Communities, and Eric Pickles, the State Secretary for Community and Local Government, suggests that any prospect of cooperation rested on mutually-accepted expectations and personal connections. First, I will discuss the issue of Islamophobia and the MCB's successful interaction with Warsi. Second, I will examine the issue of national efforts to combat hate crimes and MCB's less fruitful attempts to re-engage with the Home Office in the aftermath of the Rigby affair in the summer of 2013.

The desire to combat Islamophobia provided a particular meeting point for the MCB and the Coalition. In its approach to dealing with hate crime, the Coalition government engaged more with the issue of Islamophobia than the Labour administration (Allen 2013). By moving away from the idea of equality as conceptualised by New Labour, the problem of Islamophobia was aligned with manifestations of general hatred against any religion (ibid.: 7). The establishment of such cross-sectional platforms as the All Party Parliamentary Group on Islamophobia, the Cross-Government Working Group on Anti-Muslim Hatred and TELL MAMA (a public service for measuring anti-Muslim attacks) was in line with the Coalition's pluralist approach to enhancing integration and social cohesion. However, it has also provided an opportunity to address the problem of anti-Muslim crime within the broader agenda.

Sayeeda Warsi was put in charge of the Faith Engagement Team. She held a cross-departmental brief and liaised with the Home Office and the Department for Communities and Local Government. Her approach to faith reflected the Coalition's conservative approach of 'doing religion' not on the basis of guaranteeing equality of individual faiths as bounded categories, but rather as a way of defending individual citizens against any acts of hatred, regardless of their religion. Reportedly, she criticised Labour's initiative to set up Young Muslims Advisory Group on the grounds that this was 'another example of the Government engaging with the British Muslim communities on the basis purely of their faith' rather than considering other issues facing young people such as 'drugs, unemployment and housing' (Warsi 2008).

In her new mediatory capacity, she provided the missing link between the Coalition and the MCB, particularly by praising the efforts of both parties on the issue of Islamophobia. In 2011, she made her famous speech suggesting that 'Islamophobia has now passed the dinner-table-test' to become socially acceptable in Britain (Warsi 2011). The MCB praised the renewed interest in condemning Islamophobia and welcomed Warsi's critical words on the role of the media in 'normalising Islamophobia' (Murad 2011).

The tragic events of the Rigby murder and the Woolwich crisis in 2013 helped reconcile some of the differences between the MCB and the British government. While criticising Labour for their 'hyperbolic statements about the war on terror' and questioning the usefulness of a 'them and us' mentality,

Baroness Warsi praised David Cameron for being 'statesmanlike and sensible, careful to use non-emotional language [and] very protective of Britain's Muslim community' (cit. in Odone 2013). Similarly, she spoke highly of the MCB's response to the Woolwich attack and gave the Council some positive publicity in the media. In her interviews to the press, she highlighted the speed and the manner in which the MCB condemned the attack, indicating that 'Muslim spokesmen are not tacitly supporting jihadists in our midst' and that 'the Council has learned from its past mistakes' (ibid.).

The MCB welcomed these statements and applauded her 'firm response to some Islamophobic assertions in the House of Lords' (Muslim Council of Britain 2013c). These verbal and written exchanges may not have signalled a full-scale cooperation between the Coalition and the MCB. However, they indicated that shared positions, backed up by personal relations, provided good opportunities for dialogue.

A joint condemnation of Islamophobia has led to a degree of cooperation between the MCB's leaders and senior politicians. However, the nature and the scope of efforts required to deal with a security-sensitive wave of anti-Muslim violence was a different matter. A brief illustration of the MCB's correspondence with Eric Pickles reveals some of these differences on combating terrorism in its different forms. Following the murder of Lee Rigby and the ensuing wave of anti-Muslim crimes in West Midlands, the MCB wrote a series of letters, including one to Eric Pickles and the other to Theresa May.[9]

In his capacity as Secretary General, Farooq Murad raised a series of concerns of the MCB's affiliates on the lack of national response to these hate crimes (Murad 2013a). The importance of these letters for the MCB's communication with the government was two-fold. First, it revealed that the MCB saw the issue of anti-Muslim hatred as a matter of national, rather than local security. Second, it showed that in light of the seriousness of the incidents, the MCB wished to re-establish a more direct engagement with the government. Acknowledging that any 'formal response from the government to the MCB has been muted in the last three years' the MCB leader emphasised that the organisation was ready to 'extend ... hand of cooperation and work together in this regard' (ibid.).

A copy of the same letter was sent to the Home Office, suggesting to 'meet ... as soon as possible to discuss and agree a strategy to ensure peace and harmony are maintained within our communities' (Murad 2013b). The same day, the MCB's leader issued a statement, calling for a 'coordinated, national response to ensure that these sorts of attacks never happen again' (Muslim Council of Britain 2013a). He went on to question the government's response to the escalation in anti-Muslim violence by adding that '[i]t cannot be right that a minority community is allowed to be targeted in this manner' (ibid.).

In response to Farooq Murad's letter, Eric Pickles (2013b) reassured the MCB that the government strongly condemned the attacks and their words 'received coverage in national press and was published online by several mosques.' He mentioned the role of Baroness Warsi in officially condemning the attacks and collecting views on what more could be done by the government. He added that his Department had funded the 'Tell MAMA' project as a way of tackling 'anti-Muslim hatred' (Ibid.).

As a way of demonstrating that the MCB's previous claims have not gone unanswered, Pickles recalled that the government had 'funded the first ever Srebrenica Memorial Day event to commemorate the genocide ... to warn of the consequences of when religious hate crime and intolerance goes unchallenged' (Ibid.). This was one of the key issues on which the MCB had campaigned in the past. And yet, quite a dry tone of the letter suggested that the Department preferred to remain neutral in its engagement with the MCB. There was little indication that the MCB's invitation to work together was accepted. Instead, the MCB was treated as one of many important Muslim voices representing a segment of Muslim population. This was reinforced by the final words of the letter:

> I hope this reassures you of our commitment to preventing and addressing hatred and extremism and hope you will communicate these assurances to your affiliates.
>
> (Ibid.)

There was no clear indication that there would be a coordinated national response to protect Muslim communities as was suggested by the MCB. There was a shared understanding that such types of incidents should not be allowed to happen. There was, however, little agreement on whether this was a matter of national or local importance. In his earlier speech on integration, Eric Pickles (2013a) made it clear that the Coalition's position on faith was that it 'provides a moral compass' and helps 'galvanise our communities.' However, unlike its predecessors, there was a strong belief that 'integration occurs locally and can't be imposed by Whitehall' (ibid.).

Conclusion

Over the last fifteen years, the MCB's engagement with the British political establishment was rather mixed. Its initial engagement with the Labour Party was facilitated by the latter's preoccupation with mainstreaming faith in the public sphere. Moreover, the MCB came to occupy a rather unlikely position as the government's preferred interlocutor through personal relations with individual ministers as well as a match in ideological preferences for communitarian equality and social cohesion. The nature of relations was altered once the idea of mainstreaming faith gave way to securitising Muslim identity in light of national terrorist threats and the militant rhetoric of some of the MCB's representatives. With the government's tighter controls on Muslim communities and co-optation of its leaders, it is not surprising that increased friction resulted in the eventual disengagement towards 2009.

Under the Coalition, the MCB's engagement with the government appears to have come full circle. Conservatives' preference for treating Muslims as individual citizens, coupled with a decentralised, local approach to community relations provided a new challenge for the MCB to remain an important Muslim voice in state-Muslim relations. The Coalition's refusal to engage with Islamist ideology and its U-turn from block-representation conceptualised under New Labour encouraged the MCB's search for alternative partners and political platforms from which to lobby the government. Personal connections and a shared agenda became important once again with the issue of combating Islamophobia and preventing hate crime, particularly in the aftermath of the Rigby affair.

The MCB's peaceful rhetoric and keen participation in interfaith events helped the organisation to keep its foot in the door of British politics. And yet, unlike its previous efforts to unite British Muslims in the days of the Rushdie affair, similar calls for national-level protection of the Muslim community in the aftermath of anti-Muslim attacks proved difficult to deliver. Increased pluralisation and maturity of Muslim communities, combined with the government's reluctance to repeat some of its past mistakes called for a more nuanced and diversified mode of engagement.

Notes

1 For more detailed accounts, please see Gilliat-Ray (2010), Radcliffe (2004) and Vidino (2011).
2 Prior to London bombings in 2005, the level of engagement was high in spite of occasional disagreements over the British foreign policy.
3 For a more nuanced exploration of New Labour's policies on faith, please see Allen (2011) and O'Toole et al. (2013).
4 New Labour's approach to religious governance contained a series of features which are more readily identified with a corporatist mode of engagement with specifically selected 'peak' organisations. Schmitter (1974: 86) defines these as 'associationally organised interests of civil society' with direct links 'with the decisional structures of the state'.
5 A further discussion on the MCB's insider status can be found in Radcliffe (2004).
6 For further details please see an updated version of these arguments presented in Sherif (2011).
7 See further discussions in O'Toole et al. (2012) and Thomas (2010).
8 The controversy centred on the issue of justifying violence against Israel and British troops.
9 Lee Rigby of the Royal Regiment of Fusiliers was attacked and killed by Michael Adebolajo and Michael Adebowale in Woolwich, southeast London on 22 May 2013. On anti-Muslim attacks, please see *Independent*, 'Woolwich Backlash: Ten Attacks on Mosques Since Murder of Drummer Lee Rigby', 28 May 2013, www.independent.co.uk/news/uk/crime/woolwich-backlash-ten-attacks-on-mosques-since-murder-of-drummer-lee-rigby-8633594.html (accessed 5 January 2013).

Bibliography

Allen, C. (2011) "We Don't Do God': A Critical Retrospective of New Labour's Approaches to 'Religion or Belief' and 'Faith'", *Culture and Religion*, 12(3): 259–275.

Allen, C. (2013) 'Passing the Dinner Table Test: Retrospective and Prospective Approaches to Tackling Islamophobia in Britain', *Sage Open*, 1–13.
Amin, M. (2011) 'The Muslim Council of Britain's Need for Constitutional Reform', January, available at: www.mohammedamin.com/Community_issues/MCB-constitutional-reform.html (accessed 2 January 2014).
Archer, T. (2009) 'Welcome to the Umma: The British State and its Muslim Citizens Since 9/11', *Cooperation and Conflict*, 44(3): 329–347.
Bari, M. (2006) 'Letter to Mrs Ruth Kelly', 14 October, available at: www.mcb.org.uk/uploads/rksgpav3.pdf (accessed 24 December 2013).
Bari, M. (2007) 'Secretary General's Address to the Annual General Meeting of the General Assembly', 16 June, available at: www.mcb.org.uk/uploads/SGAGM2008.pdf (accessed 6 January 2014).
Bari, M. (2012) 'It is Time for an Inclusive Politics', 8 March, available at: www.mcb.org.uk/features/features.php?ann_id=2232 (accessed 5 January 2014).
Birt, J. (2006) 'Good Imam, Bad Imam: Civic Religion and National Integration in Britain', *The Muslim World*, 96: 687–688.
Blair, T. (2001) 'Faith in Politics', Speech at Westminster Central Hall, London. Available at: www.britishpoliticalspeech.org/speech-archive.htm?speech=280 (accessed 5 January 2014).
Bunglawala, I. (2005) 'Muslim Council of Britain E-Newsletter', 1 May, available at: www.mcb.org.uk/media/view_issue.php (accessed 5 December 2012).
Bunting, M. (2010) 'The MCB's Wonderland Election', *The Guardian*, 18 June, available at: www.guardian.co.uk/commentisfree/belief/2010/jun/18/the-mcbs-wonderland-election (accessed 3 January 2013).
Cesari, J. and McLoughlin, S. (eds) (2005) *European Muslims and the Secular State*, Aldershot: Ashgate.
Commission on Integration and Cohesion (2007) 'Themes, Messages And Challenges: A Final Analysis Of Key Themes From The Public Consultation', June, available at: http://collections.europarchive.org/tna/20080726153624/http://www.integrationandcohesion.org.uk/~/media/assets/www.integrationandcohesion.org.uk/themes_messages_and_challenges_final_analysis%20pdf.ashx (accessed 5 December 2012).
Communities and Local Government (2004) 'Working Together: Co-operation Between Government and Faith Communities'. Available at: http://webarchive.nationalarchives.gov.uk/20120919132719/www.communities.gov.uk/documents/communities/pdf/151393.pdf (accessed 5 December 2012).
Communities and Local Government (2012) 'Creating the Conditions for Integration'. Available at: www.gov.uk/government/uploads/system/uploads/attachment_data/file/7504/2092103.pdf (accessed 19 January 2014).
Conservative Party's Group on National and International Security (2007) 'Uniting the Country: Interim Report on National Cohesion', Interim Report.
Gilliat-Ray, S. (2010) *Muslims in Britain: An Introduction*. Cambridge: Cambridge University Press.
Glynn, S. (2009) 'Liberalising Islam: Creating Brits of the Islamic Persuasion'. Available at: www.sarahglynn.net/Liberalising%20Islam.html (accessed 10 March 2011).
Hansard (2003) 8 September. Available at: www.publications.parliament.uk/pa/ld200203/ldhansrd/vo030908/text/30908w06.htm (accessed 2 January 2014).
Hawkins, W. (2013) 'Faith in Government', *Publicspirit*, 7 October, available at: www.publicspirit.org.uk/faith-in-government/ (accessed 17 December 2013).

HM Government (2009) 'Pursue, Prevent, Protect, Prepare: The United Kingdom's Strategy for Countering International Terrorism', March, available at: www.official-docum ents.gov.uk/document/cm75/7547/7547.pdf (accessed 14 December 2013).
HM Government (2011) 'Prevent Strategy.' Available at: www.gov.uk/government/up loads/system/uploads/attachment_data/file/97976/prevent-strategy-review.pdf (accessed 10 December 2013).
Home Office (2013a) 'Home Secretary Statement on West Midlands Attacks', 21 July, available at: www.gov.uk/government/news/home-secretary-statement-on-west-midla nds-attacks (accessed 7 January 2014).
Home Office (2013b) 'Security Minister Visits West Midlands Following Terror Incidents', 24 July, available at: www.gov.uk/government/news/security-minister-visits-west-midlands-following-terror-incidents (accessed 6 February 2014).
House of Commons (2005) 'Terrorism and Community Relations', *6th Report of Session 2004–2005*, Volume 1, 22 March, available at: www.publications.parliament. uk/pa/cm200405/cmselect/cmhaff/165/165.pdf (accessed 5 January 2014).
Interview 2, Leeds, 11 January 2012.
Interview 5, Leicester, 26 January 2012.
Interview 6, Leicester, 26 January 2012.
Interview 9, London, 6 February 2012.
Interview 10, London, 7 February 2012.
Interview 11, London, 26 February 2012.
Kelly, R. (2006) 'Britain: Our Values, Our Responsibilities', Speech to Muslim organisations on working together to tackle extremism, London, 11 October, available at: http://ukingermany.fco.gov.uk/en/news/?view=Speech&id=4615992 (accessed 5 December 2013).
Kepel, G. (1997) *Allah in the West: Islamic Movements in America and Europe.* Cambridge: Policy Press.
Milmo, C. and Morris, N. (2013) 'Woolwich Backlash: Ten Attacks on Mosques Since Murder of Drummer Lee Rigby', *Independent*, 28 May, available at: www.indep endent.co.uk/news/uk/crime/woolwich-backlash-ten-attacks-on-mosques-since-murder-of-drummer-lee-rigby-8633594.html (accessed 5 January 2013).
Murad, F. (2011) 'MCB Welcomes Baroness Warsi's Comments', *News Release*, 20 January, available at: www.mcb.org.uk/index.php?option=com_content&view=a rticle&id=1066&Itemid=54 (accessed 19 January 2013).
Murad, F. (2012) 'Secretary General's Address to the Annual General Meeting of General Assembly', Annual Report. Available at: www.mcb.org.uk/uploads/FINAL%20 MCB%20Annual%20Report%20Mar%202011.pdf (accessed 2 December 2013).
Murad, F. (2013a) 'MCB's Letter to Eric Pickles', 22 July, available at: https:// docs.google.com/file/d/0B0dlvxkBijyZT2VSUDV4SHpEbWc/edit?pli=1 (accessed 8 December 2013).
Murad, F. (2013b) 'MCB's Letter to Theresa May', 22 July, available at: https:// docs.google.com/file/d/0B0dlvxkBijyZdzlOM2JJTVQ0Ync/edit?pli=1 (accessed 8 December 2013).
Muslim Council of Britain (1998) 'MCB Hosts Luncheon Meeting with Jack Straw', *Press Release*, 2 December, available at. www.mcb.org.uk/media/archive/news021298. html (accessed 10 January 2014).
Muslim Council of Britain (2000) 'A Recognition Of Faith Identity', *Press Release*, 16 June, available at: www.mcb.org.uk/media/archive/news160600.html (accessed 5 December 2012).

Muslim Council of Britain (2001) 'The Common Good', *The Newsletter of the Muslim Council of Britain*, 1(4).
Muslim Council of Britain (2005) *Newsletter*, 56(1), May, available at: www.mcb.org. uk/media/view_issue.php (accessed 5 December 2013).
Muslim Council of Britain (2007) 'Briefing Paper: Our stand on Multiculturalism, Citizenship, Extremism and Expectations From the Commission on Integration and Cohesion', January, available at: www.mcb.org.uk/downloads/MCB%20ReDoc% 20Briefing%20Paper%20PRINTRUN.pdf (accessed 5 December 2012).
Muslim Council of Britain (2012a) 'MCB Calls for People of All Faiths to 'Come Together to Build Trust and Work for Common Values', 16 February, available at: www.mcb.org.uk/index.php?option=com_content&view=article&id=2142&Itemid= 93 (accessed 6 January 2014).
Muslim Council of Britain (2012b) 'MCB Eid Reception in Whitehall: Celebration of Unity and Dialogue', *Press Release*, 15 November, available at: www.mcb.org.uk/ article_detail.php?article=announcement-1040 (accessed 6 January 2014).
Muslim Council of Britain (2013a) 'Anti-Muslim Terrorism: Time for a Coordinated, National Response', *Press Release*, 22 July, available at: www.mcb.org.uk/index. php?option=com_content&view=article&id=2361:anti-muslim-terrorism-time-for-a-coordinated-national-response&catid=40:press-release (accessed 8 December 2013).
Muslim Council of Britain (2013b) 'Muslim Council of Britain Eid Reception Concludes Successful World Islamic Economic Forum in London Friday', *Press Release*, 8 November, available at: www.mcb.org.uk/index.php?option=com_con tent&view=article&id=2411:mcbnewstemplate&catid=82:mcb-news (accessed 6 January 2014).
Muslim Council of Britain (2013c) 'Muslim Council of Britain Welcomes Baroness Warsi's Robust Defence of Islam and Muslims', *Press Release*, 22 November, available at: www.mcb.org.uk/index.php?option=com_content&view=article&id= 2420:pr-template&catid=40:press-release (accessed 6 December 2014).
Muslim Weekly (2004) 'Interview with Iqbal Sacranie', 19 May, available at: www. mcb.org.uk/downloads/Interview190504.pdf (accessed 5 June 2013).
O'Toole, T. *et al.* (2012) 'Balancing Tolerance, Security and Muslim Engagement in the United Kingdom: The Impact of the 'Prevent' Agenda', *Critical Studies on Terrorism*, 5(3): 373–389.
O'Toole, T. *et al.* (ed.) (2013) *Taking Part: Muslim Participation in Contemporary Governance*. Bristol: University of Bristol.
Odone, C. (2013) 'Baroness Warsi: Muslims Want to Organise Peace Meetings – This is Community Activism of the Right Kind', *Telegraph*, 24 May, available at: www. telegraph.co.uk/news/uknews/terrorism-in-the-uk/10080108/Baroness-Warsi-Muslims-want-to-organise-peace-meetings-this-is-community-activism-of-the-right-kind.html (accessed 5 January 2014).
Peach, C. (2005) 'Muslims in the UK', in T. Abbas (ed.) *Muslim Britain: Communities Under Pressure*. Zed Books Ltd: London.
Pedziwiatr, K. (2007) 'Creating New Discursive Arenas and Influencing the Policies of the State: The Case of the Muslim Council of Britain', *Social Compass*, 54(2): 267–280.
Pickles, E. (2013a) 'Uniting Our Communities: Integration in 2013', Speech by Secretary of State at an event hosted by Policy Exchange and British Future, 15 January, available at: www.gov.uk/government/speeches/uniting-our-communities-integration-in-2013 (accessed 7 January 2014).

Pickles, E. (2013b) 'Letter to the MCB', 6 August, available at: www.gov.uk/governm ent/uploads/system/uploads/attachment_data/file/226833/130806_-_Letter_to_MCB. pdf (accessed 8 December 2013).
Populus (2006) 'Muslim Omnibus', Poll of Muslims, Commissioned by Policy Exchange. Available at: www.populus.co.uk/uploads/download_pdf-131206-Policy-Exchange-Poll-of-Muslims—Living-Apart-Together.pdf (accessed 3 January 2013).
Radcliffe, L. (2004) 'A Muslim Lobby at Whitehall', *Islam and Christian-Muslim Relations*, 15(3): 365–386.
Sacranie, I. (1999) 'Secretary General's Address at Reception For Prime Minister', London, 5 May, available at: www.mcb.org.uk/index.php?option=com_content& view=article&id=1248&Itemid=96 (accessed 5 January 2014).
Sacranie, I. (2006) 'Secretary General's Speech to the MCB's Ninth Annual General Meeting', 4 June, available at: www.mcb.org.uk/uploads/SECGEN.pdf (accessed 5 December 2012).
Schmitter, P. (1974) 'Still the Century of Corporatism?', *Review of Politics*, 36(1): 85–131.
Sherif, J. (2003) 'Campaigning for a Religious Question in the 2001 Census'. Available at: www.mcb.org.uk/downloads/census2001.pdf (accessed 4 January 2014).
Sherif, J. (2011) 'A Census Chronicle – Reflections on the Campaign for a Religion Question in the 2001 Census for England and Wales', *Journal of Beliefs and Values: Studies in Religion and Education*, 32(1): 1–18.
SWP Online (2011) 'Statement on David Cameron's Multicultural Speech', 9 February, available at: www.swp.org.uk/press/statement-on-david-camerons-muliculturalism-speech (accessed 17 January 2014).
Thomas, P. (2010) 'Failed and Friendless: The UK's 'Preventing Violent Extremism' Programme', *The British Journal of Politics and International Relations*, 12(3): 442–458.
Vidino, L. (2011) 'London's Frantic Quest for the Muslim Holy Grail: The Post-9/11 Evolution of the Relationship Between Whitehall and the British Muslim Community', *Religious Compass* 3(4): 129–138.
Warsi, S. (2008) Interview, *Telegraph*, 7 October.
Warsi, S. (2011) 'University of Leicester Sir Sigmund Sternberg Lecture', Speech, 20 January, available at: http://sayeedawarsi.com/2011/01/20/university-of-leicester-sir-sigmund-sternberg-lecture (accessed 17 January 2014).

11 Muslims in Parliament
A myth of futility

Ekaterina Kolpinskaya

Introduction

The importance of Muslim parliamentary representation is two-fold. First, it is based on the assumption that, as well as good minority representation in general, it increases the quality of democracy and contributes to the country's well-being by enhancing political participation, reducing socio-political exclusion, and introduce as role models for British Muslims (Phillips 1995; Saward 2011). Secondly, it improves awareness of the political elite about the society's trivia and people's views and attitudes, whereby Muslim MPs deliver their expertise and insights on issues of concern for the Muslim minority (Saalfeld and Kyriakopoulou 2011). These ideas have been endorsed by all the main British parties and political institutions. The House of Commons, for instance, regularly publishes reports on the state of ethnic and religious representation in the Chamber and encourages the parties to facilitate access to Parliament for candidates from minority, including Muslim, backgrounds in order to ensure effectiveness and fairness of the House as a representative body (e.g. House of Commons 2009: 17–21). Responding to the call for widening representation, the main political parties pledge to bring politicians from diverse backgrounds to Parliament in their manifestos and candidate recruitment strategies (e.g. Labour Party 2010: 4; Conservative Party 2010: 2; Durose *et al.* 2011). As a result, the number of Members of Parliament from Muslim backgrounds[1] has grown from one in 1997 to nine elected at the 2010 General Election (Muslim Vote 2010).

However, despite the increasing number of parliamentarians from Muslim backgrounds, British Muslims feel as under-represented by the main parties as they did before 1997 when the first Muslim MP was elected (Heath *et al.* 2013: 95). This indicates that the growing Muslim parliamentary presence is not enough to 'rebuild trust and restore a dialogue between Parliament and those whom it represents' (House of Commons 2009: 19–20). This could be a problem relating to the parliamentary performance of Muslim MPs and their inability to exercise legislative powers and fully participate in the legislative process, which is often blamed on the constrained parliamentary environment dominated by 'white, middle-aged, middle class men' in the case of other under-represented groups (Durose *et al.* 2011: 41), which makes Muslim politicians behave like non-Muslim ones (Sinno and Tatari 2009: 124). It also casts doubts on the ability of Muslim parliamentarians to improve the representation of minority interests under the constraints of the modern political system (Saalfeld and Kyriakopoulou 2011: 246).

One way in which this representation is thought to be achieved is through increasing the access of Muslim parliamentarians to the legislative process though their inclusion in different aspects of legislative decision-making, drafting and introducing legislation. Drawing upon the analysis of parliamentary careers, this chapter identifies the types of legislative roles MPs from Muslim backgrounds hold and examines how they enable and restrict Muslim parliamentarians in contributing to the legislative process. The study argues that the legislative behaviour of Muslim MPs is determined by their parliamentary roles rather than religious background, and is affected by their parliamentary duties and responsibilities, including ministerial positions and memberships on committees. It shows that although the number of Muslim parliamentarians is small, they are disproportionally well-represented on the frontbench, which opens up opportunities to influence the legislative process and policy-making. Muslim backbenchers are also involved in scrutinising legislative proposals and policies at the committee stage. Legislative roles enable MPs from Muslim backgrounds to actively contribute to producing minority-related legislation and policies, as demonstrated in the analyses. Overall, the chapter shows that in spite of the concerns raised over the quality of Muslim minority representation (Heath *et al.* 2013), they are not a result of poor parliamentary performance of Muslim parliamentarians. Instead, Muslim MPs engage in various stages of legislative decision-making and contribute to the legislative process in accordance to their parliamentary duties and responsibilities. With this in mind, the problem of the public and minority dissatisfaction with the quality of representation could be caused by miscommunication and/or misconceptions of what constitutes better representation, and how it should be achieved.

Why are legislative roles important?

The concept of legislative roles is based on the assumption that MPs' parliamentary routines, or roles, frame their legislative behaviour in a formalised institutional environment (Strøm 1997: 158). Holding different roles allows MPs to contribute to decision-making in various ways and ensure checks and balances on legislative decision-making. Initially, this concept did not consider for ethno-religious identity (Wahlke *et al.* 1962; Searing 1994). It has, however, been recently adapted for the study of the parliamentary behaviour of migrant-origin ethnic minority politicians (Saalfeld *et al.* 2011; Saalfeld and Kyriakopoulou in Bird *et al.* 2011). This research does not consider the impact of legislative roles on parliamentary behaviour in a broader sense because of the limitations of the data and a small number of Muslim Members of

Parliament[2] – it has a more specific purpose: to identify whether and how holding a particular type of legislative role enables an MP from Muslim backgrounds to influence legislation.

Therefore, the chapter identifies the legislative roles of MPs from Muslim backgrounds and examines how these roles affect their legislative behaviour in the House of Commons. By adopting an institution-centred approach (Norton 2001), which suggests that parliamentary rules and procedures are the main predictors of individual behaviour, this study will demonstrate that Muslim MPs are able contributors to the legislative process, including the introduction and scrutiny of legislative proposals and policies.

It is expected that MPs from Muslim backgrounds hold various legislative roles that affect the way in which they engage with the legislative process, and that the influence of these roles is more significant than that of their ethno-religious background. If true, it shows that Muslim parliamentarians are enabled and constrained by their roles rather than their religious minority background. Therefore, if a particular type of role encourages and allows them to play a major role in preparing, proposing or scrutinising legislation, there is no reason to consider Muslim politicians to be deprived of opportunities to contribute the legislative process just because they are Muslim.

Previous research identifies two types of legislative roles – leadership (or frontbench) and preference (or backbench) (Searing 1994; Saalfeld and Kyriakopoulou in Bird *et al.* 2011). Choosing between the two is a trade-off between more legislative power and more freedom of political self-expression. For instance, a member of the Government is enabled to introduce legislation, but is, on the other hand, bound by collective agreement and accountable to Parliament. A backbencher has fewer opportunities to introduce legislation, but has plenty of opportunity to scrutinise government policies and legislative proposals.

Leadership roles are based upon the official positions of MPs in the Government, broadly defined as senior ministers[3], junior ministers[4], the Law Officers, and Whips[5]. In some cases a minister is known by a 'courtesy title' that has no legal or constitutional significance, but reflects on the assigned duty (Cabinet Office 2010: 20–29). Parliamentary Private Secretaries (PPSs) are not members of the Government, but are included in its structure. They are bound by collective agreement and assist ministers in conducting parliamentary business, hence, hold a leadership role (Cabinet Office 2010: 23).

Members of Parliament in leadership roles have the most opportunities to propose legislation as government business taking precedence at most sittings of the House of Commons. Depending on their duties and responsibilities, government ministers and PPSs prepare and present bills, and handle the committee stage and debates on the floor of the House. Although the contribution of a single MP to each bill is difficult to identify, it is not essential for the research; the key point is to highlight the fact that being in the Government enables junior ministers and PPS to make legislative proposals as a part of their legislative roles. In principle, bills are initiated and presented by senior ministers; PPSs and junior ministers prepare them and handle the committee stage of its scrutiny. The Whips ensure the attendance of MPs for important votes and maintain the party's voting strength which is crucial for passing legislation through the House. Overall, Members of Parliament in leadership roles propose and support the majority of successful bills.

Ministers are accountable to Parliament, which ensures scrutiny of the Government's policies and legislative proposals, which is the opportunity for backbenchers to influence the legislative process. Every government bill is read three times before being sent to the House of Lords. At the Committee (after a second reading) and Report stages (before a third reading) backbenchers and members of the Government (usually junior ministers) scrutinise bills, and suggest and negotiate amendments (Cabinet Office 2010: 42). Serving on committees is an important part of the backbench legislative role. It empowers every MP to contribute to the legislative process by considering legislative proposals in detail. This compensates for a lack of power to propose their own legislation with the exception of Private Members' Bills that rarely make it onto the statute book.

Legislative roles are dynamic. There is evidence of 'role-switching' depending on the political context, personality and career stage of an MP (Andeweg 1997). The majority of MPs start as backbenchers. Some get promoted to the frontbench, but the majority stay on the backbench or return there after spending some time in leadership positions. The career development of MPs is usually gradual; a backbencher becomes a PPS to be further promoted to ministerial positions. Returning to the backbench, if it happens, is caused by a variety of reasons from disagreement with the party leadership to age.

Data and method

Limitations of the sample and data mean that a largely qualitative approach to the analysis is required. A micro-analytic approach to studying parliamentary roles and behaviours increases the validity of the research as an exploratory, if fairly descriptive, study. It is intended to summarise what we know about the legislative behaviour of Muslim Members of Parliament so far rather than to develop a generalisable framework of what we would expect all Muslim MPs to do following election.

The primary data for this analysis include the parliamentary profiles of Muslim MPs (Parliament 2013–2013h; Guardian 2013–2013a), which provide detailed information about the career trajectories of parliamentarians, their responsibilities (such as memberships of the Select and Public Bill Committees), as well as ministerial positions. By outlining MPs' duties, the data help to identify their legislative roles. These roles are defined on the basis of their official positions in the Government and Parliament and based on the parliamentary profiles and memberships of MPs from Muslim backgrounds. Examining the effect of Muslim MPs' roles on legislative behaviour, the chapter considers their membership of the Select and Public Bill Committees

Muslims in Parliament: a myth of futility 219

and the number of Private Members' Bills they introduced. Government ministers and PPSs are considered to have a higher impact on the legislative process as the result of their work in the Government. On the other hand, if backbenchers and junior ministers serve on several Public Bill and Select Committees their impact on scrutiny of legislation is significant too.

Considering for role-switching between elections, the analysis is conducted by session rather than by Parliament. Leadership roles are assigned to MPs who have been once promoted to a ministerial or PPS position. The rest are considered to be backbenchers. The experiences of ministers and PPS as backbenchers are explored on a case-to-case basis. Importantly, the research does not examine if Muslim MPs represent minority interests, and it does not consider for the content of their proposals and contributions to debates, rather it focusses on the forms of engagement with the legislative process.

The data on legislative roles are examined and contextualised using other sources of parliamentary documentation, including the Code of Conduct of Members (House of Commons 2012a); the Cabinet Manual (Cabinet Office 2010); the Guide for Select Committee Members (House of Commons 2011); the Sessional Information Digest (House of Commons 1998–2012); the Public Bill Committees debates House of Commons (1998–2007) as well as the previous research, reports and notes on representation (House of Commons 2009; Durose *et al.* 2011; Cracknell 2012; Duckworth and Cracknell 2013).

Identifying legislative roles

Muslim MPs frequently hold leadership roles. As Figure 11.1 shows, at least one Muslim MP has been on the frontbench since the 2004–05 parliamentary session, and their presence in the Government has been growing. By 2012 four of six Labour and one of three Conservative Muslim MPs have held ministerial or PPS positions. Four Muslim MPs have been on the backbench throughout the 2010–12 session. This includes the newly elected Labour (Yasmin

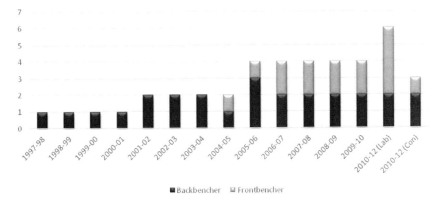

Figure 11.1 Legislative roles of Muslim MPs by session
Source: Parliament 2013–2013h; Guardian 2013–2013a.

Qureshi) and Conservative (Nadhim Zahawi and Rehman Chishti) politicians and recently retired Mohammad Sarwar. Finally, Khalid Mahmood was a PPS between 2004 and 2006, but has been a backbencher ever since.

The data demonstrate the change of legislative roles held by Muslim MPs between 1997 and 2012. Mohammad Sarwar, the first British Muslim MP, was elected in 1997 and remained a backbencher until 2010. After the 2001 election he was joined by Khalid Mahmood. Between 2006 and 2010 Sadiq Khan and Shahid Malik held junior ministerial positions, whereas Mohammad Sarwar and Khalid Mahmood remained backbenchers. In 2010 Shahid Malik lost his seat, and Mohammad Sarwar stood down. Despite losing the 2010 General Election, the Labour Party increased the number of Muslim Members of Parliament from four to six, including three female Muslim MPs elected for the first time. Two of them, Rushanara Ali and Shabana Mahmood, were promoted to junior ministers. Newly elected Anas Sarwar was also appointed as a PPS to Liam Byrne. Currently four Muslim Labour MPs are holding leadership positions, and two parliamentarians, Yasmin Qureshi and Khalid Mahmood, are backbenchers. The first Muslim MPs from the Conservative Party were elected in 2010. They include one minister, Sajid Javid, and two backbenchers, Nadhim Zahawi and Rehman Chishti.

Overall, of eleven Muslim parliamentarians, seven have held leadership roles at some point in their parliamentary careers, and four have always remained on the backbench. This shows a skew towards holding frontbench posts among Muslim politicians. It stands out in comparison with parliamentarians from other under-represented groups such as women, non-Muslim ethnic minorities, and white MPs from Jewish backgrounds (Table 11.1).

Table 11.1 shows frontbench to backbench ratios for women and minority MPs in the 2010 Parliament, which is by far the most diverse (Durose et al. 2011). The ratios are calculated to represent how many backbenchers there are for one frontbencher in each group, namely MPs with Jewish, Muslim, non-Muslim BME backgrounds and women MPs. The ratios instead of actual numbers are used to account for differences in the sizes of these groups. The number of MPs in each group is larger than the number of Muslim parliamentarians, whereby 143 women, 19 non-Muslim BME politicians and 25 MPs with a Jewish background took their seats in the 2010 Parliament, comparing to 9 Muslim parliamentarians. The ratio of frontbenchers to backbenchers in the case of those groups is lower than for Muslim MPs and never reaches 1:1. This means that there are fewer politicians in ministerial roles than backbenchers from these groups. Muslim MPs, on the other hand, being smaller in numbers and under-represented in the Chamber, are over-represented on the frontbench. The ratio of 1.25 demonstrates that there are more frontbenchers than backbenchers among parliamentarians from Muslim backgrounds.

A comparison between women and Muslim parliamentarians illustrates this best. The number of women in the House of Commons exceeds the number of Muslim MPs by almost 16 times, but women are half as likely to

Table 11.1 MPs from under-represented groups in the 2010 Parliament by role type

	Ratio fb/bb	Frontbenchers, N	Backbenchers, N	MPs, N
Muslim MPs	1.25	5	4	9
Jewish MPs	0.8	11	14	25
Non-Muslim Ethnic Minority MPs	0.7	8	11	19
Women MPs	0.6	56	87	143

Source: Cracknell 2012; Duckworth and Cracknell 2013; Parliament 2013–2013h; *The Guardian* 2013–2013a.

be frontbenchers. Due to the limited availability of ministerial positions, the number of frontbenchers does not increase when the number of MPs from the under-represented groups grows. This is reflected in low frontbenchers-to-backbenchers ratios of groups more numerous than Muslims, particularly women. This shows how the likelihood of promotion to the frontbench for women and minority MPs might drop when their numbers increase. Muslim MPs, on the other hand, are fewer. This enhances the chances for each of them to be promoted to the frontbench as a result of partly their career aspirations and partly the desire of the main parties to improve Muslim minority representation by making their presence in the House more visible. Table 11.2 shows which ministerial positions have been held by MPs from Muslim backgrounds so far. It includes six of eight Labour Muslim parliamentarians elected between 2001 and 2010, namely Khalid Mahmood, Shahid Malik, Sadiq Khan, Rushanara Ali, Shabana Mahmood and Anas Sarwar, and one of three Conservative Muslim MPs, who were first elected in the 2010 General Election.

As with politicians from other religious backgrounds, Muslim MPs gradually advanced their parliamentary careers by moving from Private Parliamentary Secretaries to ministerial positions, as shown in Table 11.2. With the exception of Rushanara Ali and Shabana Mahmood, all Muslim frontbenchers went through a government apprenticeship as Private Parliamentary Secretaries. Driven by personal aspirations, their career trajectories were, however, shaped by the parties' needs. For instance, the Conservative Party has been struggling to improve its minority representation (Cameron 2005). Mindful of this, the appointment of a Muslim ministerial high-flyer as a PPS improves the party's representation record and tests the member's loyalty and ability before further ministerial promotion. For instance, Sajid Javid was a PPS to John Hayes and George Osborne before becoming the Economic Secretary. Other Conservative Muslim MPs, Nadhim Zahawi and Rehman Chishti[6], also show ministerial ambitions, but remain on the backbench due to an unproven record of the party loyalty[7]. Rehman Chishti, for instance, joined

Table 11.2 Members of Parliament with Muslim background on leadership roles, 1997–2012

Member of Parliament	Ministerial and PPS positions
Labour Party	
Rushanara Ali	Shadow Minister for International Development 2010–
Sadiq Khan	PPS to Jack Straw as Leader of the House of Commons 2007; Assistant Government Whip 2007–08; Parliamentary Under-Secretary of State, Department for Communities and Local Government 2008–09; Minister of State, Department for Transport (attending cabinet) 2009–10; Shadow Secretary of State for Transport 2010; Shadow Lord Chancellor and Secretary of State for Justice (with responsibility for political and constitutional reform) 2010–; Minister for London 2013–
Khalid Mahmood	PPS to Tony McNulty as Minister of State: Department for Transport 2004–05, Home Office 2005–06
Shabana Mahmood	Shadow Minister for: Home Office 2010–11, Business, Innovation and Skills (Higher Education) 2011–
Shahid Malik	PPS to Jim Knight as Minister of State: Department for Education and Skills 2006–07; Parliamentary Under-Secretary of State for International Development 2007–08; Parliamentary Under-Secretary of State for Justice 2008–09; Parliamentary Under-Secretary of State for Communities 2009–10
Anas Sarwar	PPS for Liam Byrne as Shadow Minister for Work and Pensions and a Deputy Leader of Scottish Labour
Conservative Party	
Sajid Javid	PPS to John Hayes as Minister of State for Further Education, Skills and Lifelong Learning 2010–11 and George Osborne as Chancellor of the Exchequer 2011–12; Economic Secretary, HM Treasury 2012–

Source: Parliament 2013–2013h; *The Guardian* 2013.

the Conservative Party after unsuccessfully standing at the 2005 General Election as a Labour candidate (Foot 2006).

The Labour Party, by contrast, has a record of exceptionally fast promotions for Muslim parliamentarians, with the exceptions of Mohammad Sarwar and Yasmin Qureshi. For instance, Rushanara Ali and Shabana Mahmood were appointed junior ministers shortly after the 2010 General Election, missing the PPS stage. The promotion of Rushanara Ali to Shadow Minister for International Development is well-grounded in her pre-parliamentary experience; work in MPs' offices, for the Home Office and a Labour-affiliated think-tank, which ensured her expertise and loyalty to the party, and therefore, her rapid promotion[8]. Shabana Mahmood, on the other hand, had an extensive background in Law as a practicing barrister, but virtually no political experience prior to becoming the Shadow Minister. The political benefits of both appointments are obvious. The Labour Party is not only the first to get three Muslim women elected to the House of Commons, but to provide them with legislative powers and potentially a position in the Government should Labour win in 2015. The promotion of two of three Muslim female MPs to junior ministers kills two birds with one stone corresponding to the party's belief in improving both female and minority representation by increasing the numbers of respectively women and ethnic minorities in Parliament (Labour Party 2010: 9.3).

Labour Muslim frontbenchers rarely return to the backbench. The only example of role-switching is Khalid Mahmood, a PPS to Tony McNulty, who returned to the backbench after calling for a change of the party leadership in September 2006 (BBC 2006). Other Labour Muslim frontbenchers once promoted tend to remain ministers whilst in Parliament[9]. This observation cannot be extended to the Conservative Party yet, because all the Tory Muslim MPs are currently serving their first term in the House of Commons. Without a case for comparison from other parliamentary parties, the consistency of career development among the Labour Muslim MPs cannot be considered a party trend. There is a possibility for it to be extended to other parties in the following years.

Legislating as a frontbencher

Apart from improving descriptive minority representation in the Government, and the Shadow Cabinet the promotion of Muslim parliamentarians to the frontbench provides Muslim MPs with practical opportunities to legislate. MPs in leadership roles are on the frontline of the legislative process because most sittings in the House are devoted to government policies and legislation. As a result, frontbenchers, especially from the Government party, legislate the most. This does not include the Shadow Cabinet which is formed from the frontbench members of the Official Opposition party. It replicates the structure of the Government and ensures its thorough scrutiny during the parliamentary debates, on Select and Public Bill Committees. However, the opportunities for Shadow ministers to introduce legislation are limited to the Opposition Days in Parliament. In practice, the lack of opportunities to introduce legislation for the Opposition makes the legislative behaviour of Shadow Ministers similar to that of backbenchers. Examining how leadership roles enable Muslim MPs as legislators, the study focuses on members of the 1997–2010 Labour and 2010 Coalition Governments and MPs from the Governments' parties holding ministerial positions, as listed in Table 11.3, which covers the period between the 1997 General Election and the end of the 2010–12 parliamentary session.

Although there had not been Muslim ministers in the 1997 and 2001 Parliaments, the 2005 Parliament witnessed three of four Muslim MPs performing leadership roles, including Shahid Malik, Khalid Mahmood, and Sadiq Khan. All started from PPS positions, but Khalid Mahmood returned to the backbench in 2006, whereas Shahid Malik and Sadiq Khan remained junior

Table 11.3 Members of Government from Muslim backgrounds, 1997–2012

Member of Parliament	Ministerial and PPS Positions
Labour Government, 1997–2010	
Sadiq Khan	PPS to Jack Straw as Leader of the House of Commons 2007; Assistant Government Whip 2007–08; Parliamentary Under-Secretary of State, Department for Communities and Local Government 2008–09; Minister of State, Department for Transport (attending cabinet) 2009–10
Khalid Mahmood	PPS to Tony McNulty as Minister of State: Department for Transport 2004–05, Home Office 2005–06
Shahid Malik	PPS to Jim Knight as Minister of State: Department for Education and Skills 2006–07; Parliamentary Under-Secretary of State for International Development 2007–08; Parliamentary Under-Secretary of State for Justice 2008–09; Parliamentary Under-Secretary of State for Communities 2009–10
Coalition Government (Conservative Party), 2010–	
Sajid Javid	PPS to John Hayes as Minister of State for Further Education, Skills and Lifelong Learning 2010–11 & George Osborne as Chancellor of the Exchequer 2011–12; Economic Secretary, HM Treasury 2012–

Source: Parliament 2013–2013h; *The Guardian* 2013.

ministers until May 2010, and moved to the Opposition frontbench after the defeat in the 2010 General Election. Under the Coalition Government, one of the first Conservative intake of Muslim MPs, Sajid Javid is holding a position as a Secretary of State for Culture, Media and Sport and Equalities, preceded by the posts of Financial Secretary, Economic Secretary and PPS. The leadership roles of the Labour Muslim MPs suggest that they are involved in preparing legislative proposals and their scrutiny at the committee stage. The only Conservative Muslim minister, Sajid Javid, had similar responsibilities as a PPS, but is unlikely to participate in committees after being appointed Economic Secretary to the Treasury.

Although government ministers are not precluded from serving on either Public Bill or Select Committees, they avoid associating themselves with recommendations critical of the Government (Cabinet Office 2010: 30–37). These considerations, as well as time pressures, limit committee membership of frontbenchers, especially of senior ministers[10]. If ministers join a committee, it usually corresponds to their ministerial responsibilities and area of expertise. These limitations are imposed to secure the principle of collective decision-making in the Government, whereby any decision of Cabinet or one of its committees is binding on all members of the Government, regardless of their personal views (Cabinet Office 2010: 30–31). Government ministers have a right to disagree at the preliminary stages of drafting a bill, but they are bound by collective agreement once the bill goes to Parliament for further consideration. The Ministerial Code summarises the principle of collective responsibility as follows: 'The principle of collective responsibility, save where it is explicitly set aside, requires that Ministers should be able to express their views frankly in the expectation that they can argue freely in private while maintaining a united front when decisions have been reached' (Cabinet Office 2010: 31).

The Ministerial Code, therefore, constraints political self-expression of the members of Government and Parliamentary Private Secretaries, including those from Muslim backgrounds. Although Muslim MPs are limited in their ability to publicly interrogate and scrutinise the Government's legislation and policies, they, on the other hand, have more opportunities to initiate legislative proposals. Once in the Government, Muslim MPs have a responsibility to prepare legislative proposals that almost always become law because of the skew of legislative powers, which advantages the party that forms the Government. As a result, Muslim parliamentarians have as much influence on initiating and drafting legislation and policies as non-Muslim parliamentarians in similar legislative roles.

Private Bill and Select Committee membership

The Government's accountability to Parliament is ensured by the scrutiny of government policies and bills in Select and Public Bill Committees. Elected from the Members of the House, they empower backbenchers to consider and amend the Government's legislation and policies. The House of Commons Select Committees examine the work of each government department with regard to spending, policies, and administration, whereas the Backbench Business Committee schedules non-government business in the Commons. Serving on Committees in particular empowers Muslim backbenchers who have more freedom to participate and take up formal responsibilities as chairs. The majority of the Committees act on a permanent basis with members being re-elected each parliamentary session.

Public Bills Committees examine legislative proposals in detail. They are named after bills under consideration. Government ministers supply oral and written evidence to committees and amend legislative proposals after considering committee reports. They rarely serve on Select Committees, but Private Parliamentary Secretaries and junior ministers often engage with Public Bills Committees at the Committee stage of the scrutiny of legislation.

Muslim MPs' memberships on committees show that their areas of expertise include a wide range of issues such as transport, education, justice and human rights, work and pensions, and international and community development. Table 11.4 demonstrates the memberships of eleven Muslim MPs on the Select and Public Bill Committees by the types of legislative roles they hold.

Frontbenchers' committee membership, although limited, largely corresponds to their government responsibilities. For instance, being a member of the

226 Ekaterina Kolpinskaya

Table 11.4 Membership in Select and Public Bills Committees

Member of Parliament	Select Committee	Public Bill Committee
Frontbenchers		
Rushanara Ali	–	–
Sajid Javid	Public Accounts Work and Pensions	–
Sadiq Khan	Public Accounts (as a backbencher)	Business Rate Supplements Bill 2008–09 Criminal Justice and Immigration Bill 2007–08 Criminal Justice and Immigration Bill 2006–07 Crown Employment (Nationality) Bill 2006–07 Digital Switchover (Disclosure of Information) Bill 2006–07 Forced Marriage (Civil Protection) Bill 2006–07 Parliament (Joint Departments) Bill 2006–07 Finance (No. 2) Bill 2005–06 Northern Ireland (Miscellaneous Provisions) Bill 2005–06 Racial and Religious Hatred Bill 2005–06 Work and Families Bill 2005–06
Khalid Mahmood	Broadcasting Home Affairs (as a backbencher)	Crossrail Bill 2007–08 Forced Marriage (Civil Protection) Bill 2006–07 Commissioner for Older People (Wales) Bill [Lords] 2005–06 Immigration, Asylum and Nationality Bill 2005–06 Racial and Religious Hatred Bill 2005–06 Road Safety Bill 2004–05 Railways and Transport Safety Bill 2002–03
Shabana Mahmood	Work and Pensions	Identity Documents Act 2010 Terrorism Prevention and Investigation Measures Act 2011
Shahid Malik	Home Affairs (as a backbencher) Environmental Audit	Racial and Religious Hatred Bill 2005–06
Anas Sarwar	International Development Arms Export Controls	Public Services (Social Value) Act 2012 Welfare Reform Act 2012

Table 11.4 (Continued)

Member of Parliament	Select Committee	Public Bill Committee
Backbenchers		
Rehman Chishti	Justice	Protection of Freedoms Act 2012
Yasmin Qureshi	Justice Political and Constitutional Reform Privacy and Injunctions	Sports Grounds Safety Authority Act 2011
Mohammad Sarwar	Scottish Affairs (chair) Liaison	Patents Bill 2003–04 Industrial Development (Financial Assistance) Bill 2002–03 Finance Bill 1998–99
Nadhim Zahawi	Privacy and Injunctions Arms Export Controls Business, Innovation and Skills	Energy Bill [HL] 2010–11

Source: Parliament 2013–2013h; *The Guardian* 2013–2013a; House of Commons 2011; House of Commons 1998–2007.

Committee of Public Accounts implies evaluation of the economy, and efficiency and effectiveness of government bodies, which informs Sajid Javid's work at the Treasury. Memberships of different committees can also overlap. Anas Sarwar is a member of the International Development and Arms Export Controls Committees. The latter is the 'Quadripartite Committee' which includes the Business, Innovation and Skills, Defence, Foreign Affairs and International Development Committees (House of Commons 2011: 5).

With the exceptions of a few PPSs and junior ministers, the majority of Muslim MPs serve on committees as backbenchers and stand down once promoted to the frontbench. As a result, there tends not to be an overlap between backbench and leadership roles. For example, after becoming Parliamentary Private Secretaries, Sadiq Khan and Shahid Malik stood down from the Committee of Public Accounts and the Home Affairs Select Committee respectively. Whilst on the backbench, politicians from Muslim backgrounds serve as members and chairs on committees with diverse areas of expertise – from Home and Scottish Affairs to Human Rights and Justice. For instance, Mohammad Sarwar was a chair of the Scottish Affairs Committee between 2005 and 2010. As an MP for Glasgow Govan (from 2005 – Glasgow Central), he lobbied on behalf of the Scottish ship-building industry and had expertise in Scottish affairs in general (BBC 2007). As a chair of the Scottish Affairs Committee, he was involved in producing reports on the Committee system and took oral evidence from the Prime Minister serving on the Liaison Committee composed of all the Select Committees chairs.

The Committee membership of Muslim backbenchers corresponds to their pre-parliamentary experience.[11] For instance, as a practising barrister, Yasmin Qureshi serves on the Justice, Political and Constitutional Reform, and Privacy and Injunctions Committees, which suit her expertise the most. Rehman Chishti, a lawyer and a former advisor to Benazir Bhutto, is another member of the Justice Committee with a background in Law and Human Rights. The Membership of a wide range of Select Committees, that correspond to their areas of expertise, educational and professional background, allows Muslim MPs to thoroughly scrutinise government policies.

Legislative proposals are considered by Public Bill Committees. Membership of Public Bills Committees is not limited to backbenchers, but rarely includes senior ministers. Parliamentary Private Secretaries, junior ministers, and members of the Shadow Cabinet serve on committees as often as backbenchers. For instance, Sadiq Khan served on twelve Public Bill Committees before becoming a Minister for Transport attending the Cabinet in 2009. Since then he has not been a member of either Select or Public Bill Committees. Similarly, Sajid Javid is not serving on Public Bills Committees, albeit remaining a member of two Select Committees. Khalid Mahmood served on four Public Bill Committees, including the Road Safety Bill Standing Committee whilst a PPS to Tony McNulty as a Minister of Transport.

However, the Official Opposition frontbenchers, including Shabana Mahmood and Anas Sarwar, serve on Public Bill Committees, as well as backbenchers. The purpose of Committees to consider government legislative proposals in detail corresponds to the functions of the Official Opposition – to examine and challenge the Government. The Shadow Cabinet replicates the structure of the Government. This means that when a government department proposes a bill, members of the Shadow Cabinet who hold a similar portfolio are able to evaluate it making scrutiny more focused and robust.

Members of Public Bill Committees are encouraged to provide expertise relevant to particular legislative proposals. Therefore, the choice of Committees usually corresponds to the pre-parliamentary and ministerial expertise of MPs. For instance, Sadiq Khan held ministerial positions at the departments for Communities, Local Government Transport and Justice. His areas of responsibility as a minister overlapped with the Committee memberships, including the Criminal Justice and Immigration, Crown Employment (Nationality), Forced Marriage (Civil Protection), Parliament (Joint Departments), and Racial and Religious Hatred Bill Committees. Similarly, the PPS to the Shadow Secretary of State for Work and Pensions, Anas Sarwar, joined the Public Services (Social Value) Act and Welfare Reform Act Committees. Because of his background in Law and Human Rights, Rehman Chishti is a member of the Justice Select and Protection of Freedoms Act Committee.

Religious minority background is occasionally relevant to the committee choice as well. Three of four Muslim MPs – Sadiq Khan, Khalid Mahmood and Shahid Malik – served on the Religious Hatred Bill Committee, and two – Sadiq Khan and Khalid Mahmood – on the Forced Marriage (Civil Protection) Bill Committee. They referred to the personal experiences and concerns of the Muslim population in their constituencies and the country as a whole as reasons for their interest in working on those bills. For instance, during the debate of the Religious Hatred Bill Shahid Malik states that, '*I stand here today, the first British-born Muslim MP, but representing a seat* [Dewsbury] *with the highest BNP vote in the country… I have spent a lot of time and much of my working life fighting sectarianism, bigotry and hatred. My own life experiences are the third reason why I consider myself qualified to speak in the debate*' (Hansard 2005: 702), whereas Sadiq Khan explained that '*The Bill is about trying to close a loophole that far-right groups are well aware of, and outlawing incitement against the followers – the followers – of multi-ethnic faiths* [given that] *In the last few years, the far right have cynically and deliberately been targeting British Muslims*' (Hansard 2005: 734). In both cases pre-parliamentary work and personal experience – alongside concerns over the wellbeing of the British society – seemed to encourage Muslim parliamentarians to engage in the debate. These instances of Muslim MPs' engagement in discussions of issues of concern for the Muslim minority, and their contribution to drafting the relevant legislation, demonstrate their willingness to participate in the parliamentary debate on Muslim-related issues and to provide their expertise and insights on these matters.

Similarly, Muslim MPs' involvement in scrutinising migration and anti-terrorism legislation – e.g. Criminal Justice and Immigration Bill and Immigration, Asylum and Nationality Bill – indicates their interest in broader issues that concern both British Muslims and the UK population in general. Although those proposals do not target Muslims, in particular, some aspects of the bills, such as the asylum regime, family reunification, and naturalisation, are relevant for the UK Muslim population. For instance, the asylum regime, regulations and eligibility of asylum seekers concern countries of origin for parts of the Muslim minority such as Somalia and Sudan, for instance. The issues of family reunification and naturalisation as well often overlap with the widespread concerns over the Muslim family law and traditions and such practices as arranged marriages. Although legislative proposals on these issues do not necessarily go into detail, they set a general practice that overlap with some areas of concern for British Muslims related to their cultural and religious practice.

Overall, all Muslim parliamentarians, with the exception of Rushanara Ali[12], have served on various Select and Public Bill Committees. Their choice of committees has been largely affected by both ministerial duties and pre-parliamentary expertise, whereas their Muslim minority backgrounds stimulated them to contribute to the discussion on the Religious Hatred Bill Committee and the Forced Marriage (Civil Protection) Bill only. Muslim MPs' membership of Committees allows them to scrutinise government bills and policies and ensures their contribution to the legislative process. On the other hand, it does not show how likely they are to introduce legislation individually.

Private Members' Bills

Introducing a Private Members' Bill (PMB) is one of the few opportunities for non-ministers to propose legislation. They rarely become law, but may impact on legislation indirectly by increasing MPs' awareness and testing support for a particular issue or policy. There are three types of Private Members' Bills. The Ballot Bill has a good chance of becoming law due to the fact that MPs who propose them are given time by the Government to discuss their proposals on the floor of the House, which might give a bill stronger cross-party support. However, the majority of Private Members' Bills are either introduced under the Ten Minute Rule or are Presentation Bills. Neither of them is allocated time for further discussion, and stands little chance of becoming law. This is even less so for a Presentation Bill, because an introducing Member is not able to speak in support of it. Both types are often used as a campaigning tool (Priddy 2013).

As shown in Table 11.5, between 1997 and 2012, Members of Parliament from Muslim backgrounds introduced five Private Members' Bills, compared to the overall number of 1,420. Sixty-nine of them, just under five per cent, were successful.

Such a small number and a short period of Muslim presence in the Chamber do not allow for generalisation and the forecasting of Muslim MPs' behaviour in terms of proposing PMBs. However, drawing on the existing data, a few observations are possible to make.

First, Muslim MPs proposed very few Private Members' Bills – less than 0.5 per cent of the overall number. None of their proposals were either successful, or won the ballot. As a result, all the bills were introduced under the Ten Minute Rule, which decreased their slim chance of becoming a law even more. All of them were dropped or withdrawn after the first (in one case the second) reading. The limited engagement of Muslim MPs in proposing Private Members' Bills can be explained by the pressures of their ministerial responsibilities. They leave little room for extra-parliamentary activities. Furthermore, frontbenchers are enabled to initiate legislation because of the nature of their legislative role, which might make them less interested in

Table 11.5 Private Members' Bills, number per session

	1997–2001	2001–2005	2005–2010	2010–2012
PMBs introduced, N	385	348	466	221
by Muslim MPs	0	1	1	3
Unsuccessful PMBs, N	377	323	448	215
PMBs receiving Royal Assent, N	20	25	18	6

Source: House of Commons, 1998–2012.

Table 11.6 Private Members' Bills introduced by Muslim MPs

Member of Parliament	Private Members' Bill	Type of Bill	Proceedings & Result
Sajid Javid	National Debt Cap	Ten Minute Rule	1R: 12.7.2011 Withdrawn
Anas Sarwar	Resource Extraction (Transparency and Reporting)	Ten Minute Rule	1R: 1.3.2011 Dropped
Mohammad Sarwar	Prevention of Homelessness	Ten Minute Rule	1R: 16.3.2004 Dropped
	Prevention of Excessive Charges	Ten Minute Rule	1R: 29.4.2009 Dropped
Nadhim Zahawi	St George's Day and St David's Day	Ten Minute Rule	1R: 15.12.2010 2R: 13.5.2011 Withdrawn

Source: House of Commons 1998–2012.

proposing bills individually. These assumptions are supported by the fact that three of the five bills were introduced by a backbencher and PPSs. Table 11.6 summarises the data on all five Private Members' Bills proposed by four Muslim parliamentarians, including Sajid Javid, Anas Sarwar, Mohammad Sarwar, and Nadhim Zahawi, their proceeding and results.

The bills introduced by Muslim MPs were not successful, which is unsurprising given Private Members' Bills have such a slim chance of becoming law. Furthermore, the bills were introduced under the Ten Minute Rule that limits the opportunity for them to be discussed in detail. This is shown by the fact that three of the five bills were dropped and another one was withdrawn during the first reading. All of them were scheduled between 73 and 156 items of the debate, which left little chance for them to be debated on the floor of the House.

Overall, Members of Parliament from Muslim backgrounds have not succeeded in introducing Private Members' Bills; none of their proposals was successful, won the ballot, or even got past the second reading. This, however, does not seem to differ from the fate of the vast majority of PMBs proposed by non-Muslim parliamentarians. Furthermore, Muslim MPs seldom engage with this type of parliamentary activity. The lack of individual legislative proposals is balanced out by extensive engagement with other aspects of the legislative process, namely preparing and passing government legislative proposals as ministers and Parliamentary Private Secretaries, and scrutinising them as Opposition frontbenchers and Opposition and Government backbenchers.

Conclusion

This study challenges the belief that Muslim politicians lack opportunities to contribute to legislative decision-making and substantively engage with minority interests due to the constraints of the parliamentary environment (Durose et al. 2011: 41; Saalfeld and Kyriakopoulou in Bird et al. 2011: 246; Sinno and Tatari 2009: 123–124). Drawing upon an analysis of the parliamentary careers of Muslim MPs, it shows that politicians from Muslim backgrounds are both enabled and restricted by their legislative roles and responsibilities rather than their religious background. Belonging to a religious minority affects access to Westminster politics (Sobolewska 2013), but it does not determine how Muslim MPs engage with the legislative process on a day-to-day basis. The legislative roles they hold, by contrast, have a substantial influence on their legislative routines. Different types of roles empower Muslim parliamentarians to propose legislation and scrutinise bills and policies in various ways. Although the data is limited, it is clear that Muslim backbenchers and Parliamentary Private Secretaries are more likely to serve on Select Committees and introduce Private Members' Bills. Along with junior ministers they are also scrutinising government legislative proposals at the Committee stage. Government ministers, however, tend to stand down from committees as their ministerial responsibilities increase. Overall, there is no evidence that Muslim MPs lack access to certain legislative roles and committees.

Since 2004 the number of Muslim frontbenchers has been gradually increasing and they have been moving from Parliamentary Private Secretaries to junior and senior ministers. Overall, seven of eleven Muslim parliamentarians hold (or have held) leadership roles. This makes them over-represented on the frontbench compared to women and non-Muslim minority MPs, despite being under-represented in the House of Commons in general. Muslim frontbenchers are limited in self-expression in the debates and membership of committees, which makes them less vocal and often less visible on the floor of the House. However, as government ministers, they successfully propose legislation and develop policies in relevant government departments. Muslim backbenchers are also involved in scrutinising government legislation and policies in the same way as non-Muslim MPs. Since 1997 they have been serving on departmental and cross-cutting Select and Public Bill Committees. Each of the Muslim backbenchers is a member of several Select and Public Bills Committees chosen with regard to their professional background and expertise. Despite such extensive opportunities to influence the legislative process, however, Muslim MPs have had no more success than any other MPs in successfully tabling Private Members' Bills, which make it onto the statute book. The evidence from the legislative behaviour of MPs from Muslim backgrounds suggests that they are constrained by parliamentary rules and procedures, as well as non-Muslim members, and enabled to introduce and scrutinise legislative proposals, in accordance to their legislative roles. This system neither encourages nor restricts their engagement with minority interests, as long as it

Muslims in Parliament: a myth of futility   233

does not contradict their party and constituency commitments. This follows from successful involvement of Muslim MPs in scrutinising minority-related proposals supported by the party, such as the Religious Hatred Bill.

Overall, parliamentarians from Muslim backgrounds engage with the legislative process and contribute to drafting and proposing legislation in accordance to their legislative roles, whereby frontbenchers develop and propose legislation, and backbenchers scrutinise and amend those proposals during the parliamentary debates and at the Committee stage. Given that all the Muslim MPs, with only two exceptions, held ministerial roles at some point in their parliamentary career, their input in the legislative process is as substantial as the contributions of MPs from other or no minority backgrounds who hold similar legislative roles.

Notes

1 'Muslim' Members of Parliament are identified by their religious minority background. It is defined as a socio-cultural phenomenon rather than religious practice and allows including secular, non-religious and practicing politicians (Lazar et al. 2002; Sinno and Tatari 2009). Terms 'Muslim MPs' and 'MPs from Muslim backgrounds' are used interchangeably.
2 Between 1997 (when the first Muslim MP was elected) and 2010 only eleven Muslim politicians took seats in the Commons; eight MPs were elected from the Labour Party and three from the Conservative Party. This constitutes approximately 1.7 per cent of MPs.
3 Senior ministers in the Government are also the members of Cabinet. This always includes the Chancellor of the Exchequer, the Lord Chancellor, and the Secretaries of State.
4 Junior ministers include Ministers of State, Parliamentary Under-Secretaries of State and Parliamentary Secretaries.
5 The Chief Whips and their Assistants manage their parliamentary parties and are government ministers.
6 Nadhim Zahawi is a co-founder and chief executive of YouGov. Rehman Chishti was an advisor to Benazir Bhutto and Francis Maude MP.
7 As naturalised British citizens, who were born overseas, Nadhim Zahawi and Rehman Chishti have a short history of membership in the Conservative Party, comparing to the majority of the Tory MPs, whose families have been linked with the party for generations (Whiteley et al. 1994: 223).
8 Before election Rushanara Ali was a Research Assistant to Michael Young and Oona King, MP for Bethnal Green and Bow, and a researcher at the Institute of Public Policy Research (IPPR) and at the Communities Directorate of the Home Office.
9 Shahid Malik lost his parliamentary seat in Dewsbury at the 2010 General Election.
10 Currently the only senior minister among Muslim MPs is Rt Hon Sadiq Khan MP as a Shadow Lord Chancellor and Secretary of State for Justice.
11 Donald Searing (1994) identified this position as a Policy Advocate.
12 Her role as the Shadow Minister for International Development involves extensive overseas travelling, which limits her taking up more parliamentary responsibilities.

Bibliography

Andeweg, R. (1997) 'Role Specialisation or Role Switching? Dutch MPs Between Electorate and Executive', *The Journal of Legislative Studies*, 3(1): 110–127.

BBC (2006) 'Blair Hit by Wave of Resignations', *BBC News*, 6 September, available at: http://news.bbc.co.uk/1/hi/uk_politics/5319328.stm (accessed 15 March 2011).
BBC (2007) 'Sarwar Plans to Stand Down as MP', *BBC News*, 22 June, available at: http://news.bbc.co.uk/1/hi/scotland/glasgow_and_west/6228920.stm (accessed 9 August 2012).
Bird, K., Saalfeld, T. and Wust, A. (eds) (2011) *The Political Representation of Immigrants and Minorities. Voters, Parties and Parliaments in Liberal Democracies*. London and New York: Routledge.
Cabinet Office (2010) 'The Cabinet Manual: A Guide to Laws, Conventions and Rules on the Operation of Government', Cabinet Office, 14 December, available at: www.gov.uk/government/uploads/system/uploads/attachment_data/file/60641/cabinet-manual.pdf (accessed 26 June 2013).
Cameron, D. (2005) 'Until We're Represented by Men and Women in the Country, We Won't Be Half the Party We Could Be', The Conservative Party, Speech on 12 December, available at: www.conservatives.com/News/Speeches/2005/12/Cameron_Until_were_represented_by_men_and_women_in_the_country_we_wont_be_half_the_party_we_could_be.aspx (accessed 1 July 2013).
Conservative Party (2010) 'A Contract for Equalities', *The Conservative Party Manifesto 2010 General Election*, The Conservative Party. Available at: www.conservatives.com/news/news_stories/2010/05/~/media/Files/Downloadable%20Files/Manifesto/Equalities-Manifesto.ashx (accessed 7 April 2014).
Cracknell, R. (2012) 'Ethnic Minorities in Politics, Government and Public Life', Standard Note SN/SG/1156, House of Commons Library. Available at: www.parliament.uk/briefingpapers/sn01156.pdf (accessed 1 July 2013).
Duckworth, N. and Cracknell, R. (2013) 'Women in Parliament and Government', Standard Note SN/SG/1250, House of Commons Library. Available at: www.parliament.uk/briefingpapers/SN01250.pdf (accessed 1 July 2013).
Durose, C., Gains, F., Richardson, L., Combs, R., Broome, K. and Eason, C. (2011) 'Pathways to Politics', *The Equality and Human Rights Commission Research Report Series*, Research Report 65, The Equality and Human Right Commission. Available at: www.equalityhumanrights.com (accessed 10 March 2012).
Foot, R. (2006) 'Ex-Labour Election Candidate Defects to Tories', *Kent Online*, 15 March, available at: www.kentonline.co.uk/kentonline/newsarchive.aspx?articleid=25502 (accessed 10 August 2012).
Guardian (2013) 'Malik, Shahid. Guardian Politics Profile', *The Guardian*, available at: www.guardian.co.uk/politics/person/8710/shahid-malik (accessed 10 June 2013).
Guardian (2013a) 'Sarwar, Mohammad. Guardian Politics Profile', *The Guardian*, available at: www.guardian.co.uk/politics/person/4616/mohammad-sarwar (accessed 10 June 2013).
Hansard (2005) *House of Commons Debate*, 21 June. London: The Stationery Office.
Heath, A., Fisher, S., Rosenblatt, G., Sanders, D. and Sobolewska, M. (2013) *The Political Integration of Ethnic Minorities in Britain*. Oxford: Oxford University Press.
House of Commons (1998–2007) 'Standing Committees on Bills & House of Commons Public Bill Committees', House of Commons Archive, Parliament. Available at: www.parliament.uk/business/publications/hansard/commons/bill-committee-debates/previous-sessions/.
House of Commons (1998–2012) *Sessional Information Digest*. London: House of Commons Information Office.
House of Commons (2009) *Speaker's Conference (on Parliamentary Representation) Final Report*. London: The Stationery Office.

House of Commons (2011) *House of Commons Guide for Select Committee Members.* London: Department of Chamber and Committee Services.

House of Commons (2012) *The Code of Conduct & The Guide to the Rules Relating to the Conduct of Members.* London: The Stationery Office Limited.

Labour Party (2010) 'A Future Fair for All', *The Labour Party Manifesto 2010 General Election,* The Labour Party. Available at: www2.labour.org.uk/uploads/TheLabourpartyManifesto-2010.pdf (accessed 10 May 2012).

Lazar, A., Kravetz, S. and Frederich–Kedem, P. (2002) 'The Multidimensionality of Motivation for Jewish Religious Behaviour: Content, Structure, and Relationship to Religious Identity', *Journal for the Scientific Study of Religion*, 41: 509–519.

Muslim Vote (2010) 'New Muslim MP's 2010', *Muslim Vote*, 7 May, available at: www.muslimvote.org.uk/index.php?option=com_content&view=article&id=176:new-mps&catid=59:election-news&Itemid=194 (accessed 19 March 2011).

Norton, P. (2001) 'Playing by the Rules: The Constraining Hand of Parliamentary Procedure', *The Journal of Legislative Studies*, 7(3): 13–33.

Parliament (2013) 'Ali, Rushanara. House of Commons profile', Parliament. Available at: www.parliament.uk/biographies/commons/rushanara-ali/4138 (accessed 10 June 2013).

Parliament (2013a) 'Chishti, Rehman. House of Commons profile', Parliament. Available at: www.parliament.uk/biographies/commons/rehman-chishti/3987 (accessed 10 June 2013).

Parliament (2013b) 'Javid, Sajid. House of Commons profile', Parliament. Available at: www.parliament.uk/ biographies/commons/sajid-javid/84360 (accessed 10 June 2013).

Parliament (2013c) 'Khan, Sadiq. House of Commons profile', Parliament. Available at: www.parliament.uk/biographies/commons/sadiq-khan/1577 (accessed 10 June 2013).

Parliament (2013d) 'Mahmood, Khalid. House of Commons profile', Parliament. Available at: www.parliament.uk/biographies/commons/mr-khalid-mahmood/1392 (accessed 10 June 2013).

Parliament (2013e) 'Mahmood, Shabana. House of Commons profile', Parliament. Available at: www.parliament.uk/biographies/commons/shabana-mahmood/3914 (accessed 10 June 2013).

Parliament (2013f) 'Qureshi, Yasmin. House of Commons profile', Parliament. Available at: www.parliament.uk/biographies/commons/yasmin-qureshi/3924 (accessed 10 June 2013).

Parliament (2013g) 'Sarwar, Anas. House of Commons profile', Parliament. Available at: www.parliament.uk/biographies/commons/anas-sarwar/3981 (accessed 10 June 2013).

Parliament (2013h) 'Zahawi, Nadhim. House of Commons profile', Parliament. Available at: www.parliament.uk/biographies/commons/nadhim-zahawi/4113 (accessed 10 June 2013).

Phillips, A. (1995) *The Politics of Presence.* Oxford: Clarendon Press.

Priddy, S. (2013) 'Successful Private Members' Bills since 1983–1984', Standard Note SN/PC/04568, House of Commons Library. Available at: www.parliament.uk/briefing-papers/SN04568.pdf (accessed 20 July 2013).

Saalfeld, T. and Kyriakopoulou, K. (2011) 'Presence and Behaviour: Black and Minority Ethnic MPs in the British House of Commons', in Bird *et al.* (eds) *The Political Representation of Immigrants and Minorities. Voters, Parties and Parliaments in Liberal democracies.* London and New York: Routledge.

Saalfeld, T., Wust, A. and Petrarca, C. (2011) 'Immigrant MPs in Britain, France and Germany: Roles and Activities', IPSA-ECPR Joint Conference, Sao Paolo. Available at: http://saopaulo2011.ipsa.org/sites/saopaulo2011.ipsa.org/files/papers/paper-1428.pdf (accessed 5 October 2011).

Saward, M. (2011) *The Representative Claim*. Oxford: Oxford University Press.

Searing, D. (1994) *Westminster's World*. Cambridge, MA: Harvard University Press.

Sinno, A.H. and Tatari, E. (2009) 'Muslims in UK Institutions: Effective Representation or Tokenism?', in A.H. Sinno (ed.) *Muslims in Western Politics*. Bloomington, IN: University of Indiana Press, pp. 113–135.

Sobolewska, M. (2013) 'Party Strategies, Political Opportunity Structure and the Descriptive Representation of Ethnic Minorities in Britain', *West European Politics*, 36(3): 615–633.

Strøm, K. (1997) 'Rules, Reasons and Routines: Legislative Roles in Parliamentary Democracies', *The Journal of Legislative Studies*, 3(1): 155–174.

Wahlke, J.C. *et al.* (1962) *The Legislative System. Exploration in Legislative Behaviour*. New York: Wiley.

Whiteley, P., Seyd, P. and Richardson, J. (1994) *True Blues: The Politics of Conservative Party Membership: The Politics of Conservative Party Membership*. Oxford: Oxford University Press.

12 The political behaviour of minority councillors across London boroughs
Comparing Tower Hamlets, Newham, and Hackney

Eren Tatari and Ahmet Yukleyen

Introduction

Western European countries, Canada, and the United States are host to numerous minorities. These groups may identify themselves by their religion, ethnicity, race, gender, sexual orientation, disabilities, and their immigrant status. Most are socio-economically and politically disadvantaged. As such, minority groups pressure their governments to accommodate their particular needs. Yet the responses of Western democracies to minority demands vary significantly. Some countries, like Britain, take a *pluralistic* approach and strive to accommodate minority needs. Others, such as France, pursue an *assimilationist* strategy and do not grant group rights. What is more puzzling is that government responsiveness to minority interests varies significantly even within countries. This presents an intriguing research problem; what explains the variation in government responsiveness to minority demands? In this chapter, we explore this puzzle by analyzing the factors that influence local government responsiveness to Muslim demands in London.

Although Muslims in the West is a flourishing research area, there are few rigorous studies on the political representation of Muslims in Western Europe. Moreover, most studies focus on ethnicity rather than the sociopolitical Muslim identity. Hence, this chapter investigates the dynamics of effective Muslim political representation in a liberal democracy. We define effective political representation as high levels of congruence between policy preferences of voters and elected officials. These research questions are significant for a number of reasons. First, there are an estimated 15–20 million Muslims living in the EU, and close to 3 million of whom reside in Britain (Open Society Institute 2010). Recurring riots, violent backlashes and increasing religious extremism demonstrate that the accommodation of Muslim minorities is a pressing issue for European governments. Dovi (2007: 5) argues that the primary goal of a democracy is resolving conflicts fairly, which ensures its legitimacy and stability in the eyes of its citizens; 'For if a disgruntled minority or majority holds that democratic institutions are unfair, then such groups are likely to employ undemocratic practices – for example, violence – to settle their political conflicts'. Hence, the sociopolitical integration of Muslims is of considerable importance for the future of British civic life.

Currently, there are ten Muslims in the House of Commons, eight in the House of Lords, and three in the European Parliament representing Britain. More strikingly, since 1980, the number of ethnic minority city councillors in Britain increased by more than 700 per cent.[1] As of January 2010, we estimated that there are approximately 146 Muslim councillors (thirty-six of whom are women) in London. Yet the number of Muslim councillors and government responsiveness to minority needs vary drastically across local councils. The aim of this chapter is to explore which factors facilitate or hinder effective Muslim political representation in Britain, and how representation styles of Muslim elected officials shape these factors. To this end, we study the political incorporation, party fragmentation, experiences and perceptions of Muslim councillors in London as well as their impact on government responsiveness to minority needs. In particular, we investigate whether the increasing number of Muslim councillors in Britain leads to substantive representation of Muslim interests. We argue that descriptive representation of minorities leads to improved government responsiveness to minority interests contingent on the percentage of minority representatives, the level of their party fragmentation and political incorporation, and the electoral competitiveness of the district.

We evaluate the specific process of their interaction through comparative analyses of the London Boroughs of Tower Hamlets, Newham, and Hackney, while also investigating the role of representational styles of Muslim councillors on their political effectiveness. The findings suggest that:

a   Muslim identity has become strong and politicised in Britain and shapes political behaviour.
b   Identity based on faith impacts day to day practices, which are governed by legislation (i.e. *halal* food provision at hospitals, schools and other public agencies, accommodation of Islamic practices in public schools, Islamic dress code or provision of prayer time and space).
c   Despite substantial in-group diversity, British Muslims share common concerns and needs.
d   Muslim elected officials are likely to advocate for the accommodation of unique demands and needs of the community and to mediate when conflicts arise with local and national governments.
e   Local government responsiveness to Muslim interests is likely to be higher in boroughs with a higher proportion of Muslim councillors who are less fragmented along party lines and more politically incorporated.

Scholars point out that political representation is one of the highly effective means of minority integration. As Lovenduski (2005: 3) argues, political representation 'underpins the legitimacy of democratic states' and 'claims for representation are part of the process of claiming membership of a polity'.

Political empowerment literature cites that electing a minority representative can alter the political attitudes and behaviour of minorities, improve the perceived legitimacy of the system, enhance trust in government by signalling that their concerns are taken seriously and decisions will reflect their input, and increase their sense of belonging. Therefore, the openness of British political institutions to influence from minority groups is significant for theories of democracy and representation. As such, Muslim political representation is an important venue for the inclusion of Muslims in the democratic process.

After the 1989 Rushdie Affair, Muslims emerged as a political group pressuring the British government for equal rights. Such conflicts have acted as an impetus for Muslims to seek public office, most effectively at the local level. They sought being part of the system to make political and socio-economic change for their communities. This chapter will examine whether Muslim political representation has been only symbolic or not.

Exploring these research questions at the local level, as well as the national level, is important. Muslims have been particularly successful in getting elected to local councils that affect their day-to-day lives and their long-term socio-economic status (i.e. councils have jurisdiction over local education authorities). On the other hand, national legislatures have jurisdiction over immigration, foreign policy, and national security, and they have more visible and prestigious posts. Most scholars agree that 'ethnic minority immigration identification with the host country is a function of three main factors: socio-economic status, social engagement in the mainstream culture, and political/civic participation ...' and that political and civic participation will 'increase the likelihood of identifying with the nation through acceptance of national symbols, institutions, and tangible involvement and investment in the community ...' (Maxwell 2006: 4–5). Likewise, Dovi (2007: ix) argues that '... the ability of democratic institutions to approximate their ideals depends, in no small part, on *who* represents democratic citizens and *how* they represent them'. Therefore, assessing the effectiveness of minority representation at both the local and the national level would provide invaluable insights about the 'continuing struggle by an excluded racial minority to win inclusion and influence in the nation's preeminent representative institution[s]' (Fenno 2003: 1).

For the purposes of this study, which seeks to explain the causal mechanisms of policy outcomes in relation to state accommodation of Muslim demands, *Muslim* is used in the broadest sense to encompass all who self-identify as Muslim. *Descriptive representation* refers to how much and in what ways the representatives resemble the represented; whereas *substantive representation* involves actions of the represented on behalf of the represented, which is assessed through policy outcomes. Haynie compares descriptive and substantive representation as follows:

[Substantive representation refers to] ... the degree of congruence between the actions and behaviour of a representative and the policy preferences of her or his constituents. It concerns what the representative does rather than what or who he or she is ... descriptive representation, which simply focuses on the degree to which a representative reflects or mirrors the distinctive social characteristics of the constituents that he or she represents- characteristics like race, ethnicity, gender, social class, or religion ... the emphasis is on who or what the representative is, rather than on what he or she may actually do.

(2001: 16)

This chapter primarily explores the relationship between descriptive and substantive representation among Muslims in London.

The case for Muslim political representation

Why are Muslim elected officials necessary? Does religious identity supersede ethnicity or gender? How is religious group representation justified in a liberal democracy? First, studies in the United States on constituent-elected representative relations find high levels of convergence between the political behaviour of elected officials and constituent preferences. This is particularly true for highly salient issues like civil rights and welfare policies (Fenno 1978; Erickson 1978). Yet most scholars emphasise the need for group representation to ensure such congruence.

A vast body of literature has demonstrated that descriptive representation leads to substantive representation of group identities based on gender, race, and ethnicity. For instance, Ross (2002) claims that there are four main justifications for increasing the role of women in politics; namely, democratic justice, maximisation of resources, representation of the special interests of women, and being role models. On the other hand, for the political representation of African Americans in the US, the expectation has been that 'black legislators would provide African Americans with substantive representation by articulating and advocating something called 'the black interest,' and that these legislators would be agents of economic, social, and political advancement for all black citizens, regardless of where those citizens happened to reside' (Haynie 2001: 16).

Despite rejecting totalising essentialism, and acknowledging that socialisation, culture, family, schooling and personal traits render different interpretations and practices of Islam, British Muslims share common concerns and needs, which call for Muslim representation. What are the group-specific concerns, accommodations, and interests of British Muslims that require Muslim political representation? Some of the policy issues that arise in several Western European countries are *halal* food provision at hospitals, schools and other public agencies, and the accommodation of Islamic practices in public schools, i.e. dress code or provision of prayer time and space (Tatari 2009). This was candidly acknowledged as far back as 1981 in a Bradford Council

Report that demonstrated the need for group representatives. The Bradford Council stated that it had:

> ... no direct knowledge of Asian needs and requirements, and we have no automatic way of knowing the issues they feel important... (we need) some new channel of communication between the Council and the communities – something to compensate for the lack of political representation.
>
> (Lewis 1997: 103)

Furthermore, the size and nature of the Muslim community also plays a role in necessitating group representation. Muslims constitute 5 per cent of the total population of Britain, and 13.5 per cent of London (Office for National Statistics 2012). According to data from the Muslim Council of Britain (MCB) based on the 2001 Census, there is one parliamentary constituency (out of 529) with 49 per cent Muslim population, two with 30–40 per cent, six with 20–30 per cent, thirty-one with 10–20 per cent, sixty-one with 5–10 per cent, and 468 with 0–5 per cent Muslim constituents (see Table 12.1).

Islamophobia on the part of governments and societies shape this debate and impact policymaking unconstructively such as polarising the public debate. For instance, when Western governments propose initiatives to liaise with their Muslim populations in policy-making, the role of Muslim elected officials becomes indispensible. Pluralism entails multiple groups thriving within the same polity, not through policy silences, but through active policy-making. Moreover, sociopolitical, ethnic, linguistic, cultural, and religious plurality can move beyond mere co-existence through constructive pluralism and interaction.

Finally, Swain (2006: 3) claims that the ability of governments to address minority needs is a test of representative democracy. The same holds true for all religious minorities and Muslim elected officials. For liberal democracies that extend constitutional protection of religious belief and expression,

Table 12.1 Percentage of Muslims in parliamentary constituencies in England and Wales

Percentage of Muslims in constituency	Number of parliamentary constituencies
40–50	1
30–40	2
20–30	6
10–20	31
5–10	61
0–5	468

Source: Muslim Council of Britain.[2]

Note: See www.mcb.org.uk/vote2005/statistics5.php for the complete list of parliamentary constituencies and the percentage of Muslim constituents.

ensuring effective political representation for religious minorities is an essential test of representative democracy.

Muslim political representation across London

In this section, we present the comparative analysis of the three case studies: Tower Hamlets, Newham, and Hackney. The findings provide important insights about the explanatory factors included in the statistical analysis and the mechanisms through which they impact government responsiveness. While partially confirming the necessity but insufficiency of descriptive representation, they also introduce new variables, such as the political culture of the minority populations and the councils.

Unlike the stark divide in Tower Hamlets, the political behaviour and the representative styles of Muslim and non-Muslim councillors in Newham are rather similar. Arguably due to the political culture of the borough and the council, non-Muslim councillors are more understanding and responsive to Muslim interests and the interests of other minorities. Likewise, Muslim councillors take a more balancing perspective (compared to the group representative style of the Muslim councillors in Tower Hamlets), and they do not unequivocally support all Muslim demands at all costs but balance the interests of Muslims with the other minority groups and the borough. It seems that in the case of Tower Hamlets, there is an action (aggressive style of Muslim constituents and councillors) that causes a reaction from the non-Muslim residents and councillors. However, in the case of Newham, both Muslim and non-Muslim councillors are able to weigh the advantages and disadvantages of minority demands and council decisions for minority groups and the borough.

Among the issues of concern for the Newham Muslim community, two are particularly noteworthy for the purposes of this study; namely, the establishment of a Muslim cemetery and opposition to mosque applications, in particular, the Abbey Mills Mosque in Stratford. The key committee for both of the issues is the planning committee. Although the planning committee is independent in its decision-making, councillors do not have a lot of discretion and are advised by council officers as to what the legislation dictates. It is occasional that councillors can exercise some judgment.[3] Newham Muslims, who constitute one fifth of the population, have lobbied the Council for a separate Muslim cemetery for decades, before being granted a separate section in the only council-run burial ground in 1991. West Ham Cemetery at Forest Gate, found in 1857, is the only cemetery owned and managed by the Newham Council. It is divided into three areas, consecrated, unconsecrated, and a section for Muslim burials. Cllr. Abdulkarim Sheikh, the longest serving Muslim councillor in Newham, played a crucial role in establishing the Muslim section in the West Ham Cemetery, which is in use since 1991 (Bambery 2006). As the only Respect councillor currently, his views and political behaviour lean towards a group representative, though less so than the Muslim councillors in Tower Hamlets. He decided to be a councillor because he 'thought that the service delivery was not tailored to the composition of the population. And if you have to say something, if you stand in front of the town hall and make noise, it does not make any difference. So it is better to be involved in the decision making process'.[4] He acknowledged that although he counts on the votes of the 4,000 Muslims in his ward, he also needs the votes of other communities to get elected.

In the 2006 local elections, he fought his first campaign as a Respect candidate. He said that the campaign was not focused on Muslim issues as such but focused on specific local issues, such as Sir Robin Wales' proposal to replace an historic market with Walmart and closing down a secondary school. Contrary to common perception, he said that there were more non-Muslims helping his campaign than Muslims. Cllr. Sheikh has been involved with the Newham Alliance of Islamic Associations since it was formed in 1981. Dr Zulfiqar Ali became the chairperson of the same organisation in 2007 after being elected as a councillor. Cllr. Sheikh claimed that partially due to his involvement in this organisation, he is more aware of Muslim issues than the other Muslim and non-Muslim councillors.[5] He has tried to help out the Muslim community in the public sphere because he believes that 'To be a good Muslim, you have to be a good citizen'.[6] He added that he is the only Muslim councillor in Newham who refuses to come to evening meetings in the Council during Ramadan.

The comparative analysis of the Tower Hamlets, Newham, and Hackney Boroughs and Councils reveals the specific mechanisms through which the independent variables as well as the representation styles of Muslim councillors play out. The statistical data show that Tower Hamlets Council has the highest local government responsiveness to Muslim demands, followed by Newham Council. However, Hackney Council falls far behind and has the twelfth highest government responsiveness among the thirty-two boroughs. Although there are numerous factors that may influence this outcome, the most significant ones are summarised in Table 12.2, which compares the averages of data from 1998 to 2010 for the three boroughs studied.

Similarities. According to Newham Cllr. Graham Lane, 'The problem with London boroughs is that they are lines on a map, they don't reflect communities. Newham, Tower Hamlets or Hackney could be one borough. You wouldn't know you moved from one to the other'.[7] The data confirm his analysis in that Tower Hamlets, Newham, and Hackney are among the three poorest boroughs in London; they have the highest proportion of Muslims and Muslim councillors (the first, second, and fourth in both categories); and all three have Labour controlled councils. Moreover, they are amongst the most ethnically diverse London boroughs. Table 12.3 compares the ethnic breakdown of Tower Hamlets, Newham, and Hackney. Newham is not only the most ethnically diverse borough among the three case study boroughs but also in the whole of England. Although there is a high percentage of ethnic minorities in Tower Hamlets, an overwhelming majority of them are Bengalis, therefore it is not as diverse as Newham.

Table 12.2 Comparison of Tower Hamlets, Newham, and Hackney

	% Muslim population	Number and % of Muslim councillors	Number of parties and fragmentation index	% in majority party	Mean Seniority	Number of leadership positions	Number of committee assignments	% Majority party seats	Electoral competitiveness	% Ethnic population	Cemetery	Islamic school	Mosque	% Grant	IMD score	Political incorporation index	Local government responsiveness
Tower Hamlets	36.4 (1st)	28.7 (56.2%1st)	2.7 (0.1)	76.2	1.9	11	34.3	LAB 62.8%	90.8	49.3	0.3	11.7	36	11	50.6	2.24 (1st)	2.13 (1st)
Newham	24.3 (2nd)	10.67 (17.8%2nd)	1.33 (0.1)	92.3	5.7	5	9.7	LAB 96.1%	165.4	58.1	1	0.03	31.3	12	46.5	0.87 (2nd)	1.61 (2nd)
Hackney	13.8 (4th)	8 (14%; 4th)	3 (0.4)	65.9	5.7	3.3	5.3	LAB 68.4%	84.4	40	0	0.04	8.7	9	49.5	0.49 (4th)	0.06 (12th)

Table 12.3 Ethnic breakdown of Tower Hamlets, Newham, and Hackney, mid-2005

	Tower Hamlets	Newham	Hackney
White British	44.5	32.8	47.3
Indian	2.2	12	4.1
Pakistani	0.09	8.8	1.4
Bengali	30.6	9.2	2.9
Black Caribbean	2.4	6.8	9.2
Black African	2.9	12.8	10.6

Source: Office of National Statistics (percentages).

Divergences. Despite all their similarities, the Tower Hamlets, Newham, and Hackney Boroughs and Councils also have critical differences. For instance, Newham and Hackney has a mayor and cabinet system since 2002, compared to the leader and cabinet system in Tower Hamlets. This difference in the institutional design of the boroughs is likely to be responsible for a more efficient service delivery under directly elected mayors in Newham and Hackney compared to a slower deliberation process under the leader and cabinet system of Tower Hamlets.[8] Nonetheless, the argued advantages of the mayor and cabinet system did not yield notable results for minorities, at least in the case of Muslims. What explains the low local government responsiveness to Muslim needs in Hackney? In what ways do the case study findings confirm or disconfirm the results of the regression analysis on Table 12.2?

Fragmentation. Muslim councillors in Tower Hamlets have been least fragmented ethnically during the three terms, and their average party fragmentation is 0.1 (see Table 12.2). Muslim councillors in Newham have been more ethnically diverse compared to Tower Hamlets, yet their average party fragmentation is the same (0.1) as Tower Hamlets. On the other hand, Muslim councillors in Hackney are the most diverse ethnically and their average party fragmentation is 0.4 (see Table 12.2). The interview data strongly suggests that party fragmentation among Muslim councillors impacts their cohesion and effectiveness to increase the council responsiveness to Muslim demands. It is not uncommon to see public rivalries among Muslim councillors from different parties. For instance, among the six Muslim councillors in the London Borough of Camden, five are Labour, and one, Cllr. Faruque Ansari, is a Liberal Democrat. Only three months into his first term, Cllr. Ansari accused Labour's Muslim councillors of not speaking out for the Muslim community in a letter to the *Camden New Journal*. The Labour councillors defended themselves in a letter to the editor,

> 'We are all longstanding community activists and leaders, with a proven track record of working within our community. We have been involved for years with some of the real issues that affect our community: the need to raise educational attainment; the campaign to ensure that Camden was able to provide *halal* options in school dinners; the need for a Muslim burial ground; youth and education projects; and finally the need for a Mosque/Cultural Centre in the south of the borough.'[9]

Since all the Camden councillors and a significant majority of Camden's Muslim community are Bengali, the chair of the Bengali Men's Project, Amir Ali, responded in a letter to the editor listing the advocacy work of the Muslim councillors:

> [The Muslim councillors] worked together to introduce Islamic Awareness Week in Camden in order to address increased levels of Islamaphobia and to build bridges with others faiths. Both Nasim Ali and Abdul Hai

were elected Labour Councillors in Camden after the 9/11 atrocities. Cllr Ali, was also the first and youngest Muslim Mayor in Camden which was a great inspiration for young Muslims ... The bombings of 7th July created wide spread worry amongst the Muslim community in Camden. In particular, Muslim women were very vulnerable as they wear a distinctive Muslim outfit and can be singled out. It was also an uncertain time for young Muslim men who were under the spotlight as a result of the media frenzy linking the atrocity to Islamic groups. Many of the young Muslim men felt injustice, as they were being judged by the acts of few people who carried out the attacks. Cllr. Nasim Ali, Cllr. Abdul Quadir, Cllr. Fazlul Chowdhury, Cllr. Abdul Hai, Cllr. Nurul Islam, Cllr. Syed Hoque worked very closely with the police, community leaders, councillors, local authority and voluntary organisations to organise various meetings in order to support the Muslim community and to re-assure them by addressing their needs, issues and concerns ... On behalf of the Muslim Community in King's Cross Cllr. Abdul Hai arranged a Stop and Search Workshop in partnership with Camden Police Consultative Forum in order to address the injustice felt by many Muslim young people in light of the 7/7 attacks. This has given the Muslim young men the opportunity to engage with the police in a proactive way. We are proud of our Labour Muslim councillors who are representing the diverse community of Camden as well as representing the Muslim Community.[10]

On the one hand, the quantitative analysis on Table 12.2 exclusively focused on the impact of party fragmentation among minority representatives on substantive representation and found it to be a significant determinant. On the other hand, the case studies demonstrated that differences in religiosity, gender, and ethnicity also act as sources of fragmentation but to varying degrees. Muslim councillors, who do not consider themselves religious, nonetheless advocate for Muslim interests. However, the interviews showed that in some cases (i.e. Hackney) Muslim councillors are fragmented to the extent that those who consider themselves religious do not cooperate with the less religious ones. Gender fragmentation also plays a negative role in the cohesion among Muslim councillors. As confirmed by Newham Cllr. Rohima Rahman and Barnet Cllr. Zakia Zubairi, female Muslim councillors are not welcomed in certain circles of male councillors in general and Muslim male councillors in particular. This leads to less collaboration among Muslim councillors that hinders substantive representation. On the other hand, there was no evidence that ethnicity is a strong source of fragmentation among Muslim councillors, except in the case of Alevi Kurds and other Muslim councillors in Hackney. Yet even in this case religion and ethnicity were intertwined factors in this tension.

Political Incorporation. In terms of the number of leadership positions held by Muslim councillors, Hackney ranked third in the 1998–2002 term, second in the 2002–2006 term, and fifth in the 2006–2010 term (see Table 12.4).

Table 12.4 Hackney data

Hackney	1998–2002	2002–2006	2006–2010	Average
% Muslim population				13.76
Number and % of Muslim councillors	5 (8.8%)	10 (17.5%)	9 (15.8%)	8 (14%)
Number of parties and fragmentation	3 (0.6)	3 (0.3)	3 (0.3)	3 (0.4)
% in majority party	40	80	77.8	65.9
Mean seniority	6.4	4	6.7	5.7
Number of leadership positions	2	4	4	3.3
Number of prestigious committee assignments	0	9	7	5.3
% majority party seats	LAB 50.9%	LAB 77.2%	LAB 77.2%	LAB 68.4%
Electoral competitiveness	68.3	93	91.8	84.4
% ethnic population	40.6	40.6	38.9	40
Cemetery	0/1	0/1	0/1	0
Islamic school	3/93	4/94	4/94	0.04
Mosque	7	9	10	8.7
% grant	8	9	10	9
IMD scores	57.3	45.1	46.1	49.5

However, in terms of the mean seniority and the number of prestigious committee assignments held by Muslim councillors, it ranked considerably lower than the other two boroughs. Hackney had the third lowest mean seniority in the 1998–2002 term, fourteenth in the 2002–2006 term, and sixth in the 2006–2010 term. Furthermore, in the 1998–2002 term, Muslim councillors did not hold any prestigious committee assignments, in the 2002–2006 term, they held the third highest, and in the 2006–2010 term they held the seventh highest.

The political incorporation of Muslim councillors in Tower Hamlets is high, for they constitute the majority of the ruling party and therefore hold leadership positions and prestigious committee assignments. Although this contributes to the high government responsiveness for Muslim interests, the case study findings reveal that the political attitudes and behaviour of the Bengali councillors is partially responsible for the tension in the council and the community at large. Hence, the constellation of political incorporation indicators is more complex than what the statistical analysis presented in Table 12.2. Although Muslim councillors hold an extraordinarily high number of leadership positions and committee assignments, their seniority is exceptionally low, suggesting that those who hold these positions are relatively inexperienced. In addition, the high tension in the council and the community at large between the British Bengalis and other groups obstructs social cohesion. In comparison, Muslim councillors in Newham are highly politically incorporated without the high levels of tension. They hold a considerable number of leadership positions and prestigious committee assignments and their mean seniority is relatively high. Similarly, the political incorporation of Muslim councillors in Hackney is relatively better than most other councils and does not seem to play a significant role in the low government responsiveness.

Political Culture of the Council. The most striking divergence between the results of the regression analysis in Table 12.2 and the case studies is the view that Hackney Council is more Muslim friendly than Newham Council, a view voiced by a long standing Muslim Hackney councillor and confirmed by a Muslim councillor in Newham. Hackney Cllr. Shuja Shaikh argued that although the number of Muslim councillors is about the same in Hackney (the average is eight) and Newham (the average is 10.67), Muslim councillors in Newham are self-interested and are divided among themselves, hence due to these fault lines they are not working towards Muslim causes. Cllr. Shuja Shaikh pointed out the Muslim Housing Association, and the Islamic cultural centre where non-religious programs are partially funded by the Council, as evidence for the Muslim friendly policies of Hackney Council. Newham Cllr. Abdulkarim Sheikh confirmed this opinion, saying that:

> Hackney council is Muslim friendly. Even though there are more Muslims in Newham, Hackney has done better than us even with less Muslim councillors. The simple reason is, if you don't have opposition you don't have a healthy democracy. They have opposition and have to work with give and take. If they don't support Jewish applications or demands, then they can't get what they want. They are doing a good job. They are treating all sections of the community equally and that's what I want to see in Newham. Until the dominant party fears losing seats to the opposition in a very competitive election, we are not likely to see much change in Newham – that is politics, without the fear of losing power, you will not deliver as it should be.[11]

The comparative case study analysis reveals that the high diversity in Newham and Tower Hamlets contributes to the high levels of local government responsiveness, however, it has the opposite effect in Hackney. For instance, Tower Hamlets Cllr. Shiria Khatun explained her views on representing the interests of all minorities:

> The way I look at things is, for instance, in my ward there is an increase in the Eastern European population moving in, for me as a ward councillor, I look at how we can meet their needs. I am not Eastern European but that should not stop me from representing them, and finding out what the barriers are and how to overcome them. I represent everybody. Also we have a good percentage of Somali population that moved into the borough. The borough has always been very diverse. ... For me what

is really important is that you recognize the needs of the community, which ever cultural background they come from, you are there to represent everybody. I really hope that my views are shared by other councillors as well. Because my parents came from Bangladesh and I am of Bengali descent, doesn't mean to say that I am only a councillor for the Bengali people, that's not right at all, I am a councillor for everyone in my ward. As a matter of fact I get white and Bengali constituents from other wards who come to see me with their problems, and I don't say no to them ... Because when elections come, you are not selective, you are not just knocking on Bengali or Somali doors, or white people's doors. Because you want everyone to come out and support you and you should not forget that once you are elected. That you have been looking for everyone's support and now should be available for everybody regardless of whether they supported you. I do think that my colleagues share the same views.[12]

And contrary to the views of Hackney Cllr. Shuja Shaikh and Newham Cllr. Abdulkarim Sheikh, Newham Cllr. Rohima Rahman's explanation of the underlying political attitude of Newham Council towards minorities supports the overall findings of the case studies and the statistical analysis in that the Hackney Council has a rather minority-aversive political culture, whereas Newham acknowledges its diversity:

We try to integrate the whole community rather than dividing, that's the way we actually feel. Whether we are Muslim or Hindu or Sikh, when there is an issue affecting the Muslim community, we all unite rather than have Muslim councillors deal with it. We don't have that system here at all, I am proud of that. ... We need to set up an example for our local community. We are here to work and live together ... this person is from Pakistan or India, this is Muslim, that's where conflicts start. We don't have neighbor conflicts that much here as we hear from other boroughs ... that's why integration is valued in Newham.[13]

Electoral Competition. The case study findings confirmed the results of the statistical analysis in Table 12.2 and found that electoral competition does not have a significant impact on local government responsiveness. For instance, Newham's electoral competition index is twice as high as that of Hackney's, yet the Newham Council has a higher government responsiveness score than the Hackney Council. Moreover, the interview data suggests that factors other than the electoral competitiveness of the district influence the attitudes of the political parties and Muslim and non-Muslim councillors towards minority demands.

Representative Styles. It is clear that the Muslim councillors in the London boroughs are the primary advocates of the concerns and needs of the Muslim communities in their boroughs. However, it is also the case that these councillors do not focus exclusively on Muslim interests. The case studies provide ample evidence that Muslim legislators have distinctive representational styles, and that most are balancing the interests of Muslims and other constituencies. While they make a special effort to articulate and pursue the concerns of the Muslim community, they also devote time to working on issues that have no religious, ethnic, or racial content. Yet, the distinctive style of the Muslim councillors as a group in Tower Hamlets is group representatives; in Newham, it is balancers; and in Hackney, it is balancers as well as responsible representatives. The religious identity of the councillor is linked to the kind of responsiveness Muslim constituents get from local government exemplifying the link between descriptive and substantive representation. The findings here are highly similar to Canon's conclusion regarding US politics that:

> African American members of the House *are* more attentive to the distinctive needs of the black constituents than are their white counterparts who represent substantial numbers of blacks. ... *The race of the representative has important implications for the type of representation that is provided to a district with a significant number of black constituents.* Black members do a better job walking the racial tightrope and balancing the distinctive needs of black voters and the general interests of all voters, black and white alike. White members tend to have a more exclusive focus on nonracial issues.
>
> (1999: 244–45)

On the other hand, this finding contradicts Anwar (1991)'s characterisation of BME councillors as *party candidates*. Commenting on the achievements of BME leaders in the political process, Anwar argued that:

> In addition to the four ethnic minority MPs, at local level ethnic minority concentrations have helped to elect ethnic minority councillors in several areas, though they are still under-represented in proportion to their numbers. Generally, ethnic minority candidates are increasingly being accepted as 'party candidates' and also get white people's support. However, in some areas white electors still discriminate against ethnic minority candidates. Even the recent record of ethnic minority candidates shows that if they are given 'safe' or 'winnable' seats, they can win. Their performance has certainly improved in the last few years, as white electors are getting used to them.
>
> (1991: 59)

Muslim councillors are also *party representatives* in so far as the whip system forces them to be. The criticisms of Muslim councillors of the strong whip system, in particularly in the Labour Party, and their struggle to advocate on behalf of Muslim interests despite their parties, testify to this fact. They

Political behaviour of minority councillors 251

struggle to balance the demands of their party whips, the interests of the constituencies at large, and the Muslim community.

The conversion of inputs from constituents to policy decisions is at the heart of the policy-making process (Garcia 1997: 227). This conversion is the extent and quality of substantive representation, which 'can be determined by examining the responsiveness of the representative to his or her constituency' (Swain 2006: 5). The findings here also suggest that Muslim councillors are not just symbolic representatives or tokens of descriptive representation that is not followed by substantive representation, but are critical for effective representation of minority interests. To provide substantive representation means to act 'in the interest of the represented in a manner that is responsive to them' (Pitkin 1967: 209).

The claim that the Muslim councillors articulate the interests of the Muslim constituents in council meetings finds widespread support in the interviews. Nearly all the Muslim councillors made a link between the presence of Muslim councillors and the effective interests of Muslim constituents. They talked about how concerns of their Muslim constituents would not have been raised, or would not have been raised as vehemently, in their absence. It is apparent that Muslim constituents approach their Muslim councillors with their civic needs as well as specific group demands. Arguably, the basis for this is a shared sense of identity and a concern for Muslim interests. There is a perception and anticipation that Muslim councillors will identify with their concerns and will be more understanding. For instance, the Muslim councillors in Bradford facilitated an effective collaboration between the local authorities and the Muslim community. Lewis analysed the history and the role of the Bradford Council for Mosques, whose six founding members represented the diverse religious schools present in the city. This organisation worked closely with Muslim councillors in Bradford City Council (some of whom were also members of the Council for Mosques) and was highly successful in the 1980s in getting the local education authority to be responsive. Lewis explains the two primary reasons as follows:

> The first was the education authority's willingness to respond under the new educational banner of 'multi-culturalism'. The second factor was the political and the institutional support they could muster locally to implement anti-racist initiatives ... Local educational memoranda sought to respond to Muslim concerns about dress codes for girls, single-sex swimming and physical education; they showed flexibility over extended visits to South Asia; they provided *halal* meat for Muslim school children and capitalized on generous subventions from the Home Office to meet 'special needs' of ethnic minority children, e.g. community language teachers were employed in upper schools, a supplementary schools' officer was appointed to bridge the gap between the state school and the supplementary schools.
>
> (1997: 110–11)

At the turn of the century, Saggar and Geddes claimed that 'Minority representatives plainly have the potential to enter the mainstream but so far they have generally not done so' (2000: 25). On the contrary, the current evidence from the interviews suggests that a majority of the Muslim councillors have entered mainstream politics and mastered the rules of the game. However, an exception to mainstreaming Muslim politics occurs when political parties insist on emphasising minority identities to gain votes. As Purdam (2001: 154) explains:

> Arguably, a dynamic of 'self-organisation' has been imposed on Muslim members of some local Labour parties. Campaigns that focus on the identity of the individual can therefore become typical despite the councillors' stated attempts to run party-based campaigns. However, such positionings do not necessarily translate to the articulation of specific Muslim agendas (Purdam 2000). Muslim councillors' case-work is dominated by constituents' civic concerns – such as housing – rather than an essentialised identity politics (Purdam 2000). It is also notable that the candidacy of Muslim candidates can carry its own momentum as certain Muslim voters get involved in order to support the campaign of a fellow Muslim.

Nonetheless, a drastic increase in the political incorporation of Muslim councillors has occurred during the three terms analysed in this study. They are not only learning to successfully advocate for minority interests but are gaining leadership positions in recognition of their effective service.

Does minority political representation matter?

The literature on British ethnic minority political participation is highly divided as to the benefits for minority communities and society at large. The arguments could be grouped into three categories:

a   Minority representation is detrimental for integration by emphasising group identities.
b   Ethnic minorities do not have specific agendas; therefore minority representatives do not advocate for minority interests.
c   Minority representation is highly beneficial for minority communities and the society at large.

Some scholars argue that the political mobilisation of minorities based on ethnic ties and kinship networks furthers segregation by reinforcing ethnic and religious identities (Kepel 1997; Sikand 1998). It therefore impedes the integration of immigrants and harms both minorities and British society at large by furthering social fragmentation, particularly in the case of European Muslims. Koopmans and Statham (1999: 679) also argue that ethnic minority political participation, including that of Muslims, seeks to further minority

Political behaviour of minority councillors 253

interests at the exclusion of broader societal interests. Similarly, Duyvene de Wit and Koopmans state that 'too much emphasis on, and facilitation of, cultural difference may be detrimental to integration' (2005: 71). Saggar and Geddes present a different position and argues that neither ethnic minorities nor ethnic minority representatives have a coherent political agenda; therefore, the claim that ethnic minority representatives would exclusively represent ethnic minority issues cannot hold true (2000: 218).[14] In contrast, others, like Anwar (1986) and Adolino (1997) argue that effective ethnic minority political participation facilitates the integration process for immigrants by making them feel part of the system.

This study found that Muslim political representation in British local government benefits British society and Muslims under certain conditions, yet it does not always produce the anticipated positive results. Some of the benefits of Muslim political representation include assisting a marginalised minority and alleviating bottled resentment. Muslim elected officials also help decrease racism and discrimination in government institutions and effectively mediate between British Muslims and government agencies. They assist members of the minority who are not proficient in government red-tape. Michael contends that 'Social control and civic participation are therefore apparently vital to counter the growth of problematic groups of young people' (2004: 14). This research found that Muslim elected officials also encourage civic involvement among Muslim youth and are alternative role models instead of extremists who shun democratic institutions. Muslim elected officials also become socialised into their profession and develop a strong ethos of fairness and service to all their constituents, Muslim or not, by acting as *balancers* rather than *group representatives*. They build multi-ethnic coalitions within the electorate, their parties and legislatures. By serving in decision-making bodies, they develop a sense of institutional ownership. Moreover, contrary to Squires' claims that the separation of Church and state is 'a Western idea that is rejected by Muslims and even seen by them as sacrilegious' (2003: 87), most Muslim officials are successfully integrated into the secular democratic system and work to improve civic participation of British Muslims. However, this is not the case for all.

Conclusion

The case studies illustrated that the benefits of descriptive and substantive representation occur particularly in highly diverse districts (without a dominant ethnic group) with low racial tension like Newham, where minority representatives pursue *balancing representative styles*. Yet the case study findings also suggest that certain conditions are not conducive for all the benefits of descriptive and substantive representation to emerge. In the case of Tower Hamlets, low integration and aggressive *group representative styles* of the Muslim councillors are counterproductive, enhancing tensions in the council and exacerbating social conflict in the borough. Moreover, as the case of Hackney illustrates, high fragmentation among the minority councillors and the political culture of the council that leans towards the aversion of minority demands diminishes the benefits of descriptive and substantive representation.

Another key finding of the study involves the role of political parties in minority political representation. Although this study demonstrated that the case of Muslim representation in Britain supports the political incorporation thesis, it also found strong evidence that political parties play a significant role in determining levels of government responsiveness to minority interests. The strong whip system in British political parties and their role as gatekeepers (not only in the candidate selection process but also in leadership and committee appointments) influences whether descriptive representation of minorities leads to substantive representation of their interests. This finding calls for the modification of the theory of political incorporation by taking into consideration the role of political parties. In other words, if political parties determine the extent of minority politically incorporation, then political incorporation becomes an intervening variable in explaining government responsiveness.

In sum, this study confirmed the argument that descriptive representation is a necessary but not a sufficient condition for the representation of minority interests. Substantive representation of minority interests is contingent upon not just the presence of minority representatives but also requires them to be politically incorporated and less divided among party lines. This study also demonstrated that the presence and advocacy of minority representatives acting as *balancers* leads to a more responsive decision-making body as a whole.

Notes

1 Le Lohe (1998) reports the number of ethnic minority councillors in London boroughs increased from 35 in 1978 to 213 in 1994.
2 See www.mcb.org.uk/vote2005/statistics5.php for the complete list of parliamentary constituencies and the percentage of Muslim constituents.
3 Interview with Graham Lane, 14 July 2009, Newham Council, London.
4 Interview with Abdulkarim Sheikh, June 2006, Newham Council, London.
5 Ibid.
6 Ibid.
7 Interview with Graham Lane, 14 July 2009, Newham Council, London.
8 Tower Hamlets has also elected its first directly elected mayor who has executive rather than ceremonial functions on 21 October 2010.
9 'Politics and Religion Should Not Be Mixed', *Camden New Journal*, 7 September 2006, www.thecnj.co.uk/camden/090706/letters090706_05.htm.
10 Ibid.
11 Interview with Abdulkarim Sheikh, 12 June 2006, Newham Council, London.
12 Interview with Shiria Khatun, 13 July 2009, Tower Hamlets Council, London.
13 Interview with Rohima Rahman, 14 July 2009, Newham Council, London.
14 Saggar and Geddes notes four distinct positions on the expectations placed on ethnic minority representatives and their capacity and willingness to represent ethnic minority political interests versus their constituency at large; a) to represent ethnic minorities exclusively; b) to identify with and represent certain

political issues; c) to promote specific positions on certain political issues; d) the mainstreamer position which argues that 'distinctive interests can be defended across a number of issues that have no immediate racial or ethnic dimension' (2000: 218).

Bibliography

Adolino, J.R. (1997) *Ethnic Minorities, Electoral Politics and Political Integration in Britain*. London: Pinter Press.
Anwar, M. (1986) *Race and Politics: Ethnic Minorities and the British Political System*. London: Tavistock Publications.
Anwar, M. (1991) 'Ethnic Minorities' Representation: Voting and Electoral Politics in Britain, and the Role of the Leaders', in P. Werbner and M. Anwar (eds) *Black and Ethnic Leaderships in Britain: The Cultural Dimensions of Political Action*. London: Routledge Publishing, pp. 28–42.
Atkinson, H. and Wilks-Heeg, S. (2000) *Local Government from Thatcher to Blair: The Politics of Creative Autonomy*. Oxford: Blackwell Publishers.
Bambery, C. (2006) Respect Councillor: 'We Are the Opposition to New Labour Here', *Socialist Worker*, 20 May.
Canon, D. (1999) *Race, Redistricting, and Representation: The Unintended Consequences of Black Majority Districts*. Chicago, IL: University of Chicago Press.
Dovi, S. (2007) *The Good Representative*. Oxford: Blackwell Publishing.
Duyvene de Wit, T. and Koopmans, R. (2005) 'The Integration of Ethnic Minorities into Political Culture: The Netherlands, Germany and Great Britain Compared', *Acta Politica*, 40: 50–73.
Erickson, R. (1978) 'Constituency Opinion and Congressional Behaviour: A Re-examination of the Miller-Stokes Representation Data', *American Journal of Political Science*, 22: 511–535.
Fenno, F.R. (1978) *Home Style: House Members in their Districts*. Boston, MA: Little, Brown.
Fenno, F.R. (2003) *Going Home: Black Representatives and their Constituents*. Chicago, IL: University of Chicago Press.
Garcia, F.C. (ed.) (1997) *Pursuing Power: Latinos and the Political System*. Notre Dame, IN: University of Notre Dame Press.
Haynie, K. (2001) *African American Legislators in the American States* New York: Columbia University Press.
Kepel, G. (1997) *Allah in the West: Islamic Movements in America and Europe*. Stanford, CA: Stanford University Press.
Koopmans, R. and Statham, P. (1999) 'Challenging the Liberal Nation-State? Post-nationalism, Multiculturalism, and the Collective Claims Making of Migrants and Ethnic Minorities in Britain and Germany', *The American Journal of Sociology*, 105(3): 652–696.
Le Lohe, M. (1998) 'Ethnic Minority Participation and Representation in the British Electoral System', in S. Saggar (ed.) *Race and British electoral politics*. London: UCL Press, pp. 74–97.
Lewis, P. (1997) 'The Bradford Council for Mosques and the Search for Muslim Unity', in S. Vertovec and C. Peach (eds) *Islam in Europe: The Politics of Religion and Community*. New York: St. Martin's Press.
Lovenduski, J. (2005) *Feminizing Politics*. Cambridge: Polity Press.

Maxwell, R. (2006) 'Muslims, South Asians, and the British Mainstream: A National Identity Crisis?', *West European Politics*, 29(4): 736–756.

Michael, L. (2004) 'Leadership in Transition? Issues of Representation and Youth in British Muslim Communities', ESRC/ODPM Postgraduate Research Programme, Working Paper 12.

Office for National Statistics (2012) *2011 Census Snapshot: Religion*, Census Information Scheme, GLA Intelligence. Available at: http://data.london.gov.uk/datastorefiles/documents/2011-census-snapshot-religion.pdf.

Open Society Institute (2010) *Muslims in Europe: A Report on 11 EU Cities*. New York: Open Society Institute.

Pitkin, H. (1967) *The Concept of Representation*. Berkeley, CA: University of California Press.

Purdam, K. (2000) 'The Political Identities of Muslim Local Councillors in Britain', *Local Government Studies*, 26(1): 47–64.

Purdam, K. (2001) 'Democracy in Practice: Muslims and the Labour Party at the Local Level', *Politics*, 21(3): 147–157.

Ross, K. (ed.) (2002) *Women, Politics, and Change*. Oxford: Oxford University Press.

Saggar, S. and Geddes, A. (2000) 'Negative and Positive Racialisation: Re-examining Ethnic Minority Political Representation in the UK', *Journal of Ethnic and Migration Studies*, 26(1): 25–44.

Sikand, Y. (1998) 'The Origins and Growth of the Tablighi Jamaat in Britain', *Islam and Christian-Muslim Relations*, 9(2): 171–192.

Squires, J.E. (2003) 'The Significance of Religion in British Politics', in W. Safran (ed.) *The Secular and the Sacred: Nation, Religion and Politics*. London: Frank Cass Publishers, pp. 78–95.

Swain, C.M. (2006) *Black Faces, Black Interests: The Representation of African Americans in Congress*, enlarged edn. New York: University Press of America Inc.

Tatari, E. (2009) 'Theories of State Accommodation of Islamic Religious Practices in Western Europe', *Journal of Ethnic and Migration Studies*, 35(2): 271–288.

Index

Abdullah, Daud 203
Abdul-Matin, Ibrahim 107
Abu Hamza 54
Abu Qatada 54
activism: civic 94–5; environmental 115; of genuine believers 109; Islamic 105; of Muslim women 87, 89, 92–8; political 150; *see also* 'microactivism'
Adib, Mahdi 46
Adolino, J.R. 253
Afghanistan, invasion of (2001) 105
African Americans, political representation of 240
Ahmed, Maulvi Rafiuddin 32–3
Ahmed, Nazir (Baron) 4, 40
Ajeeb, Muhammad 4
Akhtar, P. 22
Ali, Aftab 33
Ali, Amir 245–6
Ali, Nasim 245–6
Ali, Rushanara 20, 220–2, 226, 229
Ali, Zulfiqar 243
All Party Kashmir Group 4
Allen, Chris 182
Alley, Surat 33
Alli, Lord 4
Allievi, Stefano 3
Al Qa'ida 54
Altikriti, Anas 127, 131–5, 186, 188
al wala wal bara concept 179
Anderson, J.W. 165
Anglo-Asian Conservative Society 34
Ansari, Faruque 245
anti-war movement 124–35, 153
Anwar, Muhammad 1, 18–19, 22, 34, 36, 38, 250, 253
Archer, T. 196
asylum seekers 91–2, 177–8, 185

auto-photography, use of 142
Azam, Tre 45

Back, L. 158
balancers 253–4
Bari, Muhammad Abdul 202, 205–6
Batten, Gerard 143
Bayat, Asef 106
Benn, Tony 132
Beyerlein, K. 55–7
Bhutto, Benazir 228
biraderi networks 15–16, 21–8
biraderi-politicking 23–8
Birmingham 94–5, 135
Birt, Jonathan 128, 131, 134, 179–80, 197
Blair, Tony 40, 133, 181, 197
blasphemy 126
Blears, Hazel 201
Bloemraad, I. 68
Bolognani, M. 134
Bosnia 128
boyd, d. 160–2
Bradford 1–2, 4, 125–6, 240–1, 251
bridging and *bonding* 56, 58, 167
British Muslim Forum 201
British Muslim Initiative 45, 134–5
British Muslims for Secular Democracy 156
British National Party 182–3, 185
British Social Attitudes surveys 58–9
Britishness 148, 153
Brown, Gordon 47
Brown, J.A. 133
Bryant, M. 108
Burns, N. 89–90
Bush, George W. 130
Byrne, Liam 220

258 Index

Cabinet Ministers, Muslim 5
Calhoun-Brown, A. 56
Cameron, David 47, 147, 206, 208
Campaign for Nuclear Disarmament (CND) 132, 134
Campbell, D.E. 55
candidates, Parliamentary 42
Census of Population 39–40, 43, 48–9, 62, 66, 199
Central Islamic Society 33
Centre on Dynamics of Ethnicity 61
Cesari, J. 196
Chaves, M. 55
Chishti, Rehman 219–22, 227–8
Chowdhury, Fazlul 246
church attendance 58–61
Church of England 126, 198, 203–4
citizenship 147–8, 153, 185–6
civic activism 94–5
civic engagement 89–91
civil society 117–18, 125, 135; definitions of 106
'clash of civilisations' 174–5
Clegg, Nick 47
climate change 111–12, 114
collective decision-making within the Government 224–5
Commission on Integration and Cohesion 200–1
Commission for Racial Equality (CRE) 34
Commonwealth Immigration Act (1962) 33
communitarianism 197
community leaders 4, 97–8
community relations 181, 210
Community Relations Commission (CRC) 33
community representation, mistrust of 16
congregations, religious 55–6
Conservative Muslim Forum 5, 206
Conservative Party 33–4, 48
consumerism 110–11, 114, 116
convergence in political behaviour 240
Corbyn, Jeremy 206
Cordoba Foundation 135, 188
councillors: of London boroughs 237–54; Muslim 1–2, 20, 26
Crewe, I. 19, 24
critical discourse analysis 109
Crossley, N. 109
cultural diversity 197
Cutts, D. 57

da'wa 178
deenport internet portal 187
DeHanas, D.N. 108–9
Demireva, N. 68
democracy, concept of 17
Denham, John 203
Discrimination Law Association 184
Djupe, P.A. 56
Dovi, S. 239
dress, Islamic 85–6, 92–4, 131, 163, 176, 240
Duffy, Gillian 48
Durose, C. 20
Duyvene de Wit, T. 253

ecology 115–16
The Economist 48
Ellison, Jane 48
Ellison, N.B. 160–2
emel (magazine) 186
English Defence League 167, 169
English language 185
environmentalism 103–19; Islamic discourse of 106–8
ethnic groups, differences between 2
Ethnic Minority British Election Study (EMBES) 58–63, 69–78
European Parliament 238
European Union 183

Facebook 158–70
Faith Community Liaison Group 197
feminist scholarship 89
Fenno, F.R. 239
Finsbury Park Mosque 54
foreign policy 141–2, 154, 169, 181–2, 184, 188
Fraser, Nancy 168
freedom of expression 126, 177–8, 183–4
Friends of the Earth 104, 117–18

Galloway, George 5, 48–9
Garbaye, R. 22
Geddes, A. 28, 252–3
German, Lindsey 133
Giddens, Anthony 169
Gilbert, C.P. 56
Gilliat-Ray, S. 58, 108
Glynn, S. 197
Gohir, S. 86
Goodall, Kay 183–4
Green Lane Mosque 54
Greenpeace 104, 117–18
Gulf War (1991) 38, 127, 134

Index 259

Habermas, Jürgen 116
Hackney 242–6, 253–4
Hadith 108
Hague, William 41
Hai, Abdul 245–6
Hain, Peter 206
halal food 240
Hannigan, John 104–5, 109
Harris, F.C. 55
Hart Dyke, A. 54, 59
hate crime 94, 207–10
Hawkins, W. 204
Hayes, John 221
Häyhtiö, T. 165, 169
Haynie, K. 239–40
Heath, A. 19, 57, 65, 68, 134
Hipp, J.R. 56–7
Hizb-ut-Tahrir 38, 133, 179
Holocaust Memorial Day 201–2
Honeyford, Ray 1, 125
Hoque, Syed 246
House of Lords 183–4, 218, 238
Howard, John 147
Howard, Michael 40, 126, 196
Hussain, D. 176
Hussain, Karamat 4
Hussain, Muzammal 109–16

identity *see* Muslim identity;
    national identity; religious identity
identity politics 146–50, 174, 188
Idris, Mohamed 110
iENGAGE group 135
imams 54, 116
immigrants' identification with
    the host country 239
immigration policy 181, 185, 188
incitement to religious hatred 183–4
India League 33
integration 238
'intense' political activists 95–7
Internet technology and usage 156–60,
    163–70, 187
Iraq War 5
Islam 53, 153–4
Islam, Nurul 246
Islam Awareness Week 182
Islam Expo (2005) 187–8
Islamic environmental organisations
    (IEOs) 103, 107–8, 113, 118–19
Islamic Foundation for Ecology
    and Environmental Sciences (IFEES)
    104, 108–18
Islamic Party of Britain 176

Islamic Society of Britain 126, 187
Islamisation 3
Islamophobia 49, 64, 97, 133, 159,
    175, 180, 182–3, 188, 195–8,
    205–10, 241
Israel 151, 153
Istanbul Declaration (2009) 203

James, H. 106
Javid, Sajid 220–2, 224, 226–8, 231
Jenkins, Roy 33, 36
jihad and *jihadists* 179–80
Jones-Correa, M. 57
Al-Judai, Shaykh Abdullah 145
Juergensmayer, Mark 106
Just Peace group 128–33

Kandiyoti, Deniz 92
Kashmir Human Rights Committee 4
Kay, Jeanne 108
Kelly, Ruth 201–2
Khalid, Fazlud 107–16
khālifa role 107
Khan, Hamira 24–5
Khan, Sadiq 5, 42, 220–4, 226–9
Khatun, Shiria 248
Khilafa Conference (1994) 179
Khomeini, Ayatollah 135
King, Oona 5
kinship networks *see biraderi*
Kitchener, K. 163
Klausen, J. 27
Kohler, D. 22
Koopmans, R. 252–3
Kurds, Alevi 246
Kushin, M.J. 163

Labour Party 3–4, 22, 27–8, 33, 35, 38,
    40
Lamington, Lord 33
Lane, Graham 243
Layton-Henry, Z. 23
Leal, D. 57
Leeds 94
legislative process 215–33; roles in 219–23
Lewis, Philip 1–2, 125, 251
Liberal Democrats 48
Liberty 184
lifestyles and lifestyle values 104, 110
Linton, Martin 48
Livingstone, Ken 187, 206
London bombings (7 July 2005)
    135, 141, 157, 199
London Central Mosque 54

260 Index

London demonstration against the Iraq war (2003) 124
Lovenduski, Joni 18, 238

Maan, Bashir 4
McAndrew, S. 57
McLoughlin, S. 196
McNulty, Tony 223, 228
MADE in Europe movement 135
Mahmood, Khalid 25, 41–2, 220–4, 226, 228–9
Mahmood, Shabana 20, 48, 220–3, 226, 228
Major, John 179
Malcolm X 25
Malik, Hanzala 24
Malik, Shahid 5, 42, 220–4, 226–9
Mandaville, P. 165
Mansbridge, Jane 17
Marichal, J. 169–70
Marqusee, Mike 133
Marsh, D. 19, 157
Marx, Karl 104
Mawlawi, Sheikh Faysal 148
Maxwell, R. 147, 239
mayors, Muslim 4
Measuring Anti-Muslim Attacks (MAMA) 169
Members of Parliament (MPs), Muslim 4, 48, 215–33, 238
Merkel, Angela 147
Miah, Abjol 48–9
Michael, L. 253
'microactivism' (Marichal) 169–70
Ministerial Code 225
Ministers 218; Muslim 5
minority groups: government responsiveness to 237; *pluralistic* and *assimilationist* approaches to 237; political institutions' openness to influence from 239; within minority groups 19
mizān concept 107
mosques 53–78; attacks on 127; attendance at 62; data on 69–78; political mobilisation at 62–4; social distance and political engagement at 64–7; social segregation in 61–2
Mouffe, Chantal 168–9
Moussaoui, Zacarias 54
Muhammad the Prophet 108
multiculturalism 20–1, 37, 68, 85, 147, 206
Murad, Farooq 203, 205, 208
Muslim Association of Britain (MAB) 124, 131–5, 182, 186

Muslim-consciousness 176
Muslim Council of Britain (MCB) 32, 40–2, 45, 126, 131, 156, 177, 181–6, 195–210, 241; and the Coalition government 203–10; creation of 196; engagement with New Labour 196–9; New Labour's disengagement from 199–203
Muslim Defence League 158–9, 169
Muslim identity 1–3, 85–6, 161, 168–9, 175–6
Muslim Institute 135
Muslim Parliament 126, 128–9, 176
Mustapha, Shabnum 24, 27–8

nasheeds 187
Nasr, Seyyed Hossein 107–8
national identity 148
National Interim Council for Muslim Unity (NICMU) 177
National Lottery 39–40
Near Neighbours programme 203, 205
new social movements (NSMs) 104, 109, 113, 116
Newham 242–5, 253
newspapers, Muslim 186
Nineham, Chris 124, 133
Norris, Pippa 18, 90, 167

Offe, Claus 113, 118
Operation Black Vote 18, 43, 49
Osborne, George 221
O'Toole, T. 40, 158, 204

Paltridge, B. 109
Papacharissi, Z. 163
parliamentary representation, Muslim 215–33
participation: civic 178–9; political 93, 154
Pasha, Syed Aziz 34–8
Patel, Ismail 44
People's Justice Party 4
Percival, Ian 34
Philips, Trevor 25
Phillips, Anne 17
Phillips, M. 146
Phillips, R. 132–4
Pickles, Eric 207–9
Pipes, Daniel 143
Pitkin, Hilary 17, 251
Pola Uddin, Manzila 40
Policy Exchange 54
political activity, definition of 89–91

political engagement 152–3, 158, 254; lack of interest in 22, 156; symbolic importance of 24–5
political representation 176, 238–9, 242–53; concept of 17–20; forms of 17; importance for minorities 252–3; of Muslim communities in London 242–52
political violence 141–6, 153
politicisation of Muslims 92–3, 141
Powell, Enoch 33
Prevention of Violent Extremism (PVE) programme 54, 86, 98, 200, 203
private members' bills (PMBs) 230–2
Public Bill Committees 225, 228, 232
Purdam, Kingsley 2–3, 18, 20, 27, 252
Putnam, R.D. 55

Q-News 156, 186
Quadir, Abdul 246
Quilliam Foundation 54
Qur'ān, the 107–8, 115, 145, 154
Qureshi, Yasmin 20, 219–20, 222, 227–8

Race Relations Act (1976) 33–7
Racial and Religious Hatred Act (2006) 184
racism and racial discrimination 49, 68, 94, 182–3
Rahman, Rohima 246, 249
Raza, M. 21
Rees, John 133
Rees, Merlyn 34
refugees *see* asylum seekers
Reid, John 202
Reid, Richard 54
religious hatred, criminalisation of 184, 188, 202, 233
religious identity 2–3, 141, 151; *see also* Muslim identity
representation, *descriptive* and *substantive* 239–40, 254; *see also* political representation
Respect Party 4, 42–3, 46–9, 135, 186
Ridley, Yvonne 186
Rigby, Lee, murder of (Woolwich, 2013) 141, 145, 207–8, 210
Rinne, J. 165, 169
role models 16, 24, 95
role-switching by parliamentarians 218–19, 223
Ronson, J. 180
Ross, K. 240
Rucht, D. 124

Runnymede Trust 48, 183
Rushdie, Salman 125–6
'Rushdie affair' (1989) 1, 38, 125–7, 134–5, 175–7, 185, 196, 210, 239
Ryder, Richard 35–6

Sacranie, Sir Iqbal 40, 198–9, 203
Saggar, S. 28, 252–3
salaam website 187
salafis 179
Saleem, Farooq 4
Saleem, Shahed 128–30, 134
Sands, K.Z. 165
Sarkozy, Nicolas 147
Sarwar, Anas 220–2, 226–8, 231
Sarwar, Mohammad 4, 24, 40–2, 219–20, 222, 227–8, 231
The Satanic Verses 38, 125–6; *see also* 'Rushdie affair'
Schlozman, K. 89–90
secular Muslims 27
security concerns and securitisation 174, 181, 188, 200, 209
Select Committees 225
September 11th 2001 attacks 85, 87, 93, 97, 128, 157, 174, 180–2, 188
Shadow Ministers and the Shadow Cabinet 223, 228
Shaikh, Shuja 248–9
sharia law 62, 66, 148, 154
Shaw, Alison 21
Sheikh, Abdulkarim 242–3, 248–9
Sherif, Jamil 199
Siddiqui, Asim 135
Siddiqui, Ghayasuddin 129, 135
Siddiqui, Kalim 126
Sigelman, L. 55
Singerman, D. 106
Snow, D.A. 108
Sobolewska, M. 57
social capital 56
social media 157
social movement theory (SMT) 103, 117–18; *see also* new social movements
social networking sites (SNSs) 160–2, 166
Socialist Workers Party 133–4
Squires, Catherine 168
Squires, J.E. 253
Srebrenica Memorial Day 209
Statham, P. 134, 252–3
'stay-home' political activists 93–4
stereotyping 97

Index

stop-and-search powers 41
Stop the War Coalition (StWC) 124, 128–35, 182
Storm, I. 57–8
Straw, Jack 40, 184–5
Sufi Council 201
Swain, C.M. 241, 251
Syria 153

Tamimi, Azzam 132–3
Taylor, Charles 20
television debates 47
TELL MAMA project 207, 209
Ten Minute Rule 230
terrorism and counter-terrorism 41, 54, 85–6, 92, 94, 97, 181–2, 200; *see also* 'war on terror'
Thatcher, Margaret 34, 37, 206
Thrasher, M. 20
Tower Hamlets 242–5, 253
Trade Union Congress (TUC) 206
Trom, D. 108

Uddin, Manzila (Baroness) 4, 205
UK Action Committee for Islamic Affairs (UKACIA) 32, 38–40
Union of Muslim Organisations (UMO) 32, 34, 36–9
United Kingdom Action Committee on Islamic Affairs (UKACIA) 126
United Shades of Britain 158–9, 164, 169

Van Ingen, E. 56
Van der Meer, T. 56
Vawda, Shahedah 128–35
Verba, S. 64, 89–90
vignettes, use of 142

Voas, D. 57
voting behaviour 150–3
voting rights 22

Wales, Sir Robin 243
Walgrave, S. 124
'war on terror' 41, 85, 87, 174, 182, 188, 207
Warsi, Sayeeda (Baroness) 5, 24, 204, 207–9
Waugh, Auberon 33
Weatherill, Bernard 34
websites, Islam-related 160
Wells, H.G. 33
Werbner, Pnina 127
Whips, parliamentary 218
Wiktorowicz, Q. 105
Wilcox, C. 55
Winter, T.J. 148
Wisdom in Nature (WiN) 104, 108–18
women from Muslim communities 85–98; activism of 87, 89, 92–8; politicisation of 92–3
women politicians 18–21
women's organisations 86, 89
women's role in politics 240
Wright, M. 68

Yaqoob, Salma 42–3, 48, 135, 186
YouElect project 42–9
Young Muslims Advisory Group 207
Yousaf, Humza 24–5
Yusuf, Sami 187

Zahawi, Nadhim 219–21, 227, 231
Zubairi, Zakia 246
Zukin, C. 89